David A. Baptiste Jr.
Editor

Clinical Epiphanies in Marital and Family Therapy
A Practitioner's Casebook of Therapeutic Insights, Perceptions, and Breakthroughs

Pre-publication
REVIEWS,
COMMENTARIES,
EVALUATIONS . . .

More pre-publication
REVIEWS, COMMENTARIES, EVALUATIONS . . .

"**C**linical Epiphanies in Marital and Family Therapy is compelling reading for students and experienced practitioners alike. It presents sixteen case studies as described by the primary therapist along with commentary on the narrative by two other and unrelated experienced practitioners.

For each case, background information about the therapist and commentators is given, including gender, age, and theoretical orientation used in discussing the case example.

The result is a rich presentation of how therapists from a variety of theoretical perspectives see and manage some very difficult clinical cases. At the heart of it, the case for the common factors associated with therapy across theoretical models emerges. These cases highlight the importance of patience, respect, acceptance, caring, and the client's readiness to change. In this book, therapy is not pretty. Rather it is presented as a somewhat messy business where changes can occur as the result of family members' actions as much or more than because of what the therapist actually does in a given treatment. As such, I think it is a reasonably accurate example of how therapy really proceeds in the day-to-day work of most family therapists."

D. Russell Crane, PhD
Director, Family Studies Center,
Brigham Young University,
Provo, Utah

"**B**aptiste has collected a bonanza of provocative case studies that are presented by some of the best-known family therapists in the United States, from a wide variety of theoretical perspectives. One of the refreshing features of this collection is its emphasis on people and their relationships, instead of abstract theorizing. Critical incidents seem to have little to do with the particular school of thought used. They should teach all clinicians to be humble and be less likely to pontificate. In fact, these stories seem to argue that it is warm, positive regard paired with readiness to face reality and work hard that serves clients well. In the end, Clinical Epiphanies does what a good book is supposed to do. It makes you think."

David L. Weis, PhD
Professor of Human Development
and Family Studies,
Bowling Green State University, Ohio

The Haworth Clinical Practice Press
An Imprint of The Haworth Press, Inc.
New York • London • Oxford

Clinical Epiphanies in Marital and Family Therapy

A Practitioner's Casebook of Therapeutic Insights, Perceptions, and Breakthroughs

HAWORTH Marriage and the Family
Terry S. Trepper, PhD
Executive Editor

Clinical Epiphanies in Marital and Family Therapy
A Practitioner's Casebook of Therapeutic Insights, Perceptions, and Breakthroughs

David A. Baptiste Jr.
Editor

The Haworth Clinical Practice Press
An Imprint of The Haworth Press, Inc.
New York • London • Oxford

Published by

The Haworth Clinical Practice Press, an imprint of The Haworth Press, Inc., 10 Alice Street, Binghamton, NY 13904-1580.

Cover design by Marylouise E. Doyle.

Library of Congress Cataloging-in-Publication Data

Clinical epiphanies in marital and family therapy : a practitioner's casebook of therapeutic insights, perceptions, and breakthoughs / David A. Baptiste, editor.
    p.   cm.
   Includes bibliographical references and index.
   ISBN 0-7890-0105-5 (alk. paper) — ISBN 0-7890-1565-X (alk. paper)
   1. Marital psychotherapy—Case studies. 2. Family psychotherapy—Case studies. I. Baptiste, David A.

RC488.5 .C5835 2002
616.89'156—dc21

                                                                           2001039563

To my family
Nancy, François, Gabrielle, and Émile
in appreciation for their forbearance and encouragement

CONTENTS

ABOUT THE EDITOR

David A. Baptiste Jr., PhD, is a psychologist with the New Mexico Corrections Department and in the private practice of marriage and family therapy. He received his BA from Howard University and his PhD from Purdue University. He previously served as Senior Family Therapist, River's Bend Adolescent Treatment Center, Las Cruces, New Mexico; Associate Director, Southwest Counseling Center, Las Cruces, New Mexico; Clinical Director, Sun Valley Psychiatric Hospital, El Paso, Texas; Counseling Psychologist, New Mexico State University; and Family Therapist, Massachusetts Department of Corrections.

Dr. Baptiste has served in executive positions on a number of professional and editorial boards. He is an AAMFT clinical member, approved supervisor, fellow, and past member of the Commission on Accreditation for Marriage and Family Therapy Education. He is co-founder of NCFR's ethnic minority section and AAMFT's ethnic minority committee. His principal research and clinical interests are stepfamilies (both gay and straight), single parents, racial and cultural minority families, biracial issues, immigrants, and pregnant adolescents. He has published articles and book chapters in these areas.

CONTRIBUTORS

Primary Contributors

Marc N. Barney received an MS in Marriage and Family Therapy from The University of Louisiana at Monroe. He is currently employed by Youth and Family Centered Services of Utah and LDS Family Services. His clinical interests include parent-adolescent relationships and adolescent development.

Gregory Brock is Director of the Marriage and Family Therapy Program and Professor in the Department of Family Studies at the University of Kentucky. His PhD in Human Development and Family Studies is from The Pennsylvania State University. His current research interests include practitioners' compliance with ethical codes and research integrity. He has published widely in the field of marriage and family therapy and is editor of the *AAMFT Ethics Casebook*.

Jill H. Freedman is Co-Director of the Evanston Family Therapy Center, a faculty member of the Chicago Center for Family Health, and has co-authored two books on family therapy. She received her BA from Shimer College and her MSW from Washington University. Her current professional interest is in the area of narrative therapy.

Adi Granit received her BS in social work from Bar-Ilan University in Israel and an MS in Marriage and Family Therapy from The University of Louisiana at Monroe, where she is a PhD candidate. Her areas of professional interest include brief therapy models, intercultural therapy, and supervision.

Anthony P. Jurich is Professor of Family Studies and Human Services at Kansas State University. He received his BS from Fordham University and PhD from The Pennsylvania State University. His areas of professional interest are adolescence, family crisis, sex therapy, and marriage and family therapy.

Margaret K. Keiley is Assistant Professor of Marriage and Family Therapy at Purdue University. She received her MEd in Family Therapy from the University of Massachusetts at Boston and her EdD from Harvard University. Her research interests are affect regulation, attachment, and conduct disorder.

J. Steven Lamberti is Associate Professor of Psychiatry and Director of Long-Term Care at the University of Rochester Medical Center. He received his BA and MD from the University of Missouri and completed residency and fellowship training at the University of Rochester. His current professional interest is community-based care of adults with severe mental illness.

Judith Landau is President of Linking Human Systems, LLC, and Visiting Professor at the National Jewish Medical and Research Center in Denver, Colorado. A family and child psychiatrist, she received her MB, ChB medical degree from the University of Capetown, South Africa, and a Psychological Medicine specialty degree, DPM, from Trinity College, Dublin, Ireland. Her current research, consultation, and training are focused on empowering disenfranchised families and communities through identifying natural change agents or link therapists to enhance positive attachment to family and culture of origin.

Tracey A. Laszloffy, PhD, is Associate Professor and Director of the Couples and Family Therapy Program at Seton Hill College, Greensburg, Pennsylvania. She received her MA and PhD in Marriage and Family Therapy from Syracuse University. Her current professional interests include diversity and oppression as they pertain to family therapy, and therapy with troubled teens and their families.

Janie K. Long is Assistant Professor of Marriage and Family Therapy at Purdue University. She received her MS from Duke University and her PhD from Virginia Tech. Her research interests include the experiences of lesbian and gay adolescents and their families, persons with Alzheimer's disease, MFT supervision, theory, and human sexuality.

Andres Nazario Jr. is Director of the Center for Couples and Family Development at the Gainesville Family Institute, Gainesville, Florida. He received his BA from Florida International University and his PhD from the University of Florida. His primary area of interest is oppression-sensitive approaches to training and supervision of couples and family therapy.

Kenneth E. Newell received his MS in Marriage and Family Therapy from the University of Kentucky and his PhD in Marriage and Family Therapy from Brigham Young University. His research interests include male survivors of sexual abuse and adolescent development.

William F. Northey Jr. received his BS from the University of Delaware and his PhD from Kansas State University. Currently, he is the Research Specialist for the American Association for Marriage and Family Therapy. His research interests include research methodology, mental health services delivery, and treatment for juvenile sex offenders.

Harriet H. Roberts received her BS from Savannah State University and her PhD from Union Graduate School. She is senior faculty at the Houston-

Galveston Institute in Houston, Texas; she also has a private practice. Her clinical and research interests include mandated psychotherapeutic treatment of ethnic minority families and the influence of contextual issues in therapy.

Robert G. Ryder is Professor of Family Studies at the University of Connecticut. He received his BA from Rutgers University and his PhD from the University of Michigan. His current professional interests include marriage and other intimate relationships.

Linda Stone-Fish is Associate Professor and Director of the Marriage and Family Therapy Program at Syracuse University. She received her BA from Northwestern University and her PhD from Purdue University. Her current professional interests include Jewish families and relationship development.

Volker Thomas is Associate Professor and Director of the Marriage and Family Therapy Program at Purdue University. He received his PhD from the University of Minnesota. His primary professional interests include creativity in family therapy and experiential approaches to marriage and family therapy.

William H. Watson is Clinical Associate Professor, Psychiatry (Psychology) and Neurology at the University of Rochester School of Medicine. He received his BA from Princeton University and his PhD from the Rosemead School of Psychology at Biola University. His current professional interests are in the areas of spirituality in psychotherapy, couples therapy, and mind/body issues.

Carolyn I. Wright is a Lecturer in the Program of Medical Humanities, College of Medicine, SUNY Upstate Medical University, Syracuse, New York, and in private practice. She received her PhD in Marriage and Family Therapy from Syracuse University. Current research interests include medical education, intergenerational impact of disease, and women's health care issues.

Toni S. Zimmerman is Associate Professor and Director of the Marriage and Family Therapy Program at Colorado State University. She received her BS from Ohio University and her PhD from Virginia Tech University. Her current professional interests include gender equality in marriage, parenting in gender nonrestrictive ways, and work/family balance.

Commentators

Stephen A. Anderson is Professor of Marriage and Family Therapy at the University of Connecticut. He received his MS from Northeastern University and his PhD from Kansas State University. His primary research interests are in the areas of training and supervision and family violence.

Charles Lee Cole is Professor and the Hanna Spyker Endowed Chair in Marriage and Family Therapy at The University of Louisiana, Monroe. He received his BA from Texas Wesleyan University and his PhD from Iowa State University. His current professional interests include couples therapy, and research on marital stability and quality and marriage enrichment processes.

Michael Durrant is Director of the Brief Therapy Institute of Sydney, Australia. He is a former Lecturer in Counseling and Family Therapy and Assistant Director of the family therapy clinic at the University of Western Sydney. His primary interests include teaching and supervision of brief therapy and research into students' experiences of this.

Craig A. Everett is Director of the Arizona Institute for Family Therapy and in private practice in Tucson, Arizona. He received his BA from The George Washington University and his PhD from Florida State University. His current areas of specialization are the divorce process and ADHD.

Leslie L. Feinauer is Professor of Marriage and Family Therapy at Brigham Young University and in private practice. She received her MS in Nursing from the University of Utah and her PhD in Marriage and Family Therapy from BYU. Her research interests include trauma and the development of hardiness and Jungian-oriented psychotherapy with children, adolescents, and adults.

Lisa Aronson Fontes, PhD, Director of School Counseling Programs in the Department of Psychology at Springfield College, Springfield, Massachusetts. Professionally, she focuses on cultural issues in family violence, research, and forensic interviewing. She conducts training nationwide on these and other topics.

Suzanne Midori Hanna, PhD, is Professor of Counseling and Family Sciences at Loma Linda University, teaching Medical Family Therapy in the Marriage and Family Therapy doctoral program. She received her BS in Psychology and her PhD in Marriage and Family Therapy from Brigham Young University. Her professional interests include practiced-based research of family therapy models with underserved populations in nontraditional settings.

Kenneth V. Hardy, PhD, is Director, Center for Children and Families at Ricks, Ackerman Institute for the Family, New York, New York, and Senior Adjunct Clinical Supervisor with the family therapy program, Syracuse University, Syracuse, New York. He received his BA from The Pennsylvania State University and his PhD in Marriage and Family Therapy from Florida State University. His current professional interests include working with couples and families, especially those who live on the margins of society.

Jeri Hepworth is Professor and Associate Residency Director in the Department of Family Medicine at the University of Connecticut School of

Medicine. She received her BA from SUNY Albany and her PhD from the University of Connecticut. A family therapist, she trains family physicians and family therapists and specializes in working with families with chronic illness. She is co-author of two books, *Medical Family Therapy* and *The Shared Experience of Illness.*

Thomas C. Jewell is a Senior Instructor of Psychiatry (Psychology) at the University of Rochester Medical Center and Director of Family Services Research at the Strong Ties Community Support Program. He received a PhD in clinical psychology from Bowling Green State University. His primary clinical and research interests are in the areas of families of people with severe and persistent mental illnesses as well as psychosocial treatments for schizophrenia.

Harvey Joanning is Professor and Director of the Marriage and Family Therapy Doctoral Program at Iowa State University. He received his BA from Briar Cliff College and his PhD from the University of Iowa. His professional interests include process and outcome research in marriage and family therapy and family therapy theory.

Scott Johnson, PhD, is Associate Professor and Director of Clinical Training in the Marriage and Family Therapy Program at Virginia Tech. He holds degrees from Lincoln University, Johns Hopkins University, the Peabody Conservatory, and Virginia Tech, respectively.

Patricia Keoughan is an Instructor in the Counselor Education Program at Iowa State University and President of Human Systems Consultants, Inc., Ames, Iowa. She received her Bachelor of General Studies from Auburn University and her PhD from Iowa State University. Her professional interests include qualitative research methods, process and outcome of marital therapy, and family therapy theory.

Marcia E. Lasswell, MA, is Professor of Psychology, California State University, Pomona, Clinical Professor of Marriage and Family Therapy, University of Southern California, and in private practice in Los Angeles and Claremont, California, respectively. She is a past president of the AAMFT and an Approved Supervisor.

Leigh A. Leslie is Associate Professor of Family Studies at the University of Maryland, College Park, and in private practice. She received her BS from Texas Tech and her PhD from The Pennsylvania State University. Her professional interests include ethnic minority families and issues of gender.

Kevin P. Lyness is Assistant Professor of Marriage and Family Therapy at Colorado State University. He received his BS from Texas Tech University and his PhD in Marriage and Family Therapy from Purdue University. His research interests include adolescence, substance abuse, and MFT process and outcome research.

Eric E. McCollum is Associate Professor and Clinical Director of the MFT program at Virginia Tech, Falls Church, Virginia. He received his PhD in Marriage and Family Therapy from Kansas State University. His current professional focus is family therapy in substance abuse treatment.

Susan H. McDaniel is Professor of Psychiatry and Family Medicine, Director of the Wynne Center for Family Research, University of Rochester School of Medicine and Dentistry, and in private practice. She received her BS from Duke University and her PhD from the University of North Carolina at Chapel Hill. Her special interests are patients with physical health problems, such as somatization, cancer, genetic illnesses, and reproductive health problems.

Earl F. Merritt is Director, Office of Multicultural Equity Programs, and a doctoral candidate in Human Development and Family Studies at The Pennsylvania State University. He received his BA from Kentucky State College and his MA from Western Kentucky University. Current professional interests include multicultural education/therapy and adolescent development.

Thorana S. Nelson is Associate Professor and Director of the Marriage and Family Therapy Program at Utah State University. She received her PhD from the University of Iowa. Her research interests include skills training in family therapy.

Fred P. Piercy, PhD, is head of the Department of Human Development at Virginia Polytechnic Institute and State University, Blacksburg, Virginia. He has received degrees from Wake Forest University, University of South Carolina, and University of Florida. His professional interests include qualitative research, family therapy education, HIV social science research and intervention, and professional issues in family therapy.

Karen H. Rosen is Associate Professor of Marriage and Family Therapy at Virginia Tech, Falls Church, Virginia. She received her BS from Radford University and advanced degrees from Virginia Polytechnic Institute. Her current professional interest is in the area of domestic violence.

Nancy B. Ruddy currently is in private practice as a child and family psychologist in Princeton, New Jersey. She received her BS in Psychology from the University of Iowa and her PhD in Child Clinical Psychology from Bowling Green State University; she received family therapy training at the University of Rochester. Her primary professional interests include domestic violence, collaborative care, and childhood behavior disorders.

Candyce S. Russell received her BS from Cornell University and her PhD from the University of Minnesota. Currently she is the Vera Mowery McAninch Professor of Human Development and Family Services at Kansas State University. Her research interests are in the areas of marital therapy process and outcome.

Thomas A. Smith is Associate Professor of Marriage and Family Therapy at Auburn University. He received his BS from the University of Alabama and his PhD from Virginia Polytechnic Institute. His current professional and research interests include MFT supervision and remarried family development and therapy.

Douglas H. Sprenkle is Professor of Marriage and Family Therapy at Purdue University. He received his BA from Connecticut Wesleyan University and his PhD from the University of Minnesota. His current research interests are common factors in change within marriage and family therapy, affect regulation as an aspect of change, and family factors in the success of business-owning families. He is a former editor of the *Journal of Marital and Family Therapy* and author of five books on marriage and family therapy.

Sandra M. Stith is Professor of Marriage and Family Therapy at Virginia Polytechnic Institute, Falls Church, Virginia, and in private practice. She received her PhD from Kansas State University. Her primary research is in the area of domestic violence.

Cheryl L. Storm is Professor of Marriage and Family Therapy and Director of the Marriage and Family Therapy Clinic at Pacific Lutheran University in Washington and is in part-time group practice. She received her PhD in Marriage and Family Therapy from Purdue University. Her current research interests are the supervision and training of marriage and family therapists.

Frank N. Thomas is Associate Professor of Family Therapy at Texas Woman's University. He received his BS from the University of South Dakota and his PhD from Texas Tech. His current professional interests include client and supervisees' experiences, competency and resiliency, and spirituality in therapy.

Karl Tomm is Professor of Psychiatry at the University of Calgary, Alberta, Canada. He received his MD from the University of Alberta and completed a Psychiatric Residency at McMaster University. His primary research interests are postmodern theory and practice in marital and family therapy.

Terry S. Trepper is Professor of Psychology and Marriage and Family Therapy and Director of the Family Studies Center at Purdue University, Calumet. He received his BA from California State University, Northridge, and his PhD from the University of Oregon. His professional interests are treatment of sexual disorders, family abuse, and family therapy for chemical dependency.

Lynelle C. Yingling received her BS from Texas Tech University and her PhD from Texas Woman's University. She currently is in private practice and conducts mediation and training as a consultant. Her primary professional focus is on the court system collaboration for family services, and human systems mediation training.

Foreword

Standal and Corsini's classic, *Critical Incidents in Psychotherapy,* was published in 1959 at a time when psychotherapy in the United States was still struggling to overcome the hegemony of long-dominant psychoanalysis, and family therapy was just emerging as a separate field. David Baptiste's early fascination with Standal and Corsini's work, which he encountered as an undergraduate psychology student, never left him. The indelible belief that heterogeneous approaches can lead to similar outcomes in psychotherapy was a major impetus in his endeavors that eventually produced *Clinical Epiphanies in Marriage and Family Therapy: A Practitioner's Casebook of Therapeutic Insights, Perceptions, and Breakthroughs.* Instead of the high-sounding *equifinality,* a term that family systems theory has borrowed from general system theory, Baptiste uses the homey but expressive aphorism, "There is more than one way to skin a cat."

Theoretical orientations in marital and family therapy have proliferated in the past four decades. Today's marital and family therapy practitioners clearly are not lacking in choices. The Association of Marital and Family Therapy Regulatory Boards (AMFTRB), which produces and oversees the national examination required as part of the licensure process in most states in the United States, recognizes sixteen schools or theoretical orientations with which potential licensees must demonstrate awareness. These are: behavioral, cognitive behavioral, contextual (Nagy), experiential, integrative, intergenerational (Bowen), network, psychodynamic-object relations, psychoeducational, strategic (Haley, Weakland, and Fisch), strategic (Watzlawick), structural, systemic (Milan), solution focused, narrative, and Ericksonian.

Will today's students (MFT and others) be as intrigued as Baptiste was with the notion that different ways exist to arrive at the same outcome? Baptiste attempted, in his planning of this book, to provide marital and family therapy students and trainees with the opportunity to expose themselves to multiple examples of how practitioners from various orientations within the now highly developed and differentiated marital and family therapy field seek to work with human problems. As editor of this work, Baptiste has provided a rich heterogeneity of sixteen cases presented by twenty different therapists. At the time therapists treated their critical incident case their ages ranged from twenty-four to sixty years, with a median age of forty. Their years of marital and family therapy experience at the time they saw the family of the case report ranged from one year to thirty-seven years, with a median of nine years; one primary therapist did not indicate MFT experience.

Because some of the primary therapists claimed that they used more than one theoretical orientation, four of the major MFT theoretical schools were represented, including strategic (five), narrative (two), solution focused (one), and psychoeducational (one). Two families were treated from an eclectic orientation, and one family each from approaches described by the therapist as relationship oriented, collaborative language, feminist, transitional family therapy, and oppressive sensitive. Other orientations mentioned by various therapists as part of their approach included social constructionist, transgenerational, structural, intergenerational, experiential (Satir), MRI (problem focused), and emotion focused.

Of the sixteen cases presented in this book, seven used only a conjoint family therapy format, one involved only couples therapy, one was essentially individual interviews in which the client's spouse was seen one time, and the remaining cases were seen in combined family and individual sessions. Most of the cases fit into the medium-length pattern—typically six months or less—common to family therapy, but one couple was seen for at least fifteen months.

The selections of therapists, commentators on the cases, and practice locations where the families were seen tilt the book in the direction of a university emphasis. A majority of the contributors—therapists and students—are affiliated with a university. Most of the contributing therapists are involved in marital and family educational and training programs, and some are in part-time private practice. Of the thirty-five commentators, only five are in full-time private practice; the remainder are affiliated with a university. A majority of the families (ten) were seen in clinics, including eight seen in university counseling/MFT training centers and six who were seen in private-practice offices. Approximately forty years of practice as a marital and family therapist and as a clinical psychologist and decades of teaching and supervising clinicians at the doctoral, postdoctoral, master's, and postmaster's levels in a variety of settings convinces me that frequently some important differences can be found between clients who are seen in institutional clinical settings and those who are seen in private-practice settings. However, since the target audience for this book is graduate students, the editor cannot be faulted for this university emphasis among therapists, commentators, and practice settings.

Given the difference in numbers between the commentators and the therapists, the theoretical perspectives claimed by the commentators are more varied than the treatment orientations of the therapists. Some perspectives are directly related to marital and family therapy schools, such as strategic, solution focused, and integrative, whereas a considerable number of the perspectives may more accurately be characterized as outlooks or perspectives rather than theories. As might be expected, there is significant variation in the manner in which commentators responded to the case reports. Some commentators focus primarily on the actions of the therapist, while others expound on their own theoretical orientations and ideas regarding treatment. Leaving aside the overworked and increasingly stale adjective "exciting," a more appropriate description of the commentaries, as well as the case reports, would be that this is thought-provoking material.

These case reports have in common experiences from many practice settings in that they provide little support for the notion strongly—sometimes arrogantly—expressed in early family therapy that the therapist is responsible for change. Most of the critical incidents occurred serendipitously rather than as part of a treatment plan. They occurred within the session in some instances and outside the sessions in others. With one exception, the critical incidents occurred after at least six sessions with the reporting therapist; the majority occurred after nine or more interviews. Only two critical incidents occurred after more than thirty sessions. At least three incidents occurred immediately after the therapist had conducted an interview that differed from the usual interview format—one with the spouse of a client who was being seen individually, one with a child who was seen alone by the therapist, and one after a child came in with her mother, who formerly had been seen alone.

Similarly, it seems likely that one finds little evidence in these reports that the therapeutic orientation espoused by the clinician is determinative of positive outcome in the treatment. Space limitations for the cases do not permit extensive and detailed descriptions of the therapy, thus it is moderately difficult to know explicitly what the therapists did during the bulk of the treatment. Nevertheless, it seems likely that in most instances the critical and successful actions on the part of clients were not especially related to the clinician's theoretical orientation and school-specific interventions. When therapist interventions were evocative of breakthroughs, they were as likely to originate from therapist intuition or occasional desperation as from well-thought-out plans.

Typically, it appears that growth and development are related to more general human factors, such as the establishment of a sound and solid relationship, a meaningful therapeutic relationship and occasionally treatment bargain—to use some terms that have been around for decades—and respectful treatment of the client or client system. Factors that loom large in the healing of clients under the rubric of respectful treatment and listening sensitively to the needs and values of clients include: conveying respectful caring in matters of gender and ethnicity, sensitivity to personal hurt, and striving for personal acceptance and relatedness.

Some cases illustrate strongly the importance of persistence and patience on the part of the therapist. Evidences also exist that sensitivity and caring are not necessarily manifested adequately by being solely or softly accepting of the client and client system, as vital as acceptance is in human relationships. Rather, acceptance often needs to be accompanied by an ability and willingness to face the situation openly and directly with the clients. Attempting to take care of the client actually may have the opposite or unintended effect of what is desired. A combination of caring support and facing reality in such situations actually provides conditions for the client or client system to take over and make possible the steps for change. All of this seems to be wrapped up in the readiness of the client for change, which often is related to the ability of the therapist to create a context of caring, trust, and support, which provides a launching pad for entering into a new world or new set of behaviors. Sometimes the steps toward change appear to have been taken because clients felt ready to do so with the therapist standing beside them to provide backup and help. At other times clients can move only by showing the therapist—and, hence, other important figures in their real and psychic world—that they will take a step regardless of what the therapist does or thinks.

Some cases illustrate the general therapeutic principle that sticking too strongly to one's theoretical notions or therapeutic approach may be a major source of stuck cases. Interestingly, moving away from the therapist's agenda and toward the client's issues in such instances—whether done consciously and by plan or intuitively—often results in the creation of critical incidents and change. In brief, it appears that client changes are related to a complex intermix of client-therapist interactions, and that both the client and the therapist bear responsibility for alteration of problematic situations.

In a few instances, commentators point out possible ethical problems that they detected in a therapist's behaviors. Dissimulation by the therapist and engaging in physical contact are pointed to as actions commentators consider questionable. Does the end justify the means?

At least one case report focuses significantly on a family's sibling subsystem. The sibling subsystem can have a powerful effect on the client's life, for both ill or good. It is perhaps the most neglected aspect of family structure and functioning in family therapy.

The editor, the therapists, and the commentators of this book are due our appreciation for their careful, thoughtful efforts to help the reader grasp important factors in the treatment of individuals in marital and family therapy. Both their conscious, deliberately expressed statements and the knowledge and awareness of important points that are gained by the reader otherwise certainly have the potential to remind us all that equifinality prevails—that, fortunately, there are multiple ways "to skin a cat" or to work effectively with human beings and to do it well.

In these pages the serious reader will encounter a number of important ideas and stimuli to new thinking and will need to study and critique the material and to form his or her own specific conclusions. If each reader educes at least one good idea from this book, then it was worth the time required to read it. Beyond that, wherever this intriguing book helps anyone to become aware of the importance of concentrating on the client or client system and the relationship and context of therapy instead of concentrating on the "right" techniques or approaches to therapy, David Baptiste and his colleagues have done therapists and clients alike a magnificent service.

William C. Nichols, EdD, ABPP, President
International Family Therapy Association

Preface

This book had its genesis in four widely spaced but interrelated contributions. The first of these is the book *Critical Incidents in Psychotherapy* (Standal & Corsini, 1959) that I read in an undergraduate psychology senior seminar at Howard University. That book of clinical case reports and their invited comments taught me that although therapists of similar and opposing theoretical orientations may approach the treatment of an identical presenting problem differently, they also can arrive at similar outcomes. That book also helped me to understand heterogeneity and convergence of therapeutic approaches as they relate to behavioral changes; there is more than one way to skin a cat and do it well! That idea has indelibly impressed me, and the memory of the frequently stimulating in-class discussions of the book's content has influenced me beyond the seminar.

A second contributor is the frustration I experienced several years later when, as an assistant professor, I could not find a family therapy text similar in format to Standal and Corsini's book that could help students in a dual level (undergraduate and graduate) introductory family therapy course— Family Crisis and Rehabilitation—to understand the interrelationship between theoretical perspectives. Absent a suitable text, students highly praised the alternative assignments that helped them to achieve the desired learning objectives and invariably suggested that I should consider writing a book similar in format to the course assignment, since I could not find a suitable text.

A third related contributor is my discussions with a cross section of MFT graduate students during accreditation site visits to several COAMFTE (Commission on Accreditation for Marriage and Family Therapy Education) MFT programs. Characteristically, students appeared to be wedded to a favored therapeutic approach and unable to understand but, more important, unwilling to consider that other therapeutic and theoretical approaches, in addition to those they currently were studying, could be as effective with their clients as their favored therapeutic approaches. Based on those experiences and my conversations at AAMFT conferences with colleagues who also lamented this shortcoming, the idea for this book was born. My thinking has also been influenced and nurtured by Eysenck's (1952) assertion that over time psychotherapists, regardless of their particular theoretical allegiances, tend to be very similar in their approach to therapy.

The fourth contributor is a chance discussion with Terry Trepper (editor, the *Journal of Family Psychotherapy* and senior editor of The Haworth Press's Marriage and the Family Series) subsequent to the publication of an article I had authored and for which another marriage and family therapist provided a comment. During that discussion I shared with Terry my desire to edit a book with a format similar to that used with my published article. Terry was receptive to the idea and worked with me to bring the book to fruition.

The focus of this book is clinical epiphanies, i.e., intuitive therapeutic turning points that often occur in marriage and family therapy and can change (sometimes positively, sometimes negatively) the outcome of therapy which previously had been stuck. Pittman's (1984) "Wet Cocker Spaniel Therapy" is an example of a clinical epiphany that changed positively a therapeutic outcome and is representative of the kind of positive changes featured in this book. This book is modeled after Standal and Corsini's book, and is an anthology of sixteen case reports of clinical epiphanies in marital and family therapy and thirty-two commentaries on those case reports. A majority of the case reports and their commentaries are written by experienced marriage and family therapists (a few less experienced) from varied theoretical orientations and present a cross section of approaches to clinical problems. The commentaries provide an alternative perspective to the therapists' of record approaches to treatment. The intent is to afford readers an opportunity to peep into the treatment rooms of these sixteen marriage and family therapists and to listen in as two colleagues of each therapist examine the case, then "debate" and provide their alternative points of view—one from a similar and one from a dissimilar theoretical perspective—of the therapists' of record therapeutic approaches.

Each case report presents the salient features of the case and is introduced with an overview of the theoretical perspective from which the therapist of record approached the case. Also included is information about the clients, a description of the presenting problem, the therapeutic situation up to the point of the clinical epiphany, the events that led to the clinical epiphany, the specific epiphany, outcome of the specific session in which the epiphany occurred, and the eventual outcome of therapy if the case is terminated or, if current, the progress of therapy since the clinical epiphany (all cases were concluded at the time these case reports were written).

For each case, two commentators were asked to: identify the good and the not-so-good points about the case, tell what they might have done similar to and different from the therapist of record and how they would have dealt with the critical incident from their favored theoretical perspectives. Commentators also were invited to raise any questions that might have occurred to them with regard to the therapist's approach to treatment as well as any ethical issues specific to the case. Interestingly, not all commentators followed the guidelines faithfully. However, their doing so proved to be a boon, since the results are clinically rich, stimulating, thought provoking, and make for excellent reading and discussion.

The case reports and their commentaries are organized randomly—rather than by similarity of theoretical models, presenting problem, or topic—to encourage readers to peruse the book's content rather than flipping to their "favorite topic(s)" and in doing so miss an interesting case because it did not deal with their favorite topic. A majority of the favored theoretical approaches from which the primary contributors approached treatment of the families are systemic integrative and incorporate more than one theoretical model. In cases in which the primary contributor reported using a single theoretical model, his or her commentators identified elements of at least one other theoretical model in the therapist's approach to therapy.

There is something for every marriage and family therapist (and other psychotherapists) in this book regardless of his or her particular theoretical orientation to treating families or whether he or she is an advanced or beginning therapist, teacher, or a student of marriage and family therapy. However, because of differential clinical experiences, advanced and beginning therapists and students will read this book differently and will gain different levels of insight and inspiration from these cases and their commentaries. Advanced therapists will recognize the various meanderings of the therapeutic course (of therapy) and may even see reflections of their own struggles and successes over the course of their clinical careers. Beginning therapists will find a wealth of useful information which can point them in a positive direction which can contribute to success in dealing with clinical obstacles similar to those described in this book. Equally important, information garnered from these case reports and their commentaries can help beginning therapists to feel that "I'm not alone. Others have passed this way before." For students, especially those who have not as yet adopted a preferred theoretical orientation or never have observed their teachers or supervisors conducting therapy, these case reports can help them to sharpen that adoption process and to understand and appreciate the intersection of heterogeneity and convergence of therapeutic approaches vis-à-vis theoretical models.

Of course, not everyone will like every case and some may even raise ethical as well as general practice and/or clinical concerns about some cases. However, because this book is targeted at marriage and family therapy students and trainees, I encourage teachers of marriage and family therapy to promote and encourage in-class discussions and debates of the good, the bad, and the ugly of these cases so that students may learn from them that there are other ways, in addition to their preferred ways, of skinning a cat and doing it well!

My thanks to the therapists who exposed their clinical work to colleagues for comment, and to their colleagues who graciously provided comments. Indeed, it takes a special courage to share such intimate portraits of one's clinical work and invite colleagues to comment. For doing so, my sincere thank you. My thanks also to the families whose lives are presented in these case reports. While we as therapists may have helped them to overcome some of life's difficult obstacles, they certainly have taught us through their willingness to tolerate our uncertainty and all that is part and parcel of the therapeutic process. Because of their willingness to endure an imperfect process they will continue to teach us for years to come.

Finally, my thanks to senior editor Terry Trepper and The Haworth Press for their continued support in the preparation of this book. I hope that the final product is well worth the reader's time.

REFERENCES

Eysenck, H.J. (1952). The effects of psychotherapy. *Journal of Consulting Psychology* 16(5), 319-324.

Pittman, F. (1984). Wet cocker spaniel therapy: An essay on technique in family therapy. *Family Process* 23(1), 1-9.

Standal, W.S. and Corsini, R.J. (1959). *Critical incidents in psychotherapy*. Englewood Cliffs, NJ: Prentice-Hall.

CASE 1

Try Death on for Size

David A. Baptiste Jr.

Therapist Background

Currently: sixty-one years old, black, male, PhD, thirty-two years clinical practice, twenty-seven years marriage and family therapy (MFT) practice. When I saw this family: thirty-five years old, two years MFT practice, five years predoctoral clinical practice.

Practice Setting

Currently: private practice. When I saw this family: university counseling center.

Client Characteristics

The Clarke family consisted of Karen (age forty-nine) and Leslie (age fifty-one), a white, middle-class, interfaith couple (Jew and Gentile), and their daughter, Melissa (age twenty-three), the identified patient (IP); son Wayne (age twenty-six), and daughter Wanda (age nineteen) were not directly involved in therapy. Karen was head of the high school math/science department in a Texas border city; Leslie was a senior aeronautical engineering manager for a military contractor. Wayne held an MIT engineering undergraduate degree and was a graduate student at an Ivy League university. Melissa was on a leave of absence from Wellesley College and a part-time student at a southwestern university. Wanda was a sophomore at the University of Colorado at Boulder. Mother and father were graduates of Wellesley College and MIT, respectively.

Length of Treatment

The family was seen from late April 1976 through the end of June 1977. This included ten unscheduled sessions requested by the parents because of a "crisis" with Melissa, one unscheduled session requested by Melissa after a very revealing session, and one unscheduled extended session requested by me after the critical incident. The critical incident occurred subsequent to Session 38.

Theoretical Perspective

A strategic approach was used in working with this family in concurrent family and individual sessions.

"Your nine o'clock is here. Looks like this is going to be a hot one." This cautionary statement from the receptionist introduced the Clarke family to me. Unaccustomed to such cautions, I asked, "How come?" "The girl is sitting on the floor in the hallway by the stairs, and her parents are fighting with her to come into the center and sit on a chair." I introduced myself to the parents in the waiting room; they explained the situation to me. I introduced myself to Melissa and invited her into my office. After what seemed an eternity, she got up, brushed me aside, and walked down the corridor in the direction of my office. Standing behind her, I curtly said, "The open door." The parents apologized profusely and we followed Melissa into my office.

Melissa was a very thin, gaunt, and moderately skeletal-looking young woman. She sat on the floor in the middle of the office apart from her parents and me. She gazed downward and made eye contact with no one. Her mood appeared to be depressed and her moderately unkempt appearance in part supported that impression.

PRESENTING PROBLEM

The Clarke family was referred by a former client family whom they said "sings your praise" for helping them through a difficult time. The parents identified Melissa as the IP and expressed concerns about her chronic bulimia. In a plaintive voice, Mrs. Clarke said, "Melissa has had this problem since she was about sixteen. She had been doing well but now is slipping back into her old behaviors. She is throwing up again after eating and has lost about ten pounds already. Looks like we may have to hospitalize her again. The last time we did that was about two and a half years ago. We would prefer not to do that and are trying not to. That's why we're here."

The Parents' Story

Mr. and Mrs. Clarke shared that during Melissa's early teen years, she had become progressively obstinate, oppositional, and contrary. As a result, their relationship with her was highly conflictual. Parent-child conflicts were primarily about academic issues and were much more evident and intense with the mother than with the father. Both parents admitted to having very high expectations, especially academic expectations, for their children. They believed Melissa to be much more academically capable than was evident from her attitude, effort, performance, and grades at that time; she was as academically capable as her siblings but did not apply herself. At approximately age fifteen, her contrariness ended. Then she refused to eat. At first, she was picky about what she would eat. "When we put our foot down on that, she would heap food onto her plate and eat all of it; that was the rule. But then she would throw up after eating. When we discovered what she was doing, we were concerned but thought it was another one of her phases and expected her to outgrow it. We did not fight with her because she was doing well in school. We decided to wait her out. At that time we had no idea what it was or how dangerous it could be. Then it got worse and affected her health, and her doctor referred her to therapy. That was the beginning of our nightmare and revolving doors with therapists, hospitals, treatment programs. She has been in and out of therapy with several therapists in Boston and New York, and in and out of hospitals and treatment programs at least seven times for this problem. Over the years nothing seemed to work. She seems to get better for awhile then backslides for no apparent reason. We can't keep doing this; it's getting old. We're nearing the end of our patience with her. We were told a woman would be better as a therapist for her, but she hasn't liked any of them. She usually finds fault with a therapist just as the therapist would be telling us that she is getting better. She is good at finding reasons to change therapists. Up to now she was not willing to see a male. But we're making this change because we want results, and from all we were told about you, we feel you can help us. You did well for the Thomases and the people who told them about you. We want you to help us."

In response to questions about family issues and concerns that might be impinging upon Melissa and contributing to her behaviors, Mr. Clarke disclosed that as adolescents Melissa and her brother Wayne were intense rivals. Apologetically he admitted that initially the adults had fostered that rivalry. They reasoned that a rivalry would improve the children's academic performances. Mr. Clarke offered that, "The rivalry got out of hand and was stopped but not before Melissa developed an intense dislike, perhaps closer to hatred, for Wayne. We have tried to make it up to her, but she would not budge and we still don't understand why she dislikes Wayne with such passion. Because of that, Wayne will not come home when Melissa is here. This bothers Karen to no end." It was evident that Wayne was his parents' favorite and the model child; this was especially true more for the mother than for the father. On the other hand, Melissa was, especially for her mother, the problem child. Melissa's father was moderately more accepting and understanding of Melissa's contrary ways but nevertheless doted on Wayne. Wanda's currency with her mother was less than Wayne's but significantly higher than Melissa's. For example, Wanda received an honorable mention as a National Merit Scholar and had been accepted to Mount Holyoke, Smith, and Wellesley College but attended the University of Colorado. Her mother was disappointed that she chose not to attend an Ivy League college or an East Coast university as an acceptable alternative; she fully expected Wanda to "come to her senses and transfer." Wanda's father fully accepted and supported her choice.

Individually and jointly, this couple presented as very inflexible in their approach to life and parenting. They appeared to be more comfortable with thinking than feeling. Both insisted on perfection for themselves and their children. They admitted they were strict disciplinarians and very strict with the children. Mrs. Clarke always seemed to have answers to all the questions, even those directed at Mr. Clarke and, on occasion, Melissa, who seemed not to want to speak in therapy. Mr. Clarke appeared less self-assured than his wife and at times nonverbally expressed irritation with something she had said in therapy.

Negotiating for Therapy

At this first meeting with Melissa and her parents, I felt simultaneously flattered, awed, and overwhelmed. It was clear that the parents were desperate and urgently looking for a solution, perhaps more so for their own sake than for Melissa's sake. I was bothered by their desperation and expressed expectation for me as a therapist. They were expecting great things from me. They were expecting that I would succeed in making Melissa well when others had not been able to do so. More important, they appeared to be seeking assurance that a lasting—if not immediate—solution was forthcoming this time around.

Given the family's expectations, I felt overwhelmed and feared that I really did not know how to help Melissa and could not live up to her parents' expectations for me. I felt that their expressed expectations for me as a therapist were beyond my abilities at that stage of my professional development. Accordingly, I declined to work with Melissa and her family. I told the family that I felt unqualified to help them because my clinical experiences with eating-disordered clients were limited. More important, I am male and Melissa did not want to see a male. Contributing to my decision was their reports that Melissa had been treated by some of the best therapists in Boston and New York and also had been in some very excellent treatment pro-grams. If more experienced therapists could not help Melissa, I would be in over my head; I did not want to fail. True, I had worked with a few bulimic clients during my doctoral internship and also had served as a cotherapist in treating an anorexic female during my master's externship in Boston, but I felt convinced that Melissa's situation was beyond my clinical abilities. Also, I was concerned about Melissa's lack of engagement and her silence; she seemed not to have a voice of her own.

Mr. and Mrs. Clarke turned a deaf ear to my objections and deflected my efforts to disqualify myself. Individually and jointly, they told me that they felt that I was qualified to help them. They said, "You were given high marks by the Thomases. You helped their family through a very difficult situation. You did not give up on them. We would like you to give Melissa a chance. You got her to come into your office when we could not get her to come into the center." Despite their reassurances, I continued to insist that I lacked the requisite experiences to work with the family. Paradoxically, the more I sought to disqualify myself, the more they continued to reassure me that I was qualified and implored me to work with Melissa and the family. Mrs. Clarke assured me that knowing that I attended two East Coast colleges (they learned this from the Thomases) increased her confidence in my abil-ity to help Melissa. As an incentive they offered to pay to see me in my pri-vate practice because the services of the counseling center are free to stu-dents; Melissa was a part-time student. Their desperation and the urgency of their need for help betrayed the calm of their voices.

Against my better judgement, and persuaded by the parents' entreaties and flattery, I agreed to work with Melissa and her family but provided my-self some wriggle room: I repudiated any possibility for success. I cautioned them not to expect me to be successful in changing Melissa's behaviors and not to be disappointed if I was unable to help them. I repeated this caution several times during the course of treatment. The family accepted my limi-tations and I contracted with them for both family and individual sessions. Since neither the parents nor Melissa alone was the client, my intention was to provide the parents as well as Melissa and me the opportunity to develop different perspectives of the situation. Throughout these discussions, Me-lissa contributed very little verbally except a few grunts and inappropriate giggles, even when I solicited and encouraged her contribution. Because her parents had presented her story, I wanted to acknowledge her and let her tell her own story. I asked, "Melissa, can you tell me what is happening in your life that led your parents to bring you here?" She sat on the floor and stared at it intently. Her energy was turned inward; she was disheveled, sullen, withdrawn, and appeared to be moderately depressed and dissociated. This became her usual in-session mode.

For twenty-two sessions, I saw the family in individual and family sessions and focused on many issues specific to bulimia, especially anger, autonomy, belonging, control, and depression, as these were relevant to Melissa's situation. However, despite my best efforts, no perceptible progress was occurring and the family's situation remained unchanged. Therapy with Melissa was, for me, a struggle, as I believed it was for her. I was beginning to feel stuck and in over my head; I seriously considered referring the family to another therapist in the center. If after these many sessions I had not made an impact, perhaps it was time to refer the Clarkes to another therapist. I shared my feelings with Melissa in an individual session and with Melissa and her parents in a joint session. The parents echoed my concerns about the lack of progress but encouraged me to continue when I suggested a referral. They stoically accepted that progress would be longer in coming. Melissa gave no indication that she was bothered by, or even heard, my concerns.

Our First Conversation

In the previous twenty-two sessions, Melissa spoke exceedingly little and shared only superficial personal information. Attempts to engage her verbally using techniques such as the two chairs and thought doubling (Baptiste, 1995) appeared only to anger her and to strengthen her resolve not to speak in therapy. However, at this individual session, something changed. Melissa did not sit on the floor. Instead, she paced for a few minutes and, while still standing, fixed her gaze upon me and asked, "What do you think of me?" Surprised that she had spoken more than two words, I replied, "I really don't know what to make of you. My hunch is that you are a very, very angry person who may be using your bulimia to hurt yourself and perhaps someone else. At times I question whether you are truly a bulimic or if there is more to this situation."

She maintained her gaze but said nothing. After a five-minute silence, she asked, "If I am not bulimic, what am I?"

"You tell me," I said. "You are angry; you throw up, lose weight, and are depressed, but in other ways do not behave like bulimics I have known. For example, you don't seem to be down on yourself."

She was silent again. Then she asked, "You haven't tried to get in my head like my other counselors. Why not?" I asked her what does "getting into my head" mean. She said, "My other counselors used to tell me why I am the way I am. No one knows why I am the way I am."

"I am sure you know why you are bulimic," I said, "but so far you have told no one. Will you tell me?" Looking away, she said "No!" After a long silence, I thanked her for talking and sharing. I said, "I was beginning to feel that you never were going to talk with me." She smiled in therapy for the first time and, while still pacing, she initiated a sustained conversation.

She shared her intense dislike for Wayne and her mother. She never disclosed reasons for disliking Wayne but offered that, "My mother never listens. She thinks she is a shrink and always wants to tell you what is going on in your head. And she never believes what anyone says." She expressed feelings that her mother cared more for Wayne than for her and Wanda and even for her father. She wished that she could be more like Wanda; "Wanda stuck it to Mom and went to CU. And you stick it to her, too. You make my parents come to counseling. Before, I was the only one who went. Even in the hospital, they came to counseling only a couple times. She doesn't like to come." Because of the devilish grin that followed her last comment, I asked her, was her comment a positive acknowledgment that her parents were now coming to therapy, or was she taking delight in the fact that having to come to therapy was disrupting her parents' lives? She did not reply.

She abruptly switched directions and asked to read the punch line of a cartoon on my bulletin board but asked—no, ordered—me to move away so that she did not have to be close to me. I nodded assent and moved closer to the door. After we regained our original positions—she pacing, I sitting—I asked if she was afraid of me. She replied, "Damn straight; I don't trust men. You are a man, aren't you?" A discussion about her fear and distrust of men and an exploration of her relationships with men followed. Aside from her father and brother, close relationships with men essentially were nonexistent. She neither dated nor had a boyfriend in high school. In college in Boston, she had "a three-month boyfriend." That ended when he discovered that she was bulimic. She acknowledged loving her dad but saw him as a weak person. "He always gives in to mom. He never stands up to her."

The next session, Melissa was business as usual, but for the first time she talked about wanting to die. Paradoxically, she was not *planning* to die but *wanted* to die. I pointed out the paradox and said, "You sound as though you are tired of being bulimic but either do not want to change as yet or do not know how to change."

She replied, "People who die get respect." She, however, was not looking for respect. "Maybe then everything would be clearer."

She never identified what she was looking for, what would be clearer, or for whom it would be clearer. I commented that from her point of view dying would be an answer, but if she died without confronting the person(s) with whom she was angry, that person would have won. He or she would have gotten away with whatever it was that made her angry enough to want to die. Angrily, she said, "Fuck you! What do you know? I just want to die and get it over!"

At that point, I told her I did not feel that I could help her. This was not the first that she had become angry with me. She often became angry whenever I said something that was true or perhaps close to it. I said, "We are not making any progress. So far, in most of the sessions, we do not talk. And when we do, you become angry. That is not helping the situation."

I invited her to consider whether we should continue with therapy. Gazing intently at me, she said, "That's chickenshit! Nobody ever said "fuck you" to you before? You really don't understand me!" She left the office before I could reply.

The next day, Mrs. Clarke called for an unscheduled appointment. At that meeting, the parents disclosed that they again were thinking of re-hospitalizing Melissa. "Yesterday she came home after seeing you and went straight to her room. She refused to eat anything or to talk with either of us. For most of the night she paced in her room and screamed about wanting to die." Mr. Clarke added, "She sounded like a wounded banshee." They asked if I had an explanation for her behavior. I summarized the previous day's session, shared my feelings about being stuck, my concern about the futility of continuing therapy, and, again, suggested a referral. Mrs. Clarke asked Melissa if she wanted to continue in therapy with me; hospitalization was the alternative. I asked that Melissa not be threatened with hospitalization and invited them to assess whether any progress had been made so far; I reminded them of my earlier statement regarding my lack of experience. If they felt that progress was not being made, a change of therapist might be in order. As they did in our first meeting, the parents dismissed my self-disqualification and asked that I continue with the family and not "give up" on them. They really did not want to hospitalize Melissa, but if I did not continue to work with them, they might not have a better alternative. Based on this discussion, I decided to continue to work with the family. Throughout this discussion, Melissa sat on the floor with her back to her parents and me. She was consistent in her silence and did not comment even when invited to do so.

Two weeks later, Melissa returned to therapy with me. For the next five sessions, her in-office behaviors, whether alone or with her parents, remained unchanged. During this period, the frequency of Melissa's gorging and purging increased, and her parents expressed their exasperation at the lack of progress in therapy and in her deteriorating condition. At home and in therapy, Melissa's continuing theme was wanting to die. She placed several notes around the house with her preferred inscription for a headstone: "Here lies Misunderstood." My efforts to discuss, in individual and family sessions, her wanting to die and the significance of her headstone inscription were futile. Interestingly, however, when I invited her to write the obituary she wanted, she declined. Her parents were no more informed than I about her reasons for wanting to die.

EVENTS LEADING TO THE CRITICAL INCIDENT

The next individual session began with Melissa in her usual position on the floor but much more talkative than in recent sessions. She acknowledged that she had heard me speculate with her parents about her anger and they not knowing why she might be angry. She said, "You think that I am angry that's why I want to die?" I repeated my hunch that she was hurting inside; gorging-purging, and wanting to die might be her way of punishing whomever. She denied feeling hurt but admitted wanting to die. I asked whether it was worth dying because she was angry. She responded with silence. I asked whom she felt would be happy if she died. More silence. Who would miss her if she died? "My father," was her brusque reply. He would miss her because he cared for her and worried about her. She did not believe that her mother would miss her; Melissa thought "she might even be happy." Melissa would miss Wanda. Since she did not mention Wayne, I asked her how she felt he would feel if she died. "Do I have to answer that?" I pushed her to answer, given her dislike for him. She replied, "He wants to forget, but that isn't going to happen and she is on his side." I asked her to clarify her comments.

Her response was fifteen minutes of pacing and silence punctuated by sobbing. She moved to the window, stared outside, and broke the silence. In junior high school, she was failing algebra. Her mother called her dumb because she was failing. Her father offered to tutor her but, "was too busy with work." Mother asked Wayne to tutor her. Initially, she refused to be tutored by Wayne because of their rivalry. She later agreed because she was failing and afraid of her mother's wrath. After a few tutoring sessions, "Wayne said I had to pay him. I asked how much he wanted. He said he'd show me. He told me to lie down and close my eyes and then he put his dick in my mouth. I pushed him away and said I would tell Mom and Dad when they came home. He laughed and said, 'You don't eat, I don't teach.'" Melissa attempted to tell her mother, but "she brushed me off. She never wants to hear anything bad about Wayne." She did not say in what ways her mother had brushed her off. She did not tell her dad because "he won't believe." Again, she did not elaborate.

Despite her best efforts to stop the abuse, Wayne forced her compliance through blackmail. If she did not comply, he would not tutor her, she would fail algebra for the semester, and her mother would belittle her. He also threatened to tell her friends that "I eat dick and like it." Feeling between a rock and a hard place and that neither parent was "on her side," she endured in silence, complied with Wayne's request, was tutored, and passed algebra. In the wake of this experience, she grew to hate Wayne and her mouth. Thus began her descent into bulimia. She threw up any food she put into her mouth and felt intensely dirty and angry. She felt she could not tell her father and believed her mother intentionally had "brushed her off." In doing so, her mother was perceived to have "sided with Wayne." When she ended her story, she said, "Now you know!"

Five minutes of silence followed her outpouring as I struggled to find the correct words to say to her. At last her anger, depression, and silence made sense. She had been sexually abused. I empathized with her anger and suggested that therapy now be focused on issues specific to her abuse to help her understand the effects of the abuse on her life and its relationship to her bulimia, and to allow her to vent her anger in a nongeneralized manner. We also discussed telling her parents about the abuse to give them an opportunity to deal with it and to provide meaningful support for her.

She was adamant that I not tell her parents, especially her mother. She felt it was too late for them to do anything; "they had their chance." I asked, "Are you seeking revenge?" Melissa said no, but "she is going to have to take care of me until she dies." I asked if that meant that she planned to be bulimic until her mother died or until she died. What did she hope to gain by continuing to be bulimic? She fell silent again. I wondered aloud if she was cutting her nose to spite her face. I also suggested that in telling her parents she would be punishing Wayne because he would lose status in their eyes. She would not be persuaded and asked me to promise not to tell her parents. I told her that it was not my responsibility to tell them. However, I felt uncomfortable keeping a secret, especially since that secret was tied to her bulimia. I told her, "I will leave it up to you to tell. But if your condition worsens and you become a danger to yourself, I will tell them."

She was livid. "No! No! No! I don't want you telling them. You said it is my right to tell them, so why don't you butt out?" I commented that as difficult as it was for her to hear, she might be surprised that her parents cared for her more that she was willing to believe. She screamed, "How do you know? Leave me alone! Just let me die." Again she ran from the office.

A Secret Is a Heavy Load

The next day, Melissa returned to see me. She wanted assurance I was not going to tell her parents about her disclosure. She regretted having told me about the abuse: "It is my business." I iterated that it was her responsibility to tell her parents. I asked if she believed that being bulimic was related to her being sexually abused. She replied, "If I say no, you won't believe me. If I say yes, you won't leave me alone. I don't care what you think; just don't tell my parents." I pointed out that it will be difficult for me to talk candidly with her and her parents while keeping a secret. I asked her to help me understand her objections to telling her parents. In a very controlled voice she said, "None of your business. Just don't tell her." Before I could respond, she asked, "What if it was my fault? That's what she made it sound like when I tried to tell her that night." She explained that she never was explicit about the details in telling her mother about the abuse. She had gotten as far as telling her that Wayne had done something to her but before she could say any more, "she brushed me off, 'you must have done something to him first.'" I empathized with her feelings of being brushed off and emphasized that she was not responsible for the abuse. I also emphasized the importance of being heard now. She reaffirmed her position: "Don't you tell."

For four weeks, Melissa did not return to see me. During that time, I met with her parents. They shared that Melissa's condition had become more anorexic than bulimic; she was not eating at all. "She infrequently would eat a small salad, then for several days she won't eat." In addition, she had not left the house in approximately three weeks. She neglected her personal hygiene and was silent for longer periods. When she did talk, it was about wanting to die. To dramatize her desire to die, she often laid on her bed or the living room floor, arms folded across her chest, "to see how death looked." This behavior bothered Mrs. Clarke. "She is frightening us with this kind of behavior." At that juncture, I realized Melissa was achieving her goal of making her mother suffer. She was holding the possibility of her death over her parents' heads and, in doing so, was making life unpleasant for her mother. Her parents were unsure of their next move, but hospitalization was becoming an imminent possibility because of Melissa's worsened condition. During each session, Mrs. Clarke cried uncontrollably and consistently asked, "What have I done to deserve this?" She talked about the anguish she felt seeing Melissa in such pain and about feeling helpless to do anything to stop it. Mr. Clarke empathized with his wife and shared his feelings about Melissa's condition. Despite his frustration with the situation, he was optimistic that the family and Melissa would "get through this thing." I felt very restrained in talking with them and was very careful lest I inadvertently break my promise to Melissa. I shared with them my feelings of being stuck and briefly considered telling them of Melissa's disclosure and its likely relationship to her deterioration. Instead, I told them that despite the obvious gloom, some progress was being made, albeit slowly. I pointed to Melissa's increased verbal production in therapy as one indicator of progress. They were pleased that she and I were talking after so many months of silence. I cautioned them that in many cases things often get worse before getting better.

Two weeks after those sessions, Melissa dropped in to see me without an appointment. She looked even more skeletal than in past months. Her primary concern was, "What did you tell her when I wasn't here? She doesn't think that I'm serious about dying. Did you tell them that?" I assured her that I did not. I suggested that what she heard may have been her mother's loving concern for her well-being. Despite what Melissa believed about her mother, she cared for Melissa and wanted her to live. I also told her I had kept my promise about her disclosure and asked if she was any closer to telling her parents. She replied, "Thanks. You still don't understand, do you?" I invited her to help me to understand. Still standing, she looked at me in silence for awhile then left without responding.

THE CRITICAL INCIDENT

Four days later, Melissa and her parents were seen in an unscheduled session. Mr. Clarke spoke first. "Something has to be done now! We are at the end of our patience. Melissa has gotten way out of hand. She won't tell us what is going on inside of her, so we can't help her. And you can't seem to make a dent in whatever is going on with her. We don't want to put her in the hospital, but looks like we don't have a choice." Mrs. Clarke elaborated. Since our last meeting, Melissa had not eaten; her screaming, pacing, and not talking had increased. She now lay for longer periods in her death posture on the living room floor. The previous day, she had lain in her death mode in the backyard and also had called Wanda and told her what to wear to her funeral. According to Mrs. Clarke, "That frightened Wanda because we have not told her what has been going on. Now she is worried, and that bothers me. This has got to stop!"

I shared with the parents that Melissa was hurting but as yet had not found a safe way to share what it was that was hurting her. I suggested that all may not be lost given that they were able to get Melissa to come with them today. Apologetically, Mr. Clarke admitted, "We threatened to put her in the hospital today if she did not come with us." During this session, Melissa sat on the floor but closer to her father than her mother. She looked unkempt and sleep deprived, and her mood was severely depressed compared to past meetings. I asked Melissa how might I help her tell her parents what was hurting her. Her response was a piercing stare and silence. Her communication consisted of grunting, tossing her head, rolling her eyes, and incessantly asking, "Can we go now?"

The parents' frustration struck a responsive chord with me. I also was feeling frustrated and stuck. In the void of not knowing, I quickly devised a plan to bring the reality of death to Melissa. I told her, "You seem intent on taking control by wanting to die. Planning your own funeral is the final control and responsibility you will have. I want you and your parents to visit a funeral home and see what goes on after you die so that you can plan your own funeral." This prescription caught the family off guard. No one spoke for awhile. The parents said that the invitation was "weird" and questioned its purpose. Melissa refused to take the tour; "That's stupid," she determined. I pointed out that Melissa will die if she continued not to eat. Since she had been preparing the inscription for her headstone, she could go a step further and plan her funeral. Both Melissa and her parents were still unpersuaded, but I asked them what they had to lose and strongly encouraged them to go. "Right now we seem not to have anything better to offer, and Melissa wants to die and will die if she continues down this path." They agreed to the visit; in their presence, I called a funeral home director I knew and scheduled the visit for two o'clock that day. After the family left, I called the director again to clarify my reasons for referring the family. When I initially spoke with him, I knew by his questions that he, too, may have thought my request "weird."

THE AFTERMATH OF THE CRITICAL INCIDENT

Approximately 4:30 p.m. that day, Mr. Clarke called. He was irate. He questioned my professionalism, accused me of being crazy and of trying to kill his daughter. After he calmed down, I learned that Melissa had run away as a result of an incident at the funeral home. I invited the family to come in later that afternoon. Initially, he refused, but I persuaded him to do so.

I immediately called the director to inquire about the incident and was referred to the associate who conducted the tour. I learned that the tour was unremarkable until the casket room. There the associate invited Melissa to get into a casket and "try it on for size." When he attempted to lift her into the casket, she bolted, with her parents in pursuit. I listened in stunned silence as I visualized the scene and tried to imagine what Melissa must have felt. The very thing for which she had been asking but did not want was staring her in her face. My initial concern was that the incident might have pushed her over the edge; I would be held culpable if any harm had befallen her. Several emotions flooded my consciousness; like a drowning man I saw my career passing before my eyes. However, despite my feelings of gloom and doom, I decided to wait until I met with the family before my final self-chastisement. I informed my supervisor about the situation. He initially was concerned about the potential for harm to Melissa. He concluded, however, "It might be the best thing that happened. Now she knows what death is all about. You can handle it. You have been doing well so far."

At 5:30 p.m., Melissa and her parents arrived. Mr. Clarke was much calmer; Mrs. Clarke was very reserved. Surprisingly, Melissa sat on a chair between her parents, her head on her mother's shoulder. I apologized to the family for the incident and asked how I could help them cope. Angrily, Mrs. Clarke said, "That was a terrible thing to happen to her. It scared her out of her mind. I can't believe you would put her through that knowing what she is going through." Melissa sat up and took notice of her mother; she said nothing.

Before I could respond, Mr. Clarke defended me. He said, "That was not his doing. You heard what he said when he called. That man got carried away." Chuckling, he said, "You must agree it has its humorous side." Melissa screamed, "It wasn't funny! You think I want to die?" Mr. Clarke looked at her in disbelief. She hung her head and fell silent. I did not respond, hoping Melissa would say more; she did not. Mrs. Clarke then shared that she had found Melissa and spoke with her before Mr. Clarke caught up with them. She said, "I now know that she doesn't want to die, but I still don't know why she made such a production about wanting to die." Melissa remained silent as did I. I remarked that there appeared to be a breakthrough in the parent-child—especially the mother-daughter—relationship. I offered as evidence Melissa talking with both parents and sitting close to her mother. Mrs. Clarke acknowledged that, "There is a break in our cold war, but I don't think we're out of the woods yet." I commented that only Melissa could say for sure whether the family was out of the woods or how much farther they had to travel. She did not respond. During this meeting, Melissa did not talk with me directly; she communicated through her mother. At this juncture it was clear that an in-group (the family) and an out-group (me) had developed in therapy as the parents rallied around Melissa, and as a family they began to coalesce in response to the crisis created by the funeral-home incident. I invited the family to return because I believed Melissa was still in physical and psychological danger from not eating. The parents agreed to return and asked Melissa if she wanted to continue to see me. She agreed to see me only with her parents present. Mrs. Clarke interjected, "She doesn't like you much right now. She's afraid of you." I asked Melissa to share her reasons for fearing me. She blurted out, "You bully me into talking. You sent me to that man." I apologized for the incident and emphasized that putting her into the casket was neither a part of my plan nor an expectation for the tour.

During the next session, Melissa again sat between her parents and received much attention from her mother. I learned that the mother-daughter relationship continued to improve. Melissa had begun to eat more than salad, was talking more to both parents, had cleaned her room, and had not mentioned wanting to die since the funeral-home visit. Despite this glowing report, the session was very somber and tense. Melissa had told her mother and later her father about the sexual abuse. Both parents were outraged that Wayne had abused Melissa. They blamed themselves for fostering the rivalry between the siblings. Mrs. Clarke was harsher in her self-chastisement. She blamed herself for not listening more carefully to Melissa and vowed to "be there for you from now on." Although not as self-chastising as his wife, Mr. Clarke apologized to Melissa for "not being there for her when it counted." Switching direction, Mrs. Clarke thanked me for "hanging in there with Melissa. It must have been hard knowing this and not being able to tell us. I know that she has gotten this off her chest and know that I did not brush her off, willfully or not. But are we out of the woods?" I acknowledged that much progress had been made in a short time. However, I emphasized that therapy needed to focus on helping Melissa to regain her emotional strength and to overcome the effects of the abuse and her negative feelings about her family, especially her mother. To that end, I provided them with relevant literature and information about the emotional aftermath attendant to being sexually abused. I asked Melissa how she felt about the situation now that she had shared the secret. Looking down at the floor, she said, "It's OK, I guess. I guess I didn't really tell her before. I still don't like Wayne."

Mrs. Clarke concurred, "I don't blame you. Right now, I don't like him either." Crying, she added, "All these years we all suffered because of his horrible behavior. I can't forgive him." I invited the family and Melissa in particular to return to therapy. The focus would be on helping her to deal with the effects of the abuse, her feelings toward Wayne, as well as her feelings of being unloved by her parents, especially her mother. Melissa continued to refuse to see me individually.

DISCUSSION

Characteristics of the Case Relevant to the Outcome

As I review this case, several characteristics are specific to the family as well as to me that are relevant to the outcome. Some of these were evident as I worked with the family; others became evident only in hindsight. The first factor was my limited experience with eating-disordered clients. Although negative at one level, on another level it proved to be a positive factor in the eventual outcome of the case. My "not knowing" allowed me to approach therapy with fewer preconceptions about the nature of Melissa's illness and to be free to follow paths wherever they led. Telling the family that I could not help them (i.e., not knowing) also provided me with an advantage that was relevant to the outcome. It is highly unusual that a professional would declare himself or herself unqualified and the consumer would convince the professional that he or she is qualified and, despite the professional's declaration, contract with him or her for services. However, since the family had convinced me that I could help them, they now were invested in coming to therapy and following my prescriptions no matter how "weird" they were. Interestingly, despite my then limited knowledge about the interplay of sexual abuse and eating disorders, my hunches that Melissa might really not be bulimic and that there was more to her behavior were, as it turned out, steps in the right direction. More important, because Melissa knew what really was fueling her behavior, she became angry whenever I came too close to the truth. She wanted her parents to discover the source of her anger and concomitant illness.

Second was Melissa's disclosure of the abuse to me and her injunction against telling her parents. Her disclosure was a turning point for both of us.

It allowed me to narrow my focus and allowed her to unload her secret after approximately seven years of therapy. However, her injunction made me a holder of a secret and raised an ethical dilemma for me. Like Melissa, I knew something her parents did not know. In keeping her secret, I knowingly was colluding with Melissa in deceiving her parents. Not disclosing to her parents allowed them to continue worrying about her and kept us from focusing on the central issue of sexual abuse.

Third, the family's dynamics—e.g., the favorite child (Wayne) versus the problem child (Melissa)—and the rivalry fostered by the parents was one characteristic that directly contributed to the drama and its unfolding. Because of their respective positions in the family, Wayne felt that his behavior would be overlooked, and Melissa was convinced that her hurt was minimized and disqualified by her mother. Melissa's anger at being a second-class child in the family was relevant to her decision not to disclose to her parents and certainly affected the outcome of the case. Melissa's bulimia and her concomitant behaviors could be seen as a test of her parents' love and caring for her. For approximately ten years, she had felt like the problem child in the family: unloved and uncared for by her parents. She saw their lack of caring demonstrated in: (a) the parental instigation of a rivalry with a brother whom she believed to be academically superior to her; she could not win; (b) a father who would not make time for her needs (e.g., tutor her) but would, "stop the world if Wayne wanted something," and (c) a mother who doted on Wayne but loved Melissa only when she followed her mother's plans for her (e.g., attend Wellesley College) and "brushed her off" when she sought her protection and support. Melissa felt wronged by these three members of her family, primarily her mother and Wayne. Anger became her main weapon because, despite all she had done (e.g., used her illness to get their attention) and was doing then (e.g., being silent, asking to die), she felt that she was not being heard in the manner in which she wanted to be heard.

Fourth, the parents' decision to engage a male therapist, despite having been made to believe that a female therapist was better suited to work with Melissa, was a significant contributor to the unfolding of the case. Previously, Melissa had refused to see a male therapist. Although the parents had acceded to popular wisdom and Melissa's wishes with regard to the importance of a female therapist, they now departed from that wisdom and engaged a male therapist. The change in the therapist's gender removed the comfort—if indeed she was comfortable—of a woman and replaced it with a man with whom she would be uncomfortable. In the past, Melissa had demanded to change therapists for reasons known only to her. Given her history of "firing" therapists, I was surprised that she never attempted to fire me or actually fired me despite the fact that I repeatedly made her angry and often suggested referring the family to another therapist.

Fifth, the parents' desperation and urgency for "results" were also relevant to the outcome. Had they not been to the "therapeutic well" so many times previously without obtaining the desired results, they may not have been as open as they were to continuing therapy despite not seeing any perceptible progress. More important, it may have been their desperation for "results" that allowed them to agree to visit the funeral home, despite their doubts about the value of doing so.

Sixth, the actions of the funeral-home employee who did not follow the "script," were perhaps the most significant contributor. I often tell clients and students that God has a wild sense of humor. That employee's well-meaning disregard for directives certainly is an excellent example of God's sense of humor. He never could have imagined the unintended consequences he set into motion through his attempt at humor. However, in the end, it was that reckless act of attempting to put Melissa into a casket that proved to be the catalyst which moved her off dead center, allowed her to reveal the secret to her parents, and thawed the mother-daughter relationship.

Finally, Melissa's perception of me as different from any of her previous therapists in ways other than gender was an important factor in the eventual outcome. She was prepared for "more of the same" with regard to the therapeutic process and did not have a schema against which to evaluate me as she had done with her female therapists. For example, she was surprised that I neither told her why she was bulimic, demanded that she get better, nor asked her to give up her anger. The opposite was true. I told her I did not know what to make of her illness, empathized with her anger, and required that her parents come to therapy, when previously they were not required to do so with any regularity.

The Role of the Critical Incident in Getting Therapy Unstuck

Clearly, the funeral-home incident was the catalyst and the critical incident that played a pivotal role in eventually getting therapy unstuck by creating a crisis principally for Melissa but also for her parents. This crisis helped Melissa to discover some truths about herself (she did not want to die) and her parents (given a fair chance, they would protect and defend her). Predictably, her parents rallied around her and provided the support she felt she never received from them. Their doing so challenged Melissa's perceptions of them, especially her mother, as not caring for her. It also allowed her to trust them, share her secret, and repair the mother-daughter relationship. Prior to the critical incident, therapy was still stuck despite Melissa's disclosure to me of the sexual abuse as the major contributor to her bulimia. Because she refused to tell her parents and continued in her anger and concomitant behaviors, Melissa's negative perceptions of her parents as uncaring, and their anguish about her suffering, continued. Indeed, subsequent to her disclosure, the situation actually got worse; the intensity of her anger and its manifestation in her physical behaviors increased. Although I was aware that she really did not want to die despite her continuing mantra, it was not until Melissa was about to be placed into that casket and stare death in the face that she became fully cognizant that she really did not want to die. I learned that immediately prior to entering the casket room Melissa's composure was shaken while visiting the embalming room. Consequently, it may have been the cumulative effect of seeing an actual embalming and the incident in the casket room that resulted in the critical incident. Whether singular or cumulative, the positive role of the critical incident in getting therapy unstuck cannot be overemphasized.

Implications of the Critical Incident for Therapy

The implications of the critical incident are remarkable despite therapy still being stuck. That incident facilitated the family's coalescence (i.e., unifying against a common enemy) that occurred at home following Melissa's disclosure of the abuse to her parents prior to returning to see me after the funeral-home visit. Subsequent to that incident and the disclosure, the direction of therapy as well as the family's relationship, especially the mother-daughter relationship, changed dramatically. Rather than wanting to die, Melissa had to deal with living. And living involved putting aside her anger and its manifestation—her bulimia—and rebuilding the parent-child relationship not as a problem child, but as a child loved and cared for by her parents. This was new for her, given the years spent feeling uncared for and unloved.

POSTSCRIPT

I saw the family for approximately fourteen more sessions. Since Melissa's bulimia was under control, at least 75 percent of those sessions focused on issues specific to the parents. For example, Mrs. Clarke addressed issues related to her feelings of guilt at "not being more understanding of Melissa" as an adolescent and as a young adult. Both parents dealt with their anger at Wayne as well as their indirect contributions to the attitude that fostered his behavior. They saw Wayne's behavior as a negative reflection on them as parents: "Those things only happen in other families. How can we even tell other people about this? What will they think of us as parents?" Of importance to them was what could they do to help Wayne to understand the consequences of his behavior and mend the sibling relationship. They openly questioned whether that rift could ever be mended. During one session with the parents alone, Mr. Clarke stopped midsentence and began to laugh lustily. He said, "You, you son of a bitch! You knew that sending Melissa to that funeral home would turn out the way it did, didn't you? No wonder you were so calm when we came back here." Mrs. Clarke looked at him in disbelief; then she looked at me. She said, "Come to think of it, you didn't seem to be really worried when we came back. You planned that all along, didn't you? We can't thank you enough for all you have done. Life for Melissa and us is so much better now. All those years seem like a nightmare." I pleaded innocent; "the funeral home incident was a serendipitous occurrence." They were not persuaded. Instead, Mr. Clarke said, "You can be modest all you want, but you did a damn fine piece of work. For that, we thank you."

Final Comments

Following the termination of therapy, the parents remained in the area for approximately two years. During that time, I had one follow-up contact and two informal contacts with them. I learned that Melissa no longer was bulimic. She had gained weight and returned to Wellesley College. Since terminating with me, she had seen a male therapist in Boston to deal with issues related to the sexual abuse. Melissa and Wayne were "still on the outs," and Wayne was in therapy. The parents reported that Melissa remembers the funeral-home incident and frequently refers to it as the time "you scared the hell out of her." They continued to believe that I had staged the funeral-home incident. It was recounted to their friends as "the greatest trick they had ever seen" and has become a part of the family's legend.

REFERENCE

Baptiste, D.A. (1995). Therapy with a lesbian step family with an electively mute child: A case report. *Journal of Family Psychotherapy,* 6(1): 1-14.

Commentary

A Therapeutic Hail Mary

Douglas H. Sprenkle

Commentator Background

Fifty-nine years old, white, male, PhD, thirty years MFT practice.

Practice Setting

Full-time university-based MFT training program; limited private practice.

Theoretical Perspective

A common factors approach was used to examine this case.

As fate would have it, I began to write this commentary after watching my university win a startling come-from-behind victory in a football game. Well into the fourth quarter, little had gone right and the team seemed dispirited and ineffectual. Through some lucky breaks, however, they were only twelve points behind. The momentum shifted dramatically when, with only two minutes remaining, the team blocked the opponent's punt and went on to score. Following the ensuing kickoff, the opponent failed to score but tied up the clock so that my university was twenty-six seconds from defeat on its own ten-yard line. Plays on the first three downs went nowhere. With only a few seconds remaining, with defeat staring him in the face, our quarterback unleashed a desperation "Hail Mary" pass. The wide receiver, defenders swarming around him (any one of which could have intercepted the ball had it been a fraction of an inch off course), caught the pass with one outstretched hand and sealed a miracle finish.

The case presented here is no less dramatic, and the stakes were much higher. Baptiste felt dispirited and ineffectual. It was well into the game and defeat stared him in the face. The momentum shifted when Melissa shared with him the source of her bulimia. Nonetheless, defeat seemed imminent as her symptoms worsened and she refused to tell her family about her sexual abuse. With the clock running out, Baptiste offered the "Hail Mary" funeral-home intervention. A dramatic rapprochement ensued between Melissa and her family; she was victorious in her seven-year battle with bulimia, and the therapist went from goat to hero.

This is therapeutic drama at its best! In twenty-eight years of reading case studies, I do not think that I ever found one to be so gripping and compelling. In this commentary, I first will reflect on the ethical implications of what I am calling a "Hail Mary" approach to intervention. Then I will comment on why I believe the therapy proved to be effective, utilizing the lens of a common factors approach to marriage and family therapy. I have chosen this framework in part because it might be tempting to dismiss Baptiste's account as simply a special case with few links to other successful therapies. I will conclude with why I believe Baptiste calling his approach "strategic" may be only one way of punctuating what occurred in this case.

ETHICAL DIMENSIONS

Little doubt exists in my mind that Baptiste sought to conduct this case ethically. He was very straightforward with the clients about his limitations and urged the family on several occasions to seek alternate treatments. He utilized a supervisor in the case. He struggled with the limits of confidentiality following Melissa's revelation of abuse by her brother. Clearly, he kept the best interest of the clients paramount in his thinking. Nonetheless, one must make the distinction between unethical therapy (which this was not) and high-risk, potentially litigious therapy, which this probably was. Following the "Hail Mary" funeral-home intervention, when Mr. Clarke was irate and questioned Baptiste's professionalism, I was not surprised that "like a drowning man" Baptiste saw his career passing before his eyes.

I am fairly confident that I never would have delivered such an intervention. Furthermore, I probably would have hospitalized Melissa well before the thirty-eighth session when the critical intervention occurred. Alas, I also am fairly confident that my treatment would also have been the eighth treatment failure experienced by this desperate young woman and her family.

In the world of investments, one law says that rewards are proportional to the risks one is willing to take. One will not, for example, typically get a great rate of return on an insured certificate of deposit. Risky investments, like aggressive growth stocks, have the potential for enormous returns, but potential also exists for financial ruin. Baptiste's "Hail Mary" intervention was, in my judgment, clearly "high risk/high reward." It could have led to ruin (Melissa's death, the demise of Baptiste's career), but instead the payoff was remarkably positive. The critical intervention, in the context of other crucial factors I will describe, may well have saved the family's collective life. Was this due to luck, powerful clinical intuition, other factors, or, in

Baptiste's terms, "God's wild sense of humor"? Although we will never know for sure why this intervention worked, I do believe it demonstrates that there may be a trade-off between creativity/risk and therapeutic reward when it comes to difficult, intractable cases such as this one. Stories of miracle cures by Milton Erickson and Carl Whitaker have the same high risk/high reward flavor. Is my therapy more ethical because I would have hospitalized Melissa or just more bullet proof from malpractice? This is a vexing question, but I am thankful that Melissa and her family consulted Baptiste and not me.

A "COMMON FACTORS" LENS
FOR EXAMINING THIS CASE

After a quarter century teaching family therapy theoretical models as though they were responsible for change in therapy, I have converted to a common factors approach, which emphasizes variables that are found in a variety of therapies, regardless of the therapists' alleged theoretical orientation. In individual psychotherapy, decades of comparative clinical trials in which the leading models were pitted against each other produced an unexpected "bonfire of the vanities" (Hubble, Duncan, and Miller, 1999). Although occasional significant findings occurred for a particular therapy, the preponderance of evidence revealed no compelling general superiority of one approach versus another. This cleverly was called the "Dodo Bird Verdict." Taken from *Alice's Adventures in Wonderland,* it states: "Everyone has won and so all must have prizes" (Luborsky, Singer, and Luborsky, 1975). Left with little evidence to recommend use of one type of therapy over another, psychotherapy researchers and therapists redirected their attention to common factors that were not unique to particular orientations.

Research also exists which suggests that techniques unique to particular models in MFT do not explain the efficacy of these models. As Shadish and colleagues (1995) put it, on the basis of the most comprehensive meta-analysis of marital and family therapy research to date: "Despite some superficial evidence apparently favoring some orientation over others, no orientation is yet demonstrably superior to any other. This finding parallels the psychotherapy literature generally" (p. 348).

Regrettably, family therapy has paid little attention to common factors that underlie therapeutic efficacy. Perhaps because family therapy began as a maverick discipline that was oppositionally defiant to the prevailing therapeutic zeitgeist, and because the early family therapy pioneers were forceful personalities whose theories were an excellent match for their unique personalities, our field has tended to emphasize differences rather than similarities. Throughout most of its history, the family therapy field has been a coterie of competing religions built around charismatic individuals. Furthermore, because the field has not been particularly influenced by research, these leaders were never required to offer evidence for the alleged superiority of their models.

Until demonstrated otherwise, I will believe that change which occurs during family therapy has much less to do with the unique aspects of our sacred models than we believe it does. In the section that follows, I will delineate the factors that I believe are responsible for change and relate each of these to Baptiste's case. My list is a modification of the model developed by Michael Lambert (1992) to explain change in psychotherapy.

Elements of the Common Factors Lens

Client Factors

I believe that far too much attention has been paid to what the therapist does and not enough emphasis has been paid to client characteristics, such as their level of motivation, their willingness to do assignments, their courage, and so forth, that contribute to change. Smith, Glass, and Miller (1980), the authors who completed one of the first major meta-analyses of controlled studies of psychotherapy, reached a similar conclusion. These authors assert: "The possibility ought to be considered more seriously that the locus of those forces that restore and ameliorate the client in psychotherapy resides more within the client himself and less within the therapist and his actions. What the client brings to psychotherapy—the will to solve a problem or be rid of it, the intelligence to comprehend contingencies and relationships, the strength to face weakness, the confidence to trust another person, may contribute more to the success of therapy than whether it lasts twenty sessions or ten . . . or whether the therapist pays obeisance to Fritz Perls or Joseph Wolpe" (p. 188).

Clients are the real heroes in psychotherapy (Tallman and Bohart, 1999). Although therapists do play significant roles—they provide a healing context for change, and they help to remove the barriers and impediments to the clients' own natural processes of healing—I believe that clients ultimately heal themselves; therefore, client effort is probably the most important common factor in psychotherapy.

I also believe that client characteristics surely played a major role in the success of this case (as Baptiste clearly acknowledged). Their tenacity in the face of discouragement, their motivation to find a solution, their flexibility and willingness to try new things (even Baptiste's "weird" intervention), and their caring for each other that was hidden beneath the tension undoubtedly were crucial factors.

Extratherapeutic Events

Extratherapeutic events are factors that are part of the clients' environment that occur independent of therapy. Fortuitous events may have more impact on our clients' lives than our cherished interventions. In a two-year follow-up study of behavioral marital therapy, Jacobson, Schmaling, and Holtzworth-Munroe (1987) found that the differences between clients who maintained gains versus those who relapsed were unrelated to the type of treatment received (or to therapist characteristics). Rather, the presence or absence of stressful external events made the difference. Many therapists are humbled by the fact that extratherapeutic events, such as a client getting a job or watching an episode of *Oprah* or experiencing the death of a parent, can be more influential in producing change than what the therapist does.

As Baptiste acknowledges, the clients' treatment history probably had a significant bearing on the outcome. Furthermore, the fortuitous occurrence of the "wrong" person conducting the funeral-home tour may well have been decisive. Had this person not suggested that Melissa get into the coffin, the emotional impact of the tour might have been lost. In any event, this fortuitous twist was clearly an extratherapeutic event not under Baptiste's control.

Expectancy

It makes a difference if clients expect therapy to help and if they believe in the therapist. Whether because of Baptiste's history of helping another family known to the Clarkes, the Clarkes' desperation, or elements of Baptiste's therapeutic style (and it may not matter), the parents (and probably Melissa as well since she "hung in") believed that Baptiste was their best hope. Although it is possible that Baptiste's self-depreciation paradoxically enhanced this belief, as Baptiste suggested, it is also possible that this diminished the common factor of expectancy.

The Therapeutic Relationship

Consistent evidence suggests that the therapeutic relationship contributes powerfully to therapeutic outcome both in psychotherapy in general and marriage and family therapy in particular. In the largest outcome study ever completed in MFT (3,956 cases), Beck and Jones (1973) reported that the counselor/client relationship "was found to be twice as powerful a predictor of outcomes as any other client or service characteristic" (p. 8). Recently, attention has been given to the "therapeutic alliance," which includes not only the emotional bond between therapist and client but also client/therapist consensus on therapeutic tasks and goals. With regards to the tasks or interventions used by the therapist, it is not so important what they are but it is crucial that they are deemed credible and helpful by the clients (Sprenkle, Blow, and Dickey, 1999). Goals also need to be formulated collaboratively so that therapist and client believe they are working in the same direction.

I believe that in his analysis Baptiste minimized the role of the therapeutic alliance he created with the Clarkes. With regards to bonds, even highly reluctant Melissa cared about what Baptiste thought about her. She confessed her darkest secret to him. The family valued Baptiste even in the absence of overt progress. I feel quite confident that they felt his caring and this served as the anesthesia for the painful process of opening space to learn to care for each other. I believe that Baptiste's extraordinary, almost-heroic patience in the face of silences, attacks, and other forms of resistant client behavior (not to mention the felt lack of progress from Baptiste's side) created a holding environment for the clients' self-healing.

I believe that Baptiste's "not knowing" stance was powerful because it enhanced the tasks dimension of the therapeutic alliance. Melissa's other therapists had believed that they knew what was wrong with her. This destroyed their credibility with her and hence severely damaged the therapeutic alliance. By correctly identifying Melissa's goal even before she was able to articulate it (working on her anger), Baptiste also enhanced the goals dimension of the alliance. Without a strong therapeutic alliance, I do not believe the family would have complied with the "weird" critical intervention nor probably benefitted from it.

Generic Interventions

Although many therapists tend to think of their interventions as unique expressions of their cherished models, most model-based interventions can be recast as expressions of generic skills. Garfield (1992), for example, believes that most interventions can be categorized as some form of: (a) affective (emotional) experiencing; (b) explanation, rationale, or interpretation; (c) reinforcement; (d) desensitization; (e) facing or confronting a problem; or (f) information and skills training. Although space does not permit me to analyze all of Baptiste's interventions by these categories (and I believe he used all of them), let us examine one: facing or confronting a problem. The overall results of Baptiste's treatment was to get the family to face the unmentionable abuse and its consequences; the effect of the critical intervention was to get Melissa to face the reality of death (and thereby reject it).

Common Factors Specific to MFT

I believe that only three unique common factors exist in MFT.

Relational conceptualization. Marriage and family therapists translate human/family difficulties into relational terms. They try to keep the whole system (or systems) in view when relating to any part of a system. Furthermore, MFTs typically try to relate in a positive way to all parts of the system, regardless of who is in the therapy room (Wampler, 1997). This conceptualization may also help to explain why Baptiste succeeded where others failed. The other therapists may have thought of the problem as something residing solely within Melissa and may have missed the crucial web of influences related to Wayne's abuse and Melissa's perceived lack of support from her parents.

Expanded direct treatment system. MFTs typically expand the "direct" (Pinsof, 1995) client system (persons physically present in treatment) while also paying attention to the "indirect" systems (persons not physically in treatment). The parents' direct involvement (downplayed by previous therapists) was crucial to Melissa's therapeutic alliance with Baptiste: ("And you stick it to [Mom], too. You make my parents come to counseling. Before, I was the only one who went. . . . She doesn't like to come.") and also made possible the emotional reconnection that followed the critical incident.

Expanded therapeutic alliance. When the direct treatment system is expanded, not only do individuals have an alliance with the therapist, but also subsystems have an alliance that is different than the sum of individual alliances. Karen and Leslie Clarke had a parental alliance with Baptiste in addition to how they related to him as unique individuals. This alliance seemed to benefit the therapy because when one parent took an extreme position, the other tended to balance it.

I believe that all other interventions family therapists use are only unique (vis-à-vis individual therapy) to the extent that they work through these common factors of systemic conceptualization, expanded direct treatment system, and expanded therapeutic alliance. Therapists also help clients to: (a) *regulate their behavior* (by changing interactional patterns or dysfunctional sequences, modifying boundaries and changing family structures, learning new skills, behaving more supportively, and learning to empower self and others), (b) *achieve cognitive mastery* (by gaining insight, understanding, or new meaning about interactional processes within themselves and the family, between the family and other systems, and across generations) (Wampler, 1997), and (c) *regulate their affect/emotions* (by regulating or experiencing emotions and making emotional connections with themselves and with each other). Our various models differ in the extent to which they privilege one of these three interrelated tasks (Sprenkle, Blow, and Dickey, 1999).

ARE OUR MODELS IN THE EYE OF THE BEHOLDER?

Baptiste describes his approach to this case as strategic. To me, however, that means he "privileged" the disrupting of behavioral sequences (what I believe is the hallmark of the strategic approach). That also means that he emphasized (a) from the previous list ("regulate their behavior"). He interrupted Melissa's deathwatch and the alienating behaviors between her and her parents. However, I believe I could argue just as convincingly that Baptiste's approach really privileged (c) from the same list ("regulate their affect/emotion"). The therapy and the critical intervention may have been successful because they created a new emotional connection between Melissa and her parents (which was facilitated by Baptiste's own emotional connection with his clients). Viewed through this lens, Baptiste was more an emotion-focused therapist. It goes without saying that Melissa and her parents also came to think about themselves and each other differently (b) from the list, ("achieve cognitive mastery"). Therapists who privilege cognition, e.g., narrative therapists, might say that therapy with this family was successful because Baptiste helped the parties construct more empowering stories about themselves. My point is that it is somewhat arbitrary to say what is a behavioral (e.g., strategic), affective (e.g., emotion-focused), or cognitive (e.g., narrative) approach and that our models are only one way of punctuating what we are doing.

CONCLUDING THOUGHTS

Baptiste has presented a gripping saga of high risk/high reward "Hail Mary" therapy. Because the case is unique, it is tempting to view it from the vantage point of "difference" and uniqueness. In this commentary, I have chosen instead to analyze the case from a common factors perspective, which emphasizes similarities and connections among the work of successful therapists. The paradox of life and therapies is that although we are all very different, we also are very much the same.

REFERENCES

Beck, D.F., and Jones, M.A. (1973). *Progress on family problems: A nationwide study of clients' and counselors' views on family agency services.* New York: Family Service Association of America.

Garfield, S.L. (1992). Eclectic psychotherapy: A common factors approach. In J.C. Norcross and M.R. Goldfried (Eds.), *Handbook of psychology integration* (pp. 169-201). New York: Basic Books.

Hubble, M.A., Duncan, B.L., and Miller, S. (Eds.) (1999). *The heart and soul of change: Common factors in effective psychotherapy, medicine, and human services.* Washington, DC: The American Psychological Association.

Jacobson, N.S., Schmaling, K.B., and Holtzworth-Munroe, A. (1987). Component analysis of behavioral marital therapy: Two-year follow up and prediction of relapse. *Journal of Marital and Family Therapy*, 13(2), 187-195.

Lambert, M.J. (1992) Psychotherapy outcome research: Implications for integrative and eclectic therapists. In J.C. Norcross and M.R. Goldfried (Eds.), *Handbook of psychotherapy integration* (pp. 94-129). New York: Basic Books.

Luborsky, L., Singer, B., and Luborsky, L. (1975). Comparative studies of psychotherapy: Is it true that "Everyone has won and all must have prizes"? *Archives of General Psychiatry*, 32(4) 995-1008.

Pinsof, W.M. (1995). *Integrative problem-centered therapy*. New York: Basic Books.

Shadish, W.R., Ragsdale, K., Glaser, R.R., and Mongomery, L.M. (1995). The efficacy and effectiveness of marital and family therapy: A perspective from meta-analysis. *Journal of Marital and Family Therapy*, 21(4), 345-360.

Smith, M., Glass, G., and Miller, T. (1980). *The benefits of psychotherapy*. Baltimore: Johns Hopkins Press.

Sprenkle, D., Blow, A., and Dickey, M. (1999). Common factors and other non model-driven technique variables in marriage and family therapy. In M.A. Hubble, B.L. Duncan, and S. Miller (Eds.), *The heart and soul of change: Common factors in effective psychotherapy, medicine, and human services*. Washington, DC: The American Psychological Association.

Tallman, K.L. and Bohart, A.C. (1999). The client as a common factor: Clients as self-healers. In M.A. Hubble, B.L. Duncan, and S. Miller (Eds.), *The heart and soul of change: Common factors in effective psychotherapy, medicine, and human services* (pp. 91-132). Washington, DC: The American Psychological Association.

Wampler, K. (1997). Systems theory and outpatient mental health treatment. Paper presented at the Inaugural AAMFT Research Conference, Santa Fe, NM. August 2, 1997.

Commentary

The Patience of a Saint

Cheryl L. Storm

Commentator Background

Forty-nine years old, caucasian, female, twenty years MFT practice. Taught and supervised beginning marriage and family therapists for seventeen years.

Practice Setting

Full-time university-based training MFT program; part-time private practice.

Theoretical Perspective

My preferred theoretical perspective is an integration of strategic, solution-focused, feminist, and postmodern influences. However, I attempted to match Baptiste's theoretical perspective at the time he worked with this family. Initially, a strategic lens was used to examine the case, followed by a rethinking of the case from the perspective of my current preferred ideas and way of practicing.

As I read this case, I could not help but appreciate the value of patience for a therapist. Being patient frequently runs counter to my brief orientation to therapy, my need for immediate signs of improvement, and the pressures I feel to facilitate change quickly. This case reminded me of those times that I have forgotten that change comes in many forms and at many speeds. Baptiste met with Melissa and her parents for more than twenty-two sessions before any sign of movement, much less improvement occurred. Baptiste struggled with his desire to give up and concluded several times that referral was in order. Each time he proposed referral to the family, they convinced him to continue with them. Given the length of the case and the seriousness of the presenting problem, it would be easy to find fault with Baptiste claiming it was therapist hubris that kept him involved, and argue that he should have stood his ground and referred the family to someone more effective. However, when the family's history of "revolving doors of therapists, hospitals, and treatment programs" is taken into account, it may very well be Baptiste's patience that made the difference.

Baptiste's patience was evident in his "stick-to-it-ness" with this case over the long haul of over forty sessions in one year. Not only did there seem to be a lack of progress and sense of going nowhere, but at times Melissa's symptoms were escalating to the point that her life could have been at stake. Baptiste continued to meet with whomever would be involved and patiently waited. When Melissa refused to say much of anything of substance, he steadfastly attempted to engage her and waited for her to develop a trusting relationship with him. He kept information secret from Melissa's parents at her request but told her she needed to find a way to be the bearer of the news. He waited and did not reveal the secret even when Melissa quit coming to therapy and her parents reported that she was not eating, was isolating herself, and was incessantly talking of death. Once again he waited. He gave her more time even though he had no way of knowing how, when, or if she would hold up her end of the bargain. He truly had the patience of a saint.

THE STRATEGIC SAINT:
IN DEFENSE OF CLASSIC STRATEGIC THERAPY

I begin this commentary by joining Baptiste in his preferred strategic theoretical orientation. In some ways, my response is a defense of strategic therapy, an approach that currently is somewhat out of favor in the field. This case reminded me of the usefulness and elegance of many of the strategic ideas, and that the strategic approach is really about a way of thinking about change rather than creation of clever, tricky, manipulative interventions, for which strategic therapy has become known. I hope my comments will invite some readers to revisit and reconsider these ideas so that the important contributions of this earlier model do not become lost as we endorse the more contemporary models of therapy.

The initial discussion between Baptiste and the family could be viewed as a classic strategic move. The more Baptiste expressed that he was not the appropriate therapist for the family, the more the family became invested in working with him. He maintained his maneuverability by "repudiating any possibility for success," cautioning them regarding any expectations that he could do any better than their previous therapists and telling them not to be disappointed if nothing changed. I've always believed strategic moves should evolve from the interactions of the participants similar to what occurred in this case rather than to be contrived interventions a therapist or group of therapists work hard to design. Baptiste felt overwhelmed, was not convinced that he could be of much help, and sincerely wanted a gracious way out. It was from this authentic position that he could engage in this paradoxical interchange. The more he said he could not help, the more the family was convinced he could. In this process of convincing Baptiste to stay on (which occurred at several points during the case), the family appeared to become increasingly invested in the therapeutic process, which was a necessary and significant precursor to change.

That clients tell us how they want to be helped is a widely accepted tenet of strategic therapy (Haley, 1976; de Shazer, 1985; Fisch, Weakland, and Segal, 1982). Accordingly, if one believes this to be true, then clearly the family was telling Baptiste how to respond. Melissa complains that her mother "never believes what anyone says." She tells Baptiste that when people die, they get "respect." Her fantasized headstone reads "Here lies Misunderstood." Melissa pleads with Baptiste not to tell her parents her secret. At one point, Melissa ordered him to move to the other side of his office so she could read a cartoon; he politely did so without making it an issue. Melissa appears to have been asking for a therapist who was committed to understanding her as a unique person, not as a bulimic. Because Melissa is so adamant in her request, Baptiste agrees to keep her secret even when he questions his own judgment in doing so. Baptiste listened. He gave Melissa his utmost respect. The parents desired a therapist "who did not give up on them" because they believed progress would take time. Family members wanted unscheduled sessions; he found time to accommodate them. He did not give up even when he felt a referral was the best option. The family seemed to be requesting a patient therapist. Baptiste answered with patience.

Similarly, if one adopts the strategic view that Baptiste's job is to interact in a way that matches the clients' responses with an additional something new (Storm, 1991), change occurs when Baptiste matches the family and adds a twist. Progress appeared to occur when Baptiste joined the family by focusing on how Melissa's behaviors should stay the same rather than suggesting ways it should change. Change appears to begin when Baptiste begins an interchange about dying (Melissa's chosen language). At the end of a session, he asks her to write her own obituary. She declines but begins to be more talkative during the next session. When Baptiste focuses on why she is angry, therapy seems to stall once again, but when he shifts to discussing how family members will react if she dies, Melissa engages once again. This discussion culminates in her telling her secret of sexual abuse by her brother. Baptiste's not disclosing the information to the parents continues the process of matching the client, but he insists that she must tell her parents. Almost in an act of desperation at a crisis point in therapy, Baptiste continues his strategy of focusing on the way things should not change by directing the family to tour a funeral home so that Melissa can plan her own funeral.

This maneuver is a classic paradoxical intervention for which strategic therapy and its practitioners have received so much bad press in the field. Out of context, it sounds manipulative, clever, and tricky; in context, I believe it shows respect for the family. The beauty of this intervention is that Baptiste is listening intently to the chosen language of the family and responds in kind. Interestingly, Baptiste notes "paradoxically, she was not *planning* to die but *wanted* to die." Melissa could be viewed as conveying a message to Baptiste that he should be paradoxical. In my view, Baptiste's response is a paradoxical communication of an artist. It was not given because Baptiste is enamored with paradoxes as a technique to be used on a family, but it was a response that seemed to be guided by the family-therapist interactional patterns over time. The more direct Baptiste was in suggesting change, the more therapy stalled. The more Baptiste talked of Melissa's dying, the more progress occurred. The more Baptiste responded in like ways to the responses of the family, the more the family changed their interactions.

In addition to being framed in the family's language, Baptiste's directive subtly instructs the family to unify to find a mutual solution rather than an individual—Melissa—solution. Until then, it appeared that the parents were focused on changing Melissa's eating habits rather than understanding their daughter and working with her to find a solution. In response, Melissa felt that her parents would never understand her experience so she continued to deal with her secret by eating and purging. The more Melissa binged and purged, the more her parents became anxious and focused on finding a way to change her; this in turn contributed to Melissa becoming more closed off from her parents. By directing the family to tour the funeral home together, Baptiste was interrupting this pattern. All family members felt the directive was "weird" and "distasteful." For the first time, the parents and Melissa were united in a common endeavor.

The funeral-home associate's accidental directive to Melissa to get into a casket "to try it on for size" was a continuation of Baptiste's intervention. When Melissa bolted from the room, her parents searched for her. When her mother found her, they interacted somehow differently than before. This may have set the stage for the secret to be shared. Having her mother running after her may have allowed Melissa to experience her mother's concern in a new way that all the talking in therapy could not have achieved. As Baptiste notes, the intervention helped the family to coalesce and begin to communicate directly to one another rather than through a therapist. It appears that the intervention provided a way for the mother and father to really listen to their daughter who for so long felt misunderstood by them.

SOLVING THE PUZZLE:
A CONTEXTUAL UNDERSTANDING OF THE SYMPTOM

This case reminded me of a simple but very important idea I learned from Auerswald (1968, 1971) early in my career. This idea has had an indelible and profound effect on how I conduct therapy and continues to influence my work today. According to Auerswald, therapists are explorers who are solving the puzzle of understanding a symptom by learning how it makes sense within the context. As a result, Auerswald does not turn to mental health knowledge regarding diagnosis but steadfastly believes that clients communicate important messages about their contexts. He continually is curious and looks intently for clues to be used in solving the client's puzzle. Auerswald's writings are filled with fascinating cases in which symptoms that initially appear unexplainable make perfect sense when considered within their contexts.

The puzzle regarding Melissa's bulimic symptom is solved and makes perfect sense when one understands *her* context. In our culture, brother/sister incest is considered revolting; a woman who has experienced incest is viewed as damaged for life. Women receive messages that they are to accommodate men. The most intelligent people are considered to be those who are educated at Ivy League schools. Melissa's symptom makes sense when these messages are coupled with the family's interactional pattern of Melissa's brother as the favored child who can do no wrong, a mother-daughter relationship that lacks closeness, and parents who expected high achievement in school and encouraged competition among the siblings. It makes sense that Melissa would succumb to the pressure of giving sexual favors to her brother in exchange for tutoring in math but also that she would feel "intensely dirty and angry" and begin a habit of throwing up her food as a result of this interaction.

Baptiste's journey toward solving the puzzle of how the symptom makes sense becomes critical. Baptiste concludes midway through therapy that Melissa does not behave like other bulimics he has known. Accordingly, he spends much time in therapy attempting to understand Melissa as a unique individual within a family living in a larger context. For me, this case underscores the ways our experience in treating similar cases or expert knowledge in the field can limit our ability to connect fully and be in relationship with our clients. Baptiste initially questions his own ability to help this family because of his limited experience with bulimics. Yet it seems it is only when Baptiste throws out his expert knowledge of bulimics that a real connection with Melissa occurs. She notes, "My other therapists tell me why I am the way I am." Therapeutically, I believe it is not important whether Melissa is showing bulimia or sexual abuse or depression (other than to satisfy a larger context that requires this type of individual categorization). However, it is critically important for therapists to be curious about how whatever symptoms are being shown make sense in context.

One of the important puzzle pieces seems to be the influence of gender. Baptiste discusses how gender was a factor in the choice of therapist. He suggests gender as a significant contributor and hypothesizes that therapy was augmented because Melissa was in a therapeutic relationship with a male with whom she may have been uncomfortable. He notes this counters the conventional wisdom that bulimics do better with female therapists. I wonder if the opposite was true and Melissa was actually more comfortable with a male therapist. Melissa frequently expressed anger during her sessions—at times even telling Baptiste to fuck off. In our society, there tends to be more permission and acceptance for men than women—especially middle-class women—to express anger through vulgar language. Consequently, would Melissa have felt as free to express her anger to a female therapist as she did with Baptiste? Did Melissa feel freer to test Baptiste to determine if he could handle the intense emotions attached to her secret? Did Baptiste pass the test when he allowed her to express her anger without defining it as "sick" behavior and was not angry about it? We can only speculate about Melissa's interaction with her previous female therapists, but perhaps, like me, they were more comfortable with women clients expressing hurt rather than anger. It is interesting that none of the female therapists appeared to gain Melissa's trust in the way that Baptiste eventually did. However, it is possible that Melissa may have fired her previous therapists because she also trusted them with her secret and they were pressing for her to disclose to her parents. Of course, only Melissa knows the answers to these musings.

In his reporting of this case, Baptiste makes only passing mention of the Jewish heritage of the mother and the Gentile heritage of the father. But I found myself curious about and questioning whether cultural influences were another important piece of the puzzle. Because the parents are an interfaith couple and we are given little information about how they chose to address their differences, the degree to which the Jewish heritage is influencing the case is unknown. At the risk of thinking too stereotypically about this family, the mother's responses become easily understandable when her Jewish heritage is considered. Traditionally in Jewish families, mothers have been "viewed as their children's primary educator who inculcates in them the values of education and achievement" (Rosen and Weltman, 1996, p. 624). Melissa's trouble is described as beginning during her teenage years when she and her parents, especially her mother, had intense conflict specific to her in-school achievements. Competition and intense sibling rivalry existed between Melissa and her brother; this is a common pattern that can naturally evolve in Jewish families because of the importance of achievement as the means to please one's parents (Rosen and Weltman, 1996). The mother more than the father is described as having been highly concerned about Melissa's school difficulties, intent on the children attending the "right colleges," and distraught when Melissa's symptoms escalated. Melissa seems to be more upset and angry with her mother than with her father; daughters in Jewish families frequently feel they cannot live up to their mothers' expectations (Rosen and Weltman, 1996). The father is said to share the mother's high expectations with regard to achievement, but he is described as more accepting of his children's decisions and more optimistic that everything will work out. One could hypothesize that the mother struggles more with Melissa's difficulties because they reflect more significantly on her success as a parent given her cultural background than on the father's perceived success as a parent. The couple's stance regarding therapy also becomes understandable from the point of view of the Jewish culture. Although Jewish families are major consumers of therapy (Herz and Rosen, 1982), they tend to place a lot of emphasis on finding the right specialist who may need to be patient since their "verbal facility, intellectualizations, cynicism, and intensity sometimes make progress slow and illusory" (Rosen and Weltman, 1996, p. 629).

REJECTING THE SIZE OF DEATH:
OTHER ALTERNATIVES

If I were to see this family today, given my solution-focused leanings, I would approach it in the more positive stance characteristic of current therapeutic approaches. I would have searched for exceptions within and outside of therapy. When Melissa's previous therapy was most helpful, what was happening? There were times when Melissa did better between her treatment programs. What was different during these symptom-free periods? Although the parents reported that her relapses seemed to occur for no apparent reason, my hunch is that a careful discussion would reveal some important differences about the family's interaction and Melissa's relationships outside the family during these times. Questions such as these would be key: When Melissa was doing better, how did the parents each interact differently with her? How was interaction different between Melissa and her siblings? Between her parents and siblings? With others outside of the family?

Reading the case report, it is unclear what suggestions were made to the parents about how they could handle the situation (with the exception of not threatening to hospitalize Melissa). If I had seen this case when Baptiste did, my goal as a strategic therapist would have been to suggest alternative responses for any family members who appeared invested in change. As a result, I would have focused on suggesting new ways the parents could respond to Melissa. Traditional strategic therapy would view them as the customers—those most interested in changing the situation. For example, when Baptiste suggested that Melissa write her own obituary, I would have suggested that Melissa and her parents, not Melissa alone, write the obituary. Or since her father was more accepting of the status quo and her mother was pushing harder for resolution, the father could have been asked to try to get Melissa to eat. This would have increased the intensity and connection of the father-daughter relationship and made the father rather than the mother push for change. The mother could have been asked to discuss with Melissa how she would sit *shiva* after her death. Mother and daughter could speculate about who would mourn her death and what would be said. The mother could share with Melissa what she would say about the accomplishments Melissa achieved in her lifetime. This may have created a different mother-daughter interaction; an alternative to the mother telling Melissa what she needed to accomplish to get better. There are, of course, numerous possibilities but no magic bullet.

PERHAPS NOT SO CRITICAL AN INCIDENT

I found myself speculating how differently the case could have unfolded if the father instead of the mother had found Melissa when she fled from the funeral home. Since Melissa had a slightly better relationship with her father than her mother, would she have shared the secret with him? How would Baptiste have responded if Melissa and all the men in the family knew the secret, but the other women (i.e., mother and sister) did not? How would the course of therapy have been different in this scenario?

Most important, I wonder which event was really the critical incident. Was it the incident related to the cartoon, which seemed to be a turning point in Melissa's trusting Baptiste, that really was the serendipitous event? Was it the directive of touring a funeral home that changed the outcome of therapy? Was it, as Baptiste proposes, the funeral-home employee's attempt at humor that was the turning point in therapy or would have Melissa reacted similarly at some other point in the tour? Did the critical incident occur when the mother rather than the father found Melissa after she fled from the funeral home and gave the mother an opportunity to show Melissa her concern? Or was it Baptiste's incredible patience at numerous junctures in therapy? My bet is that it was all of these critical incidents that combined in *unplanned, unpredictable,* and *synergistic* ways within a caring, solid therapeutic human relationship that created a context for change. As a therapist, it is these unexpected serendipitous events that keep the mystery in therapy and keep me scheduling my next clients.

REFERENCES

Auerswald, E. H. (1968). Interdisciplinary versus ecological approach. *Family Process*, 7(2), 202-215.

Auerswald, E. H. (1971). Families, change, and the ecological perspective. *Family Process*, 10(3), 263-280.

de Shazer, S. (1985). *Keys to solution in brief therapy*. New York: Norton.

Fisch, R., Weakland, J., and Segal, L. (1982). *Tactics of change*. San Francisco: Jossey-Bass.

Haley, J. (1976). *Problem-solving therapy*. New York: Harper and Row.

Herz, F. and Rosen, E. (1982). Jewish families. In M. McGoldrick, J.K. Pearce, and J. Giordano (Eds.), *Ethnicity and family therapy*, First edition (pp. 365-392). New York: The Guilford Press.

Rosen, E. and Weltman, S. (1996). Jewish families: An overview. In M. McGoldrick, J. Giordano, and J.K. Pearce (Eds.), *Ethnicity and family therapy*, Second edition (pp. 611-630). New York: The Guilford Press.

Storm, C. (1991). The remaining thread: Matching change and stability signals. *Journal of Strategic and Systemic Therapies*, 10(3/4), 114-117.

CASE 2

Little League: The Feel of Dreams

Jill H. Freedman

Therapist Background

Currently: forty-nine years old, white, female, MSW, twenty-six years MFT practice. Then: forty years old, MSW, seventeen years MFT practice.

Practice Setting

Currently and when I saw this couple: private practice.

Client Characteristics

Jim (age twenty-six) and Leah (age thirty-two) were an unmarried white middle-class couple who had been dating for nine months. Jim was employed as a computer specialist; Leah was completing an MS degree in biology at a Midwestern University and applying to other universities to study biology. This couple sought therapy because Leah felt the relationship "wasn't going anywhere."

Length of Treatment

This couple was seen for fourteen sessions from May 1992 through January 1993. The critical incident occurred between Sessions 10 and 11.

Theoretical Perspective

A narrative, social constructionist approach was used in working with this couple.

PRESENTING PROBLEM

Leah requested therapy for herself and Jim because she had been feeling that their relationship "wasn't going anywhere." The couple had been dating for nine months prior to beginning therapy. Leah was experiencing some urgency about the future of the relationship because she was completing a master's degree and applying for admission to doctoral programs across the country. Consequently, she wanted to know where the relationship was going so that she could decide if she should either restrict her choice of graduate programs to be with Jim or entertain the idea of Jim going with her if she went away to graduate school. Jim acknowledged the importance of his relationship with Leah but was willing to "let it take its course." He encouraged her to go ahead with plans for graduate school and believed that "thinking about their relationship in making her choice was premature." Jim believed that "if the relationship warranted it, when the time comes [more than a year after the couple entered therapy], they would decide what to do."

THE THERAPEUTIC SITUATION PRIOR
TO THE CRITICAL INCIDENT

In the early interviews with this couple, Leah told stories about Jim "not measuring up" to her ideal for a male partner. In one of her stories, she told about asking Jim to go grocery shopping to buy something to prepare for dinner. He returned with bags of groceries but nothing that Leah thought could be put together to make a meal—at least nothing that she would be interested in eating. She also told other stories about Jim's wavering after he had committed to do something with her—for example, going away together for the weekend. Leah found these incidents to be frustrating because she believed that she and Jim were compatible in other ways and well suited to each other. She emphasized that she "needed someone she could rely on." Together we wondered if we could name "frustration" as one of the problems plaguing Leah and the relationship.

Jim told a different version of the story of going grocery shopping. According to Jim, as he walked through the store he was attracted to many possibilities, but he kept remembering that Leah did not eat a variety of foods and often experienced difficulty finding something she wanted in a restaurant. As a result, he walked around the store in a muddle. Finally, he "threw snack foods into the cart." All the way home he worried about what he had bought and felt angry by the time he entered the apartment. He told stories about Leah expressing disappointment with him and his feelings of helplessness in the face of her disappointment. He also told stories about similar experiences at work when he felt like he never really knew what his boss wanted or expected of him. We tentatively named the problems fear and self-doubt.

Other stories the couple told wove through these two sets of stories. These stories accentuated the differences between Jim and Leah's age and experiences. Leah is six years older than Jim. She previously had been married and divorced. The couple told a very poignant story about their experience of visiting Jim's parents in another city. Jim was very concerned about his parents' reaction to him dating a divorcée six years his senior. Consequently, at his request, Leah did not mention her age or her divorcée status. They speculated about moments and conditions in which questions about Leah's age and/or past relationships could arise. It appeared as if they both held their breath and, miraculously, those moments passed. Jim's parents appeared to like Leah very much and approved of the relationship, but Jim continued to be concerned about their reactions should they discover the truth. The "conspiracy of omission" seemed to color the relationship for Jim. Once Jim and Leah began to tell their stories and name their problems, I was interested in helping them to deconstruct or "unpack" the stories. I asked questions that I hoped might expose how the stories and problems had been constructed and how those constructions were shaping their stories of the possibilities for their relationship. I asked about events that had fueled the frustration, fear, and self-doubt, how their relationship was taken over by these experiences, and what effects they had on the relationship.

Leah and Jim began to see that cultural expectations of what a couple "should be like" and how each member of a couple "should behave" had created an idealized set of standards that they both felt unable to fulfill. This in turn led, in part, to feelings of frustration, fear, and self-doubt. The couple was not sure what they might appreciate in their relationship if they were able to look at it through the perspective of what fit for them rather than what was prescribed by society, but they were eager to find out.

EVENTS LEADING TO THE CRITICAL INCIDENT

In the first nine sessions, Jim and Leah recounted a number of experiences that carried knowledge of what is appropriate for them. Some of the incidents that stood outside of the problematic story included stories of how they met and felt at ease with each other almost immediately, stories of camping together and working well as a team, and stories of successfully working out misunderstandings even though the conversations were difficult. These alternative stories did not erase or take the place of the problematic stories that brought the couple to therapy. Rather, they allowed Leah and Jim to see themselves, each other, and their relationship in different and less problematic ways. They continued to inhabit these new perspectives at times between therapy meetings; at other times, they found themselves immersed again in the problematic stories.

The tenth session was focused on fear and self-doubt because although both partners agreed that they had made some gains in therapy and both saw the relationship as having potential, fear and self-doubt were inhibiting Jim from planning a future with Leah. As a result, they both experienced some time pressures about envisioning a future; Leah needed to make decisions about graduate school. More immediately but of less intense concern, fear and self-doubt seemed to be keeping Jim from entering as fully into the current relationship as both of them said they would prefer. Frustration was coloring Leah's experience once again: she had learned that Jim would be attending a wedding in his hometown and had not invited her to accompany him.

I offered Jim the opportunity to construct alternative stories about himself—stories that would not be dominated by fear and self-doubt. I did this, in part, by asking him at what time in his life or in what context was he most free of self-doubt. Jim took the question quite seriously, thought about it for some time, and then answered in a definitive tone, "Little League—When I played Little League." In response to my questions, he regaled us for the greater part of the session with stories from his four years playing on the Modern Appliance Company Little League baseball team.

On that team, he was the catcher and also was a very dependable hitter. Neither Leah nor I knew much about baseball, so Jim assumed a teacher-like role to explain what his responsibilities were and described how confidently he was able to handle them. He recounted working closely with the pitchers, giving them signals to decide what sort of pitches they needed to throw and when. This meant that he had to know the strengths and weaknesses of each of the pitchers on his team. It also was useful if he knew the strengths and weaknesses of each batter his team faced. He told us he had studied the key players on all the other teams and, by the fourth year of Little League, the coach and the pitchers looked to him to make the final decision in these matters.

Asked if fear or self-doubt took over when he was called upon to make these decisions, Jim said, "Not at all," and described how his self-confidence grew with each year's involvement in Little League. I asked what he had learned about himself from his Little League experiences that he might not have known if he had not played Little League. After some thought, he replied, "That I am a competent person, that I can handle responsibility, that there is a kind of a groove that I can get into where I expect things to go right, and they usually do." My questions were directed both by curiosity and the desire to help these past events in Jim's life become stories that spoke to him of his life and identity rather than events about which he rarely thought. Jim acknowledged that although he was not the most powerful hitter on his team, he was confident of his batting ability because he was the most reliable. He seemed to have a knack for putting the ball into the open spaces between fielders.

Jim's team won the city championship the last two years he played. He talked with pride about the final game the first time his team had won the championship in his third year of playing Little League. According to Jim, it was a very close game against the previous year's champions. His team was leading by one run in the bottom of the ninth inning. There were two players from the opposing team on base when the batter hit a short grounder toward the shortstop. Jim's confident catch and tag of the player coming from third was the key move in the double play that ended the game. The detail with which Jim described his Little League career to Leah and me was not because of his loquaciousness as a storyteller. Rather, the details were prompted by the kinds of questions I asked. I wanted to invite Jim not only to retell the experience but to *relive* it as well.

Leah listened to Jim's stories with rapt attention and commented that she wished she could have seen him play. I asked her if through those stories she had gained a new perspective of Jim that she had not seen before. She said that she had. Listening to the stories, Leah began to envision the younger Jim as having a keen sense of intuition, confidence, and a clear notion of who he was. Further discussion led Leah to include leadership ability on the list. When I asked her what difference it would make if she held on to this image of Jim and continued seeing him in this light, she laughed and said, "I'd better watch it or I'll strike out. . . . No. I could count on him more and that would mean that I could relax." I asked Jim if he agreed with Leah's list. After some thought, he said that he did. We explored what life would be like for Jim if he owned the qualities Leah had named. He believed that the major impact would be his decisiveness in small ways as well as in larger ways. As he sat and pondered his answer, he discovered that there already had been times in the relationship when he had been decisive and sure of himself.

I asked Jim about those times when he had been decisive and sure of himself. He told one story about a surprise camping trip he had planned for Leah. He revealed his plans to Leah only after gathering the necessary provisions and making all the arrangements. I was surprised to hear about this trip because it appeared to be quite a risk to plan a trip for someone else, deciding where to go and what to take without that person's input. I commented that Jim's planning of this trip gave me an image of him that was very different from the one I had of him wandering around the grocery store not knowing what to buy. I wondered what they each made of the differences.

Leah was first to answer. She said that the images were really different and recalling how Jim planned the trip put her back in touch with characteristics that contributed to her being attracted to Jim. We talked about how the frustration stood in the way of her acknowledging these qualities about Jim or even seeing them at times. Again I wondered if societal expectations played a role. She agreed they did and were a significant contributor to her frustration. She acknowledged that such expectations were manifested in the belief that she and Jim *should* be together in a particular way, *should* each have particular roles, *should* live in the same city, and *should* be moving in the direction of living together and eventually marrying. As the interview was ending, Jim and Leah were looking at each other appreciatively until Leah said, "But I'm still not happy that he didn't invite me to the wedding this weekend." In response, Jim mumbled, "It would be a drag, Leah. I'm bad at parties. You wouldn't know anyone there. It just would be awkward." This turn in the conversation refocused the session in the direction of the problematic story. As a result, I felt that we all left the session feeling individually and collectively that the old stories of self-doubt, frustration, and time pressure were so powerful that we might still be stuck in them. Certainly the couple and therapy were stuck.

THE CRITICAL INCIDENT

Several weeks later, we met for the next session. Jim entered the room beaming and began to speak before he sat down. He said, "You won't believe what happened. I was in my hometown for the wedding, and I really got into watching a basketball game in the hotel bar. I looked up and realized I was probably going to miss the ceremony. So I took off. The hotel was just a couple of blocks away. I was half running, half walking, and then I realized I could cut through this field and save some time. So I did and suddenly I was right in the middle of my old Little League diamond—you know, where we played our home games. And I was there! Frankie Dubin was playing first base; Ray Brown was pitching. . . . I could feel the ball in my mitt and hear the sound of it landing there. I was playing good ball. My vision was clear. The world was crisp. And I was competent. I had to sort of come back to realize I was on my way to a wedding. But I kept the mood all the way through the weekend."

I asked Jim how different was it to go through the wedding in the "Little League mood." He replied, "All the difference in the world," and described feeling friendly and confident at the wedding and party, introducing himself with ease, talking to people, and enjoying himself. He contrasted this experience with his more usual experience of feeling awkward and disconnected, not attempting to interact much or talking to others but wondering if his conversation felt like an intrusion. Throughout my conversation with Jim, Leah was smiling. When asked what she was thinking about she said, "I love hearing Jim talk about a party this way. I was disappointed that he didn't ask me and I started out not wanting to hear about his weekend at all, but he came back different in a delightful way." Asked what she meant by "different in a delightful way," Leah said, "Jim seemed more spontaneous, more fun, and more at ease." I commented that perhaps Jim was reclaiming some forgotten aspect of himself. That hypothesis made sense to them. We spent the remainder of the hour talking about what differences Jim's reclamation of this aspect of himself had made to Leah and to their relationship. The effects and possibilities were far-reaching.

Leah was experiencing herself in relation to this "new Jim" as lighter, funnier, and willing to risk more. These qualities were not completely new in Leah's experience, but they were relatively new in this relationship. She told stories about other times in her life when she had experienced herself this way. It was as though the "younger Jim" and "younger Leah" were meeting and falling in love with each other for the first time. These other versions of themselves were creating a relationship that felt more joyous and more flexible and would support these reclaimed qualities that they valued in themselves.

Clearly, everyone involved believed that the déjà vu Jim experienced when he stumbled upon the Little League diamond was a turning point in the therapy. An unexpected outcome of Jim's reclamation of his confidence through this incident was his decision to change jobs. Previously, his fear of not being able to find a good job was one of his primary concerns about moving with Leah if she went away to graduate school. Now, however, through confident eyes the situation looked quite different. Now Jim openly acknowledged that in many respects his job did not suit him and that it was time to move on regardless of whether he decided to move with Leah. He believed he could find a job wherever he went and declared that would not be a factor in his decision about how to pursue the relationship. By their report, the relationship was better than ever.

Jim and Leah came to the next two sessions with stories about new good times together, discoveries about each other that they admired, and tales of now doing things together with ease that in the past had not gone as well. Not surprisingly, the couple decided that Jim would move with Leah to which ever city/town she moved to attend graduate school. Together, the two of them made the final decisions about where Leah would apply. Much more surprising to everyone was the couple's plan for how they would move together. Reflecting on some of the earlier therapy discussions about fear, frustration, and especially the impact of societal expectations for relationships, Leah and Jim realized that they wanted to be together and to continue the relationship but did not feel ready to make a bigger commitment. Accordingly, they decided to move together but to live separately and not take the move as an indication of expectations for the future. They discovered that although this idea suited them it was not an easy one to implement. To their respective families and, to some extent, friends, moving together implied a larger commitment. In their conversations with me about moving, they resolved to take control of their relationship rather than allowing it to be shaped by the expectations of others. Each time they had a conversation with someone and retained their own vision of their relationship and their own idea of what the move would mean, they added a chapter to their lives in which they were in charge of their relationship. At the same time, they were expanding the audience to their story.

DISCUSSION

My work with this couple is grounded within social constructionist ideas (Berger and Luckmann, 1966; Gergen, 1985; Hoffman, 1990) and narrative practices (Freedman and Combs, 1996; White and Epston, 1990; White, 1995; Monk et al., 1997; Zimmerman and Dickerson, 1997). In the beginning of therapy I am interested in hearing each person's account of the problem and naming these problems through questioning. Rather than thinking about people as being problematic or containing problems, I think about problems as acting on people, coming between them, and I perceive the larger culture as creating a context in which problems develop (Laird, 1989; White, 1995).

The Role of the Critical Incident in Getting Therapy Unstuck

One of the organizing tenets of narrative therapy is that stories are not about life, they *are* life (White, 1991). Nevertheless, not all events about which we ask questions become vivid and real enough to stand against or overshadow the problem stories that bring people to therapy. Although the Little League stories that Jim told in Session 10 seemed very helpful and fitting, they could easily have been forgotten and lost in the shadow of Leah's anger and frustration about not being invited to the wedding and the time pressure about applying to graduate school. When Jim happened upon the actual baseball diamond where these episodes in his life occurred over the course of four years, they were recalled prominently and with such vividness that little possibility existed of them being lost. It was also helpful that a potentially uncomfortable situation (the wedding and wedding party) occurred immediately after this incident. Jim's experience (his combined perceptions, thoughts, feelings, and actions) at the wedding and party was so different from his usual ways of being that it heightened the meaning of his Little League story and the identity it supported.

It is important to point out that as this incident became a turning point in the therapy for Jim and therefore for Leah, it also influenced *my* story of the therapy. That is, the parts of therapy I am writing about and those I am omitting are determined at least in part by which experiences led up to this event in the Little League field and which ones were influenced by it. A completely different account could be written. For example, I could have focused more on Leah's stories. However, to continue with this version of the story, Jim's entry into the world of meaning was supported by the Little League story, especially when combined with Leah's witnessing of it, and made very positive differences in their relationship. It made it possible for them to move beyond the problems that had brought them to therapy. The stories they then began to live out together were ones that pleased them both for quite some time.

Implications of the Critical Incident for Therapy

An important idea in narrative therapy is that of the numerous events one experiences in life, only a relative few are given meaning and storied. A tremendous number of unstoried events could be storied and could speak to the person or family of different identities and possibilities. So, while I usually begin by asking questions to deconstruct a problematic story, I am always looking for "unique outcomes" (White, 1988)—openings to alternative stories. That is, I am interested in finding events or moments that would not have been predicted by the problematic stories. As such moments or events are found, I ask questions that invite people to expand them into experientially vivid stories—to make meaning of them and to tell and retell them. Working together in this way, we construct alternative stories. Once people are situated in preferred stories, narrative therapy becomes a process of telling and retelling new stories that thicken and expand the preferred stories of people's lives and their relationships.

In the work with Jim, I fully expected to find a time in his life that did not fit with the problematic story. Identifying the Little League years and telling and retelling the stories of Little League were expected parts of the work. It was quite unexpected and serendipitous that shortly after these particular recountings, Jim stumbled onto the Little League diamond where he "had lived" these stories. It was this vivid experience of reliving the Little League stories on the diamond that was the turning point in the therapy.

In the conversations that I facilitate in couples therapy, I am interested in alternative stories becoming part of each member's knowledge of the other. It is only as this happens that stories such as the Little League stories can affect a couple's relationship. For this reason, I was careful to solicit Leah's reflections on Jim's stories of stumbling onto the baseball diamond and then feeling different at the wedding festivities. Her subjective experience that Jim came back "different in a delightful way" (more spontaneous, more fun, and more at ease) had far-reaching effects on their relationship. It brought forth a side of herself that was lighter, funnier, and willing to risk more.

As people begin to experience alternative stories of themselves and their lives, they often remember past events that support the new stories (Bruner, 1990). Leah showed how this can happen when she told stories about other times in her life when she had experienced the more spontaneous, more fun version of herself. When Jim heard these stories, it further enriched the version of his identity that had been so vividly reawakened on the baseball diamond. It was as though the "younger Jim" and "younger Leah" were meeting and falling in love with each other for the first time.

The Outcome of Therapy

Therapy ended on a good note, and Jim and Leah telephoned me before the move to tell me where Leah had decided to attend school and to which city they would be moving. In the December following the move, I received a holiday card from the couple.

POSTSCRIPT

I heard nothing more from Jim and Leah for many months, but the following school year I heard from them separately. Leah sent a holiday card in which she informed me that she and Jim were no longer together. Upon relocating, she and Jim had decided to live together. Accordingly, he moved in with her into an attractive house that she had bought with money from her divorce settlement. Their relationship continued to flourish for several months after the move. However, the arrangement of Jim living in Leah's house became increasingly uncomfortable for both of them. Although she was a student, she owned the house. Whereas Jim, six years younger and still building his career, was living in her house. She wrote, "I think those societal expectations got us again" (I assume that her reference to societal expectations was her recognition that had the situation been reversed so that Jim owned the house, the same kind of discomfort might not have been present). According to Leah, the relationship began to deteriorate and they mutually agreed to separate. Leah was feeling good about her life and her graduate school experiences.

Some months later, Jim called to talk with me about making a difficult work-related decision. In the course of that conversation, I asked him about his relationship with Leah. He acknowledged that the relationship had deteriorated and that he and Leah had amicably agreed to go their separate ways. Since that time he had remained in the town to which he and Leah had moved. They continue to be friends. He expressed feeling good about the relationship and did not regret moving with Leah. He did not want to get back together with Leah, thought positively of the relationship, and felt better prepared for another relationship. Although the couple did not ultimately stay together, the positive developments in their relationship made for stories that each valued, and those stories enriched their respective futures.

REFERENCES

Berger, P. and Luckmann, T. (1966). *The social construction of reality*. New York: Doubleday.

Bruner, J. (1990). *Acts of meaning*. Cambridge: Harvard University Press.

Freedman, J. and Combs, G. (1996). *Narrative therapy: The social construction of preferred realities*. New York: Norton.

Gergen, K. (1985). The social constructionist movement in modern psychology. *American Psychologist*, 40(3), 266-275.

Hoffman, L. (1990). Constructing realities: An art of lenses. *Family Process*, 29(1), 1-12.

Laird, J. (1989). Women and stories: Restorying women's self-constructions. In M. McGoldrick, C. Anderson, and F. Walsh (Eds.), *Women in families: A framework for family therapy* (pp. 427-450). New York: Norton.

Monk, G., Winslade, J., Crocket, K., and Epson, D. (Eds.) (1997). *Narrative therapy in practice: The archaeology of hope*. San Francisco: Jossey-Bass.

White, M. (1988). The process of questioning: A therapy of literary merit? *Dulwich Centre Newsletter*, winter, 8-14.

White, M. (1991). Deconstruction and therapy. *Dulwich Centre Newsletter*, 3, 21-40.

White, M. (1995). *Re-authoring lives: Interviews and essays*. Adelaide, Australia: Dulwich Centre Publications.

White, M. and Epston, D. (1990). *Narrative means to therapeutic ends*. New York: Norton.

Zimmerman, J. and Dickerson, V. (1997). *If problems talked: Narrative therapy in action*. New York: The Guilford Press.

Commentary

If You Reframe It, They Will Come

Thorana S. Nelson

Commentator Background

Fifty-three years old, female, white, PhD, twenty-one years MFT practice.

Practice Setting

University MFT clinic and private practice.

Theoretical Perspective

My current preferred theoretical perspective is an integration of structural, strategic, Bowen, solution-focused, and narrative practices. I reviewed this case from a strategic perspective.

INTRODUCTION AND CONCEPTS

Confusion between paradigms, theories, models, and techniques or practices has contributed to questions about which kind of therapy is being conducted. But, as this commentary demonstrates, therapy can simultaneously be understood from many perspectives (e.g., narrative and strategic), thus making admirable stories, such as Freedman's, accessible to more of us.

Before beginning my commentary I briefly will define the concepts I have used in examining Freedman's case. I consider Cloe Madanes' (1981) explication of strategic therapy to be one of the clearest I have read. It is informed by her work with Jay Haley (1976; 1980) and her familiarity with the mental research institute (MRI) model (Watzlawick, Weakland, and Fisch, 1974).

Important concepts from the MRI include:

1. *First-order change*—change within a system;
2. *Second-order change*—change of the rules of the system so that it becomes a different system; and
3. typical interventions include *directives,* both direct and indirect or paradoxical, and *reframing.*

Important concepts that Madanes added include:

1. The *therapist is responsible* for planning the therapeutic strategy.
2. Therapy focuses on and intervenes in the client's *social context.*
3. The *unit of interest is several people.*
4. The problem is defined as "a type of behavior that is part of a *sequence* of acts *between several people*" (Haley, 1980).
5. The first task is to *define a solvable problem.*
6. Therapy emphasizes and focuses on changing *analogic* or *metaphoric* communication.
7. The therapist is concerned with *hierarchy.*
8. The goal of therapy is to interrupt or prevent repetition of nonproductive sequences that metaphorically can change communication in many areas, *introducing complexity and alternatives.*

PRESENTING PROBLEM AND THERAPEUTIC SITUATION

Through the title of her case, Freedman introduces us to the idea of *metaphor:* "The *Feel* of Dreams." Through this metaphor, we understand, at least for this couple, that Freedman found some experiences to be important. As we come to understand later in the case, Jim's experiences on the baseball field of his youth significantly contributed to a change in the sequence of thoughts and behaviors that shaped his life. The change did not occur directly but metaphorically, in his communication patterns with Leah. For Leah, Jim's changed responses provoked a change in her experience of Jim, their relationship, and herself. I believe that this legitimately could be labeled *second-order change,* a change in the system of Jim, Leah, and their relationship. Freedman might not have been consciously thinking this way, but this is the approach I am taking: the *application* of strategic principles to understand her work and to suggest how a strategic therapist might work.

Beginning with the presenting problem, a relationship that "wasn't going anywhere," strategic therapists would argue that this is not a clear problem and that it needs to be reframed into a solvable one. The strategic therapist would want to reframe this problem quickly into one that is clearly defined and involves at least two people. The behavioral indicators and sequences of the problem are clear. Leah asked Jim to go grocery shopping. He was befuddled in the grocery store because he was "attracted to many possibilities" and was concerned about finding something that Leah would want to eat. In frustration, he finally simply "threw snack foods into the cart," worried about what he had done, and was angry when he arrived home; Leah was disappointed with Jim and with his feelings of helplessness. We are not told what happened next, but one could surmise that these feelings of anger and disappointment contributed to Leah and Jim becoming discouraged, and feeling distanced from each other and unable to reconnect. Jim also described similar experiences at work, suggesting a possible pattern in communication for him.

In terms of *social context,* the MRI clinical group and other strategic writers typically mention relationships and life-cycle stages. Freedman introduces issues of family and societal expectations specific to relationships, relative age of partners, gender, and divorce. Although Jim and Leah had been able to visit Jim's parents without experiencing the overt negative effects of these societal expectations, the expectations still were present in the sequences of thoughts, behaviors, and beliefs that fueled the patterns of their communication around certain topics. Madanes (1981) would be interested in the particular metaphors represented in the symptoms. It is not difficult to see that grocery shopping in the context of this relationship in which the female is older could elicit messages about hierarchy—specifically, despite Jim and Leah's desire to have an egalitarian relationship, hierarchical issues with regard to who is in charge of what and who gets to decide whether a job is performed well persisted. The *shoulds* and unspoken rules about their relationship seem to have helped them to maintain a pattern of distancing from each other. The conversation about grocery shopping represents the problem and, at the same time, is a failed attempt to resolve it.

With the couple's cooperation, Freedman reframes (labels) the problem as "fear and self-doubt" that inhibited Jim from planning a future with Leah. Although Haley cautions that labeling contributes to the generation of the problem, Freedman uses this label as a way of helping Jim and Leah discover exceptions, times when they are able to prevent the externalized problem from intruding into their relationship, resulting in increased distance. Indeed, this labeling by Freedman, in cooperation or collaboration with the clients, suggests a hierarchical arrangement such that the externalized problem, "fear and self-doubt," has had the upper hand and its metalevel communication has, at times, reinforced its dominance in the relationship. By taking over the prerogative of naming the problem, Freedman and the couple in effect regain control, thereby changing the problem and concurrently making it more solvable. As a consequence, Jim and Leah are now able to metacommunicate in ways that permit and affirm exceptions rather than absolutes. Such communication reinforces the metamessage that Jim and Leah wish to and can regain control of their relationship to the problem.

Freedman also uses metaphoric or analogic communication as a way to help the couple to understand a different time in Jim's life when he was in control of his own "fears and self-doubts." Their recognition of this relationship introduced new information into the system of "fear and self-doubt." Subsequently, Jim could at least temporarily regain his previous position vis-à-vis the problem, by interrupting the sequence in which fear and self-doubt played a significant part in his relationship with Leah. The language that Freedman uses in writing her story of Jim's and Leah's therapy suggests further metaphorical language of which Milton Erickson would approve. In this regard, Freedman's use of words such as "catcher," "dependable," "knack for putting the ball into the open spaces between fielders," "very close game," and "Jim's confident catch and tag of the player" convey hypnotic suggestions about Jim's relationship to the problem as well as new information for the adult Jim, Leah, and Freedman. These suggestions, if absorbed well into the system, could stimulate new behaviors that might renew Jim's relationship with himself and Leah's relationship to dismembered aspects of herself. Such behaviors can also interrupt the unfortunate patterns of communication between Jim and Leah. Indeed, this narrative restorying itself interrupted dysfunctional sequences.

Freedman asked more questions about those times when Jim had been more confident of himself; Jim provided additional information. With these questions, Freedman might have been helping the couple to find a factor that would make a difference in the apparent stagnation of their relationship. She also introduced information related to the context of the couple, including their own, their families', and society's expectations related to gender, unmarried couples, age, and the question of who is in charge. These questions enlarged the couple's problem context from one specific to themselves and their communication to one that included other aspects of their families and societal (cultural) relationship. Haley is very clear about the "third party" in couples' relationships, which includes other people. This could easily be interpreted to include other persons as well as behavioral, cultural, and contextual influences on the couple. The couple seemed to absorb this new information well. Leah, however, still was unhappy that Jim had not asked her to his friend's wedding. Some systemic therapists might interpret Leah's complaints as negative feedback intended to maintain the homeostasis of the relationship. At this juncture in therapy, Freedman acknowledges that the couple *and* therapy were stuck.

THE CRITICAL INCIDENT

During this stuck time, Jim attended an old friend's wedding in his hometown. There, an event occurred that reinforced the remembered information about his sense of confidence and efficacy in his youth. After figuratively tripping over his adolescent memories, which became very vivid for him, Jim was introduced to new information in his social system with people other than Leah. As a result, he discovered that he could feel friendly and confident. Although this might have been no surprise to Jim's friends, it was new information for his relationship with Leah. This information introduced even more complexity into his relationship with Leah and suggested new alternatives. Jim was able to maintain these rediscovered feelings in such a way that required Leah to take notice. His behaviors and Leah's reactions to them constituted a changed sequence that was reinforced by Leah observing how *her* behavior was new to the relationship, if not entirely new to her. Prior feelings that had been dismembered from her context were now remembered. Freedman notes that the "younger Jim" and "younger Leah" were "falling in love with each other for the first time."

This radical change in the relationship between Jim and Leah could be viewed as second order change. That is, the previous rules of the relationship demanded inequality, distance, and disappointment in the way they related to each other with regard to certain topics. The added complexity did not remove these as possibilities but *added* new possibilities for them to be confident, spontaneous, and fun loving with each other. The previous rules demanded a prescribed sequence in relation to specific topics (e.g., when someone was "supposed" to be in charge). This often lead to confusion and disappointment in their interaction. The new rules allowed for greater variety in the couple's responses to each other.

This change is evidenced by Jim spontaneously changing his job and receiving work-related positive feedback that reinforced his new attitude of confidence and courage. Although this change may have been sufficient for Jim and his relationship to his own ideas about himself, it might not have been sufficient to sustain the changes in his relationship with Leah.

Viewed from a different perspective, the changes experienced by Jim and Leah, i.e., the introduction of new behaviors to an existing sequence, may have been first order. However, the system rules about expectations from self, family, and society may have remained unchanged. In new circumstances, these rules would prevail. Alas, Jim and Leah were unable to maintain their new relationship in the face of a move together for Leah's schooling. The hierarchy of the problem of "fear and self-doubt" to the couple may not have been sufficiently reversed to allow Jim and Leah to take charge when they wanted to and remain together. On the other hand, their separating might be viewed as desirable second order change, taking charge over the problem in a different, more confident way.

With regard to therapy, it is interesting to note that the critical incident occurred at a time when Freedman also was feeling stuck. Up to this point, therapy had been fairly usual for Freedman. Intervention consisted of the assignment of new labels, new perspectives on relationships, adding complexity to the system by externalizing the problem, and calling attention to the relationship between the couple and problem rather than simply the relationship between Jim and Leah. Freedman's usual way of intervening was not working; first order changes of observing new but already existing aspects of both Jim and Leah and of the relationship were not sufficient. Somehow, Jim's "finding himself" on the baseball field, recalling his youthful feelings of confidence and competency, and his experience at the wedding added new information to the therapeutic system. Here we can speculate about contributors to this new information: the reinforcement of ideas from the therapy session prior to the critical incident, information from *outside* the therapeutic system, or Leah's response to Jim's new persona. I claim not to be a modernist any longer. However, I wonder if the spontaneous occurrence of something outside of therapy surprised even Freedman, who, at that time, may not have been as aware of the possibilities of the out-of-therapy events. Freedman might have been jolted into genuine surprise at the change in both Jim and Leah, which was a positive feedback reinforcer of the change. This is not to suggest that Freedman is not or was not genuinely surprised at "sparkling moments" that are/were revealed in therapy but simply that the quality of her reaction was different in some way.

DISCUSSION

In reviewing her story of Jim and Leah's therapy, Freedman suggests that her usual way of working is to "hear . . . each person's story of the problem and to name these problems through questioning." This way of working elicits reframing of problems in such a way that they are more solvable than the presenting language would suggest. By externalizing the problem in a frame that clients can accept and, indeed, embrace, clients can develop a new relationship to the problem. Often clients come to perceive the problem as more solvable than when they initially perceived it to be somehow inherently *within* them or their relationship. Observing and discovering exceptions, previous successful solutions, new attitudes, or sparkling moments in the fight against the problem introduce new information into the system of sequences. This news is of such a nature that the system cannot ignore it and simply remain in its current state. The new metarule is one that constitutes second order change in the system, becoming a system with exceptions rather than one without. Freedman did not use directives, however, a hallmark of strategic therapy. I wonder how much of her part of the conversation could be viewed as indirect suggestions in metaphorical language, which also is a part of strategic therapy.

The critical incident also introduced new information into the therapeutic system. Freedman admits that this incident influenced *her* story of therapy and thus her perception of the couple, their problem, and the nature of therapy as stuck. This may have introduced new sequences in the therapy such that Freedman, Jim, and Leah could no longer act as though there was only one way to "do" their relationship *or* the therapy. I wonder how Freedman has incorporated her understanding of this spontaneous incident into her therapy and how it has changed her as a therapist.

WHAT I MIGHT HAVE DONE DIFFERENTLY

I'm not sure what I would have done differently had I been a strategic therapist with this couple. I probably would have worked to find a nonexternalizing label, one that would suggest new categories of solutions. I might have surmised that Jim and Leah's manner of communicating with each other maintained some kind of relationship balance that was maintained at great cost. The style of communicating was effective but it cost the relationship a great deal. For example, Leah's occasional dissatisfaction and belief that the relationship was "going nowhere" might have kept her in the simultaneous one-up and one-down position of failed person in charge. That is, she requested something from Jim and he failed to comply, thus giving her the upper hand. This incongruent relationship also defined Jim as simultaneously in a one-down and one-up position. Their communication pattern that did not include metatalk—talk about the way they dealt with problems—served also to maintain the status quo of the relationship. Their solutions are not clear but probably included not talking—applying more of the same or applying a first instead of second order solution.

With regard to their communication style, I might have assisted them behaviorally to learn more effective ways to communicate with each other as well as ways to metacommuncicate that would bring them closer as a couple, without stifling their individual autonomy. Were I an MRI therapist, I might have used directives that instructed Jim intentionally to become befuddled in the grocery store and to bring home grocery items that clearly were silly. This would have disrupted their usual pattern of relating around such issues, especially if, concurrently, I instructed Leah to do something different, such as to make a casserole of whatever Jim brought home and to serve it with candles and incense. If I were aware of the gendered expectations on this couple, I might have instructed Leah to do the grocery shopping herself, to report to Jim about the price of items and the details of shopping. I also would have instructed Jim to remain at home, to help Leah to carry the bags into the kitchen upon her return from the grocery store, and to listen intently to her story about grocery shopping. This might have exaggerated their incongruent but invisible hierarchy and stimulated new ways of relating specific to these issues.

If I were using Madanes' interventions, I might instruct the couple to pretend to have poor communication, with Jim pretending to shop ineptly, pretending to be angry when he came home, and Leah pretending to be disappointed and to withdraw. Most likely, I would assist the couple in adding metacommunication to their repertoire of communication styles and to recognize and detoxify the contextual and conflicting messages of gender and age. I also might have assisted them in using new skills for different, less intense topics of difference so that they might metaphorically be able to use them in these critical areas, thus changing their typical sequences and leading to more direct and satisfying communication.

CONCLUDING REMARKS

As this case report demonstrates, Freedman's narrative approach can capitalize on fortuitous events outside of therapy and expand their effects in people's lives. However, many ways exist in which therapists can use the identical material with which they are presented in therapy. Whether using narrative, strategic, or intergenerational ways of thinking or practicing, as therapists we all strive to help our clients in the best possible way. For example, a therapist who subscribes to a different theoretical perspective might have used these identical or similar events in therapy in an entirely different way. Yet a different therapist might not have noticed these events or included them in therapy. For me, the outcome of this case demonstrates that equifinality, i.e., multiple pathways to a desired outcome, is alive and well. Therapists, MFT and otherwise, can use multiple perspectives of single events to the advantage of their clients and the therapy process. This is an essential point of this commentary and the editor's goal for this book. Indeed, there are many ways of skinning a cat and doing it well!

REFERENCES

Haley, J. (1976). *Problem-solving therapy*. San Francisco: Jossey-Bass.

Haley, J. (1980). *Leaving home*. New York: McGraw-Hill.

Madanes, C. (1981). *Strategic family therapy*. San Francisco, CA: Jossey-Bass Publishers.

Watzlawick, P., Weakland, J., and Fisch, R. (1974). *Change: Principles of problem formation and problem resolution*. New York: Norton.

Commentary

Hit the Next Good Pitch

Frank N. Thomas
Michael Durrant

Commentator Backgrounds

Forty-seven years old, white, male, PhD, twenty-two years MFT practice.

Forty-seven years old, white, male, registered psychologist, twenty-two years clinical practice.

Practice Setting

Thomas: University MFT and counseling clinic; limited private practice. Durrant: University counseling and family therapy clinic; private practice, Sydney, Australia.

Theoretical Perspective

Both of us teach and practice from a competency-based model of therapy and our commentary comes from this perspective. The competency-based model of therapy is a social constructionist approach primarily informed by the "brief, interactional" approaches such as MRI and brief solution focused.

We accept that every therapeutic approach has its limitations, and all reports of therapy, oral or written, are of necessity selective. Consequently, Freedman could not tell the reader everything that occurred in her work with Leah and Jim. As a result, the tendency to read other points into the textual account is not only easy but inevitable. Accordingly, our purpose for this commentary is to consider other ways of approaching treatment and to suggest other important ideas that, in our opinion, relate to the social constructionist tradition rather than to negate the excellent work Freedman has done with this couple.

We perceive our therapeutic approach to be similar to yet different from Freedman's. We hold to assumptions about reality that we believe fit well with Freedman's social constructionist stance and its focus on the importance of context and language. However, we follow (with differing degrees of allegiance) a model or framework for therapy that appreciably is different from Freedman's narrative approach. Our designated approach competency based, is informed by de Shazer (1991) and Berg's (DeJong and Berg, 1998) solution-focused brief therapy and shares some underlying assumptions with White's narrative approach. We acknowledge that it is hardly fair to comment on a case from within a therapeutic framework different from the one the therapist of record used when he or she worked with the family. However, just as Freedman sees these clients through the lens of her approach, so we see her work with this couple through the lens of our framework. Moreover, debate continues about the extent to which the narrative and solution-focused models are similar and the extent to which they are different. As a consequence, throughout our commentary we will highlight some of the differences between our perspective and the narrative perspective.

GOOD POINTS ABOUT THE CASE

Freedman describes well her work with this couple. She elicits stories from the couple, deconstructs them, and creates new stories with the couple that allow for different futures. Her use of textual metaphors, such as "adding a chapter to their lives" and "expanding the audience to their story," is consistent with her particular version of narrative therapy and are important aspects of narrative development. We also appreciate her focus on therapy becoming "a process of telling and retelling new stories that thickens and expands the preferred stories of people's lives and their relationships" because doing so is consistent with the tenets of narrative therapy.

ISSUES WITH WHICH WE STRUGGLED

Freedman's creation of the labels "fear" and "self-doubt" as ways to understand Jim's experience is one of the primary issues with which we wrestled as we examined her work with this couple. From our perspective, these labels, as ways of understanding, appear to be incongruent with the description of Jim's reaction to the grocery store incident. One could cogently ask, why isn't Jim simply "pissed off" at Leah or "angry and worried" about the situation? Accordingly, we question the need to create a deficit concept with regard to Jim's reaction when a reactive construct might be less enduring regarding his character? Self-doubt is pervasive rather than situational. Consequently, labeling Jim's reaction as pervasive rather than situational has the potential of exacerbating that experience by generalizing his Leah-centered experiences into pervasive or even permanent attributes.

Based on Freedman's case description, we struggled with the possibility that she may have privileged Leah's perception of the status of the relationship over Jim's perception. From the first session, it was clear that Jim did not perceive that a problem existed in the couple's relationship—more important, *his* problem did not exist. It was Leah who was "experiencing some urgency about the future of the relationship" and wanted to know "where the relationship was going"; Jim was willing to let the relationship "take its course." However, after the couple and therapist spent ten sessions talking about the future of the relationship, Jim admitted a problem existed. Subsequent to that admission, the problem was defined as "fear" (Jim's) and "self-doubt" (Jim's) "that was inhibiting Jim from planning a future together with Leah." In light of this, we question, whose responsibility is it to decide whether a relationship is problematic? In a collaborative approach, surely the problem is openly negotiated among all parties present from the beginning of the first session. If Jim did not embrace Leah's conceptualization and experience as a problem worth pursuing, a collaborative therapist would negotiate a problem that both could agree from the outset was worth pursuing *or* meet individually with the family member requesting a particular change. For example, if both Leah and Jim agreed to explore the problem as Leah had defined it (i.e., wanting to know "where the relationship was going"), we would have developed a goal focused on exploring this need and presented it in the following way: "The three (or two) of us will meet to examine Leah's struggles with the future of this relationship." We also differ from Freedman in regard to her focus on a problem (externalized) as opposed to a focus on future and goals. Jim and Leah differed on what they believed was a problem (or the existence of one). They may not have differed quite so much on how they wanted things to be in their relationship. A pressure to "name" an externalized problem tends to reinforce the focus on the problematic and so the polarization between the two views becomes entrenched. It appears that in finding a name for the externalized problem, Freedman made it principally Jim's problem.

What We Might Have Done Differently

When discussing "serendipitous moments" in therapy, it is important to consider whether we wait for a source of the random (Bateson, 1979) to enter the therapeutic context, or is it our responsibility as therapists to coax or even create such moments into being (doing what Lynn Hoffman [1985] has so eloquently suggested, "Give it a bump and see how it jumps")? From a competency-based perspective, we believe we must be purposive in creating therapeutic realities. Consequently, we might have proceeded differently in the following areas:

Goal orientation. A competency-based approach (Durrant, 1993; Thomas and Cockburn, 1998) would highlight clear goal orientation negotiated between the couple and the therapist. Based on Freedman's report, we are unclear whether the couple had a clear idea of what life, views, and interaction would be like when therapy was completed. It appears that of the fourteen total sessions they spent together, the first nine contained no goal, no symptom, and no active decision making. In our approach, these would have received the greatest attention. Although most of Freedman's work on this case appears to set the stage to talk about externalized realities and societal gaze, we believe it is most important that people experience agency and positive change. Therefore, we would have focused on what each partner wanted in therapy, how each one had experienced parts of these outcomes, and what could be done to achieve them (intentional activities and interactions based on resources, abilities, and past successes).

Focus on competence. Stories of competence can be identified within Freedman's description of Sessions 1 through 9. Our focus would have highlighted their competencies both as individuals and as a couple, and we would have spent less time on accounts relating struggles and failures. For example, Freedman states that multiple times in the first nine sessions Leah and Jim told "stories of . . . working well as a team and stories of successfully working out misunderstandings." Similar to Freedman, we would have focused attention on these exceptions to the problem. In addition, we might have negotiated between-session tasks for Leah and/or Jim to possibly create additional experiences of success from which to define their futures.

Couple communication. In Freedman's account of the case, Leah and Jim express difficulties and frustrations with each other, especially in response to what had become a defining event—Jim's trip to the grocery store. With regard to this event, we might have negotiated an agreement that focused on each person's unstated expectations. Doing so would have led naturally to an examination of their communication process. However one stories it, we believe that occasionally people get into repetitive interactional patterns that hinder change. For example (with some fictional license!), Leah states, "Please go to the store." Jim hears, "Get whatever you want at the store." Jim does not ask Leah for specifics, but he is frustrated because he knows he needs more direction from Leah with regard what he needs to purchase. Leah's response to Jim when he returns with junk food is, "I don't like what you bought." We perceive this malcommunication to be more related to a couple problem than what became known as Jim's self-doubt or fear.

An alternative focus on Leah. Leah's perceptions of Jim as "not measuring up" could have become the focus of therapy, with or without Jim. Consequently, we question the need to direct the focus of therapy; instead, why not address, alter, adjust, or inform Leah's perceptions of the ideal mate?

An alternative "societal expectation." Increasingly, more women in the United States are choosing to remain single after divorce (Coontz, 1997). As a result, it would have been appropriate to focus on "societal expectations to remain single and independent." As one current joke stated: "For men, it's called 'a fear of intimacy;' for women, it's called 'being choosy.'" With a "societal expectation" for Leah to remain a single woman, the focus of therapy might have been on other aspects of their (or her) experiences of jobs, graduate school, and relationships.

Exploring each person's understanding of an experience. We see many possible understandings of Jim's weekend away from Leah. Based on Freedman's report, we do know that Jim attended a wedding and Leah was upset that Jim did not invite her to accompany him. Upon Jim's return, both he and Leah report that he was "different" in a positive sense. Of the many possible explanations for Jim's change is that perhaps having the weekend alone was the difference! That is, perhaps being away from the pressure to make the relationship "happen" was as important a contributor to the change observed as was the storied experience of the baseball diamond. We can only wonder if the renewed therapeutic focus on methodically examining the relationship stupefied Jim's change and stifled his spontaneity.

Successful outcome. We believe that clients perceive an outcome to be successful when they experience themselves both as having agency and as having taken significant steps toward resolving a difficult situation. Because of this focus, we see client motivation as a key to positive outcomes and wonder about each partner's motivation with regard to the change process and, specifically, how Leah and Jim perceived the outcome. Consequently, were we the therapists working with this couple, we might have focused on accessing their individual and mutual experiences of therapy through posttreatment interviews and client feedback. In doing so, we would have been informing ourselves regarding the clients' perspectives on success, which in turn informs our own stories of a successful case.

ETHICAL ISSUES

Other aspects of this case that pique our clinical curiosity fall into what the editor calls "the ethical." Here, it is important to point out that we raise these issues not as accusations or criticisms of Freedman's work but as alternative ideas to be considered in examining this case.

Viewpoints of "Truth"

The format of this book raises an interesting question for us. When presenting, orally or in writing, a clinical case, who among the participants, clients, and therapist decides the importance of an event? Are clients' viewpoints considered regarding the critical incidents in therapy? If so, how? In this regard, Freedman has written (with Gene Combs) about collaborative research with her clients. She asserts, "One particular purpose of this (client/therapist) co-research is that of evaluating the ethics of the beliefs, attitudes, and practices that constitute our work" (Freedman and Combs, 1996, p. 287). Increasingly, the current therapeutic literature is replete with reports of therapists writing collaboratively with their clients (e.g., "Jeremy" and Epston, 1992; Metcalf, et al., 1996; St. George and Wulff, 1998; Thomas, 1994), thus we wonder how accounts of this particular critical incident reported by Freedman would be written by Jim or Leah or a collaborative team of Jim, Leah, and Freedman. It is not simply a question of difference. Rather it is highly possible that clients may actually benefit from researching and recollecting their experiences of therapy (Gale, 1993, 1992). Given the importance of examining the ethics of participation, we discuss the following three additional ethical issues specific to this case:

Autonomy

This relates to each client's right to make informed decisions as long as those decisions do not harm others; we believe that autonomy needs to be of primary concern for helping professionals. In light of our emphasis on clients' rights to make informed decisions, we can only wonder if Jim had or believed that he had clear choices as to whether or not he wanted to pursue the direction therapy took.

Gender

In Freedman's therapeutic approach, the therapist's sensitivity to gender is an important factor in his or her work with families. Accordingly, as we observed—through her case report—Freedman's attention to gender issues in working with Jim and Leah, we question some of her actions and suggest another perspective. What might have been the outcome of therapy had Freedman labeled Jim's difficulty in making decisions "flexibility" rather than labeling it "self-doubt"? We believe no neutral position exists from which to conduct therapy (Watzlawick, Weakland, and Fisch, 1974). Consequently, it is important that therapists continually examine—and invite others to examine—the possibility of bias outside of their awareness; we believe Freedman would agree with this perspective. However, given that Jim did not initially present with a problem but became a primary focus during the course of therapy, we wonder if this is an attempt to unilaterally apply a narrative sense of justice in this case. Although in the minds of many "justice" is fair and equal treatment, some narrative perspectives hold to a more intentional stance of righting wrongs and reversing normalized situations (Cowley and Springen, 1995). Accordingly, we question whether Jim felt or actually was fully informed of the possibility that he would be placed in a position of responsibility for the relationship's problems and be affected by therapy in ways to which he might not have agreed.

Culture

We question whether Freedman considered the specific culture of each partner as an important contributor to the unfolding of this case. What, if any, were the explicit and/or implicit familial and/or cultural factors that perhaps influenced this couple's experiences? We know that Freedman applied a more general idea of "societal expectations," but could this be more prescriptive than experiential? As readers, we are left wondering. In this regard, could it be that the dating relationship Jim and Leah had established was sufficient for them? Did either Leah or Jim express any views on social pressure to be a couple, or was this Freedman's frame that was imposed without knowledge of the clients' views? When the couple decided to move but live separately, Freedman writes that it defied "social expectations." We wonder, was this the couple's experience of the event or Freedman's? We may wonder, why isn't this defined as "wisdom" rather than "defying social expectations"?

FINAL THOUGHTS

With this commentary our intent was to expand upon Freedman's clinical account of therapy with this couple and to suggest alternative ideas and understandings, not to criticize or correct her work. Our work is informed by social constructionist ideologies, and theorists such as Kenneth Gergen (1998) are moving away from the exclusive use of language metaphors and have begun to include those aspects of human experiences that may not readily be reduced to language. In this commentary we have strived to be both respectfully curious and goal driven. Accepting that all approaches to therapy are biased and incomplete, we acknowledge that as the therapist in vivo Freedman had a better view of the actual goings-on with this couple. Accordingly, we hope that we have not detracted from what she has accomplished with Jim and Leah but instead have added to the possibilities the reader sees in this account of a critical incident in therapy while avoiding the creation of dichotomies or controversies.

REFERENCES

Bateson, G. (1979). *Mind and nature: A necessary unity.* New York: Bantam.
Coontz, S. (1997). *The way we really are: Coming to terms with America's changing families.* New York: Basic Books.

Cowley, G. and Springen, K. (1995). Rewriting life stories. *Newsweek*, April 17, pp. 70-74.

DeJong, P. and Berg, I.K. (1998). *Interviewing for solutions*. Pacific Grove, CA: Brooks/Cole.

de Shazer, S. (1991). *Putting difference to work*. New York: Norton.

Durrant, M. (1993). *Residential treatment: A cooperative, competency-based approach to therapy and program design*. New York: Norton.

Freedman, J. and Combs, G. (1996). *Narrative therapy: The social construction of preferred realities*. New York: Norton.

Gale, J. (1992). When research interviews are more therapeutic than therapy interviews. *The Qualitative Report*. Available online at <http://www.nova.edu/shss/QR/numbers.html>.

Gale, J. (1993). A field guide to qualitative inquiry and its clinical relevance. *Contemporary Family Therapy*, 15(1), 73-91.

Gergen, K.J. (1998). *Transformative dialogues*. November 19. Salesmanship Club Youth and Family Centers, Dallas, TX.

Hoffman, L. (1985). Beyond power and control: Toward a "second-order" family systems therapy. *Family Systems Medicine*, 3(4), 381-396.

"Jeremy" and Epston, D. (1992). A problem of belonging. In D. Epston and M. White (Eds.), *Experience, contradiction, narrative and imagination* (pp. 97-103). Adelaide, South Australia: Dulwich Centre Publications.

Metcalf, L., Thomas, F.N., Miller, S.D., Hubble, M.A., and Duncan, B. (1996). Client and therapist perceptions of solution-focused brief therapy: A qualitative analysis. In S.D. Miller, M.A. Hubble, and B. Duncan (Eds.), *Handbook of solution-focused brief therapy: Foundations, applications, and research* (pp. 335-349). San Francisco: Jossey-Bass.

St. George, S. and Wulff, D. (1998). Integrating the client's voice within case reports. *Journal of Systemic Therapies*, 17(4), 3-13.

Thomas, F.N. (1994). The experience of solution-oriented therapy: Post-therapy client interviewing. *Case Studies in Brief and Family Therapy*, 8(1), 47-58.

Thomas, F.N. and Cockburn, J. (1998). *Competency-based counseling: Building on client strengths*. Minneapolis: Fortress.

Watzlawick, P., Weakland, J., and Fisch, R. (1974). *Change: Principles of problem formation and problem resolution*. New York: Norton.

CASE 3

You Might Get What You Wish For

Anthony P. Jurich

Therapist Background

Currently: Fifty-two years old, white, male, PhD, twenty-seven years MFT practice. Then: Thirty-eight years old, PhD, thirteen years MFT practice.

Practice Setting

Currently and when I saw this family: University family therapy clinic.

Client Characteristics

Gary (age thirty-nine), Marge (age thirty-seven), and their three children, Cindy (age sixteen), Charlie (age thirteen), and Carol (age eight), are a white upper-middle-class family; Cindy was the IP. The family sought therapy because Cindy, a high school student, had been complaining of a variety of somatic ailments and as a result experienced difficulty attending school and completing her in-school academic work. Prior to seeing me, Cindy and her parents had consulted with three other mental health professionals respectively for a total of six therapy sessions without any appreciable changes in Cindy's complaints and/or behaviors. Gary was employed as an electrical engineer and Marge was employed as a secretary in an insurance firm. Charlie and Carol were students in elementary school.

Length of Treatment

Prior therapists: "A"—three sessions; "B"—two sessions; "C"—one session. Present therapist: Cindy and her parents were seen for eight sessions during spring 1985. The critical incident occurred in Session 2.

Theoretical Perspective

A strategic approach integrated with transgenerational techniques was used in working with this family.

PRESENTING PROBLEM

As I glanced over the yellow intake sheet, I saw that Marge had called the family therapy clinic to seek help for Cindy. Accordingly, I called the family to schedule an appointment. During that conversation, Marge reported that "Cindy had been a good student until this past year, when the work had gotten more difficult for her. Beginning this past fall, Cindy began to fake being ill to avoid the consequences of not completing her schoolwork." As the year progressed, Cindy's complaints of illness became more frequent and more dramatic. Numerous trips to physicians yielded no obvious medical reasons for the various symptoms about which Cindy was complaining. Consequently, the family physician had suggested that Cindy's symptoms might be psychosomatic in origin.

As a result, the parents and Cindy consulted a male counselor who, after three sessions, suggested that Cindy was using her physical symptoms as a coping technique to get out of doing schoolwork. Upon hearing that conclusion, Cindy refused to return to see the counselor. The parents then consulted a male psychologist who, after a battery of tests, came to a similar conclusion as the physician and the counselor. Once again, Cindy refused to continue therapy. The parents consulted next with a female social worker who arrived at the same conclusion as her male colleagues. However, when she saw that Cindy was very upset at hearing the same diagnosis again, she suggested that the family consult with me, "because I had a reputation as a therapist who worked effectively with adolescents and was nontraditional in my approach to therapy with adolescents." At the end of her story, I invited Marge to bring in the entire family for at least the first therapy session.

THE THERAPEUTIC SITUATION PRIOR
TO THE CRITICAL INCIDENT

As I awaited the family's arrival for our first session, I anticipated having to join quickly with Cindy to live up to my "reputation" of being "nontraditional," as reported to the family by my social work colleague. Accordingly, to emphasize my "nontraditional image," I wore blue jeans, a golf shirt, and boots. As the family entered the therapy room, I immediately noticed that Charlie and Carol were absent. I asked Marge why the younger children were not present. She responded that she saw no reason to "drag" the other two children to therapy when it was Cindy's problem. Furthermore, she was afraid that the younger children might learn Cindy's poor coping strategies if they came in and listened to her ailments.

At the beginning of the session, Marge informed me that it required much arm twisting by both parents before Cindy agreed to see me. She then recited a litany of situations in which Cindy "faked being ill" to get out of schoolwork or going to school. I had to interrupt her to ask Gary if he concurred with her perception of the problem. Gary replied that he "more or less" agreed with Marge's definition of the problem. I then asked Cindy to describe "her family's situation." Her response was recitation of a long list of symptoms and complaints of "how stressful school was to her." Some of her symptoms were easy to debunk. For example, she claimed to have had a fever although the thermometer showed a normal temperature. Other symptoms, such as earaches and constant fatigue, were more difficult or impossible to disprove. In my opinion, the array of symptoms she described could not logically be linked together. I asked Cindy if all aspects of school were stressful to her or only the academic parts. She replied that only the academic parts of school were stressful and that she, in fact, enjoyed her friends and the more social aspects of school.

I told Cindy and her parents that I could not tell what was going on in the family and that I needed at least one more session to sort things out. In the interim, I asked each family member for his or her respective help. I asked Cindy to monitor her illness for the next week, to keep a diary of her symptoms, and to bring the diary to the next therapy session. I asked Marge to uncover evidence that she believed would demonstrate that Cindy was "faking." Finally, I asked Gary to be responsible for bringing Carol and Charlie to the next session because they would be good observers of what was going on. The stage was set for the following week.

EVENTS LEADING TO THE CRITICAL INCIDENT

The next session, all five family members were present. I reintroduced myself to Cindy, Gary, and Marge and, with a ceremonial handshake, I introduced myself to Carol and Charlie. I was dressed as I was the previous week, with one exception: I had exchanged the golf shirt for a black T-shirt advertising a local restaurant. I thanked Gary for completing his homework in ensuring that Carol and Charlie were present and asked Cindy and Marge if they had completed their assignments. Cindy nodded affirmatively and clutched her notebook diary, and Marge said, "Yes," and waved a notepad in front of me. I was about to ask Cindy to begin, but Marge cut me off by launching into her "proof of Cindy's faking." Since Marge already had taken the floor, I let her run with it. At the end of ten continuous minutes of accusations, I stopped her by waving my hands and telling her, "I've got the picture." She protested that she was not even halfway through her list. I thanked her for her report and told her that I wanted to hear from Cindy.

Cindy appeared relieved that I was willing to hear her views. As she began to list her symptoms and the stresses connected to them at school, I intentionally increased my attention to her and demonstrated increased concern about her symptoms. When she began with her descriptions, I was relatively relaxed and leaned back in my seat. As she progressed, I intentionally leaned forward, furrowed my brow, and fixed my eyes on her face with my best look of concern. I began to make specific remarks of concern, such as "No, really?" and "God, that must have been hard for you!" After listening to her for about ten minutes, I stopped her and told her that I was seriously concerned. I asked her if there were any other "unusual" symptoms or if the rest of her diary was similar to what she just had told me. She reported a few more "unusual" symptoms.

At that point, I cupped my hands together over my nose and mouth, took a big deep breath, and turned to Gary and Marge. I focused exclusively on Gary and Marge and specifically kept Cindy and her siblings out of my direct line of vision. Because I have excellent peripheral vision, I could see Cindy's face, but she could not tell that I could see her. In my most serious voice, I told Gary and Marge, "We have a major problem here." I told them that I had done my homework and had researched Cindy's symptoms in medical books and consulted with my colleagues. In a very solemn tone I said, "What we have here with Cindy is a case of acute chronic fatigue syndrome." I told them that it was very rare but very dangerous. Gary and Marge looked shocked but concerned. Out of the corner of my eye, I could see Cindy beginning to smile for the first time.

For the reader who may want to research acute chronic fatigue syndrome, it will not be found. I made it up. All that Cindy had told me about her symptomatology had convinced me that my colleagues probably were correct: Cindy was using physical ailments as excuses to cope with the stress of academics. However, I believed that had I verbally reported that as my diagnosis, the situation would have been more of the same and Cindy predictably would have terminated therapy. Accordingly, I needed to hook Cindy into the therapeutic process so that she could not dismiss me as just another callous adult in a suit. If her symptoms were valid, many of them could have been symptomatic of chronic fatigue syndrome. Since the family also had defined the situation as "acute," I opportunistically combined the terms and created acute chronic fatigue syndrome, which I now bestowed upon Cindy. I explained to Gary and Marge that acute chronic fatigue syndrome was exacerbated by stress of any kind. Therefore, I announced to them that their daughter was simply too sick to go to school, since Cindy had reported being severely stressed by academics. In addition, since academics was such a central cause of stress, Cindy could do no homework either. Marge was still in a state of shock; Gary was beginning to become perceptibly annoyed with me; Cindy, whom I could still see in my peripheral vision, was now smiling broadly. Her smile appeared to be saying, "Yes! I finally got this guy to agree with me." As Gary glanced over at his daughter, his expression made it clear that he was becoming observably more irritated with me.

Ignoring both Gary and Marge's observable responses, I pressed on. I told them that in clinical experiments with patients who exhibited acute chronic fatigue syndrome, the only success that physicians had in overcoming the ailment was the complete reduction of stress. Out of the corner of my eye, I did a quick check on Cindy. She still was smiling broadly. I went on to explain to the parents that the best way to reduce stress with an adolescent was "complete bed rest." Suddenly, Cindy's smile was not quite as broad. I also informed the parents that stress was caused not only by negative stimuli, such as academics, but also by anything that would excite Cindy. I explained that Cindy would have to stay in bed, probably with the curtains drawn. I asked if Cindy had a telephone in her room. Marge said yes. I strongly recommended that the phone be taken out of her room and that she be restricted from all telephone calls. I told them that nothing is more stimulating to a young teenage girl than talking to her friends on the phone. Both parents agreed. I stressed that such stimulation was entirely too stressful for Cindy in her delicate condition. From the corner of my eye, I could see that Cindy no longer was smiling.

I next asked if Cindy had a television or a radio in her room. The parents shook their heads affirmatively. Again, I said, "Those will have to go too." Although Marge still seemed confused by all this, Gary gave a first glimmer of recognition as to where I was headed with my recommendations. In the spirit of the prescriptions, Gary reported that Cindy also had a cassette tape deck in her room upon which she played hard rock. I tried to strike a concerned, yet thoughtful pose. To Gary and Marge, I explained that it was okay to leave the tape deck in the bedroom, but they had to keep a vigilant watch over what was played. Accordingly, I said, "The heavy metal tapes have to go." Cindy could listen to "Montovani or Hollywood Strings but nothing more exciting." I also suggested that they would have to restrict the kind of materials Cindy read. "No magazines or comic books are allowed, but she could read some of the great classics, provided that they were not too exciting. Perhaps *Great Expectations* by Charles Dickens would be a good choice." For readers not familiar with Montovani or the Hollywood Strings (music often heard in elevators) or *Great Expectations*, I purposefully suggested music and literature that most teenagers would find boring. Gary began to take notes on my suggestions, while Cindy looked very concerned at the direction in which this conversation was headed.

Continuing, I said, "Food could also be too stimulating. Although we can get Cindy a more balanced meal in a few weeks, for the time being, we should try something bland, like milk toast." "What?" Cindy exclaimed. Without taking my eyes off Gary and Marge, I replied, "Milk toast. It's where you toast a slice of white bread and let it soak in a bowl of warm milk." Cindy shouted, "You're full of shit!" Again, without raising my voice or taking my eyes from her parents, I replied, "That reminds me, going to the bathroom can also be too stimulating. So, we'll have to get her a bedpan." Cindy huffed in exasperation. I continued, "Marge, Gary, I assume you know how to help Cindy use a bedpan? You probably will have to wipe her bottom when she defecates . . ." Cindy shouted, "Enough! I'm not going to have my father wipe my ass when I go to the bathroom! It would be easier to go to school!" Charlie and Carol began to giggle. For the first time since I initially had expressed my concern, I turned my body toward Cindy and looked deep into her eyes. She was red with frustration. I spoke softly, "But, Cindy, if you have acute chronic fatigue syndrome, this is what it's going to take to get you well." She replied, "Well, maybe I don't have it that bad?" I cautioned that if she had it at all, being extreme about the cure would be the only way to treat it. I said, "It seems to me that we have one of two choices—one, using physical symptoms as a coping device or two, acute chronic fatigue syndrome. If you or the family has any other suggestions, I'm all ears."

THE CRITICAL INCIDENT

After a few moments of silence, Carol said, "Maybe Cindy's just lazy and she got sick to get out of schoolwork." I turned to Carol and thanked her for her suggestion. I then turned back to Cindy and said, "Okay, three choices, although you don't strike me as someone who's lazy." Cindy looked lost and tears welled up in her eyes. At that juncture, Marge began to get up out of her seat and started to say, "Oh, baby, . . . " but I cut her off with my hand raised in a "stop" gesture and motioned her to sit down. I said to Cindy, "If this *is* a coping technique, where did you learn it?" Cindy cast her eyes down and sniffled. The silence was deafening.

In a quiet, soft voice, Charlie half whispered, "From Mom." For a second, the entire family appeared to be frozen in shock in response to Charlie's serendipitous pronouncement. Marge quickly began to sputter and rhetorically asked, "From me?" Gary rose to her defense. Turning my body toward Charlie and silencing both parents with a wave of my hand, I fixed on Charlie's eyes and said, "That's a good observation. Tell me about it." Charlie swallowed hard and, focusing his eyes only on me, explained that, "when Mom is afraid that Dad is going to yell at her, she gets sick." He quickly added that sometimes Carol does the same thing, too. I responded, "So, you think that there's a rule in this family that, for the women, when the going gets tough, the girls get sick?" Charlie nodded in agreement. I turned to Gary and said, "As the other male in this family, do you agree with that?" Gary sputtered and stammered: "Well, no. At least I don't think so. But maybe—I don't know." I interrupted him and asked, "Well, at least you don't disagree with it?" He shrugged his shoulders and said, "I guess not."

I turned to Marge and asked, "If there is such a rule in this family, it didn't spring up out of thin air. I wonder if you could tell me if such a rule was present in the family in which you grew up?" Marge got less defensive in her posture and thought about my question. Carol left her seat and tried to get into her mother's lap. Marge pulled Carol into her lap, held her tightly, and said that her mother and sister were both sick quite often. She confessed that she was "the healthy one" in her family of origin. Carol added that her grandmother and aunt were still sick a lot. With her right hand, Marge began to massage her temples. I asked her if that meant that she was having some pain in her head. When she replied that she was, I asked if that was some evidence that the rule we were discussing did, in fact, exist? She winced and replied, "Maybe it does."

I pulled back my chair and thanked the entire family for working so hard. I told them that even if it did not feel like it, they had accomplished a lot in this session. I thanked Gary and Marge for being concerned parents and for trying to do the right thing for their daughter. I thanked Charlie and Carol for being such good observers who were willing to help the family when it got stuck. Last, I thanked Cindy for doing the hardest job of all. I explained that, "The rule we discussed today, 'when the going gets tough, the girls get sick,' was a family secret that had the potential to cause a lot of pain to your family. Somebody had to bring that secret out into the open. You chose the role of being the 'symptom bearer' for the family to help your family uncover this secret and deal with it. That takes a lot of guts. Thank you!" I then told the family that in the next few weeks, we would explore whether such a rule existed in their family. I

had a hunch that if it did, it would be found going back several generations in both families. If that were true, it would take an heroic effort on
their part to stem the tide of generations before so that such a rule would
not do such damage to their children or their children's children. I said,
"This is a strong family with strong individuals. If we can pull together as
a team, we can do it! We can change that rule!" With smiles on their
faces, they all agreed to continue therapy and scheduled an appointment
for the following week.

DISCUSSION

Although the critical incident occurred in the second therapy session
with me, it is clear that this case had been stuck prior to Marge's initial telephone consultation with me; previously, Cindy and her parents had consulted three other therapists for a total of six sessions. Consequently, by extension, I began therapy stuck in the middle of a triangle. The first leg was
three previous therapists who were not allowed to "get on base" beyond providing a tentative/plausible diagnosis. The second leg was a teenager who
summarily "fired" her therapists because their diagnoses did not meet her
approval. The third leg were parents who were at their wits' end about how
to solve the problem and a mother, in particular, who used accusations when
all else failed. In actuality, then, the critical incident occurred not in the family's second therapy session but rather in their eighth session. I believe that it
is important to make this clarification lest my actions be perceived as capri-
cious and based only on a limited sampling of the family's presenting problem.

Characteristics of the Case Relevant to the Outcome

Several characteristics of this family situation contributed to making
them ripe for the occurrence of a critical incident. The family as a unit did
not accept ownership of the problem as a family problem but, instead, labeled Cindy as the IP and thus responsible for the problem and its solution.
On one level, this is an accurate perception. Cindy *was* using illness as a
mechanism to free her from the responsibility of doing her schoolwork. This
maladaptive coping technique *did* have major consequences, both on Cindy's
life and on the family as a whole. If Cindy had persisted in her course of action, there was an increased risk of her not completing high school. Failure
to complete high school could have had a devastating effect upon her path
toward a career and her ability to be a self-supporting adult. Such a scenario
would have potentially contributed to both Marge and Gary feeling that they
had failed as parents. It also could have provided a very negative role model
for Carol and Charlie. So on one level Cindy *was* the IP, because she was en-

gaging in a behavior with negative repercussions for both her family and her future.

However, on another level, Cindy and her coping technique of using illness to avoid responsibility were emblematic of a greater family pattern. On some level, Cindy was being very loyal to her family's method of dealing with responsibility and the anxiety that responsibility creates. She had chosen a coping technique that previously had been used in the family by Marge—one which Gary, because of the patterns of behavior in his own family of origin, had learned to expect to be used when anxiety was on the rise in the family. Cindy indirectly was influenced by these expectations in subtle and often not-so-subtle ways. True, no one ever formally explained to Cindy "these are the coping techniques utilized by our family." However, Cindy experienced this coping strategy by observing her mother's behavior and recognizing her father's normalization of that behavior by his lack of opposition to it. These patterns were also reinforced by her extended family, who held similar values with regard to this coping technique. Therefore, Cindy also was the "symptom bearer" for this maladaptive coping tradition not only for her immediate family but also for her extended family. Her behavior was the logical consequence of a family tradition.

The first six therapy sessions with three different therapists all focused only upon Cindy as the IP. Indeed Cindy as the IP was reinforced by her parents' decision to exclude Carol and Charlie from the initial session, despite my request that the entire family be present for it. In addition, Marge came to the session assuming an "accuser" or "prosecutor's" role; Gary supported her role. Because the family, especially Marge, appeared to have such a stake in defining the problem as Cindy's problem and accepting that it belonged only to her, I began to feel as though all of that armor was protecting some greater family secret. Consequently, it was for those reasons that in my first session with the family I set the wheels in motion for later strategic interventions. In my homework assignments to the parents and Cindy, I "called for the symptom" with both Cindy and Marge by asking the mother and daughter to continue to do what they already had been doing. Each was given permission to gather evidence to support her own position. I brought Gary into the situation by asking him to subvert the family's (especially Marge's) attempts to define the problem as only Cindy's problem, because I was unclear about his role in the family drama. To that end, I charged him with bringing the other two children to the next therapy session.

In the second session, Charlie and Carol respectively played crucial roles in the therapeutic process by unveiling the tightly held family secret (out of the mouths of babes). I believe that, at some level, Gary, Marge, and Cindy were all aware of that secret. However, I do not believe that any of them would have or even could have brought that secret out into the open in a therapy session. It took the two children who were not directly involved in the specific presenting problem to disclose the family secret. In this case, the change from individually oriented therapy to family therapy was distinctly advantageous in helping to create a critical incident in the therapeutic process. Previously, the three individually oriented therapists were unable to move the family off dead center because they were fired abruptly; they were too focused on the individual as IP rather than the family as IP.

Cindy, as the IP, and her mother both held onto their respective rules with great tenacity. They both demonstrated their power in the family by doggedly playing out their rules. Cindy overtly was being the troubled child and covertly being the family symptom bearer. Marge was being both concerned mother and tradition protector. By refusing to participate in therapy, Cindy single-handedly derailed three therapeutic processes. Marge demonstrated her power and emotional investment by pushing her daughter into a fourth therapeutic process, despite Cindy's refusal to continue any previous attempts at therapy. These were two very powerful women headed on a collision course with each other. Any therapist standing between them attempting to reconcile their differences surely would be run over. Consequently, instead of taking sides or trying to reconcile their positions, I chose to use their energy and redirect it to unbalance both Cindy and Marge. Three previous therapists had, in essence, sided with Mom's position that "all would be well if Cindy simply stopped using sickness as an excuse." They all summarily were fired and therapy ended in a dead end. Being aware of their fate, I elected to upset the apple cart by siding with the daughter. This derailed mom's position. I then sided with Cindy to such a degree that it became impossible for Cindy to accept the logical, though somewhat extreme, consequences of her position.

As stated in Jurich (1990), I established rapport with each family member especially Cindy. I analyzed the leverage points I felt I had by examining the family dynamics. By agreeing with Cindy, especially since no previous therapist had done so, I hooked her into agreeing with my logic, which was an extension of her own logic. My "slam" was to carry out the logic of her physical ailments beyond her comfort level. All of a sudden, both Cindy and I were arguing her into a position in which the "cure was worse than the disease." I "juiced" the "slam" by making it more and more extreme, thereby also making it increasingly uncomfortable. Finally, Cindy herself had to stop me from turning up the heat when she acknowledged that maybe she was not so sick after all. Simultaneously, this strategy also derailed Marge's position. How could she disagree with me for being so concerned for her daughter's physical well-being that I was suggesting bed rest for Cindy? When Cindy finally suggested that maybe she was not so ill after all, Marge was stunned. Cindy had come to agree with Marge's position without any yelling or screaming but, instead, with a soft voice and tears in her eyes. Marge was so ready to do battle with her daughter that she did not know how to cope with a quiet victory. By trying to protect Cindy, I believe that Marge was also trying to protect the family secret and, therefore, protect the status quo. So, Marge also got what she wanted, only to discover that it really was not what she wanted. This combination of forces within the family, with the help of a little strategic pressure from the therapist, made a critical incident a probable occurrence within therapy.

The willingness of all family members to participate in therapy, even if reluctantly, also gave rise to the possibility of the occurrence of a critical incident. Although I could have worked with Cindy as a single client, having the entire family present enabled me to work with the IP in the presence of the entire family. In so doing, the entire family could bear witness to the process of therapy. When working with adolescents in individual therapy, they can choose how they want to share the process of therapy with their parents. They also can lessen or reinterpret the more uncomfortable aspects of therapy. In family therapy involving adolescents, the presence of parents and other family members in the room, participating in the process, tends to turn up the "therapeutic heat" on the adolescents. Cindy may have exclaimed, "Enough!" in an individual therapy session. But would "surrendering" to the therapist have had as much of an impact on Cindy as having her father in the room taking notes and having to listen to the therapist give him directions on how to help her use a bedpan? Similarly, how much did the giggles of her younger siblings contribute to Cindy's felt "pressure to change"? Would the critical incident have been left dangling if Carol and Charlie had not unveiled the family secret? We may never know for sure but can speculate with reasonable certainty that the presence of her parents and siblings in the therapy room did accelerate Cindy's momentum toward change.

In addition, the willingness of the entire family to participate allowed me to help the family, rather than Cindy alone, take responsibility for the problem. The dynamics shifted from Marge's trying to force Cindy to admit that she alone had the problem, with Gary, Charlie, and Carol watching as spectators, to a more useful formulation of the problem. The problem was a legacy, passed down from previous generations through no fault of their own. Rather than splintering up the family and forcing them to choose sides, this new formulation allowed them to externalize the problem and unite as a team, with a little guidance from the therapist, to take on this curse from previous generations. This reconstruction of the problem (Michael White would be happy) allowed the family to unify against a common enemy, the legacy, for the common good—namely, future generations.

The Role of the Critical Incident in Getting Therapy Unstuck

This critical incident shifted the direction of therapy dramatically. The family eagerly appeared for the third therapy session. Marge and Cindy had telephoned some of Marge's relatives to ask them about the rule of sickness in their family, especially among the women. Gary began to observe when Carol would get sick when "the going got tough"; Charlie continued to be an excellent observer. He identified his own frustrations with the family's rules; in accordance with those rules, he was not allowed to use the illness excuse to cope with stress. He also pointed out Gary's frustrations at Marge's varied symptoms and appropriately observed that Gary often "got back at Mom" indirectly. Charlie also asked the very important question: In Gary's family of origin, did they also have the rule that when the going gets tough, the girls get sick? That question prompted Gary to ask questions among his relatives; he discovered that indeed a similar rule also existed in his family of origin.

THE OUTCOME OF THERAPY

I met with the family for six more sessions and Cindy was removed from IP status; instead, the entire family became the IP. In these sessions, we discussed issues specific to the intergenerational transmission of the behaviors which we had labeled "when the going gets tough, the girls get sick" and explored ways to change and replace those behaviors with more appropriate and adaptive behaviors for coping with stress. We also spent time on repairing the mother-daughter relationship as well as helping Cindy to make a self-esteem-enhancing transition back to being a healthy teenager able to cope with the stresses and strains of high school academic requirements and being able to appropriately ask for assistance (e.g., from her dad) when she felt overwhelmed by the high school academic grind.

POSTSCRIPT

The family terminated therapy at the end of Session 8. At that time, Cindy was attending school regularly and had discovered that she could talk with Gary about her academic difficulties; she rediscovered her dad as a resource. She had forgotten how "neat he is to talk to" when she stresses about academics. The three females in the family became more conscious of their use of illness as an escape mechanism. The family developed a new vocabulary that they used to identify two types of symptoms—(1) illness and (2) "stressness." Illness was defined as occurring when the symptom has a physical genesis. "Stressness" was defined as a symptom being generated as a reaction to stress. They discovered that although the female members of the family were more prone to stressness, the males also exhibited some stressness on occasion. The greater discovery for Gary and Charlie was that they often reacted to stressness by Marge, Cindy, and Carol through indirect methods, such as pouting or making snide remarks. Everyone took responsibility for identifying these symptoms because everyone played a part in the family drama that maintained the symptoms.

In a short time this family had come a long way from the family that was depicted on that yellow intake form nine weeks earlier. They had learned to be "careful what you wish for —you just might get it." However, they also learned that "you can't always get what you want. But, if you try, sometimes you just might find you get what you need" (M. Jagger and K. Richards, 1969).

REFERENCE

Jurich, A.P. (1990). The Jujitsu approach. *Family Therapy Networker*, 14(4), 42-47, 64.

Commentary

Let's Do Another Study

Scott Johnson

Commentator Background

Forty-nine years old, African-American, male, PhD, thirteen years MFT practice.

Practice Setting

University MFT clinic and limited private practice.

Theoretical Perspective

My preferred perspective is eclectic. My commentary for this case is grounded in a structural framework coupled with a feminist perspective.

This case is an excellent example of the power of working successfully with relationships, but as with any relational experience, the relationships in this case—within the family and between the family and therapist—can be viewed in a number of different ways. From a strategic perspective, Jurich did a fine job, but, inevitably, several alternative approaches might have been taken.

MALINGERING AND STRUCTURAL ISSUES

Jurich identifies treatment as beginning with the family's consultation with three mental health professionals—the male counselor who saw the family for three sessions, the male psychologist who tested Cindy, and the female social worker who eventually referred the family to him. Unlike Jurich, I tend to see treatment as beginning much earlier—with the "numerous trips to physicians" and the examination by the family physician, all of whom reached the identical conclusion: Cindy was faking. "Faking's" technical, DSM-IV name is *malingering,* with which I am familiar through the work of my wife, a clinical psychologist at a veteran's administration hospital. The feigning of physical and mental illness by patients seeking disability payments is a common problem at the hospital. I was surprised that neither the physicians nor mental health professionals consulted identified Cindy's behaviors as malingering, although their descriptions of her behaviors fit such a diagnosis. Had malingering been explicitly identified earlier in therapy, as it easily could have been, the family might never have been referred to Jurich, and perhaps the situation never would have gotten beyond the physicians or the counselor. Once a diagnosis of malingering—faking— had been made, Cindy's refusal to attend future therapy sessions would have been superfluous, because *there would not have been any future sessions to attend.*

Beginning with the social worker who referred the family to Jurich, little doubt existed about three things. First, several physicians had unequivocally found nothing medically wrong with Cindy. Second, a counselor, a psychologist, and a social worker had each concluded that Cindy had no discernable psychological problem. They agreed that she was feigning illness simply to avoid attending school. Consequently, unless someone discovered a compelling reason for her not attending school, e.g., she was being threatened by bullies (a possibility one hopes the previous professionals had explored), no problem exists with Cindy refusing to continue therapy since a diagnosis of malingering is the end of the case. More therapy for Cindy is, in fact, contraindicated. What is called for after malingering is diagnosed is for Cindy's parents to say to her, "Honey, it's official. The doctors, a counselor, a psychologist, and a social worker all say you're faking. Get up, get dressed, and get ready for school."

What requires more therapy is not Cindy's malingering but her parents' refusal to act appropriately on the results of the repeated consultations that they had sought from medical and mental health professionals. The parents' behavior, in this sense, is similar to that of public officials who commission studies to determine whether the government requires a tax increase. When repeatedly the answers are yes, they commission more studies in the hope that the results of the newer studies may be different, to spare them the burden of voting to raise taxes. From this perspective, the family's problem is structural, rather than needing the strategic approach taken by Jurich. The issue is not that the *family* would not own the problem but that the parents refused to exercise their executive authority and tell their daughter that she has to go to school or face realistic consequences. Instead, they allowed her to "fire her therapists" and be rewarded with additional mental health consultations.

This family's situation screams out Minuchin's now famous question, "Who's the sheriff here?" Interestingly, although the parents believed that Cindy was faking illness and their beliefs are corroborated by a host of medical and mental health professionals, they did not make an attempt to impose realistic consequences for her behaviors. Instead, Cindy was allowed to maintain the status quo, as evidenced by the privileges of using the telephone, watching television and playing her radio and tape deck, which she continued to enjoy throughout her "illnesses." No matter how many times these parents received the verdict on Cindy's actions—fraud—they continued to return Cindy to court (a new medical or mental health consultation) hoping a new judge (a medical or mental health professional) might see the situation differently. In the interim, they delayed enforcement of the necessary sentence by failing to act on the consequences of Cindy's behaviors. Paradoxically, Gary and Marge were willing to deny Cindy phone privileges based on Jurich's facetious diagnosis of acute chronic fatigue syndrome but made no attempt to do so on the basis of what they themselves believed was irresponsible behavior. They appeared unable or unwilling to say something as simple as, "Until you behave more responsibly, we're not paying for your phone calls," or, "Cindy, dear, no school, no television." In addition, there is no indication that Gary and Marge attempted to enforce any other consequences for Cindy's theatrics, such as no school, no dates, or no school, no movies. Part of the beauty of Jurich's intervention is that although working from a strategic rather than a structural perspective, he arrives at the same concern of the parents' reluctance to impose logical consequences on Cindy for her behavior, which is critical to creating change.

In this regard, the parents were, as Jurich suggests, fundamentally in league with their daughter, since even if Jurich had said—seriously (not strategically)—"Yes, there really is something medically wrong with Cindy," what logical reason could they have for choosing Jurich's view over the previous physicians and therapists? (And, as an aside, what family therapist who does not want to risk losing his or her license for practicing medicine without a license would want to contradict the earlier experts?) To repeat, from a structural perspective, this was not Jurich's approach; this family's problem is relatively clear. The compelling question is not "what's wrong with the family?" but "what's wrong with the parental sub-system?" Why are both the mother and father not behaving like effective parents?

WHAT I MIGHT HAVE DONE DIFFERENTLY

Couples Sessions

Taking a structural view, I would have been inclined not to meet with the whole family but to meet only with the parents at least for a few sessions. I probably would have moved Cindy out of the therapeutic picture very quickly. Doing so would have made irrelevant her refusal to come to therapy. Treatment from this perspective would then focus on what kept the parents from behaving as responsible adults—that is, why did they continue to commission "studies" for their daughter yet repeatedly ignore the results and implications of those studies?

The catalytic question that Jurich asked in the course of therapy—"where did Cindy learn to react to stress by faking illness?"—is of course a question that can be asked in couples work with the parents alone as well as with all family members present. The beauty of Jurich's approach in having everyone present in the room is the ability to have the question answered quickly, through the insight of thirteen-year-old Charlie, although it is possible that Gary and Marge might have had their own individual and couple answers also. Perhaps one of the parents might have pointed not to Marge, as Charlie did, but to one of Marge's relatives as the theatrical role model. One of Marge's stated reasons for not "dragging" Charlie and Carol to the first therapy session was her fear that the younger children would "learn Cindy's poor coping strategies." To me, this suggests that Marge is aware on some level that Cindy's behavior has an intergenerational quality to it. Although it is unlikely that Marge would have pointed the finger at herself, it also would be highly likely to expect that she and Gary might have reached similar or even identical conclusions that women in both Marge and Gary's families of origin had learned to cope with stress by feigning sickness.

At some point, however, it would be important that Cindy and her siblings be informed of this and other family patterns. One could argue that permitting the parents themselves to decide how this occurs might be just as useful as having the children come to therapy to discuss it. Having the children present throughout treatment, however, certainly seems efficient, and obviously worked very well for this family and for Jurich.

Behavior and Gender

I also would want to explore in greater detail some of the gender issues that this case presents. Although the family's rule that women should cope with stress by pretending to be sick is obvious, I also would want to explore other rules that Jurich touched upon but did not pursue in depth. For example, I would want to explore how men in this family are expected to cope with stress. Charlie discloses that as a male in this family he felt he was not allowed to use illness as an excuse for coping with stress. Thus a related question would have been, "were men in the family allowed to get sick at all?" Is sickness for men equated with not being able to handle things? As Bowenians would note, feigning sickness is a way of distancing. Conversely, feigning health when one is genuinely ill also could be perceived as distancing—in this case, perhaps, distancing by the males in this family. Either way, one is not being who one really is with one's family members.

Similarly, Jurich notes that Charlie disclosed that Gary "[got] back at Mom" for feigning illness by "pouting" or making "snide remarks"—in effect, by behaving childishly. These are important behaviors to point out because they undermine the notion that women's learned behaviors are weak or immature, while men's learned behaviors are really strong. In my perspective, it would have been intrinsically as well as therapeutically important to underscore the point that neither males nor females in this family have (in this instance) behaved maturely, because of the press of family rules on both sexes. If secret rules exist for women, by extension, secret rules exist for men, and neither set of rules is likely to be health enhancing.

Looking explicitly at gender also might lend insight to the issues Jurich notes about mother-daughter and father-daughter relationships specific to schoolwork. For example, Cindy reports that she had forgotten how neat Dad is to talk to when she stresses academically. This raises the question of how she forgot. I wonder not just how women and men are expected to cope with school stress, but how are they expected to cope with school period? Are women expected to be stressed because of academics, and men expected to manage it nonchalantly? And are both males and females expected not to cross gender lines to talk about it? In other words, how real was the stress that Cindy experienced about school in the first place? Was she genuinely having difficulty, or were there other, perhaps gender-coded, messages about "dumbing down" circulating through the family system? This is not a point to beat to death, but it is worth a few minutes of thought.

ETHICAL ISSUES

As with any strategic intervention, the clinical maneuvers used in working with this family raise a number of ethical questions. The first is the issue of practicing medicine without a license, raised earlier in this commentary. When Jurich "diagnosed" Cindy with the spurious disorder, "acute chronic fatigue syndrome," it was difficult for me not to imagine a state medical board official somewhere just itching to get a case like this to prosecute. Although it might be difficult to prove actual damages because the family rather quickly realizes that Cindy is right, Jurich is "full of shit"—or at least full of hooey—like she is, and although there is no question that Jurich does not believe that he is making a real medical diagnosis, a host of "what ifs" ought to be cause for some ethical discomfort.

What if Jurich, or simply a less skillful therapist, for example, misjudged the family's gullibility and the family really did believe that Cindy had an actual disease? What if the family members were not able, as they seemed to be, to discriminate between a genuine medical diagnosis and Jurich "pulling their legs" through a strategic maneuver? What if Gary had believed that Jurich's in-session recommendations for Cindy, such as removing the phone, the television, the radio, playing Montovani (yuck!), feeding her milk toast, etc., were genuine and had implemented them with Cindy only to learn after a week that the therapist is as much a fake as Cindy? We can only guess at the negative consequences that might have occurred had any of this happened, the least of which might have been the family's distrust of family therapists.

It is important, however, to keep in mind that Jurich worked with this family in 1985, at a time when strategic therapy was a clinical technique with great appeal, especially among MFTs, and dazzled the field with paradoxical interventions and the uses of therapist "power." In their 1987 book with Lynn Hoffman and Peggy Penn, Milan therapists Luigi Boscolo and Gianfranco Cecchin discuss consulting on a case in which the family had a secret that the therapeutic team and everyone else working with the family assumed was ongoing incest. However, at the time, neither Boscolo nor Cecchin considered reporting the incest to authorities. Rather they attempted to create a system in which the incest would stop. Compared to that intervention, any qualms I might have about Jurich's intervention with this family pale. But Jurich's work still raises questions about the use of deception with clients, its unintended consequences even if it is successful, and its immediate consequences should the intervention backfire. Despite Jurich's success with this family, the ethical problems of the use of deception in therapy remain, for me, an ongoing concern.

As an alternative to the strategic maneuver Jurich uses, the family could have been asked very basic solution-oriented questions such as: "Who in the family thinks Cindy's faking?" and "Who else in the family fakes?" or "Does anyone else in the family fake?" These questions might eventually have produced a response similar to Charlie's ("Mom") but without the risk of appearing to play the family for fools. Again, it is important to emphasize that these are not criticisms of Jurich the therapist or of his clinical skills. Jurich's strategic approach was masterfully and professionally implemented, undoubtedly successful in its outcome, and classical in its adherence to strategic theory. Rather my point is about the use of strategic techniques and their questionable ethics. In the heyday of the strategic approach many of its adherents produced any number of ethically questionable interventions in its name. During my own strategic period, I once put a very mildly suicidal client out on a forty-foot-high bridge as part of a trance-induction ritual—it worked, but I never would try anything like that again. As engaging as this case is, Jurich's approach in working with this family is not an approach I can imagine myself taking or advocating that another therapist take.

CONCLUDING THOUGHTS

Jurich deserves praise for providing a solid example of a strategic intervention and its contribution to a critical incident in therapy. His explication of the dynamics of the family and the therapeutic process are clearly and powerfully argued. And his skillful handling of the case obviously was central to its positive outcome. Despite Jurich's success, however, this is a case that, at least in the new millennium, I would have approached differently. My principle interventions would have focused on the parents' executive problems and downplayed or sidestepped the question of whether Cindy was faking illness. I also would have explored more deliberately the issues of gender and the behaviors that family members believed were mandated because of their assigned gender roles. For ethical reasons, I would have avoided paradoxical interventions. That said, it is important to point out that this does not mean the outcome of therapy would have been any more expeditious or helpful than it was for Jurich. It might well have been worse. My approach is simply another direction in which therapy and the therapist might have proceeded. Of one thing I am sure, however: I would have declined the parents' request to conduct "another study" of a question they already had researched into the ground.

REFERENCE

Boscolo, L., Cecchin, G., Hoffman, L., and Penn, P. (1987). *Milan Systemic Family Therapy*. New York: Basic Books.

Commentary

With Creativity We Engage Them

Cheryl L. Storm

Commentator Background

Forty-nine years old, Caucasian, female, PhD, twenty years MFT practice.

Practice Setting

Full-time university-based MFT training program; part-time private practice.

Theoretical Perspective

My preferred theoretical perspective is an integrated approach heavily influenced by Bateson's writings, the strategic and solution-focused models of therapy, the feminist perspective, and postmodern ideas. This approach does not incorporate many intergenerational ideas, although I am comfortable with and appreciate the creative ways in which colleagues use these ideas in therapy. My current interest in the process of how therapists enhance or hinder clients' willingness to participate in the therapeutic process heightened my interest in how Jurich was able to engage this family when three other therapists had failed to do so. One of the most interesting aspects of this particular case is the manner in which Jurich engages this family initially and keeps members engaged throughout the course of therapy while provocatively challenging them and their interactions. The family already had attended six therapy sessions with three different therapists. If Jurich could not engage them quickly, especially the adolescent IP, and continue to do so throughout the course of therapy, he was at risk for being the fourth therapist to be fired by the family on command of the IP.

THE FIRST FEW MOMENTS:
THE NONTRADITIONAL PROFESSIONAL

I believe Jurich's initial strategy for establishing a relationship with this family in the first few moments of therapy was central to him being able to engage them in treatment. Since they were consulting him because of his "nontraditional approach with adolescents," he believed it would be important to find a way to quickly fulfill this expectation in the eyes of the parents and the adolescent. Essentially, he had to be different from the cultural image of a therapist. In this regard, Crane, Griffin, and Hill (1986) found that the greatest predictor of successful therapy was that therapy fit the expectations of clients. Jurich begins developing an initial strategy by thinking about how to live up to his reputation. But how does a thirty-eight-year-old Caucasian male who is highly educated and a recognized expert in marriage and family therapy become nontraditional? To accomplish this he uses nontraditional clothing. His willingness to step outside of a "therapy suit" into more casual dress of boots and jeans probably did convey an immediate positive impression to Cindy that this therapist was different from the other therapists she saw previously. Because the parents were forewarned that Jurich's approach was nontraditional and they were seeking someone different, his dress was probably reassuring to them also. Even at first glance he was not like the other professionals they had seen previously. This may have raised some hope that therapy would be helpful this time. Is this a universal engagement strategy? Are the best therapists quick-change artists who have a wardrobe of various clothing from jeans to business suits into which they change to portray the "right image" to each client? Or should all therapists follow teenage trends in clothing and dress accordingly when working with families and their adolescents? Of course not, but the first few moments of therapy can set an important tone that helps or hinders engagement in therapy. For example, a client and his wife sought therapy with me because they were court ordered to do so if they were to regain custody of their children. During the initial call, the father told the intake worker that he was a reluctant client and "could put any therapist through the wall." After giving this situation a great deal of thought and feeling a little fearful of meeting this couple, I decided to approach the couple in the following manner. After introducing myself, my first remark to the father was: "I understand that you and I have the problem of convincing the court that you and your wife are capable parents, that you should get your children back, and that you do not need me in your life." There was a moment or two of absolute silence then he jumped in with a full description of what we faced together. Apparently, I had achieved my goal of immediately conveying that I was on the couple's side. Like Jurich, I spent time thinking about how best to go about meeting the challenge of establishing a relationship within the first few moments of therapy.

In both cases, it probably is not accidental that Jurich and I have been heavily influenced by strategic ideas. Early strategic proponents (Haley, 1976; Watzlawick, Weakland, and Fisch, 1974) asserted that therapists should take charge of the therapeutic context and always listen carefully and watch for signs from clients with regard to how best to help them, then use that information to guide their responses. Both Jurich and I used information obtained in our presession contact with the clients to formulate an initial strategy to engage them in therapy. Our strategies were purposeful and planned, and proactively executed. In these postmodern times, some therapists often perceive such actions as distasteful because they are so intentional. Yet I believe our actions were authentic because they stemmed from a sincere desire to help these clients. Jurich did not purchase a new wardrobe to make himself appear more likable to this adolescent client; rather, he pulled out of his closet clothes he wore at other times in different contexts, thus sharing a different part of himself with his clients. Jurich's initial careful, purposeful consideration and assessment of the initial relationship context and the challenges presented by this case, in my opinion, were significant contributors to the occurrence of the critical incident.

NO MORE "MORE OF THE SAME": SETTING THE STAGE FOR THE CRITICAL INCIDENT

Although the first impression was important, it was only the beginning of engaging this family. Jurich notes that although he agreed with the previous professionals' assessments regarding the situation, he had to refrain from "doing more of the same" of what previous therapists had done and to find ways to be different from them. He does so in several ways. At the end of the first session, Jurich asks for more time and the family's help in figuring out things. He asks each family member to be responsible for a specific task that fits his or her view of the problem. In doing so, he validates each member's experience and perspective. He also requests that the younger children attend sessions, thus he began to shape as a family problem that which the family had come to believe and to accept as "Cindy's problem." Following through with scheduled appointments and completing homework assigned by therapists usually are clear indicators of client engagement (Cunningham and Henggeler, 1999). The second scheduled session begins with family members having fully completed all assigned homework. Cindy and Marge were asked to bring specific information to the session. Both arrived with paper in hand and a willingness to spend significant time going over in detail their respective assignments. This family has become significantly engaged in therapy. I believe the real test of Jurich's ability to maintain their engagement by meeting their expectations of a nontraditional therapist is at this point in the process of therapy. He refrains from offering the family the identical diagnosis as did the previous professionals. Instead, he creates an alternative one, "acute chronic fatigue syndrome," thus making his approach appear very different from those of the previous therapists. In his discussion of the case, Jurich describes how this diagnosis keeps him engaged with Cindy and her parents while also challenging their individually held view of the situation. As he describes the cure for her symptoms, he paradoxically prescribes Cindy's solutions to her difficulty regarding school and takes it to the extreme. Now not only will she need to stay at home, but she must be confined to her bed without contact with her friends, eat a diet of milk toast, and so on. Slowly the parents (and Cindy) begin to see this nontraditional therapist at work. Many strategic therapists would have stopped here and waited until the next session for the family's response to the intervention, but Jurich adds a creative twist. He offers the family a choice of symptoms: the previous diagnosis that Cindy is using physical symptoms as a coping device, his current diagnosis of acute chronic fatigue syndrome, or wonders if perhaps the family has an alternative one? Here Jurich moves from an "expert's" position into a more collaborative one by asking the family to join with him to figure out what is happening. (This is consistent with the tone he set early in therapy when he asked for the family's help at the end of the first session.) After Cindy indicates she is leaning toward the first diagnosis, Jurich then asks the question that leads to the critical incident. If Cindy is using physical symptoms as a coping device, where did she learn the behavior?

ENGAGEMENT AND THE CRITICAL INCIDENT: CHARLIE TAKES A RISK

Jurich identifies the critical incident as occurring when Charlie whispers that Cindy learned from Mom to cope with stress by being sick. With a little encouragement from Jurich, Charlie shares an alternative perspective that results in the formulation of the hypothesis that the rule in the family is, "when the going gets tough, the girls get sick." As I read the case, I wondered how Charlie had become so engaged in therapy that he would take such a risk. (The reaction of Charlie and the family seems to support that this was risky for Charlie to do, especially since this is his first therapy session.) Several answers probably exist to this question. Little is said about the interaction between Jurich and Charlie other than that Jurich introduced himself with a ceremonial handshake. Perhaps Jurich's unconventional dress made an impression on Charlie, also an adolescent. Perhaps Jurich's willingness to take his suggestion regarding the cure for acute chronic fatigue syndrome to the extreme (Charlie laughed at one point) intrigued

Charlie. Perhaps seeing his parents and sister so invested in the therapy process paved the way for Charlie to offer his own opinion. Most likely it is a combination of some of these factors that led Charlie to take the risk and to engage in therapy.

Engaging While Challenging: The Use of Intergenerational Patterns

Jurich follows Charlie's lead and begins to explore the idea that Cindy learned this troublesome behavior from her mother. At this point in therapy, Jurich appears to be most challenging. I wondered if he would lose Marge because she felt blamed for Cindy's problem. I also wondered if Cindy would feel that Jurich had sided against her by agreeing with her previous therapists that she was using physical illness to cope with her anxieties about school. I also wondered if Gary would remain on the periphery, being viewed as neither a part of the problem nor a part of the solution. Yet Jurich's exploration of intergenerational patterns seemed to continue to effectively engage the family, especially Cindy, Marge, and Charlie. Jurich asserts that it was easier for the family to engage in the change process by viewing "Cindy's problem"—coping with stress with physical symptoms— as a family legacy. Family members could stay engaged easily because the problem was shared by all and therefore could only be solved by all family members. Jurich also contends that this perspective provides the family an opportunity to unite to confront its problem and to seek a solution.

Engaging by Placing the Responsibility on the Women

Although therapy is progressing well and a family that is difficult to engage appears to be fully invested in therapy, I am concerned that it is the women who initially are defined as the problem and the family members needing to change. Minimal attention appears to be paid to the male family members', especially Gary's, participation in the rule until much later in sessions. As a female who is sensitive (perhaps even hypersensitive) to the often unintentional blaming of mothers for family problems and thus making them accountable for the solutions, I was uneasy with the conceptualization of the rule. From my perspective, the rule seemed to place full responsibility for the problem and its solution squarely on the women, particularly Marge. The rule seemed to revolve around the women and their responses to responsibility and stress, while the men remained outside of the process, essentially free of responsibility. This actually may have promoted engagement with the men in the family since it is easier for one to be invested in anything when one is not being challenged to change. I found myself wanting the rule to be more balanced by including the male members of the family. I would have preferred an initial formulation framed more inclusively. For example, "when the going gets tough, the girls get sick and the boys become jerks" or "when the going gets tough, the girls get sick and the boys do not know what to do." Jurich notes that later on in therapy the men's behaviors are addressed and Gary and Charlie realize that they "pout" or make "snide remarks" when the women respond to stress with physical symptoms. Interestingly, it is Charlie who takes another risk and involves his father in the rule by asking if Gary's family had a similar family rule. I cannot help but wonder if the women's responses resulted in part because they believed that they cannot depend on the men to do their share during stressful times. If this is a traditionally oriented family in which parents subscribe to the culturally sanctioned gender-role socialization of white middle-class families, perhaps it was the father, not the mother, who was not providing the guidance Cindy needed to be successful in the outside world of school.

In fairness to Jurich, what initially is perceived as Cindy's problem does evolve into a family problem as therapy progresses and the male family member's contributions to the problem are addressed and they become an integral part of the solution. My wish is that the involvement of the men would have occurred sooner and that therapists replicating Jurich's creative integration of strategic and intergenerational ideas will work to include both genders in whatever intergenerational patterns are focused on in therapy.

Engagement As the Saving Grace

Jurich reminds us that this case really involved fourteen sessions, six with three other therapists and eight with him. Jurich is able to engage the family beyond a couple of sessions when others could not. During the first session and first part of the second session with Jurich, it appears to me that the family is deciding whether to fire him or to go the distance with him. One by one, they seem to decide to go the distance. Because Jurich engages all family members, he can count on them staying with him. This, then, enables him to provocatively challenge family members, to be extreme in his interventions, to entice family members to share risky perceptions, and to turn tense moments into important times of reflection by family members. In my opinion, Jurich's ability to persuade the family to engage in therapy with him was a necessary and significant precursor for the occurrence of the critical incident.

REFERENCES

Crane, D.R., Griffin, W., and Hill, R.D. (1986). Influence of therapists skills on clients' perceptions of marriage and family therapy outcome: Implications for supervision. *Journal of Marital and Family Therapy, 12*(1), 91-96.

Cunningham, P. and Henggeler, S.W. (1999). Engaging multiproblem families in treatment: Lessons learned through the development of multisystemic therapy. *Family Process*, 38(3), 265-281.

Haley, J. (1976). *Problem solving therapy*. New York: Harper and Row.

Watzlawick, P., Weakland, J., and Fisch, R. (1974). *Change: Principles of problem formation and problem resolution*. New York: W.W. Norton.

CASE 4

Being There

Tracey A. Laszloffy

Therapist Background

Currently: Thirty-one years old, white, female, PhD, eight years MFT practice. At the time of this case: twenty-five years old, MS, two years MFT practice.

Practice Setting

University marriage and family therapy training clinic.

Client Characteristics

The Sanders family consisted of Bill (age forty-three) and Janet (age forty-one), a white, upper socioeconomic couple, and their daughter, Becky (age thirteen). Bill was an executive officer for a computer graphics company and traveled a great deal. Janet was recuperating from a back injury and unemployed; she had been a dress shop manager prior to her injury. Becky was a junior high school student. Two older daughters Diane (age nineteen), a paralegal in Michigan, and Kelley (age seventeen), a freshman at an out-of-state college, completed the family but were not involved in therapy.

Length of Treatment

Janet and Becky were seen for ten sessions, Bill attended two therapy sessions. The critical incident occurred in Session 6.

Theoretical Perspective

A strategic/structural approach was used in working with this family.

PRESENTING PROBLEM

"Every morning we go through the same ordeal. I wake Becky up and tell her to get ready. She does, but then when it's time to catch the bus she starts crying and refuses to go out. After she misses the bus I drive her to school. She cries the whole way there. Sometimes I am able to convince her to go by telling her she won't have to go the next day. I've tried other things, too. I've tried talking to her the night before and telling her how I need her to go to school in the morning, and she promises me she will try. Sometimes she keeps the promise and other times she doesn't. No matter what, though, every morning is an ordeal and most days I can't take it, and I give up. I need help. I just don't know what else to do. The school counselor recommended therapy, so I'm hoping this will be able to help us."

Janet Sanders' plaintive plea for help introduced me to the Sanders family. Over the phone, I could hear the exasperation in Janet's voice as she described her struggles with Becky, who refused to go to school. I told Janet that I felt optimistic about the potential of therapy but cautioned her that I could not make any promises of success. I also informed her that as a family therapist, it was my preference to work with the family rather than with the child alone. I shared with her my belief that each family member plays an important role in the life, especially the maintenance, of a problem. Consequently, the more family members I could include in the therapy process, the more effectively I felt I would be able to map and eventually help them resolve the problem. Bill did not participate in this conversation, but Janet expressed confidence that "we could probably arrange to have him come to some of our meetings if we plan in advance. I know he couldn't come for another month at least, until he completes an intensive project for work."

Despite knowing that Bill would not be a part of therapy for at least one month, we agreed to begin therapy immediately because of Janet's expressed urgency to find a solution to the presenting problem. Janet was concerned that with each passing day Becky was getting farther behind in school; Janet needed something to be done soon. Janet's urgency aside, I emphasized the importance of Bill becoming involved in therapy as soon as possible. We scheduled our first meeting for a week later and agreed to meet every week thereafter; Bill would attend our fourth therapy session within a month.

THE THERAPEUTIC SITUATION PRIOR
TO THE CRITICAL INCIDENT

To begin our first session, Janet repeated her initial telephone complaint that Becky was refusing to attend school, and I asked Becky for her understanding of the problem and when her struggles with school began. She said, "I hate going to school. I don't like it. I don't have any friends. All the kids tease me and tell me I'm fat and I don't learn anything in school anyway because I don't like being there. I would like for my mom to teach me at home. I think that would be better for me because my mom's home almost every day now anyway since her accident." Continuing, she explained that she never liked school, but she did not begin to feel uncomfortable until this school year. She said, "Kids always stayed away from me because I'm overweight, but this year they're worse. Now they laugh in my face and make fun of me."

In response to my questions about her accident and being at home, Janet replied that she previously managed a dress shop; four months ago, she fell from a ladder in the shop and injured her back. As a result, she left her job because "we didn't need the money and, besides, I was tired of that line of work. I'd been doing it almost ten years. It was more important to me to take the time to heal. Eventually, I hope to find something different to do."

At this juncture, I noted that Becky's school-related difficulties began at approximately the same time as her mother's accident and unemployment. I wondered about a possible relationship between these two occurrences. I also wondered about the absent Sanders family members. To this end, I asked, "Becky, you have two older sisters, don't you?"

BECKY: Yes. Kelley just turned seventeen and Diane is nineteen. Diane lives with her boyfriend in Michigan so we don't see her much. She's a paralegal. Kelley is away at her first year of college.

THERAPIST: And what about your dad? What does he do for a living?

BECKY: He works for a computer graphics company. He's always busy. He works all the time because he's an executive. That means he has to travel a lot, too.

I asked Becky, "If the other members of your family were here, what do you feel they would say about you not wanting to go to school?" She said, "Kelley would say I'm a baby and I need to grow up. Diane would probably say she feels bad for me and she knows how I feel since she used to be overweight, too, but now she's lost a lot of weight and she looks anorexic. I don't know what Dad would say. Probably that I should go to school."

During the next two sessions with Janet and Becky I attempted to better understand the anatomy of Becky's aversion to school. As we spoke I became curious as to why attending school had suddenly become so difficult for Becky. With that question in mind, I pushed Becky to recall her earlier experiences in school. She remembered her classmates laughing at her even then, but she did not perceive their behaviors as the crisis it had become as of late. Given Becky's acknowledgment that being teased by her classmates was not a new experience, I assumed that other contributors must have led to the formation of the current problem. What had changed between then and now? This was the question I planned to explore in the next two sessions. One possible hypothesis was that Janet's sudden unemployment and her newfound time at home might be a contributor, because these events coincided with the emergence of the presenting problem.

EVENTS LEADING TO THE CRITICAL INCIDENT

Bill did not attend the fourth session as had been agreed. Only Janet and Becky were present. Janet apologized profusely for Bill's absence and explained that a business emergency occurred that needed his attention. She assured Becky and me that Bill would attend the following week's session. I accepted her explanation and met with her and Becky per usual.

The following week, Bill again did not attend the session. Because of my commitment to include as many family members as possible in the therapy, I was disappointed that he had missed two consecutive meetings. I had been looking forward to meeting him and observing the family's interactions, especially Bill's interactions with Becky and hers with him. I was curious about how Bill fit into the presenting problem. Accordingly, I decided to give him another opportunity to attend a therapy session with his wife and daughter. I met with Janet and Becky on the condition that Bill would join us the next week.

THE CRITICAL INCIDENT

Session 6: As they had done for the previous five visits, Janet and Becky arrived on time for their appointment. I eagerly looked behind them to see if anyone approximating a male person was following them. Sadly, despite Janet's assurances of the previous week, Bill was absent. Using my best Lieutenant Colombo imitation, I asked Janet, "Is Bill parking the car or is he in the men's room?" Perceptibly embarrassed, Janet stuttered, "I am so embarrassed. He was in a meeting that went over. First he called from his office and said he'd just drive here directly and meet us. Then he called from his car and said he was held up because of an accident. He doubted he would get here in time."

Faced with Bill's third consecutive absence, I felt a wave of irritation surge through my body. I was convinced this was more than an unavoidable emergency, a coincidence, or a mishap that could not be helped. This definitely was a pattern. My mind whirled as I thought about how I should handle this situation. I was sure this was a clinical issue that needed to be addressed, but I was unsure how to proceed. I briefly considered refusing to meet with Janet and Becky until Bill was present. An awkward silence hung in the room and, suddenly, the first serendipitous moment in working with this family occurred. I was struck with an unplanned and unexpected question. And without the benefit of contemplation, I blurted out to Becky, "Do you think you are more or less absent from school than your father is absent from your family?" A deafening silence followed my question. Becky and Janet stared at me, their faces frozen. Then slowly—ever so slowly—a soft smile began to emerge at the corners of Becky's mouth. But before she could say anything, Janet retorted, "Are you suggesting that Bill avoids our family the same way Becky avoids school?" I looked at her but did not say anything. Continuing, she said, "I just think I need to set things straight here because if that's what you're saying, you're way off. It's true Bill doesn't spend a lot of time at home with us, but he's working. He's trying to support our family. I don't think it's fair to Bill to suggest that he doesn't care about our family." I looked at Becky, who was staring at her mother. Her soft smile had faded and now she seemed very pensive. I asked her what she was thinking. Looking at Janet, she said, "Mom, it sounds like you're defending Dad. You're making excuses for him." Janet appeared stunned. She said, "I'm not making excuses; I'm just explaining how things are."

BECKY: But you're saying that Dad never comes home because he cares about our family and is trying to take care of us.

JANET: Well, that's true, Becky.

BECKY: I can't believe you're saying this. I thought it bothered you as much as me that Dad never comes home. I thought you were sad that he always leaves you alone. But now it doesn't seem like it bothers you.

Janet shifted in her chair, uncrossed and recrossed her legs, folded her arms across her chest, looked intently at Becky with a confused expression, and said, "Of course it bothers me. I would like to see more of your father, but I understand what he's doing."

I was pleasantly surprised by what was occurring in the therapy room. At my first meeting with Becky, she appeared deferential, shy, and demure. However, in this exchange with her mother, I was beginning to see another side of her; she was being confrontational and in her eyes was a glint of anger. Coming from Becky, this was an emotion most unfamiliar to me. I commented to her, "I could be wrong, but it almost seems as if you're a little irritated with your mom. Maybe even a bit angry?"

BECKY: I guess I am a little angry.

THERAPIST: Can you say what you are angry about?

BECKY: Well, I think I am just surprised by my mom. I don't know why she is making excuses for my dad. I always thought it bothered her that he never spends any time with our family. But now she's making it seem like it's okay. I'm just surprised.

Janet shifted in her chair and said, "It does bother me that your dad has to work so much, but I understand why he does it."

BECKY: Well, I don't understand. We have more than enough money. It's not as if we need so much more. Sometimes I feel like I don't even have a father.

JANET: That's a terrible thing to say, Becky. You have a father who loves you very much and works hard to take care of you.

With eyes downcast Becky said, "I know dad loves us, but I miss him and I thought you did, too. I heard the two of you argue awhile back. You told him you were lonely and you wished he didn't work so much. I felt bad for you because I know how you felt. But now it doesn't sound like you really feel that way."

Janet's eyes welled up and after a few moments she cried in earnest. Angrily she said, "You never should have heard that conversation. That was private. It was between adults. I'm sorry that you heard that, Becky. I don't want you to think I am unhappy with your father. I love him. He's a good man and he loves his family. You should never forget that. Just because I sometimes feel lonely does not mean I am unhappy with your father."

"Well, all I know is I am never going to marry a man who leaves me. I don't think that's showing someone you love them," replied Becky.

At that point, a second serendipitous moment occurred in the session. I asked Becky another spontaneous question. "Becky, your mom says that your dad's absences from your family are because he's working and trying to take care of the family. And I hear you challenging her for making excuses for him. You're challenging her about protecting him from having to face up to his responsibilities. At other times, I've heard your mom do the same thing with you. She has made excuses for you about your school absences. She has protected you from facing up to your responsibilities as well. In both cases, I think your mom works overtime to protect you and your dad because she loves you both a lot. I'm wondering, has she always worked this hard in your family to take care of everyone?" Becky paused for a while and gazing intently at me said. "Yeah, always, I think."

THERAPIST: It must be tiring for her to have to work so hard to protect every-one. It must be especially exhausting because by protecting one person, sometimes it hurts another. For example, she has worked very hard to protect your dad when he's absent from the family, but that doesn't help you and probably not even her because you both miss him. When she protects you when you're absent from school, in the long run that doesn't help you because you need to go to school and learn. And I doubt it helps her because it just makes her take up a lot of time worrying about you and making her feel like maybe she isn't a good mom.

BECKY: I never thought of it like this before.

Janet sat quietly while tears streamed down her face. I asked her what she was feeling. She replied, "I guess I do try to take care of everyone and you're right; it's never enough. No matter how hard I try, I always fail someone, including myself. But what can I do?"

THERAPIST: What do you think would happen if you didn't work so hard to make excuses for everyone and protect them from being responsible for their decisions?

JANET: I don't know.

At this point, we were well out of time. As a result, I said, "Maybe you can think more about my question and let's discuss it next week." We scheduled our next appointment for the following week. I left the session feeling energized. I knew something significant had occurred, and I also knew it had been completely unplanned on my part.

CONFRONTING CHANGE
AFTER THE CRITICAL INCIDENT

One week after the critical incident, Bill attended his first therapy session. For the first time in months, Becky attended school three of five school days; this was a record for her. I asked Becky what was responsible for the change. Beaming, she said, "My dad helps me. He drives me to school now every morning and gives me a motivational talk in the car. That helps me get ready for school."

At that moment, Janet interrupted. She said, "Bill and I had a talk last week and we decided that he would drive Becky to school. It was a little tricky to work out because now he leaves a half-hour later than normal, but I told him I really needed his help, and he was willing to do it." Concurring, Bill said, "It was no problem to change my schedule around a little. I just stay a half-hour later in the evening, which I don't mind if it helps Becky.

This way I can give Becky a pep talk to get her in the right frame of mind. I'm pretty good at that because I have to do the same type of thing with my staff at work. People just need the right attitude to do their best. Whether it's family or work, the right attitude is important." In light of these changes, I asked Becky if her dad's new approach had made a difference for her and if she felt better now about going to school.

BECKY: I still don't like school that much, but my dad is helping me see how I can be more confident and not let it get me down.

THERAPIST: How does your dad help you feel more confident? What exactly does he do that has been so helpful to you?

BECKY: Well, he told me about when he was a boy and he was overweight and kids made fun of him, too. He told me how he used to cry, but then he realized that it was their problem if they were that mean, and he wasn't going to let them ruin his life. He told me how he pretended not to hear them and that made them look stupid and eventually they got bored teasing him. He also told me how, when he got a little older, he started running and then lifting weights and he lost weight. He's going to show me how I can maybe exercise and that way I could lose some weight, too.

I commended Bill's use of his motivational skills and boyhood experiences to connect with Becky to motivate her and to give her hope and confidence. Bill's approach with Becky resonated with Janet. Sounding much like a person recently reprieved, she said, "It's been great for me. I can't tell you what it means to me to know that I don't have to have a sense of dread every morning when I wake up. After last week, I asked myself, why do I drive myself crazy trying to take care of everything myself? I just decided I wasn't going to be the only one responsible for getting Becky to school. This whole family is out to lunch and I've been caught holding the bag. I told Bill that I needed his help. Now, it's his job to get her there in the morning. I still help get them up and out in the morning in terms of making breakfast, ironing clothes, stuff like that. But he's the one that deals with actually making sure she goes to school. And if she doesn't, like last week she missed two days, he has to deal with that. I feel a hundred times better."

Given the changes that had occurred, I was curious about how Bill and Janet, but especially Bill, dealt with breakdowns in the new approach to getting Becky to school. With that in mind, I asked Becky to share with me what happens now on those days when she does not make it to school. She shared that on the first of the two days she did not make it to school, Bill drove her back home. The next day, they did not even get to the car because she emphatically refused to go to school. And since they were running late that day, Bill decided to leave her at home. Responding to Becky's disclosure, Bill said, "I was really upset with her after the second time it happened and so I had a long talk with her that night, and the next day we had no problem." Clearly, Bill had found effective strategies to maintain the momentum of the changes. However, despite his success in getting Becky to attend school regularly, it was an inescapable irony that Bill was compensating for the time he gave to his daughter in the morning by taking time away from her in the evening.

Now that Janet had delegated to Bill the responsibility for getting Becky to school and his approach appeared to be working, I was curious how Janet was feeling about how Bill was dividing his time between family versus work. I said to her, "I know I challenged you earlier about the ways in which you have been overresponsible in the family. Now I'm wondering how much of this has been related to Bill's overresponsibility at work. For example, I noticed that the only way Bill was able to give an extra half-hour in the morning to the family was by subtracting a half-hour in the evening. What do you make of this?"

JANET: You're right; he's very committed to his job; it's his top priority. That's part of why I've had to be so responsible in the family.

THERAPIST: So now that you are challenging your overresponsibility for the family, do you think Bill will be able to challenge his overresponsibility at work as well?

JANET: That's a good question. I don't know.

BILL: Are you saying that I put my work before my family?

THERAPIST: I'm just wondering if you would still be willing to give that extra time in the morning to your family without taking away from your time with them in the evening?

BILL: My job is very demanding. I wish I had more time for my family, but I have a lot of responsibilities at work.

THERAPIST: Sounds like you've answered your own question about which comes first for you.

It was evident that Bill had been affected by this conversation, and my hope was that he would begin to challenge the ways he put work before family. Consequently, rather than continuing to challenge him, I decided simply to leave him thinking about this issue and trust that over time his newfound awareness would permeate deeper layers of his consciousness and disrupt the "out-of-balance" balance he had created in life between his work and his family.

DISCUSSION

After five sessions with mother and daughter, therapy appeared to be stuck or at least stymied, and we seemed not to be making much progress. However, in Session 6, in an uncensored moment, I experienced a spontaneity that resulted in a serendipitous question that clearly stimulated a dramatic shift in the course of therapy. This question expanded the definition of the problem from Becky's school absences to a larger pattern of absence in the family that included her father's absence. Redefining the problem in this manner triggered several unexpected reactions.

1. It aroused Janet's instinctive reaction to protect her husband.
2. It provided Becky with a different way of seeing each of her parents, thus affecting how she also saw herself. With regard to her mother's defense of her father, Becky was simultaneously shocked and surprised. This defense challenged Becky's previously held belief that her mother was upset with her father's absences. As she heard her mother defend her father, Becky began to question whether her mother really was as distressed by her father's absences as she previously had thought. Once Becky's perception of her mother was challenged, it allowed her to get in touch with and express the sublimated anger she felt toward her mother. This was a novel experience for Becky.
3. With regard to her father, it is clear that Becky had been angry with him for some time because of his excessive absences from her life. Now, however, she was able to see the similarities between his behavior and her own. Later, it became clear that this was disturbing to Becky because she did not wish to repeat a pattern of behavior that she found undesirable in her father.

Later in Session 6, I was inspired by a second spontaneous question that challenged Janet's overresponsibility in the family. This question further expanded the definition of the problem to include the role that Janet played in enabling Bill's absence from the family and Becky's absence from school. More important, however, it did so in a way that cast Janet in a sympathetic light and had the following unanticipated effects:

1. Helped to expose the frustration that Janet had been suppressing as she attempted to take care of and protect everyone in her family even though it was impossible to satisfactorily meet everyone's needs.
2. Gave Becky a different perspective of her mother's struggles as she strove to be the consummate caretaker. Whereas previously Becky

perceived Janet as a lonely women in need of companionship, now she saw her as an overburdened women who needed the people around her to start being more responsible for themselves so she could have more freedom to live her life.

Implications of the Critical Incident for Therapy

It would be fair to say that therapy was a success. But whose success was it? Initially, at least, I did not feel I could claim the outcome of this intervention as an example of my therapeutic skills or expertise because, in all honestly, I am not exactly sure what allowed this family to resolve their presenting problem. I believe the pivotal moment occurred in Session 6 when I asked Becky two spontaneous questions. However, even if I attribute the pivotal moments to myself and those two questions, it is an unsettling feeling to realize that those questions were little more than pure, unanticipated inspiration—maybe even dumb luck. My interventions were not informed by a sophisticated strategy, calculated wit, or intentional skill. In fact, I think my first question was inspired more by reactivity that by rationale. I remember the irritation I was feeling when the first question appeared in my mind and exited from my mouth. So what is the therapeutic moral to the story? One possible implication is that not all that is therapeutically significant can be planned. This is an unsettling thought for me because, as my family and friends have pointed out, I tend to score rather high on "orientation toward control" scales. I entered graduate school committed to learning as much theory and technique as possible so that one day I would be able to master the forces of change and become a "skilled therapist." A part of me would rather not succeed unless I have carefully calculated the process, just as a way of affirming my illusion of control. Working with families such as the Sanderses (and the many others since then) has been a humbling experience for me. It forced me to acknowledge the fact that there is a huge part of therapy that I do not and cannot control nearly as precisely as I would prefer.

I take solace from working with families like the Sanderses because although I did not plan the interventions that seemed to be most helpful, I nonetheless played what appeared to be an important role in helping to induce change in this family. In other words, something inside me, while I was not aware of it and did not plan it, "worked." This has lead me to consider the importance of trusting in oneself. In the years that have passed since working with the Sanderses, I have learned a lot more about the power of serendipity—the unplanned moment. I have challenged myself to trust that when the moment arrives, I will find the questions, insights, and answers, and no amount of planning can or will ever fully prepare me for that moment. Some piece of therapy is inspiration and this lesson applies to situations outside of therapy as well. Prior to this experience, I tended to plan every word of a workshop presentation, a speech, or a classroom lecture. Now I approach these tasks with a general outline and trust that I will find the specific words in the moment.

The idea of trusting the moment (or of trusting myself in the moment) is still somewhat unnerving to me and, in all honesty, it does not always work. I have had moments that I would rather forget, but I also know that in the long run I have gained more than I have lost. I have been able to experience insights, interventions, inspired orations, and other strategies/maneuvers that would have been unimaginable had I been trying to plan them in a space and time removed from the moment in which such things had to come to life. My experience with the Sanderses, then, like others since, was one step along my pathway to understanding the power of the unplanned moment. Such moments played a powerful role in showing me that I may have what I need within me, but I will not necessarily know it until the precise moment that I need it. Until that moment arrives, I just have to trust it will be there.

A second implication might be that questions can be a powerful therapeutic intervention. I find it intriguing that both of the moments I perceived as pivotal in this case were set into motion because of questions I had asked. I neither lectured the Sanderses about their family dynamics, provided my opinion about the anatomy of the presenting problem, nor shared any "great insight" or analysis of the case with the them. I simply asked two questions which came from a position of seeking, rather than from professing knowledge. In retrospect, I have wondered, for example, how different the outcome would have been had I made a statement like: "I notice, Becky, that you struggle with school absence and your dad seems to struggle with family absence. It seems that absence is a major theme in your family." Would the outcome have been the same, or was there something qualitatively different about asking a question? I am inclined to believe that by asking the question, Becky was challenged to confront the issue of absence in the family directly and actively. She was not merely the passive recipient of therapeutic insight but was an active agent who had to grapple with the issues that had been put on the table, namely her family's relationship with absence.

Yet another possible implication may be that our emotions, even our emotional reactivity, may not always be the nemesis that I was trained to believe it is. Although clinically I tend to proceed from the premise that reactivity clouds therapeutic efficacy, I honestly believe that had it not been for my reactivity, I may never have stumbled upon and asked the first pivotal question in that critical session. It is also possible that I am completely overestimating and misjudging the role these two serendipitous questions played in helping this family to change. Based on my careful review of the clinical tapes and notes of my sessions, I feel confident that these questions did in fact form the critical moment in therapy, but how could I ever truly know this? My only indicators are the clients' responses to the questions in therapy, their willingness to return one week later, and the significant changes they reported. Quite possibly it may have been something else of which I was, and maybe they were, unaware that enabled them to shift gears and change their behaviors.

This brings me back to my first possible implication. The more I ponder this case, the more that I do not know. It is hard to feel even a measure of security when I realize how much I am assuming without knowing and how much I will never know irrespective of how hard I try to know. So I find myself having to fall back on faith in trusting that even if I cannot inventory my therapeutic skills and meticulously plan when and how I will use them, if I trust myself, they may come forth and assist me when I am most in need. It amuses me to realize that this essentially is what I always have believed about the families with whom I work—that they have inside of them much of what they need and therapy merely creates the context, "the moment," in which these resources are activated and organized in ways that ultimately help them to change and grow. Such moments are never planned, but somehow, more often than not, they happen.

THE OUTCOME OF THERAPY

Arguably, the changes the Sanders family had experienced in a single week were dramatic. Consequently, I met with them for three more sessions to track their progress and to help them work through the nuances of the changes they had made in their lives. Janet, Bill, and especially Becky appeared to be comfortable with the changes they had made as individuals and as a family. By what was to become our last session, Becky had missed only three days of school in three weeks. Accordingly, the family and I agreed to terminate therapy because for all practical purposes the presenting problem had been resolved. We terminated with the understanding that they would call the center if they felt they needed help again.

Follow-Up

A year later, Janet called to update the family's progress. Becky was doing fine, attending school regularly, getting good grades, and had formed a friendship with another student whom she really seemed to like. Janet was employed in a small advertising company and enjoyed it. For her, therapy was a turning point despite daily struggles not to regress into her former role. However, despite her best efforts, she occasionally stumbles. She remains cognizant of the need to push herself not to overfunction for everyone in the family. Bill continues to spend a great deal of time at work but remains faithful to his commitment to spend more time with Becky (more than he did previously). The time Bill devotes to work continues to distress Janet.

She seriously was considering entering therapy with Bill to address her frustration with his limited availability to her as a husband. Janet was thankful for having been involved in therapy; she felt everyone profited from the experience.

Commentary

Seduced by Urgency

Craig A. Everett

Commentator Background

Fifty-eight years old, white, male, PhD, thirty-four years MFT practice.

Practice Setting

Private practice.

Theoretical Perspective

An integrative systemic approach is used in the discussion of this case.

I am not sure that the task of dealing with absent and/or resistant parents and spouses in the therapy process is as much a function of clinical orientation as it is of clinical experience. I believe that most family therapists would support this therapist's desire to work with all of the family members. I also believe that most experienced therapists utilize whatever means have been successful for them in the past to engage an absent family member, theoretical orientation notwithstanding.

GOOD POINTS ABOUT THE CASE

Little can be critiqued in the specific case presentation. I commend Laszloffy for achieving a reasonably successful outcome in a short period of time. She also describes the case in a clear and reflective manner that is refreshingly free of clinical jargon. Her therapeutic approach appeared to be primarily structural in focusing on the mother-child subsystem and reflecting on the similarity of clinical dynamics that existed in the child's school-phobic behaviors and the father's apparent family-phobic behaviors. Without addressing hierarchical issues in the family system, Laszloffy identified the central enabling and mediating role that the mother played within this family triangle.

I am curious, however, about Laszloffy's use of rather dramatic language when she described the mother's request for therapy. She used such phrases as "plaintive plea for help," "exasperation in Janet's voice," "Janet's expressed urgency to find a solution," "Janet needed something to be done soon." It is likely that Janet is quite skilled at using enabling behaviors to manage interactions and to gain the outcome that she wants. Perhaps Laszloffy (then a graduate student) was seduced by the mother's urgent needs for her child and enabled by her "plaintive plea for help." After all, the case continued through six sessions with the mother defending the father's absences until Laszloffy addressed the issue more clinically. This dynamic leads, of course, to the primary feature in the discussion of this case—the therapeutic management of a resistant parent.

WHAT I WOULD HAVE DONE DIFFERENTLY

Typically in a case such as this, I make every effort to engage both parents in the therapeutic process, beginning with our first therapy session. My reason for doing so results directly from having been "burned" too many times in the past when I have ignored my instincts and allowed one parent to dictate the terms of the other parent's involvement or by simply failing to make the effort to engage the other parent. Admittedly, most of my cases do not resolve themselves as easily as this one with the father, when he finally did make his appearance, behaving in an extraordinarily appropriate manner by taking over transporting the child to school. In my experience, the absent parent more typically either continues to sabotage clinical changes from a distance or appears in therapy, having felt left out of the process, and sabotages because of resentment toward the therapist and/or the family for moving on without her or him.

I must say that I felt much more urgency about the clinical need to engage this father than was expressed by Laszloffy, which is what led me to comment earlier that Laszloffy may have been seduced into playing along with the mother's enabling behaviors. Perhaps I am simply less patient, but I would not have agreed to the early scenario presented by the mother that the father would be unavailable until the end of the month. First, I clearly perceive this as a red flag with regard to her role and enabling behaviors in the family. Second, this excused the father's participation in therapy, which was another red flag regarding family dynamics.

The enabling role of the mother, demonstrated from the beginning, would seem to suggest that putting more pressure on her to gain the father's involvement, as Laszloffy did rather gently, would not be successful. Early in my career I was more cautious in approaching absent family members—

perhaps that was a lack of confidence, inexperience, or more patience. I absolutely prefer to utilize the dynamics and resources of a family system to deal with issues such as this. However, when the specific dynamics of the system preclude their use to achieve a certain outcome, I feel that the therapist must be willing to intervene more directly. Having worked with many high-risk adolescents over many years of practice, I have learned that immediate and direct interventions are often necessary, particularly if concerns exist about suicide, drug use, and/or delinquent behaviors. In most cases, the therapist does not have the luxury of "waiting out" a resistant family member (managed care notwithstanding). Thus, I might have used two alternative methods:

1. At the conclusion of the initial interview, I might have offered to call the father—at his work—to invite his immediate participation. I would not have waited to call him in the evening at his home because that would have simply supported the mother's protection of his escape to his work setting. I would have given him the benefit of the doubt and approached this conversation as simply a matter of scheduling an appointment with me, assuming that being involved in the evaluation of his daughter's problematic behaviors was a priority for him. If initial resistance was shown by the father, I would have dramatized my concerns about his daughter's behaviors—perhaps her behaviors are indicative of an underlying mood disorder or broader developmental concerns. The decision to call him at his work establishes my authority to talk to him there and conveys the seriousness of the matter. I have found that very few absent parents turn me down after such a conversation and I would have expected him to be present at the next session.

2. Difficult cases certainly exist in which resistance to participation would continue even after the above engagement. Accordingly, an alternate strategy would be to step back and avoid a power struggle by approaching this issue from a different structural angle. Many absent fathers believe that it is the mother's role to take care of the children's everyday needs—this would include taking them to medical and dental appointments, when necessary, and to a therapist. I have found it helpful, in such cases, to change the focus from the mother-child dyad to other subsystems.

In this case, at the conclusion of the first interview, I might have said to Janet that the next step in the therapy process would be for me to see Becky individually (I routinely do this with older adolescents) to understand what she was experiencing. "After I meet with her, I need to see you and your husband to get some of your daughter's and your family's history." When making this request, I am clear that I need the father's reflections and input in that session, along with the mother's. I will also make a similar call to the father, if necessary. However, I have found that many more absent fathers are willing to meet with the therapist if the focus clearly is on their child's history and not on them or their marriage. They perceive a greater sense of "safety" when their participation is defined as a sort of consultant for their child. However, in a few exceptional cases when an absent parent continues to be unavailable, I have invited his or her parents—the grandparents of the children—into a session to help me with the family's history. Using this more dramatic strategy, I never have had an absent parent continue to be unavailable when her or his parents were coming to a session.

In many cases in which an adolescent is the IP, I prefer this approach of scheduling interviews with the subsystems even when no parent is absent. This strategy is helpful to break up coalitions and power struggles and to diffuse scapegoating and/or parentification. If this strategy had been used in this case within the first two or three hours of therapy, it could have provided a view of the adolescent's perceptions of her family and a firsthand experience of the parents' interactional patterns, as well as a glimpse of the parents' underlying marital dynamics.

Other Questions I Would Have Asked

Clearly Laszloffy relied primarily on interactional process in the interviews; as a result, the collection of background data was minimal. Were I the therapist of record, I would have wanted to pursue several areas of additional clinical data at the onset of the case. Further, such data in specific areas would be helpful in providing a clearer picture of explicit family roles and patterns, identifying potential underlying family resources, and suggesting early clinical strategies:

1. I would have sought a more explicit description from the adolescent regarding her morning behaviors to avoid school. Most of this information is provided by the mother. Later, the adolescent identified her concerns about peers but not about the morning struggles.
2. I would have inquired more about the mother's parenting efforts and style. We know that she has not been effective in getting the adolescent to go to school, but what has she tried, what has worked, and what has failed?
3. I would have inquired a little more about the historical as well as present parenting strategies between the mother and father, e.g.,

—has the father played a more effective role in the past?

—did the parents consult with each other with regard to the rearing of their older daughters?

—do they consult with each other with regard to issues specific to this child?

—what were the parenting issues in the family when all three children were at home?

4. I would have sought more clinical data on the past and present marital dynamics, even if this was provided only by observation rather than direct questioning.

5. I would have asked a few early questions about family-of-origin patterns and dynamics for both spouses. For example, did the mother learn her enabling role from one of her parents? Did the father learn his workaholic behaviors from his family of origin?

6. I would have asked more questions about this family's developmental dynamics, e.g., how did they handle the losses related to each of the older sisters' departure from the family? Could the mother's enabling behaviors be a response to these prior losses? Laszloffy effectively brought the sisters' presence into the discussion of the presenting problem but stopped short of addressing their earlier and broader roles in the family.

LOOKING AT THE CRITICAL INCIDENT

I believe Laszloffy dealt well with the clinical process that led to the questioning which produced the critical incident. It was a good recovery for Laszloffy to regain control and focus in the therapy (no matter how serendipitous it was), and it produced effective results. I support her analysis of these interactional dynamics which produced the favorable outcomes. However, I am concerned that underlying marital issues, which were clearly present, were not addressed directly by Laszloffy and that these issues potentially could resurface (and probably will) at a future time. In addition, the specific etiology of Janet's enabling behaviors may trace back to her family of origin; some objective recognition of this from the therapy experience might have been quite helpful to her in the future.

Finally, I feel that Laszloffy is much too hard on herself in analyzing (second-guessing) the "serendipitous turning points" in this case. Certainly many serendipitous phenomena occur in family therapy, and the skills and experience of the clinician will determine how effectively they are used to enhance the clinical process and its potential outcomes. However, I believe that a therapist's clinical instincts form the real basis for accurately reading the subtle dynamics in a family as well as knowing the right moment and the right manner in which to respond to them. I believe that Laszloffy demonstrated good instincts with regard to the parent-child dynamics and responded in a manner that clearly produced change for this family.

Commentary

Winning the Battle, but Losing the War?

Karen H. Rosen

Commentator Background

Fifty-four years old, white, female, EdD, sixteen years MFT experience.

Practice Setting

University MFT clinic and limited private practice.

Theoretical Perspective

Structural-strategic through a feminist lens.

Who can argue with success? In nine sessions, the presenting problem—a case of refusal to attend school—was solved. Laszloffy skillfully helped her client family to reorganize itself sufficiently to get mother and daughter "back to work" and to enhance the relationship between father and daughter. One of many ways to look at this case, theoretically speaking, is that when the overfunctioning mom stopped overfunctioning and allowed the dad to share some of the child-rearing responsibility, the child responded by going to school.

GOOD POINTS ABOUT THE CASE

I commend Laszloffy for helping the family to make important shifts that led to solving the presenting problem. How did this happen? By asking a few seemingly simple questions—the critical incidents—Laszloffy was able to challenge the system. She asked the daughter, "Do you think you are more or less absent from school than your father is absent from your family?" This question seemed to be a catalyst for an honest exchange between mother and daughter about the "pink elephant in the room," which was the father's psychological absence from the family along with his minimal physical presence. When Janet made excuses for Bill's behavior, Becky confronted her for making excuses for him and for Janet's mixed messages about the issue—on one hand, Janet apparently had expressed anger toward Bill, yet protected him on the other hand. After this exchange, Laszloffy made yet another bold move. She suggested to Becky that her mother's protection of her father from facing up to his responsibilities in the family might be similar to how the mother protects Becky from facing up to her responsibilities at school. This intervention is a kick to both mother and daughter. It puts Becky in a bind because she had just stated that she did not like her father's behavior, yet her behavior is perceived to be similar to her father's. This comparison also puts pressure on Janet for condoning the inappropriate behavior of both father and daughter. As Minuchin (1974) has suggested, the "kick" is accompanied by a "stroke" to the mother. Laszloffy pointed out that Janet's behavior is well intentioned. However, the down side to her well-intentioned behavior is that the family suffers in several ways—Janet and Becky both miss Bill; Becky does not go to school; and Janet ends up feeling as though she has failed. Clearly, Laszloffy's suggestion to Janet that she think about what would happen if she "didn't work so hard to make excuses for everyone and protect them from being responsible for their decisions" prompted Janet to ask Bill for help in a way that he could not refuse. As a result of Janet asking Bill for his help, he took charge of getting Becky to school. An interesting note, however, is that Janet, Becky, Laszloffy, and Bill all gave Bill the credit for Becky's changes, and the family went happily on its way.

WHAT I WOULD HAVE DONE DIFFERENTLY

Despite the positive outcome, aspects of this case bother me when I view it from a feminist perspective. Although the presenting problem was solved and the family made important shifts, the members left therapy with the gender-power imbalance and stereotypical gender roles intact. Perhaps even worse, Becky may have learned that men know how to solve problems and all women need to do is to be needy. Although Laszloffy's question—"So now that you [Janet] are challenging your overresponsibility for the family, do you think Bill will be able to challenge his overresponsibility at work as well?"—did attempt to confront indirectly the fact that Bill continues to shortchange his family in favor of his job, Laszloffy does not seem to have had much of an impact. Bill simply claimed that he had no choice. Laszloffy decided to "leave Bill thinking about this issue, and trust that over time his newfound awareness would permeate deeper layers of his consciousness...." I have my doubts that such a shift will occur on its own.

I believe it would have been helpful for both mother and daughter and perhaps the father as well if Laszloffy had gone a step further and had given

Janet credit for initiating the changes that the family made. From a feminist perspective, Janet's statement—"I just decided I wasn't going to be the only one responsible for getting Becky to school. This whole family is out to lunch and I've been caught holding the bag. I told Bill that I needed his help"—provided a wonderful opportunity for Laszloffy to give Janet credit for her courage to take a position with her husband or to point out how powerful Janet could be when she makes up her mind to do something. Laszloffy could also have asked Janet what was that experience like, how did she decide to do it, and what did she learn about herself? And Bill could have been asked what it was like for him to have his wife be so clear about what she wanted from him or what it was like to know that he had the good judgment (fortune) to choose a strong-minded woman or something to that effect. She also could have explored with Bill some of the ways his well-intentioned behavior, devoting himself to his job, shortchanged him and his family.

Imbuing Feminist Values

Laszloffy could also have used the evidence of Janet's strength as a way to put Becky in touch with her own strengths. Perhaps this young girl could learn something from her mother about tackling difficult problems. Instead, Becky's struggles to deal with the spoilers at school and her own weight problem was left solely in the hands of her father. How can this young girl grow up to value and trust herself if she fails to appreciate the strengths of her mother and the contributions her mother makes to the family? This family's problem and solution could have been a teachable moment with a broad impact on this young girl's views about the roles of men and women and helped to expand her notion about the contributions and capabilities of women.

Integrating feminist theory and family therapy can shift therapy from just solving the presenting problem to solving it in a way that leaves the family less patriarchal and less absent of a father (Luepnitz, 1988). From my perspective, overlaying a feminist lens when working with families within a structural or strategic framework means that family members are viewed as gendered, and therapists notice how men and women view themselves and each other. I believe it also means that, in addition to resolving the presenting problem, it is important that therapists work to provide family members with a wider array of choices about how to live as men and women. Clearly, the father in this family is seen as the entitled hero. He is viewed as doing the important work of providing the financial security for this family and having a job as an executive. It seems like the women in this family came into therapy and left therapy believing that they simply needed to understand this arrangement and to accept the husband/father's absence and appreciate his contributions. The father's hero position may have been reinforced by the fact that his efforts were viewed as key to solving the presenting problem, and he also was the one to help the daughter deal with the spoilers at school. Perhaps this was a case of winning the battle but losing the war. The presenting problem was solved, but stereotypical gender roles and gender-power imbalances were reinforced.

Other Questions I Would Have Asked

Because I view this case through a feminist theoretical lens, I would ask Laszloffy additional clinical questions. These questions point to theoretical possibilities given a structural-strategic perspective and may be helpful in obtaining a sharper image of this family. Perhaps other avenues of change had been explored and were unsuccessful. These questions suggest a different focus for the solution to the presenting problem.

1. Did Laszloffy explore other ways to help this family make changes that did not lay the blame on the mother's shoulders for enabling the inappropriate behavior of both father and daughter?
2. Did Laszloffy explore other ways to empower the mother?
3. Did Laszloffy try to help the mother be more competent in the role of getting the daughter to school?
4. Was the mother helped to be more assertive in getting the father to attend therapy in a way that did not indirectly blame her?

Instead of pointing out the isomorphic behavior of the father and daughter, Laszloffy could have noted how Becky might be taking care of her mother. Laszloffy could then ask Janet if she needed or wanted Becky to take care of her as a way to empower Janet to be more assertive with both her daughter and her husband. Clearly, the route Laszloffy took involved the entire family while the questions I would have posed focus on the mother-daughter dyad and on empowering the mother.

THE PERSON OF THE THERAPIST: GENDER AND AGE

The manner in which this case unfolded may in part have been due to Laszloffy's age and gender. Like Janet and Becky, Laszloffy, who is a young woman, initially seemed reluctant to confront Bill's behavior. Although from inception Laszloffy made it clear that Bill's participation in therapy would be important, it was six sessions before this issue was confronted directly. At first I wondered why it took so long for Laszloffy to see that if she did not draw a bottom line about Bill's participation, neither would Janet. Then it occurred to me that if she had confronted the issue sooner, perhaps not enough intensity would have surrounded the issue to have as powerful an impact as it did when it *was* confronted. Maybe Laszloffy needed to experience some of that intensity herself to gain the energy to push herself and Janet past their respective comfort zones. In a sense, Laszloffy joined with Janet as a woman who does not confront the behavior of a powerful man; from that position, she then used another tact to confront the issue.

LOOKING AT THE CRITICAL INCIDENT

Despite Laszloffy's expressed reluctance to credit herself for the interventions that clearly were the catalyst for the shift in the family, I again commend her for the work she has done with the family. Of course, the family made the changes, but I believe Laszloffy provided the impetus. She perceives it to be a serendipitous event, perhaps even "dumb luck." Contrary to her modesty, I think the phenomenon is more aptly described as "having a method to one's madness." Although Laszloffy's questions might not have been preplanned, they seem to have been well grounded in the structural-strategic theoretical perspective. Laszloffy discloses that she "entered graduate school committed to learning as much theory and technique as possible." I believe the interventions described in this case report speak to the fact that she did just that; the systemic theoretical perspective has become part of who she is and how she views people and their problems. Perhaps getting in touch with her own irritation with Bill's absence provided the impetus to confront his behavior instead of continuing to take the less risky, more predictable route she had been taking. I agree with Laszloffy's assessment that "our emotions, even our emotional reactivity, may not always be the nemesis that I was trained to believe." Indeed, therapists' personal reactions to specific family dynamics are increasingly becoming valued as assessment tools and aids in formulating appropriate clinical interventions, as they were in this case (Haber, 1990).

Laszloffy stated that she learned from this case to trust the moment and to trust herself—as well she should. She seems to have good instincts that are based on sound theoretical ground and substantial skills to make change happen in the therapy room.

REFERENCES

Haber, R. (1990). From handicap to handy capable: Training systemic therapists in use of self. *Family Process*, 29(4), 375-384.

Luepnitz, D. A. (1988). *The family interpreted: Feminist theory in clinical practice*. New York: Basic Books.

Minuchin, S. (1974). *Families and family therapy*. Cambridge, MA: Harvard University Press.

CASE 5

Be a Man

Robert G. Ryder

All people are more simply human than otherwise.

Harry Stack Sullivan

Therapist Background

Currently: Sixty-seven years old, white, male, PhD, forty-four years clinical experience, a majority of these in MFT. Then: Sixty years old, thirty-seven years clinical experience.

Practice Setting

Currently and when I saw Joe: family and couples private practice.

Client Characteristics

Joe (age thirty-eight) and Jane (age thirty-six) are a working-class white couple married approximately twenty years; they have one daughter (age five). Joe was employed in a local factory and moonlighted as a member of a rock band. Jane was employed in a secretarial position in the local town bureaucracy. Joe sought therapeutic assistance because his wife had been involved in an extramarital relationship and "his world was falling apart."

Length of Treatment

Joe was seen individually for approximately thirty sessions over twelve months, with occasional sessions after that. I saw Jane once, but she was in individual therapy with another therapist (not MFT oriented) during and beyond this period. The critical incident occurred in Session 15.

Theoretical Perspective

A relationship-oriented approach described in *The Realistic Therapist* (Ryder, 1987) was used in working with Joe. Central to this approach is the development of a candid and positive client-therapist relationship. Practiced interpersonal tactics (active listening, circular questioning, etc.) in fact are likely to have the negative effect of diminishing the reality of this relationship. Choice of technique is a relatively minor matter except for its impact on the therapeutic relationship.

PRESENTING PROBLEM

Joe's world collapsed with the discovery that his loving wife and partner of twenty years had made love to someone else. Joe was a blue-collar fellow from a blue-collar town—not the sort of person who usually voluntarily walks into a therapist's consulting room. But Joe was desperate. He could get help from someone like me or rely on his buddies at work. He could not bring his wife with him. As a result, I saw him individually although he was having a marital problem. Joe was part of a social category—white, male, working class—often not so well thought of by contemporary psychotherapists. If you believe the newspapers, the precipitating crisis was prone to excite such a person's worst behaviors.

Background to the Presenting Problem

Jane, like Joe, was a white, working-class person. As a child she had been quiet and attractive with a reputation for being well behaved. She grew up in a small New England town that once had been prosperous in the days when New England textile mills were busy and successful. In her time, however, the town was poor and her people were employed but also poor. In high school, she met a young man who was lively, exciting, and also gentle. He actually had a functioning rock band and had an income from it. She adored him and was his girlfriend for several years. They then were married and apparently were happy for fifteen years, until the events that led Joe to seek therapy. After ten years of marriage, they became parents of a daughter.

Subsequent to disclosing her extramarital relationship, Jane had begun to have bad dreams, which were so troublesome that she sought professional help. The therapist she consulted hypnotized her and apparently uncovered memories of years of terrible sexual abuse. Assuming the accuracy of these memories, she repeatedly had been raped from age seven until age ten or eleven. The primary perpetrator was her maternal uncle, who lived in the same home with her, her parents, and her sister (who seemed to have been unharmed). A second perpetrator, the uncle's male friend, joined him in abusing Jane. The end came when Jane's father discovered what was going on. He was a simple man who did not deal much with lawyers or the police. He beat up the uncle and threw him out of the house. A few months later, both the uncle and his friend were killed in an automobile accident. Joe and Jane believe that Jane's father had some involvement with this "accident." No one will ever know the truth, since Jane's father is now dead and has taken his secrets with him. Jane and Joe also believed that Jane's mother knew what was happening all along, but did nothing. Strangely, Jane maintained a polite relationship with her mother and even used her as a babysitter. Joe disapproves of this arrangement but did not interfere with his wife's choices in dealing with her mother. He was very angry with his mother-in-law.

Joe's childhood was not entirely pleasant either, although in ways different from Jane's. He was born in the same town as Jane and abandoned at birth. A local couple adopted him and a biologically unrelated sister. As a child, it was impressed upon him that he had been chosen for adoption and could be unchosen again if he did not behave properly; apparently his behavior was thought to be marginal. As a result, he was beaten regularly by his adoptive mother, who also locked him in the cellar as punishment when he was of preschool age. He grew up eager to have people think well of him and felt that he had succeeded when, as a teenager, he started his own rock band. While still a teenager, his adoptive father died; a few years later, his adoptive mother died and he was orphaned for the second time.

Prior to those losses, Joe had met a young woman who became very important to him. She seemed to adore him and he relied on her to be his entire family. However, he sometimes was short with her. He seemed to have become gradually less exciting to her as he tried to maintain his band's functioning and concurrently keep a day job that actually put food on the table. At the time I became involved with this couple, both Joe and Jane were employed outside the home. The total family income was approximately $45,000, including income from Joe's band. When Jane began experiencing emotional difficulties and sought help, Joe was supportive although concerned about the unreimbursed $100 per session cost. Jane saw her therapist at least once and sometimes twice a week.

The financial cost of Jane's therapy was nothing compared to the really bad news she gave Joe a few months after she began therapy. She reminded him of the time, several years ago, when he and the band went to a series of performances on the West Coast. One night she attended a party by herself, drank too much, and had sex with another man. Joe was seriously shaken by this news. In his worldview, it was one more abandonment—one that left him with nothing to bolster his shaky regard for himself. He worked hard to reconstruct this event to minimize its impact. He told himself that it had to do with the beginnings of his wife's returning memories of childhood abuse.

He also told himself that he was responsible for Jane's extramarital relationship, because he went away. In other words, he tried, with partial success, to make his peace with news that in his opinion was overwhelming. Then Jane dropped the other shoe.

Jane told Joe that approximately six months after the initial incident, at a time when Joe was in town and when no alcohol was involved, she had contacted the other man and arranged a second rendezvous. Upon hearing that revelation, the floor opened up under Joe, or so it felt. He had counted on Jane's devotion to him as all he had left in place of biological parents he never had known, and his adoptive parents, such as they were, who had died. He now felt that he had been counting on a fraud and that—apart from their child—he had nothing in common with Jane. He also was afraid that now he might lose his child. Hearing from Jane of Joe's upset and anger, Jane's therapist urged her to encourage Joe to consult with a therapist. Jane's therapist himself would not see Joe; possibly he may have been slightly afraid of Joe. That is when Joe called me.

THE THERAPEUTIC SITUATION PRIOR
TO THE CRITICAL INCIDENT

The question of what to do with Joe was not easy. I knew I did not want to see Joe alone without ever hearing his wife's version of the story or seeing them interact. I knew too that I did not want to reduce Joe's opinion of himself still further. It did not seem like a good idea immediately to seek out ways that Joe's own behavior facilitated or exacerbated his situation. I suggested to Joe that he, his wife, and I should meet conjointly to see if we could make some sense of things. He agreed and promised to ask Jane to come with him to see me for this purpose. The next day Jane's therapist called me. He absolutely forbade her to see me, alone or with Joe. He contended that Jane was in a delicate condition because of her returning traumatic memories. At this point I was not doing well. The only affirmative plan I had—to hear Jane's story from her and to see the couple together—was not to be.

I knew that I wanted to build on Joe's present strengths and to help him to do the things he wanted to do. The question was: what would he want to do that he might actually manage and with which I would honestly be willing to help him? Of course—he wanted to be a man. He wanted to live up to the mythic ideals of masculine decency that he had grown up to believe. I thought that this might have possibilities. How could this happen? I could coach him. Every child who has ever played an organized sport is used to being coached and usually welcomes it. Everyone wants to play better. The plan, then, was that I would offer to play coach and to try to coach Joe into conduct of which he could be proud. This might not seem so different from telling him to knock off any bad behavior, but it is different. The difference is the distinction between enhancing something that exists and is valued and implying that his conduct is wrong. It is the difference between building pride and building shame.

I believed—correctly, as it turned out—that I could count on values slightly more noble than sex and violence. The image of manhood that I attempted to conjure up was the one that Hemingway extolled in *The Sun Also Rises*. The hero of the book, the "real man" if you will, was impotent. The violent young pugilist was the only real jerk. The strength that was important was the inner strength to behave in a decent way without whining. Tenderness is fine; complaining is not.

Just in case Joe was not buying what I wanted to sell, it seemed prudent to have a fallback position so there also would be an appeal to immediate self-interest. Joe was not sure whether he wanted to stay married. He now had seriously mixed feelings about his wife and he knew he did not want to lose his daughter, but he needed time to make up his mind, to decide whether it was best to stay or to leave. Accordingly, the fallback position was to suggest that he do nothing that would deprive him of that time—that would take matters out of his hands and make the decision for him. The concrete behavioral goals, if he bought this view, were the same. If, God forbid, he was foolish enough to become violent toward his wife; if he entered into a payback relationship with another woman; even if he maintained only an unfriendly or hostile attitude toward his wife—he could be setting into motion events that he would be helpless to stop. He needed to be decent and reasonable enough so that when he could calm down and make a decision, the show would not already be over. He had a slight problem in that it was difficult to see how this "treatment" plan was treatment in any sense of ameliorating an illness. I was leaving the health care system behind. Oh well!

What I actually said to Joe was that someday, maybe ten years away, all the present distress will be history. I said, "You have a choice to make now about how all this will look then. By what you do now, you can decide whether you will look back and shake your head sadly at how badly you handled this or look back at yourself with pride. Your choice." I added that one important objective for Joe was to keep his options open. If he said or did anything that started a ball rolling out of control—started fights, for instance—he could lose the option of keeping his marriage without actually deciding to do so. Happily, he bought it all and with enthusiasm. Joe accepted that these were meaningful goals. These were goals he could achieve even if they made no difference to Jane and whether or not the marriage stayed intact. He was particularly interested in acting in a way that would enhance his self-respect.

Joe and I spent several therapy sessions together, during which I attempted to help him to grasp the distinction between what he was trying to do and instrumental activity. He was not trying to be nice so that his wife would reciprocate or do something he wanted; that would be both transparent and false, not to mention useless. He was trying to be nice or, to put it better, nicer mainly just because he needed to do so. If self-respect was his real goal, there could not exist any ulterior motives.

In subsequent weeks, I listened to Joe's reports of interaction and coached him in behaving decently and honorably. I emphasized that the behavioral objectives would still be operative even if he decided to end his marriage. He then would still have the choice between ending it honorably or getting himself out through some sleazy back door. Coaching thus begun, we spent a dozen or more sessions examining his conduct and pointing out "nicer" and "cleaner" ways to act. I did not attempt to get him to be less angry with his wife, only to try to keep his anger focused on the actual object of his anger (losing Jane's love, as he saw it) and not attacking every target of opportunity.

A couple of subtexts were in process while Joe was attempting to improve himself through coaching. In the process, a positive and optimistic relationship developed between Joe and me. We related well to each other, and this relationship appeared to foster healing of the nurturing and narcissistic wounds that he had experienced earlier in life. The chief hazard that seemed likely to undo his improvement would be the perception of being abandoned by me, also. A second subtext was the gradual change in Joe's tone when he spoke about his marriage; thoughts of ending it faded gradually. And his anger over Jane's extramarital episodes gradually gave way to the more (but far from totally) situationally based annoyance over her continuing therapy. Jane would not tell him what was going on in her therapeutic sessions, and I did not know. And it did appear to Joe that memory after memory was being uncovered in an endless stream. He wanted her to be done with therapy. In other words, Joe's wish to have his wife back changed from a global need for history never to have happened to a focused wish that might someday actually be fulfilled. I worried that his negative affect was being crowded into a smaller and smaller space—as in a balloon—and worried that there might soon be a loud pop.

Joe began to express anger at his wife's therapist in part because of the cost of therapy, which realistically was difficult. He also was spending money for his own therapy; although Joe was spending $150 per month, it was much less than Jane was spending. Another issue was the not so small matter of intimate secrets that Jane apparently was sharing with her therapist but not with Joe. Considering the revelations already made, the thought of further secrets upset Joe substantially. Accordingly, in his mind, his wife's therapy gradually took the place of her infidelity, and her therapist took the place of the other man. Partly I believed and partly I merely hoped that this problem was more manageable, and was assured by Joe that my wish and belief were essentially correct. During this period of coaching Joe, I received another call from Jane's therapist. This time his message was different. He requested that I meet with Jane; however, there were restrictions. He asked that I meet with Jane without Joe, and just once. It appeared that the therapist had heard of Joe's anger toward him and was worried that he might be the target of physical violence by Joe. Interestingly, apart from Joe being a working-class man, little evidence existed to support such a fear. I had not discovered, and Jane's therapist seemed not to have discovered, any violent incidents involving Joe since he was a child. Jane's therapist believed Joe was biased against the ethnic group to which the therapist belonged. Contrary to that belief, Joe had uncovered enough evidence about his own biological origins to discover that, "Hell, I'm one, too." Clearly, Joe was not the only person in this situation who was tilting against a fantasy adversary. Still, I was eager to actually see Jane, and I agreed to the proposed meeting.

THE CRITICAL INCIDENT

Jane arrived on time for the session. She was a pleasant-looking woman in her middle thirties, two years younger than Joe; she initially appeared very nervous. Later, when she was more relaxed, she disclosed that when she arrived she felt as if she "was walking into the lion's den." She was not a bit frightened of her husband, nor thought it even remotely likely that he would be a danger to her therapist, so the pattern of apprehension seemed a little odd. Her therapist was afraid of her husband, and she was afraid of her husband's therapist. She was not able to articulate exactly what she was afraid would happen, and I still do not know what kind of fantasy beast I had become to her.

Overall, our conversation was pleasant and friendly; but Jane had not come just to pass the time of day. Jane was a woman on a mission. She wanted what spouses have wanted from marital therapists for as long as marital therapists have existed—namely, that the therapist change the other spouse in ways that the presenting spouse prescribes. In this particular case, Jane spent the greater part of the hour building the case that Joe should learn more patience and not be in such a rush to see her "cured." Since I already had spent several months urging her husband to be patient, I heartily agreed with her and even agreed that I would try to impress upon Joe still further the need for patience. At this juncture I suggested, as mildly as I could manage, that she wanted her husband to be more patient and to be so immediately. She looked at me as if she had not really seen me before, immediately understanding me yet acting as if this was a brand new idea that changed everything. An abrupt change occurred in the tone of our interaction. The remainder of the session was spent in much more gentle talk, reminiscing about married life with the man who once had been the boy of her dreams, before she began to hate dreaming. In retrospect, it appeared that she and Joe were at the very edge of giving up animosity; only a gentle puff of hot air (my specialty) was enough to push them past it. In other words, the steam had already left the anger, but a rationale was needed—some excuse for giving it up.

I did not see Jane again. Her therapist told me that he was relieved by her conversation with me. However, the household tensions seen by both therapists did not actually go away; instead, they dwindled and faded. Joe did not perceive the situation or anyone to have changed substantially; the difference was that now he "did not mind things as much." I attempted, with partial success, to portray recent history as really a very good break for Joe. Previously, he believed he was married to a Barbie doll. This never was true, but he saw such a small part of his wife that it might as well have been true. Now he knew that he was married to a real woman with more blemishes than Barbie but also with a lot more substance. Had he been of a slightly more generous frame of mind, he might have thought that he had much for which to thank his wife's therapist. Joe bought this line of reasoning partially and a little grudgingly, but he never really gave up the idea that the simpler life he once believed he had was not so bad.

DISCUSSION

This story about Joe brings with it a collection of subtext or, more accurately, editorials. The major political issues of gender and social-class prejudice permeate the story. The idea that the very concepts of "patient" or "mental health" can diminish people informed my decisions for working with Joe. Earlier thoughts (Ryder, 1987) about the nature of therapy and the place of technique have certainly evolved more but are still with me and are central. Questions occur about apparent turning points and what, if anything, they mean.

The Role of the Critical Incident in Getting Therapy Unstuck

I did not believe therapy to have been stuck or that the incident in question "caused" anything in particular. I, however, believe that Joe was stuck and my discussion with Jane was in a sense a turning point, but not because I had such a dramatic influence, benign or otherwise, on Jane. In other words, the existence of a change in direction does not mean that the therapist made it happen. People who work with marriages learn to expect and be cautious of apparent negative turning points. The marital relationship may appear to be getting better gradually, then something may happen that seems to set off an apparently disproportionate negative reaction, and everything comes apart. Sometimes a spouse feels that the opportunity to leave easily is slipping away and leaves before it is too late. Sometimes an important issue has been ignored; sometimes negative affect remains—but without its earlier justification—and explodes anyway. Therapists probably are not eager to take credit for making negative turning points happen; perhaps we should not take too much credit for positive ones either.

Suppose it was really true that my comment about patience "caused" some dramatic change. Why did I make the comment? Was it because I was smart that day? Was it because both of us in the room had some sense—not necessarily a conscious sense—that this was the next step in the dance we were doing? Jane's reaction suggests that the thought I was expressing was practically in the tip of her tongue. Perhaps if I had said nothing, she would have said the same thing without my prompting. In other words, I believe that my comment is best understood as just one part of a flowing process between Jane and me, which in turn was one part of a relational process involving (at least) four people—Jane, Jane's therapist, Joe, and me.

Various labels, usually metaphors, are useful in thinking about therapists. My favorite is the midwife metaphor (Ryder, 1987). Midwives make birth easier, but they do not make it happen. To say that a baby is born because the mother is on the delivery table is to reverse cause and effect. In therapy as well, what seems like a precipitating event, even a planned intervention, may be only a result or correlate of some anticipation that a birth is ready to happen. Another view is that some events in therapy *do* sometimes have a powerful effect on the later course of treatment, while they themselves are a result of earlier events. The therapist may say or do something that seems to be irregular, that is not in the program but is straight from her or his heart— the impassive psychoanalyst, for instance, who loses it and says, "Go ahead and kill yourself then, you goddamn fool!" The client hears that something exceptionally authentic has happened and is moved. Note that such events, by their nature, are not planned. They usually are a violation of any plans the therapist had made, since they are instances of a real person breaking through the professional role. Here too, the therapist does not make it happen. In fact, it happens in spite of therapist's intentions.

Implications of the Critical Incident for Therapy

Mainly I think of most such incidents only as markers. The energy gradually goes out of some complaint, but the cognitive framework that rationalizes it remains. In effect, a real tiger gradually becomes a paper tiger. It only takes a small match to get rid of a paper tiger, and the beast will probably blow away by itself. Since the tiger is still inflated and looks real before the match or the breeze hits it, its disappearance seems more magical than it really is.

THE OUTCOME OF THERAPY

Subsequent to my visit with Jane, Joe moved into what appeared to be a second phase of treatment. He gradually stopped talking about current events and reminisced about his childhood. He talked much about his history of losses and of never really feeling that he belonged anywhere. Coaching gradually faded away, as did questions about whether to remain married. To an observer, this phase would resemble traditional psychotherapy. As far as I am aware, I did not manipulate these changes into existence. If anyone made conscious decisions about what we would discuss, it was Joe. After awhile, these topics seemed to interest him less and he appeared relatively contented. At this juncture, he appeared to be more relaxed than when he began therapy and perhaps more relaxed than he had been in some time. He also appeared to be experiencing more warmth in his life and was having fun—with his wife, with his music, and in his interactions with friends at work. He shared that it felt good to make music in front of an appreciative audience. He disclosed that at his day job, a female co-worker appeared to be interested in him. He was proud that he did not reciprocate her interest; it felt good to walk away from her. Thus he got his turn to reject a person and to feel loyal to his wife, all in the same act.

Outcomes from Jane's point of view are and will remain a mystery to me. All I know is that I met with her once and she left looking happier and much less anxious than when she arrived. I did not terminate with Joe. I guess I was anxious about introducing the topic; he never did. Accordingly, for awhile I met with him biweekly instead of weekly, then monthly, and finally only at his request. Joe has not called in approximately one year, and I last heard from him and Jane via the Christmas card they sent me. I would not be surprised to hear from him again, but I would be very surprised if he were in a panic such as he was when I first saw him. I guess I indefinitely will remain a part of Joe's support system.

POSTSCRIPT

The view of therapy as relationship frees us. Our choice of what to do can be wider and more imaginative. We have to choose something, certainly, but what choice we make is to some extent personal—personal in that it is comfortable for us as individuals, and personal in the sense of it working with the kinds of relationships we have with our clients. Also, freedom from categorical prejudices against our clients translates into freedom for us to be more helpful. It is trite to say, but still true, that imagining any member of a social group to be prone to fit the group's worst stereotypes is not only objectionable, it limits us. It also limits us if we fail to see any redeeming features, anything of which to be proud, in the subculture of some social group. What we may have to pay for this kind of freedom may be a willingness to notice flaws in ourselves and maybe even sometimes to feel ashamed.

REFERENCE

Ryder, Robert G. (1987). *The realistic therapist: Modesty and relativism in research and therapy.* Newbury Park, CA: Sage Publications.

Commentary

A Patient Therapist

Sandra M. Stith

Commentator Background

Fifty-two years old, white, female, PhD, eighteen years MFT practice.

Practice Setting

University MFT clinical faculty; limited private practice.

Theoretical Perspective

I used a solution-focused approach to examine this case.

I often joke with students in our marriage and family therapy program about the miracle cases in many of the textbooks they read. After telling the students about miraculous interventions that overnight change chaotic families with drug-abusing adolescents into calm, organized families with polite, respectful teens, I often tell them, "The follow-up is that Johnny goes to Harvard and becomes a Rhodes scholar." In this case report, Ryder does not present a miracle intervention or a dramatic critical incident that turns the case from what appears to be hopeless to what appears to be a masterful success. Instead, Ryder's approach is the solid, patient work of a wise, experienced therapist who appears to trust the therapeutic process as well as trust that clients have the strength to do what they need to do to effectively heal themselves.

SOME GOOD POINTS ABOUT THE CASE

Ericksonian Influence

Ryder does not tell us and we do not have any way of knowing if his approach to therapy with Joe was influenced by the work of Milton Erickson.

However, after reading this case, I am reminded of the kind of hopeful, patient work that Erickson might have done. In this regard, I am also reminded of a story Michele Weiner-Davis tells about Milton Erickson. When Erickson was a boy, he discovered a stray horse on his family's farm. He mounted the horse and rode it back to the farm of its owners. The surprised owners asked Erickson how he knew to whom the horse belonged. He reportedly replied that he did not know; he just kept the horse on the road and the horse found its way home. Similar to Erickson, all Ryder really needed to do was to help Joe and Jane to access their individual and combined abilities to be patient; with time, they did their own work and found the solution that was appropriate for them. Of course, it was not quite that simple. Ryder's ability to relate to Joe and to build a relationship in which Joe was able to trust Ryder, trust the therapeutic process, and access his ability to be patient was a key factor. As a therapist who looks at clinical intervention from a feminist-informed solution-focused approach, I am impressed by the manner in which Ryder's patience and wisdom helped this couple to reclaim their relationship.

Patience Born of Experience

Initially Ryder wanted to see both Joe and Jane, but Jane's therapist forbade her to see him. I wondered to what extent did Jane participate in making that decision and whether her therapist allowed her to have a voice in her own treatment. Were I Joe's therapist of record, I might have been tempted to learn more about Jane's role in the decision not to see Ryder and about whether her therapist was enacting a stereotypical powerful male versus helpless female scenario with her. Ryder, however, did not raise that issue; instead, he elected to focus on what the client offered rather than what was not offered. I believe that he made the right decision.

Given Jane's therapist's refusal, Ryder accepted that his only option was to see Joe alone. In actuality, however, he had another option. He could have held a core belief shared by some family therapists—couples in therapy can only be seen conjointly. Accepting that belief as fact, he could have refused to see Joe without Jane. Arguably, had Ryder seen the couple conjointly, it is possible that therapy with them might have moved more quickly. Ryder obviously believes, as do I, that no "one way exists" to work with couples. Consequently, to take a firm, controlling stand about the "right way" to conduct couples therapy would disempower clients and in this case would have cast Ryder in the same controlling role as Jane's therapist. Rather than doing so, he trusted his experiences and did not allow the conventional wisdom about the "right way" to do couples therapy to prevent him from being helpful to the couple. He patiently saw Joe alone and waited for the opportunity to see Jane; such flexibility is a kind of learned wisdom.

Joe came to the first session feeling abandoned, desperate, and furious because of Jane's infidelity. Ryder was perceptive in understanding that although a part of Joe wanted to end the marriage, another part of him was very clear that he did not want to lose his daughter. Ryder also recognized that if Joe were going to be able to have time to make a clear decision about his next steps in the marriage, he needed to be able to keep his options open. To that end, he needed to behave calmly, not to start fights, and not to become violent with his wife. Specifically, he needed to access his ability to be patient. Ryder clearly recognized that Joe, like most humans, had within him the strength of character and the ability to be patient but needed help to make the decision to allow his patience to emerge. Ryder does not explicitly subscribe to a solution-focused approach, but his emphasis on developing/enhancing the strengths of his clients closely resembles a solution-focused approach and reverberated with me.

As the therapy progressed, the importance of Jane's past infidelity declined as a therapeutic issue for Joe. Instead, her developing relationship with her therapist became the issue central to Joe's concerns about his marriage. Again, Ryder used the theme of patience in his approach with Joe. He could have elected to overfunction and attempt to influence Jane's therapist, or he could have elected to confront Joe about his need to control Jane's access to therapy. He did neither; instead, he patiently coached Joe to be patient.

When Ryder's patience paid off and Jane's therapist permitted her to see Ryder for one session, he listened to Jane's request that Joe change his behaviors. When he gently suggested to Jane that she wanted Joe to be more patient and to do so immediately, he recognized that his suggestion struck a chord with Jane. The theme of patience again was a key factor in helping Jane to recognize that change takes time. Ryder commented that, in retrospect, Jane and Joe appeared to be at the very edge of giving up animosity, and only a gentle puff of hot air (his specialty) was enough to push them past it. In other words, the steam had already left the anger, but a rationale was needed, some excuse for giving up their animosity. This explanation reminded me again of Erickson's explanation of how the horse found its way home. Like Ryder, Erickson did not tell the horse how to get home; he merely kept the horse on track and the horse found its way home on its own.

CONCLUDING THOUGHTS

Since Jane appeared to have had a positive experience with Ryder, I wondered if there might come a time when Jane's individual therapy had been completed or was at a different stage such that the couple might decide to come together for conjoint therapy. I appreciated that Ryder left the door open to Joe and, like Ryder, I would not be surprised if Joe or the couple returned at some future time. The kind of respectful, patient work described in this case could be helpful as a brief, intermittent intervention for couples who both have experienced trauma early on and who probably could use support at various points in their life cycle.

Commentary

Be a Good Person

Kevin P. Lyness

Commentator Background

Thirty-four years old, white, male, PhD, MFT, fifteen years clinical practice, nine years MFT experience.

Practice Setting

University MFT clinic, limited private practice.

Theoretical Perspective

I used a solution-focused approach complemented by a narrative and contextual perspective to comment on this case.

This case poignantly illustrates one worrisome aspect of couples therapy—some clients often present alone for therapy to address couples and/or relationship issues. In this case report, Joe presented alone for therapy although he complained of a couples (marital) problem. Ryder, understanding the importance of "the other perspective," attempted to see Joe conjointly with Jane but was thwarted by her therapist of record. In an ideal world, therapists faced with this situation either could refuse to see clients who present for couples therapy without their spouse/partner or they would see only couples. However, as Ryder has observed, to do so would deny therapeutic assistance to the very clients who need it. Again, in a perfect world, individual therapists would cooperate so that treatment is coordinated in the best interest of the clients. Sadly, as was the case with this couple, such cooperation/coordination is not always possible.

SOME GOOD POINTS ABOUT THE CASE

Much in this case report I agreed with, much I could relate to, little I could criticize, and much I could applaud with regard to Ryder's approach to a less-than-optimal therapeutic situation; I would expect this caliber of therapy from a clinician with thirty-seven years of experience. And having experienced therapeutic situations similar to those faced by Ryder—I often struggle to find ways to help clients who present alone but whose presenting complaints are of a relational/marital problem—I commend him for making the best of the situation by being flexible and willing to work with Joe alone. I also commend Ryder for his work with Joe and the goals he formulated for Joe and Joe's relationship with Jane. He appears to have a very good grasp of how to design tasks that met Joe's needs and to construct for Joe goals that Joe readily and heartily accepted (Ryder asserts, he "bought it all"). Doing so helped Ryder to develop a strong therapeutic relationship with Joe. I admire the manner in which Ryder helped Joe to overcome his annoyance and anger about Jane's seemingly protracted therapy and continuous surfacing of memories. Helping clients to deal with such sensitive issues is very difficult and can be even more difficult when only one half of the couple is present in therapy.

POINTS OF CONVERGENCE AND DIVERGENCE WITH RYDER

Therapeutic Goal Setting and Collaboration

I approach therapy from a solution-focused and narrative perspective. Both solution-focused and narrative therapies focus on the development of well-formed treatment goals as the basis for therapy and work from a collaborative model. Consequently, when viewed from these perspectives, Ryder's description of his work with Joe raises questions for me about therapeutic goal setting and collaboration. Given the manner in which the therapeutic goals were formulated, I question, "Whose goals are these?" and wonder about the extent of Joe's participation in the formulation of those goals. Clearly, the therapeutic goals appear to be Ryder's goals for Joe rather than Joe's individually identified and articulated goals or those set by the collaboration of Joe and Ryder. In this regard, Ryder asserts, "Of course he wanted to be a man," as if this were an obvious goal. He also states, "I knew that I wanted to build on Joe's present strengths . . ." and discusses his plan to coach Joe to become a better man, as well as his plans for Joe to take his time and not make any hasty decisions or take imprudent actions that would jeopardize his marital relationship.

Typically in my clinical practice I routinely begin therapy with the client's goals for himself or herself and work with the client to achieve those goals. To that end, I directly explore the client's goals and expectations for therapy and collaboratively develop a treatment plan to achieve those goals. Accordingly, the beginning phase of therapy focuses on a collaborative search for "well-formed treatment goals" (see De Jong and Berg, 1998). Collaboratively developing viable treatment goals with clients fits well with Ryder's beliefs about the primacy of the therapeutic relationship. Although Ryder is emphatic that "practiced" techniques, such as circular questions or active listening, may negatively impact the therapeutic relationship precisely because they are "practiced," I strongly believe that working collaboratively with clients to formulate their treatment goals helps to enhance that part of the therapeutic relationship. Many conceptualizations of the therapeutic relationship identify and discuss three necessary dimensions: bond, task, and goal. Based on these conceptualizations, a viable therapeutic relationship would include the development of a collaborative agreement in each of the three areas. However, for Ryder, as demonstrated in this case, the building blocks of a viable therapeutic relationship appear to be focused more on the bond dimension and less focused on the task and goal dimensions.

With regard to therapeutic collaboration, I believe that neither therapists nor clients are solely responsible for the direction of treatment. Rather, therapists and clients are equally responsible for the direction of treatment and each may legitimately, in collaboration with the other, formulate and initiate treatment goals. In this regard, Duncan, Solovey, and Rusk (1992) have asserted that the client is in charge of the *content* of therapy, while the therapist is in charge of the *process*. This conceptualization recognizes that therapists are experts with regard the therapeutic process, but clients are experts on their lives. This perspective is consistent and fits well with my perception of the therapeutic process. Unfortunately, in the case of Joe and Jane, putting this conceptualization into action was difficult because although Ryder identified Joe's problem as a couples (relationship) problem, he only had Joe with whom to work.

Alternative Conceptual Frames

Ryder does not conceptualize his therapeutic approach with Joe from a narrative perspective. But that much of his work with Joe is similar to and fits well with the narrative therapeutic approach (Freedman and Combs, 1996; White and Epston, 1990) is inescapable. Specifically, Ryder's coaching process with Joe is similar to a narrative or solution-focused therapeutic approach. He essentially helped Joe to become the kind of person that Joe wanted to be (i.e., "a real man"). The primary therapeutic focus of narrative therapists is to help clients to reauthor their lives, develop alternative ways of seeing their world, see unique outcomes to their problem(s) (similar to the solution-focused notion of exceptions), and retrospectively to discover evidence that the unique outcomes may have been occurring all along. Accordingly, much like a narrative or solution-focused therapist, Ryder helped Joe to focus on those aspects of his life that were satisfactory and to direct his energies toward achieving his goals rather than to continue to be mired in those aspects that were not moving him toward his goals.

WHAT I MIGHT HAVE DONE SIMILARLY

As I read Ryder's description of therapy with Joe and his brief contact with Jane, I believe that, had I been Joe's therapist of record, my approach might have resembled Ryder's because I would have employed many of the same strategies. Ryder does not mention whether he assigned Joe any homework or out-of-session tasks. However, had he done so, I suspect our assignments might have been very similar. For example, I would have asked Joe to identify and discuss the times when he interacted with his wife in ways that made him feel good, ways when he was able to be angry with her without damaging their relationship, and ways that allowed him to connect emotionally with her. The goal would be to maximize the behaviors that contribute to those occurrences and decrease the opposite behaviors. Like Ryder, I would have worried that there "might soon be a loud pop" when Joe's negative affect finally reached a dangerously high level. However, unlike Ryder, I most likely would have addressed directly with Joe my fears that he possibly might "go over the edge" and, as a countermeasure, I would have emphasized relapse prevention with Joe. To that end, I would have discussed the realistic possibility of relapse as well as ways in which he might relapse. That discussion would have focused on the warning signs of relapse and strategies he could use to avoid problems if it appeared that he was heading toward relapse (occasionally my experience as an addictions counselor rears its head).

WHAT I MIGHT HAVE DONE DIFFERENTLY

Given my different (from Ryder) theoretical orientation and clinical approach, it is doubtful that a similar critical incident would have occurred had I been the therapist of record for this couple. However, even if a similar event had occurred and I had been their therapist, I would have punctuated the process differently. It is more likely that I would have identified another incident as critical and would have conceptualized treatment differently. Although I also may have "coached" Joe, I would have used a narrative or solution-focused metaphor, mainly because I never have participated in an organized sport and am unfamiliar with the advantages of sports metaphors.

Specifically, I would have focused on building a strong therapeutic alliance with Joe and given him credit for the changes he was making in therapy. Accordingly, therapy with Joe would have explored ways in which he was acting like the person he wanted to be and would have helped him to identify, maintain, and maximize those behaviors.

In addition, consistent with one of my frequent subtexts in couples therapy (whether with one or both partners), I would have focused on helping Joe to discover ways to feel validated and in turn to validate Jane. Based on Jane's brief and Joe's extended interaction with Ryder, clearly each member of this couple appeared to be seeking validation from the other. Joe's need for validation appears to result from his history of abandonment (a great sense of entitlement). Previous to discovering Jane's infidelity, Joe's idealized picture of his marriage and his relationship with Jane helped him to feel validated; Jane's affair was invalidating. I agree with Ryder's statements that Joe "ought to" behave well toward his wife without the expectation that she would reciprocate in kind. From a contextual perspective, giving credit is rewarding because it helps one to feel like a whole person. I believe that this is the same goal toward which Ryder was working and which he labeled building self-respect.

With regard to the critical incident, I am unsure about what I might have done differently because the incident occurred when Joe, Ryder's client, was not in the room. However, although both partners were not in the room, I firmly believe that both Jane and Joe were clients. In the session with Jane, I might have said something to her that would have helped to change the meaning of the interactions in a similar manner that Ryder's comment about patience seemed to have done. Viewed from a narrative perspective, perhaps Ryder's statement about patience did help Jane to recognize that another story existed, one in which both she and Joe played a part in effecting change. Certainly, one unique outcome of this case was Jane's changed perspective subsequent to becoming aware that she impatiently was asking for patience. Her work with her own therapist and Joe's work with Ryder very likely prepared the couple to continue to change following the critical incident. Of course, the therapy that leads up to the incident and what follows all serve to set up and solidify change. This is also the implication of Ryder's metaphor of the midwife.

PSYCHOTHERAPEUTIC THEORY, TECHNIQUE, AND CHANGE

With regard to theory and what my particular theories of change would say about the critical incident, I cannot say for certain. However, like Ryder, I believe that the therapeutic relationship is the core basis for change and often the most meaningful incidents in therapy are the ones that come from the heart—and not from a particular technique—although I might term it as "coming out in dialogue" given my contextual bent. I concur with Ryder's belief that critical incidents in psychotherapy are unplanned irregular occurrences straight from the therapist's heart and can occur in therapeutic relationships in spite of the particular theoretical perspective of the therapist.

In this regard, some of the most intense critical incidents I have experienced in my own clinical work were often highly irregular therapeutic occurrences. For example, after working with a couple for several sessions, I had been unsuccessful in interrupting their negative pattern of mutual putdowns that kept them mired in conflict. During one session in which each partner was at his or her best putting down the other, I commented to them, "You don't even fucking *like* each other!" This certainly is not recommended therapeutic intervention; had I thought about what I was about to say, I probably would not have said it. However, despite the unorthodoxy of my comment, the couple later reported that that comment was the most influential thing I had said to them throughout therapy. They experienced the comment as a "wake-up call" that motivated them to reevaluate their relationship. I believe that this is what Ryder refers to as "exceptional authenticity." The question, then, is "How do we (therapists) foster authenticity in our work?"

As Ryder notes, this view of therapy is freeing, in that we authentically can be ourselves. However, I wondered about his preceding statement that "choice of 'technique' is a relatively minor matter" and that practiced tactics have a negative impact on the relationship. Although I believe this to be true to the extent that such tactics are inauthentic, I also believe that it is important to learn techniques that are theoretically consistent to the point that they become authentic. For example, active listening is a technique that I use effortlessly and believe is very helpful in the therapeutic relationship.

I also believe that technique can be important in therapy, but it is effective only when a goodness of fit exists with the personality of the therapist and his or her beliefs about the therapeutic process. For example, I am aware that my way of conducting therapy is not identical to Steve de Shazer's solution-focused way of doing so, nor to Michael White's way of conducting narrative therapy. Rather, what I do in therapy is what fits for me. However, I learned techniques and theories in order that I would know what fits with me as a person and what does not. It is interesting to note that most of the current models of marital and family therapy are associated with a specific person or group of people. These theorists discovered a way of thinking and working that fit so well with who they are that it was effective with their clients. Accordingly, it is important that each of us as therapists discovers what fits for us in order that we can each be authentic and continue to foster critical incidents.

ISSUES OF GENDER AND CHANGE

The gender-directed title of Ryder's case report—"Be a Man"—and his statement that "major political issues of gender and social-class prejudice permeate the [couple's] story" beg comment. Not having actually worked with these clients, I believe that while gender may have been an important variable, it did not necessarily need to be. In my clinical work, I tend to take a more gender-neutral stance, I doubt that I would use such a title for a case report, and I probably never would conceptualize my cases in such a gender-typed way. Accordingly, instead of the title "Be A Man," I probably would have used, "Be the Kind of *Person* You Want to Be," or "Be a Good Person." Of course, that is not as clever a title, but it would get my message across. I believe that the same goals—giving Joe room to be a different person and to act in ways that allow him integrity—could be achieved with a less gender-directed stance. Joe does not have to be a "man" to achieve this. In fact, the characteristics, such as self-respect, he was attempting to build would be laudable goals for anyone. On the other hand, there are probably times when working from a gendered perspective is important. In this case, given Joe's working-class status, perhaps this was the more viable approach to use. I am sure that it was not the only approach. I also am equally sure that the approach Ryder used is the one that is comfortable and provides the best fit for him.

CONCLUDING THOUGHTS

The description of the therapy reported here clearly is not brief therapy. In an age of managed care, therapists often do not have the luxury of thirty sessions. It is clear that Ryder may have been experiencing some of this pressure given his comment about ". . . leaving the health care system behind." From a diagnostic (i.e., DSM-IV-TR) perspective, I suspect Ryder is right. Yet this case reflects much of the work marital and family therapists do and also reflects some of the many goals, such as increasing positive self-esteem and rebuilding viable relationships, that we help our clients to achieve. I do not believe that we need to feel overly constrained by either managed care or the health care system, yet we need to find ways to work within these systems as well, in ways that do not, as Ryder notes, diminish people. Quite a task for our field, and one that raises more questions than it provides answers.

REFERENCES

De Jong, P. and Berg, I. K. (1998). *Interviewing for solutions*. Pacific Grove, CA: Brooks/Cole.
Duncan, B. L., Solovey, A. D., and Rusk, G. S. (1992). *Changing the rules: A client-directed approach to therapy*. New York: The Guilford Press.

Freedman, J. and Combs, G. (1996). *Narrative therapy: The social construction of preferred realities.* New York: W. W. Norton.

White, M. and Epston, D. (1990). *Narrative means to therapeutic ends.* New York: W. W. Norton.

CASE 6

Sentenced to Life or United in Death

Volker Thomas

Therapist Background

Currently: Fifty-one years old, white, male, PhD, twenty-two years MFT practice. When I saw this family: Forty-six years old, PhD, seventeen years MFT practice.

Practice Setting

Currently: limited private practice to complement university teaching. When I saw this family: very limited private practice—three to four clients per week.

Client Characteristics

Jim (age forty-five) and Sue (age forty-three) and their sons Sam (age nineteen) and Joe (age seventeen) were a white, lower-middle-class family that also included Sam's fiancée/wife Kim (age nineteen). Jim was a minister by training but now was employed as a sales clerk in a local hardware store. Sue was employed as a teller in a local bank. Sam attended college part time, worked part time at a local store, and was getting ready to move in with his fiancée. Joe was a high school senior.

Length of Treatment

This family was seen for fifteen family sessions, ten couple sessions, and forty-eight individual sessions over an eighteen-month period. The critical incident session occurred after nine family sessions, ten couple sessions, and thirty-five individual sessions.

Theoretical Perspective

A combination of strategic, intergenerational, and experiential approaches were used with this family.

PRESENTING PROBLEM

Initially, the Smith family came to therapy because Joe was failing classes in school, was truant, and had been arrested for drunk driving. Both parents agreed that they no longer could control Joe. They felt that it would be better for him to move out of the family's home and face the consequences of life, even if that meant that he would not graduate from high school. Sam, Joe's brother, was the only family member to defend Joe during the first session. Sam stated that Joe was a "good kid" who "got in with the wrong crowd." He asserted that if his mother and father could "get their act together" and support Joe, he could still graduate from high school and not "land in the street," as the parents predicted. Curious about the apparent generational coalitions and the wisdom Sam expressed, I asked the two adolescents, "Do you think your mother and father could make it without you, if the two of you were okay, did not get into trouble, and moved out?" Sam replied that he was engaged and he and his fiancée had just signed a lease for an apartment. They planned to move into the apartment within the next couple of weeks. Joe looked at me with an angry grin and said, "If I were to move out, too, Mom would go crazy and Dad would run away, because he could not stand it any longer."

I looked at the parents quizzically but said nothing. Jim avoided eye contact with me and Sue's face was flushed. With a deep sadness in her voice, she said, "I guess Joe is right. I don't know what's going to happen when both boys are gone. They have held this family together over the past four or five years." In response to my question about what had happened during that period, Sue told the following story.

Jim had been a minister in a small town; Sue was a homemaker, wife, and mother. Together, they managed their church with great compassion and success. Approximately five years ago a conflict within the congregation led to Jim's resignation and the family's move to the city in which they resided at the time that I was seeing them. With a friend's help, Jim was hired by another small church for a few months; the church elders subsequently forced him out because he did not meet their expectations. Discouraged and depressed, Jim took a low-paying job as a sales clerk in a local hardware store. Following this job change, Jim's personality seemed to change from that of a compassionate, calm, optimistic person to that of a withdrawn, depressed, sometimes agitated pessimist. To make ends meet and against Jim's wishes, Sue accepted a position as a teller in a local bank. As the family declined socially, Sam and Joe's school performance and behavior deteriorated such that Sam barely graduated from high school. Following high school graduation, Sam worked at a minimum-wage job in a discount store until he met his fiancée. At the time of our sessions, he was attending college part time and working at the store. Joe always had been a rather quiet and well-adjusted boy until the family moved to the present town. He stated that he missed his grandparents and friends in the town the family recently had left and expressed concern about his dad's well-being. He expressed intense anger toward his mom, whom he labeled "crazy and hysterical." He perceived her to "blow everything out of proportion."

This family's presenting problem appeared to be a fairly straightforward leaving-home case, à la Jay Haley (1980). I congratulated Joe for his concern about his parents and for bringing his worries for them to the forefront by acting out. I also thanked Sam for supporting his younger brother and for sharing his concerns for his mother and father. Given the presenting problem, I suggested that Sue, Jim, and I meet for awhile and then include Sam and Joe later when the parents were ready to let them go. The boys smiled and agreed immediately to my plan. Jim and Sue appeared confused and looked apprehensively at each other, as if they were saying, "We brought Joe to be fixed and now you send him home and tell us we are the bad guys." Sensing their apprehension, I complimented the parents for their courage to come in as a family and for their concerns about their sons. I reframed the problem as a need to feel better about themselves so that they could have the confidence to succeed in their marriage once the boys were gone. In addition, I pointed out that Joe especially needed to feel confident that he could grow up without getting into trouble as a means of keeping his mother and father from dealing with their marital issues. To allay the parents' skepticism, the family and I struck a therapeutic deal. The boys did not have to come to therapy for the next five sessions unless Joe got into trouble again. Joe agreed and Sam volunteered to keep an eye on him. Concurrently, the parents agreed to come in for five sessions of marital therapy. If successful, we planned on having a final family session in six weeks.

The five sessions with Jim and Sue went well—at least I thought so. Joe stopped acting out and his grades improved dramatically. The parents grieved the loss of their ministerial life and their social decline. They processed the shame and guilt they felt toward their sons and their family of origins and promised to support each other. During the final family session, everyone was relieved and thankful for the successful treatment that had saved the peace in the family and Joe's upcoming graduation.

Three months later, Jim called to inform me that Joe had been caught shoplifting; they had had to bail him out of the county jail. Sue became so upset about the incident to the extent that she decompensated and had to be admitted to a psychiatric hospital; she was diagnosed major depression with psychotic features and acute suicidal ideation. Jim asked if I would be willing to work with Sue following her discharge from the hospital. He was willing to come with her and to do everything that would help her to get better soon. When the couple came to see me, Sue was taking an antipsychotic and an antidepressive medication and appeared quite sedated; Jim presented as helpless and depressed. Sue expressed anger that she was the designated client now and vehemently complained about all the injustices to which she had been subjected over the years. She asked for an individual session. During this session, she disclosed that Jim had sexually abused her for many years and that she had kept silent about it because she did not want to "rock the boat" and jeopardize Jim's career while he still was a minister.

Subsequent to Jim's loss of his minister's job and when Joe began to act out and to get into trouble, it became increasingly more difficult for Sue to keep quiet. Having to keep the secret eventually "drove her crazy." Sue expressed feeling relieved that the secret was out now. She, however, did not know what to do about it. I encouraged her to express her anger to Jim in one of their sessions. When she did so, Jim patiently listened to her but did not acknowledge her anger. In response, he expressed the hope that Sue would be cured of her mental illness soon so that they could continue the "good marriage" they used to have.

Sue was outraged and decided to separate from Jim. She asked him to move out so that she and Joe (Sam and his fiancée had moved into their apartment already) could stay in the house in which they currently were living. Jim agreed to do as she asked, but, to Sue's surprise, Joe moved in with his dad. Sue had believed that beneath Joe's expressed hatred of her was a deep love for her and that he would live with her after the separation.

At that time the family felt strongly that they did not want anymore family sessions. Jim, Sam, and Joe blamed me for driving Sue into the mental institution and for pushing her to separate from Jim. Despite my confusion about who was victim and who was perpetrator in this family, I agreed to continue to see Sue individually for support. In collaboration with her psychiatrist, Sue stabilized within the next few weeks but still had a long road of pain and hope ahead of her.

THE THERAPEUTIC SITUATION PRIOR
TO THE CRITICAL INCIDENT

Sue struggled through the first four months of individual sessions. For example, she experienced frequent flashbacks of being abused by her husband and as a result was increasingly depressed and isolated herself. Jim's family blamed Sue for abandoning Jim and their sons. Sue always had enjoyed a closeness with her in-laws, but now she felt incredibly guilty and was tempted to settle into a victim's role, which she expressed through frequent suicidal ideation. Concurrently, she had lost her bank teller's job because of frequent absences and unsatisfactory work performance. In addition, she entered a downward spiral of depression and isolation, could not pay the house rent, and was forced to move out. As a result, she was homeless for several weeks until she was able to rent a small efficiency, despite being unemployed. From Sue's perspective, at the bottom of the depressive spiral loomed suicide as the only escape. Several times she was at the brink of involuntary hospitalization, but managed to pull herself together and stay alive. During this period, therapy was very frustrating for me and for Sue, and several times I considered having her hospitalized just to get a break from her—although I framed it differently at the time.

Then two unexpected events changed the course of therapy. One day, Sue came to therapy more severely depressed than usual. She reported that Jim had had a seizure at work and had been rushed to the emergency room. The family later learned that Jim had a cancerous brain tumor that had been growing slowly for years without any visible symptoms. During emergency surgery, the surgeon was unable to remove all of the cancerous tissue. As a result, Jim's prognosis was limited to six to eight months of life. He would be able to take care of himself for half of the time and then need constant care until his death. The surgeon also told Sue that the tumor may have caused personality changes in Jim over the years. Sue was devastated. She blamed herself for letting Jim down and abandoning him. She also was convinced that the tumor had contributed to Jim's abusive behavior toward her. She now felt that he was not really responsible and that it was all her fault that the family had fallen apart. I was prepared for her to decompensate as she had done a few months earlier and to have her readmitted to the hospital. Surprisingly, Sue responded very differently. She said, "I can't afford to be weak now. Jim needs me and I will take care of him for the rest of his days." She then realized that she would have to give up the independence for which she had struggled so strenuously. For a week Sue experienced the turmoil of her dilemma. Should she give up her attempt to free herself from the devastation of abuse, or should she give in and pretend nothing had happened for the sake of her dying husband? Because the past abuse was as real for Sue as was Jim's impending death, she struck a compromise. She would not live with Jim; she would stay at her place and take care of him as much as she could. Several marital and family sessions later, the family developed a coping strategy with which everyone could live and Jim could peacefully experience death.

Kim's pregnancy was the second important event that influenced Sue's life and the course of therapy. Sue viewed the pregnancy as a sign of life in the face of death and as a validation of her ambivalence about life and death. Although Sue continued to harbor death wishes ("I should be ill with terminal cancer, not Jim. I screwed up our lives."), she also was very determined to survive and to take care of the baby with whom she identified tremendously. The family moved the wedding to an earlier date to allow Jim, still an ordained minister, to marry Sam and Kim. Soon after the wedding, Jim's health deteriorated. Within a few weeks he was hospitalized. When the doctors could do no more than manage his pain, Jim was transferred to a nursing home and died there four months later.

During Jim's stay at the nursing home, Sue visited him before and after work (she was then employed as an office manager). Therapy focused on Sue's resilience, her determination to be there for Jim until his death, her guilt about having survived him, and the tiny glimpse of hope she associated with becoming a grandmother. She frequently wanted to give up and "run away," as she called it. But she hung in there. She had arranged a beautiful funeral for Jim and had reconnected with her in-laws following his death. Sue had grieved so much during the months preceding the death that the actual death brought more relief from suffering and pain than anguish and sorrow. For now, Sue was ready to move on and look forward to the birth of her first grandchild. Three months after Jim's death, Megan, a daughter, was born to Kim and Sam. Megan's birth delighted Sue; she believed that Megan represented a deeply vulnerable part within herself that had been violated and that sought healing. Sue harbored the fantasy that if she attended to and took care of Megan, she could heal herself and become a strong woman who could manage her life successfully.

EVENTS LEADING TO THE CRITICAL INCIDENT

Over the following months Sue continued to struggle to determine her place in life. After coping with the immediate aftermath of Jim's death and the excitement about Megan's birth, Sue's ambivalence about life and death returned. As a result, she increased the frequency with which she thought about "running away." Asked what "running away" meant to her, Sue offered a wide range of meanings, including killing herself, dying of cancer, moving to a different city and starting her life over, escaping to a tropical island and living a life of solitude. She figuratively ran away from two jobs by not getting along with her supervisors. The harder Sue worked in therapy not to be a victim, the more depressed she became. During one session, she shared a dream in which her father physically abused her. As she related the dream, she remembered her childhood bedroom and a "safe place" between her bed and the wall where she hid when her father was angry with her. The more memories she retrieved about her father physically abusing her, the stronger her wish to die became. Her feelings of guilt and shame about her growing-up years and her failed attempts to run away from the abuse frightened her immensely. Therapy provided her with a safe holding environment that helped her to feel some relief and to draw connections between her depression, Jim's death, her struggles about the marriage, and her childhood abuse. Working through these issues and seeing her granddaughter develop, cared for by nurturing parents, helped Sue to keep the delicate balance between life and death. Several times she called me in the middle of the night because she was ready to take an overdose of sleeping pills and painkillers. On one occasion we met in my office at 11:30 p.m. and she gave me a plastic bag of pills so she could feel safe. I believed that it was crucial for me to hang in there with her, because she might have perceived hospitalization as my abandonment of her.

Slowly Sue stabilized. Her wish to live grew stronger than her urge to die. Over the Thanksgiving holiday, she visited her parents and for the first time she was able to set boundaries successfully with her father. Doing so boosted her confidence that she had entered upon the path of healing. She disclosed that she still missed Jim, felt guilty about his death, and continued to believe that she should have died of cancer in his place. Half jokingly, half seriously we agreed that she was "sentenced to life." Accepting that "sentence," Sue discovered a glimpse of hope on the horizon. She celebrated Christmas with Joe, Sam, Kim, and Megan and was looking into the future (life) rather than being stuck in the past (death). Megan's sparkly eyes on Christmas morning gave Sue hope for new life. After the holidays, Sue reported that she again was experiencing problems at work, was afraid that she would receive a poor job evaluation, and was ready to run away again. At that juncture, she became aware that the first anniversary of Jim's death was coming up. I wondered aloud how she felt about the anniversary. In a defensive voice she said, "I have dealt with his death; the anniversary is no big deal." Other questions about the anniversary were deflected and she requested that we focus on her specific concerns about work; she could not afford to lose another job. Sue became so upset about her difficulties at work that she entered another downward spiral into the darkness of depression. She, however, asserted that her depression was unrelated to Jim and the anniversary of his death.

Over the next two weeks, all of Sue's earlier emotional gains disappeared as she again became discouraged, withdrawn, and suicidal. The shadow of the past had eclipsed the hope for the future. She wanted to run away every day, was experiencing insomnia, and her passive death wishes became active suicidal ideation and plans to drive her car off the highway or take an overdose of pills. Sue continued to assert that her behaviors were unrelated to Jim's death, despite her regression into an earlier state of mind which she perceived to be more comforting to her than life.

THE CRITICAL INCIDENT

Three days before the anniversary of Jim's death, Sue came into my office smiling. Her smile appeared to say, "Don't even try to talk me into this anniversary stuff; just let me die and get over the pain." Sue communicated her despair in a childlike rebellious manner that left me frustrated and angry. I restrained myself from giving in to the urge to ask her to leave my office and get a life. Having overcome the urge, I smiled inwardly at my reaction to tell a client to get a life when she was ready to die. I felt stuck. If I attempted to rescue her (e.g., hospitalization) I might kill her or at least our therapeutic relationship (i.e., abandonment). Accordingly, we talked about how we both felt stuck and how her depression was sucking both of us down into the spiral of darkness, depression, and death. We also talked about the dilemma of hospitalization. She confirmed (knowing the mental health system well enough) that I would not succeed in hospitalizing her involuntarily. She would deny any suicidal ideation when the police arrived to take her to the hospital. Such being the situation, Sue suggested that we make the best of it. I felt helplessly pushed into a corner, having to take a stance of which I was terribly afraid. I allowed Sue to push me to the edge of therapy. Was I supposed to react as a therapist? What was the professional thing to do? No, this went far beyond a professional relationship. I felt that someone had revealed the core of who she was to me and demanded that I respond from my inner core.

Continuing my internal dialogue, I ordered myself to quit the therapy BS and get real; use my common sense! Interestingly, in my helplessness I felt more connected to Sue than ever before. I shared my feelings of helplessness with Sue and she cried. She sobbed uncontrollably and said, "I miss Jim so much. I want to be with him; I want to die. Please let me go and be with him. I am not running away; I just want to be with him. I want to face life, but how can I be with him if I live and he is dead? Please let me go." Quietly I held her and cried with her. What was I supposed to do? I may be violating all professional ethics and civil laws if I let her go and she killed herself. Despite these feelings, I knew that ultimately no one could keep her from doing what she felt she needed to do. Inwardly, I questioned if I was willing to share the responsibility with her as she had shared her despair and pain with me. Again, we talked about the dilemma and how we both were stuck in the same dilemma.

Looking into her pleading eyes, I said, "Sue, I respect your wish to be with Jim. Despite everything that happened between the two of you, including him abusing you, you have convinced me that you love him. I trust you that you will find a way to be with him that will bring you healing. We both are familiar enough with the mental health system to know that the ultimate decision about a person's life is up to that person. I guess we are both taking the risk to get into trouble if things don't work out. Go in peace." I gave her a long hug. She then sat down, quietly wrote the check for the session's fee, and scheduled an appointment for the following week. Calm and determined, Sue left my office. I was in turmoil and called a therapist friend to process what was going on with me and to get some support.

I was prepared to be informed by the police that Sue had committed suicide. Instead, Sue called me the day following the anniversary of Jim's death. She sounded in good spirits and asked for an appointment that day, because she did not want to wait until our next scheduled appointment. Sue entered my office with a smirk and announced, "Well, I am still alive. Thanks for letting me decide." She then recounted the events of the past few days.

The night after our session she had begun to plan her reunification with Jim. She bought a fifth of liquor and 150 sleeping pills, and refilled her antidepressant prescription one last time. On the day of the anniversary, she visited Sam, Kim, and Megan, and talked with Joe by phone. At 10 p.m. that night she visited Jim's grave and talked to him for more than two hours. She had planned to drink the liquor, swallow the pills, then drive into the small lake adjacent to the graveyard. She began to drink the liquor and then thought about Megan and our last session. At that moment, she became aware that for the first time in many years someone important to her (a male someone) had given her a choice about what to do with her life. She always had attempted to please everyone else (her parents, Jim, her sons, her bosses, etc.), live the way she believed they wanted her to live, and to be how/what she believed they wanted her to be. She also became aware that because she had been so fed up with living for others, she wanted to die to purge herself of the guilt about Jim's death. It became pivotal to her that she now faced a situation in which she had to make up her own mind. No longer did she have to do or not do what others wanted. The downward spiral was broken; she did not allow it to force her into the darkness toward death any longer. She was free to make up her own mind.

Paradoxically, Sue decided that she could concurrently be united with Jim and yet live. Megan became the link between Jim's death (past) and her life (future). The baby was their flesh and blood and symbolized the life connection between them. Through Megan, Sue could be united with Jim in life without being sentenced to death. Accordingly, with renewed hope and deep sadness, she said goodbye to Jim and drove to the lake. There she cried as she threw the bottle of liquor and the pills into the water and promised herself never again to take antidepressants or sleeping pills. She then drove home, slept for a few hours, and called me.

DISCUSSION

Characteristics of the Case Relevant to the Outcome

The case of Sue and her family describes people's despair and resilience and their ability to face adversity, and bears witness to how people, clients as well as therapists, learn to hold ambivalence (even when it involves issues of life and death). A common strategy used to overcome ambivalent feelings is to polarize them (Schwartz, 1995) or to split off one extreme and project them onto others (Ackerman, 1966). The creation of a therapeutic holding environment (Winnicott, 1965) also helps clients and therapists to hold their own ambivalent feelings and work through their tendencies to polarize and to split off unbearable feelings. The presented case is full of attempts to deal with ambivalence.

Initially, when the family came to see me, Joe expressed the family's ambivalence about responsibility and accountability. These are issues that are raised when adolescents are on the verge of leaving home and challenging parents to grant them more responsibilities to conduct their lives. When adolescents perceive that parents are not ready for them to move on, many adolescents force the issue by "screwing up" and challenging the helpless parents. No one knows how to hold the ambivalence about leaving and staying. As a result, those feelings, usually about rules and privileges, often are polarized.

Sue expressed her ambivalence about Jim in many ways. First, she was ambivalent about leaving to free herself from his abuse. She continued to love Jim and acted against her personal values to remain loyal to her husband. After Jim's cancer diagnosis, she was ambivalent about her decision and often considered giving up and moving back in with him. Again, she polarized her feelings by blaming herself for his illness and trying to run away from her pain. The running away metaphor is a very powerful and almost literal symbol of the ambivalence and the attempts to polarize by running from one pole to the other and back.

The theme of being "sentenced to life" versus Sue's fantasy to be united with Jim in death reflects the ultimate ambivalence of Sue's life. The ultimate polarization is between life and death. Megan's birth in the story is a variation of the same theme. Jim's death symbolized the haunting past in Sue's life, while Megan's birth became a symbol of the hopeful future in her life. At one pole, Sue identified so much with Jim (the shadow side within herself) that life became punishment and death the only redemption. At the other pole, Sue identified so much with Megan (the innocent, vulnerable side within herself) that she could look into the future with the hope of change, growth, and healing.

Sue challenged me as a therapist to confront my professional boundaries when it comes to ambivalence. Usually therapists can hide behind their professional standards of conduct to decide how to deal with ambivalence. For example, rules inform us what to do when clients are suicidal. But, emotionally, therapists also polarize and split off. How often have therapists thought about "covering themselves" when they admit a suicidal client to the hospital? How often in such situations do they ask themselves whether they are guided by their fears rather than by the best interest of the client? How much responsibility are clients really given? How can therapists empower clients when they want to kill themselves? Similar to Joe asking his parents during our initial family session how much responsibility were they willing to give him, Sue asked me the night before the anniversary of Jim's death how much responsibility I was willing to give to her, to live or die in self-determination. I could have decided that she was too "crazy," unable to be responsible for her own actions, and admitted her to the hospital. This would have been my professional polarization as dictated by my personal fear. Intuitively I tried to hold my ambivalence and lost quite a bit of sleep over it. Fortunately, doing so created space for both of us to grow and change for the better.

The Role of the Critical Incident in Getting Therapy Unstuck

Initially I did not recognize the role of the critical incident in getting therapy unstuck. I had acted intuitively and to some degree out of despair. But I was very aware of the respect I had for Sue and her situation. I guess I knew more about her ambivalence and her desire to run away than my own ambivalence and desire to run away. But I managed not to run away from my responsibility by admitting Sue to the hospital. This process may have served as a true paradoxical intervention yet totally unintentionally. I joined Sue in being stuck and defined my professional responsibility as not to admit her to the hospital. We both knew that the usual/expected professional conduct would have been to intervene and admit her. Not doing so was acting irresponsibly and created a responsibility paradox for me. If Sue wanted to be loyal to me and our work, she had to act responsibly as well. In the context of our implicit therapeutic contract, killing herself would have been irresponsible. In addition, she had asked me to take care of her by admitting her to the hospital. My refusal to do so put the ball back into her court and challenged her to decide for herself. My confidence in her and her loyalty ultimately enabled her to choose to live and to integrate her ambivalence about life and death in a very creative way. Megan became the symbol of this integration, and the integration led to Sue, the therapist, and the therapy becoming unstuck.

Initially, Sue denied that the anniversary of Jim's death had anything to do with the crisis that challenged her at the time. It took my intuitive courage to reveal myself and to take a stance beyond my professional role. The turning point was our mutual courage to be vulnerable and to reveal the most inner cores of ourselves and, of equal importance, not to get hurt along the way. Sue had been vulnerable with her father and her husband in the past; as a result, she was abused and hurt deeply inside. For Sue, the pivotal moment in therapy was not to get abused and hurt when she was most vulnerable in a relationship with a man. Receiving respect and support instead of abuse and blame from a man in times of sorrow and pain was a healing experience for Sue.

Implications of the Critical Incident for Therapy

It took us several weeks to process the pivotal session and its consequences. Sue and I talked about trust and hope and how difficult it had been for her even to consider trusting me (after two years of therapy). How could she know that I would not ultimately abuse her if she honestly revealed herself to me? How could she in the future trust herself and her intuition especially with men, and how could she heal from the wounds of abuse? Trusting Megan was easy; she was as innocent as Sue had been when she was first abused by her father. Trusting adults—and especially men with all their power—was almost beyond Sue's imagination. Sue remained ambivalent. At times she trusted me; at times she did not. But she could talk about it and did not have to run away from the issue. During the following months we focused primarily on work-related issues. How could she trust her supervisor to have Sue's best interest in mind? How could Sue be more confident in her excellent work skills without the need for constant positive feedback from her co-workers and supervisors?

The implications of the "life and death" session were quite remarkable. Therapy and Sue's life was not about life and death any longer. She had decided to live. Now it was about the "nitty gritty stuff" of life, the mundane work issues ("How can I work more independently?"), relationship issues ("Can I ever date a man again?" and "How do I develop a good friendship with a woman?"), and education issues ("Do I want to return to school for an advanced degree?"), etc. Sue had many questions and worked hard to find some preliminary answers.

OUTCOME OF THERAPY

Sue and I continued to work together for another six months. Occasionally her sons and daughter-in-law joined us for family sessions. Sue reported feeling increasingly better about herself. Several times she brought

Megan with her to sessions and I was moved to tears to see Sue's confidence as she played with her granddaughter, the love she had for Megan, and the trust she had in herself that enabled her to care for this vulnerable yet stubborn little person. Sue remained resolute in her decision never to take pills again but continued to experience sporadic urges to run away. Now, however, the urges were minimal and her depressive episodes were shortened and had been flattened considerably. More important, she had not experienced a downward spiral for more than a year.

Following Jim's death, Joe had returned to live with Sue. Prior to doing so he had begun to drink heavily and to get into trouble again with the law. Perhaps in response to his mother's continued recovery, Joe decided to stop drinking. He obtained a job and entered college the next fall.

Sue visited Jim's grave regularly and often took Megan with her. As a family, Sue, her sons, Kim, and Megan planted a tree in Sam and Kim's backyard to celebrate Jim's life. Sue promised to teach Megan how to care for, water, and fertilize the tree as needed and also to tell her about the grandfather she never knew. I joined the family in the celebration ritual; it was a healing experience for all of us.

Eventually, we increased the intervals between sessions and phased out therapy. At our last session I asked Sue what she needed to complete our work together and to let go of therapy. After a few moments of silence she asked that I sit with her and Megan and hold both of them quietly for a few minutes. She chose to sit on the floor. I put my right arm around her shoulder and my left arm lightly touched Megan, who seemed a little confused about what was going on. I was amazed by this toddler's ability to sense the importance of the situation. She sat quietly with us for approximately two to three minutes; it must have felt like eternity to her. Then she slowly got up, toddled around the room, found some toys, and carefully observed us from some distance while Sue and I remained on the floor for another five minutes. Sue cried quietly. Then we both got up and sat on our chairs while Megan continued to play. Sue said, "I always have wanted to end a relationship on a good note. You accepted my vulnerable girl inside and I wanted you to hold her one last time. From now on I will take care of her myself. You and Megan have finally convinced me that I can do that myself. Thank you for all your caring, patience, and support. Most of all, thank you for the risks you took with me."

Follow-Up

Following the formal termination of therapy, Sue and I maintained contact primarily via the telephone. On occasion I saw her in person together with Megan who then was an energetic preschooler. When I see Sue with Megan, I am reminded of the way Sue resolved the polarization between "sentenced to life" or "united in death." Sue and Megan, as well as Sue's struggles between life and death, made me a better person and a better therapist.

Sue continues to abstain from pills. Joe has quit drinking alcohol altogether and remains sober. He works part time to support himself, is enrolled in college, and is doing well academically as a communications major.

REFERENCES

Ackerman, N. W. (1966). *Treating the troubled family*. New York: Basic Books.
Haley, J. (1980). *Leaving home: Therapy with disturbed young people*. New York: McGraw-Hill.
Schwartz, R. (1995). *Internal family systems therapy*. New York: The Guilford Press.
Winnicott, D. W. (1965). *The family and individual development*. New York: Basic Books.

Commentary

United in Therapy or United in Life

Stephen A. Anderson

Commentator Background

Fifty-two years old, white, male, twenty-eight years clinical experience, twenty-two years MFT experience.

Practice Setting

Full-time teaching in a Commission on Accreditation for Marriage and Family Therapy Education-(COAMFTE) accredited master's and doctoral programs; limited private practice and consultancy.

Theoretical Perspective

Preferred theoretical perspective is integrative, blending elements of structural, developmental, object relations, intergenerational, and symbolic experiential. A combination of intergenerational, developmental, and symbolic experiential perspectives was used to examine this case.

INTRODUCTION

There is much to ponder in this case presented by Thomas. The issues transcend the more general considerations of what he did in the case, what I would have done similarly, or what I would have done differently, although I will try to address these questions. Rather, the case raises serious questions about the limits of therapy and the boundary between the therapist's professional role and the struggle to be more fully human. Furthermore, ethical issues should be pondered here as well. Is the therapist's primary responsibility to protect clients from themselves, or is it to encourage clients to take ultimate responsibility for themselves, even if it means allowing them to choose death over life? I cannot claim to have an answer to these questions. Ultimately, I believe that each of us must answer these questions for himself or herself. However, I appreciate Thomas's honesty and courage in placing these matters before us so that they can be debated and made a greater part of our collective awareness.

My comments will address the following issues: (1) what I would have done the same, (2) what I would have done differently (3) what other questions I would have asked, and (4) whether choice of intervention method really makes a difference.

WHAT I WOULD HAVE DONE SIMILARLY

It would be presumptuous of me, after having read a synopsis of the case, to disagree with Thomas's judgment not to hospitalize Sue when she struggled with the question of whether to live or die. Such a judgment transcends the mere facts of a case and requires a careful assessment of a client's internal and social resources along with something even more intangible: the quality of the relationship between therapist and client. While considering the question of whether I would have acted in a similar manner as Thomas, I felt much the same ambivalence that he must have felt. Admittedly, my level of emotional investment in the case was far less than his. Nonetheless, I felt ambivalent about whether to support his decision. On one hand, conventional therapeutic wisdom would argue that it was essential to insure her safety through hospitalization when an indication existed that she was a danger to herself. On the other hand, I felt compelled to trust that he had the far better vantage point from which to make such a critical decision. In the end, I came to the same decision that he did: that the person who is ultimately responsible must make the call. Every situation we face in therapy is in some ways unique and unlikely ever to be repeated again in quite the same way. Thus, we have to make our best decisions at the moment without the benefit of hindsight or second-guessing.

Thomas and I agree on the importance of the relationship between therapist and client. I assume that nothing happens in therapy unless the client has a sense of trust in the therapist and the therapist has the courage to go where he or she is asking the client to go. I applauded his decision "to quit the therapy BS and get real." I aspire to have the same capacity as he showed to stay connected to my clients in their struggles and to tolerate my own intense feelings of helplessness, vulnerability, fear, or doubt. I agree that one of the most demanding aspects of engaging in a truly authentic relationship is to tolerate the full range of one's own conflicting feelings without projecting them onto the other or reactively distancing from the relationship.

Thomas referred to Winnicott's notion of a therapeutic holding environment, which helps clients and therapist to hold onto ambivalent feelings and to work through the tendency to polarize, split off, and project unbearable feelings. I think of it more from a symbolic experiential or existential perspective. It is the recognition of one's own basic aloneness that enables one to develop self-reliance rather than depending upon others for confirmation or direction. Furthermore, I believe that the greater one's capacity to stand alone and to find strength within oneself, the greater one's potential for intimate connection with others. Paradoxically, the more one dares to belong, the greater the freedom to be independent (Boylin, Anderson, and Bartle, 1992; Whitaker and Bumberry, 1988). In this case, Thomas ultimately stood alone, as did Sue, and in the process he achieved a greater sense of connection with Sue than he had experienced before. His willingness to engage with Sue in her life-threatening struggle appears to have left her with a greater sense of freedom to be independent from him and significant others in her life.

WHAT I MIGHT HAVE DONE DIFFERENTLY

The initial problem presented by the family was Joe's failing grades in classes, truancy, and arrest for drunk driving. I would have stayed with this during the early stage of therapy rather than shifting the focus to the parents' marital relationship. I would have reasoned that if, as Thomas noted, the parents were not yet ready to let their sons leave home because of unresolved conflicts between them, then they probably would not be ready to manage marital therapy right away without their sons present. I would have worried that the system would react adversely to this change when it had, in fact, presented Joe as the ticket into therapy. I would have opted to accept the family's definition of the problem rather than introduce my own therapist-constructed definition of the problem so early on. In short, I would have kept my focus on the family unit, at least initially.

Had I attempted to switch to the parents' marriage, I would have taken the couples' perceived nonverbal response—"We brought Joe to be fixed and now you send him home and tell us we are the bad guys"—as feedback to me that I was moving too quickly and to slow down. I would have been concerned that switching away from the designated patient too quickly might have provoked the system to find another designated patient rather than to shift its relationship rules (second-order change) so easily. This is, in fact, what occurred later when Joe was later arrested for shoplifting and Sue was hospitalized for major depression with psychotic features and acute suicidal ideation. I was particularly struck that Sue's reaction to this was to express "anger that she was the designated client now."

I subscribe to the notion that therapy needs to be as brief as possible and that having a contract with the family to address a specific issue is important. Should the family decide later to stay on after resolving the initial focus, we would renegotiate together a new contract for the next phase of our work together. However, I also believe that many of the issues that bring people to therapy have taken time to develop and require time to resolve. Accordingly, I usually spend time reviewing the family's history. I would have wanted to know more about each parent's family-of-origin experiences, the couple's early courtship, the family's developmental milestones and how they were managed, and the family's style of resolving conflict. I would have hypothesized that Joe's misbehavior might indicate a long-standing strategy for avoiding conflict by enlisting a "distance regulator" (Byng-Hall, 1980), emotional "detour" (Minuchin, 1974), or "triangle" (Bowen, 1978) to defuse tension. I would have wanted to explore whether this strategy had been evident in other stages of the family's development and whether the conflicts or toxic issues with which it was associated had been resolved.

OTHER QUESTIONS I WOULD HAVE ASKED

It is possible that many of my unanswered questions were in fact addressed by Thomas during the therapy and that space limitations required him to be selective in choosing the material to be included in the case presentation. In any event, there were several areas that I would have explored further with the couple or family.

1. What was the conflict with Jim's congregation five years ago that led to Jim's resignation? It appears to have been a major turning point for the family and apparently intense enough to produce shame and guilt for both Jim and Sue. It also apparently resulted in the couple becoming less supportive of each other.
2. Why was Jim forced out of the second church? What expectations of the elders did Jim not meet? The details of these two events may have shed light on one or more themes that helped to define this family's identity and the kinds of stresses with which they currently were dealing.
3. What was the nature of Jim's sexual abuse of Sue? What was the level of severity? Did it involve verbal abuse? Humiliation? Did he harm her physically? Were the boys aware of it? To what extent was Jim able to accept responsibility for his actions in therapy after his initial denial?
4. What was the nature of Joe's relationship with his mother? What was the basis for Joe's "expressed hatred" of his mother? What was the basis for Sue's belief that Joe actually held a "deep love" for her? During the initial family session, Joe expressed the belief that his leaving home would lead his mom to "go crazy." What was it that had led Joe

to that conclusion? Did he perceive some vulnerability in her? What was it that led Joe to conclude that his father would "run away" rather than live alone with Sue?

5. What were the connections between Sue's earlier physical abuse by her father and her current struggles in her relationships with her husband and sons? The most obvious one was a recurring pattern of physical abuse over two generations, but the themes of running away, shame, and guilt suggest that questions such as her sexual functioning, capacity for trust and intimacy, and comfort in establishing clear interpersonal boundaries should be explored.

6. Did Sue show any signs of depression earlier in the therapy prior to her "decompensation" and hospitalization for major depression following Joe's arrest for shoplifting?

These questions would have helped me to better understand the relationship dynamics, unresolved conflicts, and unexpressed secrets that were operating in the family system. I consider this information imperative because one of my assumptions is that unresolved conflicts and outmoded, covert relationship rules can serve to keep the system stuck and unable to move on along its developmental path. The fact that the family entered therapy when it was struggling with the leaving-home transition suggests to me that various horizontal stresses from the past may be interacting with the vertical stresses of the present (job loss, lower social status, moving away from the family home and extended family) to inhibit the family's adaptation (Anderson and Sabatelli, 1999; Carter and McGoldrick, 1989).

HOW MUCH DIFFERENCE DOES CHOICE OF INTERVENTION METHOD MAKE?

This case raised a larger question for me than what I would have done differently had I been asked to treat this family. It has to do with the limits of any approach to therapy in resolving some of the issues faced by this family. I am reminded of the concept of equifinality which holds that several pathways lead to the same outcome. The concept suggests that no matter where one begins or how one proceeds, the end result will be the same. This is not to suggest that every therapist will achieve the same outcome in every case, but is does raise the question of whether different intervention methods would have produced a different or better outcome in this case.

For instance, was there anything that any therapist could have said or done that would have changed the course of Jim's terminal illness, the personality changes he underwent, or his ultimate death due to a brain tumor? Some believe in the power of therapy to reverse the growth of cancer by tapping the person's will to live and the body's healing resources (c.f., Mahrer, 1980). However, many of us might attribute cancer to environmental or genetic factors.

Could anything that might have happened in the couple's therapy have prevented Sue's later depressive episode? If her depression was related to current situational factors, the couple's therapy may indeed have been helpful in helping her to deal with the vertical stresses that were impacting the marriage. It may also have been helpful in making the secret sexual abuse overt and amenable to resolution. However, if her depression was due to a genetic predisposition, therapy without medication may have had questionable results. Furthermore, major depression can follow an episodic and recurring course over time. If her depression could be traced to unresolved trauma as a result of her childhood abuse, then a prolonged, painful, personal, working-through process, probably in individual therapy, might still have included periods of depression. Would Sue's feelings of guilt and responsibility for Jim's death been different if the therapy had proceeded differently? Such feelings are all too common among survivors following a family member's death.

Can therapy really prevent someone from committing suicide when he or she really has committed himself or herself to that course of action? To be sure, therapy can be useful when clients express ambivalence about ending their lives, when their actions are a form of asking for help, or when they are willing to openly acknowledge and be prevented from completing their actual plans for committing suicide. But what about clients who really are quite determined to follow through with ending their lives? Can therapy really alter the outcome?

Finally, to what extent was it about the therapy that helped Sue eventually select life over death? Was it really an event unrelated to the therapy—namely, the birth of her granddaughter Megan? I do not know the answers to these questions, but I raise them because they point to the fact that limits may indeed exist to the power of family therapy, or any talk therapy, in altering people's lives. Such questions also highlight the limits of our knowledge about how therapy really works and how people really change. Perhaps in the final analysis, it is not so much what we as therapists do—that is, the interventions we implement—but rather the quality of the relationship we establish between ourselves and our clients that is the most important contribution therapy has to offer. It is in the personal relationship that the life of the client and the life of the therapist converge.

CONCLUDING THOUGHTS

The theme that Thomas selected to organize his case report was "sentenced to life versus united in death." He depicted this as the ambivalence that often characterizes interpersonal relationships. The theme of ambivalence was reflected in Joe's dilemma of leaving home or staying to keep his parents united, Sue's decision to leave or stay with her husband, Thomas's struggle about whether to hospitalize Sue or relinquish to her full responsibility for her life, and, ultimately, Sue's choice of life over death. Accompanying these dilemmas was a host of conflicting human emotions including anxiety, fear, shame, guilt, anger, doubt, hope, determination, helplessness, safety, loyalty, betrayal, abandonment, loss, failure, success, hatred, and love.

I have noted that my approach to the therapy, especially in the early stages, would have been notably different from Thomas's. Those differences were primarily in the area of therapy method. However, the depth of human emotions that were shared by Thomas and the family, especially Sue, stands out more in this case. I would argue that the critical moment depicted here transcends therapeutic method and speaks to the centrality of the therapeutic relationship over technique. I would further argue that some of the elements of this critical moment transcend the therapeutic relationship and speak to the stuff of all human relationships. Whether we choose to describe the human-to-human encounter in terms of ambivalence, one's ultimate aloneness, or the range of emotions listed above, those rare moments when we truly touch another person happen as much in life as they do in therapy.

REFERENCES

Anderson, S. and Sabatelli, R. (1999). *Family interaction: A multi generational, developmental perspective,* Second edition. Boston: Allyn & Bacon.

Bowen, M. (1978). *Family therapy in clinical practice.* New York: Jason Aronson.

Boylin, W., Anderson, S., and Bartle, S. (1992). Symbolic-experiential supervision: A model for learning or a frame of mind? *Journal of Family Psychotherapy,* 3(4), 43-59.

Byng-Hall, J. (1980). Symptom bearer as marital distance regulator: Clinical implications. *Family Process,* 19(4), 355-367.

Carter, B. and McGoldrick, M. (1989). *The changing family life cycle.* Boston: Allyn & Bacon.

Mahrer, A. (1980). The treatment of cancer through experiential psychotherapy. *Psychotherapy: Theory, Research and Practice,* 17(3) 335-342.

Minuchin, S. (1974). *Families and family therapy.* Cambridge, MA: Harvard University Press.

Whitaker, C. and Bumberry, W. (1988). *Dancing with the family: A symbolic-experiential approach.* New York: Brunner/Mazel.

Commentary

Sitting Outside the Therapy Room

Janie K. Long
Adi Granit
Marc N. Barney

Commentator Backgrounds

- Forty-six years old, Caucasian, female, PhD, sixteen years MFT practice.
- Thirty years old, Caucasian, female, MA, six years MFT practice.
- Thirty-one years old, Caucasian, male, MA, six years MFT practice.

Practice Setting

University family therapy clinic.

Theoretical Perspective

A postmodernist/social constructionist theoretical lens was used to view the case, and a solution-focused therapeutic model informed our discussions and comments.

We approached the examination and resultant commentary of this case as though we were entering the case at various junctures as a therapeutic consultation team and used a postmodernist/social constructionist perspective as the theoretical approach to guide our comments. As a team we accept that no one objective reality exists. Instead, multiple realities exist, and the realities we construct are generated through interactions with others and anchored in the language systems within which we exist (Gergen, 1985; Hoffman, 1990).

Although we particularly liked some aspects of Thomas's approach to the case, we questioned other aspects and potentially would have approached several aspects differently. Accordingly, our comments will address the following: (1) what we would have done similarly, (2) what we would have done differently, and (3) other therapeutic/clarifying questions we would have asked and the manner in which we might have framed them. Thus, with tongue in cheek as "experts" sitting outside the therapy room, we begin our commentary.

WHAT WE WOULD HAVE DONE SIMILARLY

Because our theoretical stance and preferred therapeutic approach are different from Thomas's, we believe that both the direction and the process of therapy would have been different from the beginning and we would have taken a very different therapeutic path with this family. Based on these perceived differences we find very little that we would have done similar to Thomas. We, however, concur with Thomas's decision to reinvolve Jim and the children following Sue's decision to care for Jim during his dying days; this decision is consistent with our thoughts about the direction of therapy.

WHAT WE WOULD HAVE DONE DIFFERENTLY

As might be expected and for the reasons stated above, our list of what we would have done differently from Thomas is much longer than what we would have done similarly.

1. We would have kept the family together as a unit longer in therapy.
2. We would not have maintained an individual therapeutic focus with Sue, although periodically we may have seen her in concurrent individual and family sessions.
3. We probably would have invited the entire family to return to therapy when Jim called to report that Joe had been arrested for shoplifting and that Sue had "decompensated."
4. We would not have dismissed the children from therapy as early as Thomas did.
5. We would have invited Sue to be more responsible for her decisions and, by extension, her life.
6. We would not have agreed to meet alone with Sue at the office at 11:30 p.m.
7. We would have attempted to obtain a much more explicit understanding of what this family, especially Sue, wanted from therapy.

Focusing on the Family

From our perspective, we wonder if Thomas moved too quickly to focus on the marital issues rather than on the family issues that appeared to be central. We perceive that such a change could potentially contribute to at least three unintended consequences for the family overall and for Sue and the sons. The first of these is specific to the family as a unit. We believe that keeping the family together as a unit would have provided an opportunity for the therapist to further explore other family members' perspectives of the problems and their possible solutions to the problems. Thomas's focus on the *marital unit* rather than the *family* suggests that he was not following Haley's (1979) approach in this case. However, based on our understanding of Haley, we believe that a more consistent approach would have been to keep the family together as a unit in family sessions and focus therapy on strengthening the parental subsystem to help Sue and Jim to obtain the desired behaviors from their son. Here we are not espousing Haley's approach as the preferred way to proceed with this family, only emphasizing that Thomas's approach does not agree with our understanding of Haley's approach.

Consistent with our theoretical stance in therapy, we probably would have invited the entire family to return to therapy when Jim called to report that Joe had been arrested for shoplifting and that Sue had "decompensated." We probably would have presented our invitation similarly to the following: "Sounds as if the family is going through some very tough times. We would like for all of you to come in for at least one session together. Having all of you together would give us as many perspectives as possible on this situation." A second unintended consequence of this maneuver pertains to Sue. Moving the therapeutic focus from the family to Sue may have unintentionally reinforced Jim's and the sons' beliefs (stories) that Sue was crazy, the "sick one," or the only one with the problem who needed help from the therapist. The message could also have been that other problems were not as important. In addition, their sons' beliefs that Dad was weak and would run away could also have been reinforced.

Another potentially unintended consequence of the change from family focus to couple focus pertains to Joe and Sam. At the conclusion of the first family session, Thomas dismissed Joe and Sam from therapy with the injunction that they need not return to therapy unless Joe got into trouble. Although his doing so was well intended, from our perspective there existed the potential for the dismissal to be perceived as framing therapy as a punishment for Joe. That is, "currently I do not see you (Joe) as the problem so you don't have to be involved in therapy. However, if you get into trouble, your parents and I will punish you by asking you to come to therapy."

Based on our therapeutic approach we would not have dismissed Joe and Sam from therapy so early in the process. If we did dismiss them, we would have framed the dismissal differently. For example, "As we work with your parents, you are likely to notice some changes. As things start to change at home, you can feel free to come back in if you want to offer your input regarding the changes. At the end of therapy, we all will meet again to talk about and celebrate the changes together." Concurrently, we would have attempted to find some exceptions to Joe's behavioral problems as reported by the family. Accordingly, consistent with a solution-focused model, we would have asked such questions as: (1) When was Joe doing better in school? (2) When did Joe act responsibly? and (3) What does Joe do well?

Whose Responsibility Is It Anyway?

At several points in our reading of the case we struggled with what we perceived as Thomas becoming too responsible for Sue's decisions. We believe that making her own life decisions with little or no prompting from the therapist would have been important for Sue. At the juncture at which Thomas encouraged Sue to express her anger to Jim, we believe it would have been appropriate to explore alternative ways of dealing with the issue and the consequences of each of those options. Consistent with our approach, we would have *focused on Sue's goals* thus allowing *her* to be more responsible for the situation and hopefully help us not to feel as stuck with the case. If we perceived that we were not reaching the desired goals of the client, we would have accepted that as evidence that we needed to change our approach. For example, we might have asked for a consultation with a colleague. Also, Thomas's encouragement of Sue to confront Jim about the secret that "drove her crazy" appeared to usurp her decision-making abilities. Our preferred approach would have been to encourage Sue to discover different ways for dealing with the secret. By continuing down his selected path Thomas appeared to be working much harder than Sue. As a result, Sue assumes a one-down position and Thomas becomes the caretaker.

What Do You Really Want from Therapy?

In Thomas's description of the therapeutic relationship during the first four months of individual sessions, we perceived him to be on a path of attempted solutions that appeared not to have gotten *him* the results that *he* wanted, thus leading to *his* frustration. Noting that we struggled together throughout our discussions is important because we did not feel as though we knew what Sue or the family really wanted from therapy.

Following Sue's disclosure that Jim had sexually abused her, we would have explored some options with her regarding how she had dealt with her feelings. Specifically, did she want to deal with them differently and, if so, what might be the consequence if she chose to do so? Here our purpose would have been to clarify with Sue what she wanted from therapy. This clarification would be used to establish her therapeutic goals. For us, such goals would be a compass that would help us to know if we were moving in the right direction and whether we were meeting Sue's needs by achieving her therapeutic goals.

OTHER QUESTIONS WE WOULD HAVE ASKED

We would have asked other questions of this family and Thomas because we perceive these questions to be germane to a fuller understanding of the dynamics of this case.

1. Why was the family unit not seen in therapy during the period when Jim was dying and after Jim's death, rather than initiating individual therapy with Sue following Jim's death?
2. What did being "driven crazy" mean for Sue?
3. How did Thomas respond to Jim's denial when Sue expressed her anger to him regarding his alleged sexual abuse?

We concur with Thomas's decision to reinvolve Joe and Sam in therapy after Sue decided to care for Jim during his dying days. However, our reading of Thomas's description of the events led us to the conclusion that family sessions ended when the family agreed upon an "acceptable strategy" for coping with Jim's imminent death. However, we wonder why family sessions were not continued during that period and after Jim's death. Our understanding is that therapy continued as individual sessions with Sue following Jim's death. Given this assumption, it seems logical that therapy should focus on the issues Thomas identified. However, because we would have continued to see the family even after Jim's death we may have focused therapy on how the family would reorganize itself.

We would have questioned what being "driven crazy" meant for Sue. We might also have explored whether she wanted to restory her "craziness" as having been successful at surviving a crazy situation. Part of the restorying would include searching for exceptions and positively connoting her resilience in fighting the abuse and surviving it. We are curious about how Thomas responded when Sue expressed her anger to Jim with regard to the alleged abuse. It is unclear to us how the session unfolded and how Thomas processed the issues. Furthermore, we also are somewhat perplexed about what occurred following this session that contributed to Thomas's belief that the family blamed him for driving Sue into the mental institution and for pushing her to separate from Jim. Finally, we feel uncomfortable about the therapist's use of the labels "victim" and "perpetrator" and wonder in what way it would be useful or serve the client's purpose.

THE GAME MACABRE

Based on Thomas's description, the interactions leading up to the events immediately prior to and including the critical incident could be perceived as a homeostatic game (Watzlawick, Bavelas, and Jackson, 1967). The game revolves around Sue's presentation of herself as vulnerable, helpless, and in need of someone to take care of her, and Thomas's presentation of himself as the reliable, strong, and dependable male rescuer. The game is circular. Sue invites him to take care of her and he invites her to be taken care of by him. Some of Thomas's descriptions of Sue tend to support this notion, e.g., "she entered another downward spiral into the darkness of depression" and "she might have perceived hospitalization as my abandonment of her." Descriptions of himself also tend to support him as rescuer, "I believed that it was crucial for me to hang in there with her" and "I questioned if I was willing to share the responsibility with her." Under the current rules, if either of them leaves the field, the game may end, which is too big a risk inasmuch as the players have become so important to each other. The following excerpt exemplifies this game: "I felt stuck. If I attempted to rescue her (e.g., hospitalization) I might kill her or at least our therapeutic relationship (i.e., abandonment). Accordingly, we talked about how we both felt stuck and how her depression was sucking down both of us into the spiral of darkness, depression, and death."

The game may not end without the introduction of some type of second-order change (Watzwalick, Weakland, and Fisch, 1974). From our perspective, this second-order change occurs when the rules of the game are altered, creating space for Thomas to relinquish his role as caretaker and Sue to assume responsibility for her own decisions over life and death. At this juncture the rule about who has responsibility for Sue's life shifts from Thomas's responsibility to Sue's responsibility. Sue decides whether she lives or she dies. Interestingly, our view of the critical incident in therapy differs from Thomas's view. He states, "For Sue, the pivotal moment in therapy was not to get abused and hurt when she was most vulnerable in a relationship with a man. Receiving respect and support instead of abuse and blame from a man in times of sorrow and pain was a healing experience for Sue." For us, the telling moment in therapy is described by Sue. "I always have wanted to end a relationship on a good note. You accepted my vulnerable girl inside and I wanted you to hold her one last time. *From now on I will take care of her myself* "[italics added].

ETHICAL ISSUES

Thomas acknowledges that the critical incident is full of ethical questions. As a team, we struggled heavily with our own thoughts and feelings with regard to the ethics of Thomas's decision not to hospitalize Sue and the dilemma it created for him. We did note that Sue contacted Thomas at those times when she felt suicidal, but we are unclear whether those contacts resulted from her initiative alone or was in keeping with an explicit therapist-initiated no-suicide contract. It is unclear whether Thomas developed a no-suicide contract with Sue. If indeed Thomas did not initiate a no-suicide contract with Sue, we believe that the establishment of such a contract would have been vitally and ethically important to the unfolding of the case.

With regard to Thomas's agonizing whether to hospitalize Sue, we concluded that we probably would have hospitalized her. This decision results from our belief that as clinicians we ultimately are responsible for doing everything we can to protect clients from immediate danger. We do not have any way of knowing how the consequences of a given therapist's chosen actions would eventuate. But without the benefit of hindsight, we would have felt that we had done what we legally and ethically were bound to do. Fortunately for Thomas, his chosen strategy resulted in therapy shifting in a positive direction toward a resolution of the problem. Unfortunately, he allowed their game to take him and Sue to the point at which he was faced with making such a difficult choice. Again, from our perspective, we believe that if the game had been interrupted earlier in the therapeutic process the situation may not have developed to such a point.

Another ethical issue relates to Thomas's willingness to meet alone with Sue at his office at 11:30 p.m. We believe that his willingness to do so was a calculated risk that potentially could have resulted in the client accusing him of inappropriate behaviors. To avoid this potential risk we believe that it would have been prudent to explore other options. For example, we believe that it would have been appropriate for Thomas to (a) ask a colleague to join him, (b) ask Sue to meet him at the hospital's emergency room, (c) ask one of Sue's family members to take her to the emergency room, or (d) call the police and have them transport Sue to the emergency room. That said, we also understand that Thomas may have believed that his choices were limited. Thus, meeting Sue at his office was in the moment appropriate because Sue knew the mental health system well enough to know how to avoid being admitted to the hospital. In addition, it is possible that Thomas may have believed that he and Sue had developed sufficient trust over the months of therapy such that seeing her alone did not pose a realistic risk.

CONCLUDING THOUGHTS

We want to make it clear that we admire Thomas for the exceptional work he has done with this family under difficult circumstances. Indeed, it is courageous of him to share such an intimate portrait of his clinical work with an immensely difficult therapeutic situation and invite colleagues to comment. Although we have identified areas where we would have proceeded in a manner different from Thomas, our comments are not, in any way, intended to negate the work he has done. We accept that many or all of the questions/issues that we raised may have been addressed by Thomas. However, because of space limitations and the fact that any case report is by necessity a synopsis of several months or years of therapeutic work, some information may selectively have been omitted. Early in our discussion of this case, we recognized that it was easy for us as observers sitting outside Thomas's therapy room to offer other perspectives and ideas that were different from his decisions, directions, and techniques. However, although we may have formulated, proposed, and traveled different paths in therapy with this family does not mean that we would have done anything better than Thomas, only differently. More important, as outsiders we are aware that we were not experiencing the immediate in vivo pressures attendant to this emotionally charged case and could not hope to fully understand the context surrounding the events that occurred over those months of therapy. In the final analysis, then, we accept that as the therapist of record Thomas had a better vantage point from which to assess Sue and her family and to make difficult decisions. Despite this acceptance, however, it is exhilarating to believe that one is an expert when one sits outside someone else's therapy room or is at least fifty miles away from home.

REFERENCES

Gergen, K. J. (1985). The social constructionist movement in modern psychology. *American Psychologist,* 40(3), 266-275.

Haley, J. (1979). *Leaving home: Therapy with disturbed young people.* New York: McGraw-Hill.

Hoffman, L. (1990). Constructing realities: An art of lenses. *Family Process,* 29(1), 1-12.

Watzlawick, P., Bavelas, J. B., and Jackson, D. D. (1967). *Pragmatics of human communication: A study of interactional patterns, pathologies, and paradoxes.* New York: W. W. Norton.

Watzlawick, P., Weakland, J., and Fisch, R. (1974). *Change: Principles of problem formation and problem resolution.* New York: W. W. Norton.

CASE 7

Fishing for Gender Equality

Toni S. Zimmerman

Therapist Background

Currently: Forty-years old, white, female, PhD, fourteen years MFT practice. When I saw this family: Thirty-seven years old, eleven years MFT practice.

Practice Setting

Private practice.

Client Characteristics

Gary (age forty-five) and his wife Ann (age forty-three), a Euro-American couple married fifteen years, were seen in therapy because difficulties in their marital relationship were negatively impacting family functioning and marital satisfaction. Three children, David (age fourteen), Leslie (age eleven), and Derek (age eight), completed the family but were not directly involved in therapy. David was a high school freshman; Leslie was a student in middle school; and Derek attended elementary school. At the time of therapy, Gary was self-employed as an electrician and Ann was employed part time as a secretary in the family's electrical services business.

Length of Treatment

The family was seen for fifteen sessions over a period of five months. The critical incident occurred in Session 10.

Theoretical Perspective

A solution-focused and mental research institute (MRI) (problem-focused) approach, with a metaperspective of feminist family therapy was used in working with this couple.

THE PRESENTING PROBLEM

Ann and Gary came to therapy primarily because of a lack of intimacy in their marital relationship. Ann complained that she felt disrespected by Gary, felt powerless about influencing some family decisions, and was "carrying the greater share of the workload at home" in addition to working part time outside the home. As a result, she felt exhausted most of the time. She also revealed that for the past five years she had felt a lack of sexual/loving feelings for Gary and was frustrated with their lack of closeness. Gary contended that Ann "nagged" him constantly. Consequently, he did not feel "good enough" as a husband. He acknowledged that beyond working together, he and Ann spent very little time together as a couple; he sensed her distancing from him.

The First Session

I asked Ann and Gary to discuss their strengths as a couple. They both identified their mutual commitment to and a close relationship with their children as a strength. For example, they both listened to their children's ideas, involved them in the family's decision making, and frequently participated in their extracurricular activities, e.g., sports. Ann and Gary also identified their amicable on-the-job work relationship as a strength. Ann worked part time as a secretary in the family's electrical services business; on the job, the couple was efficient, polite, and "businesslike." Ann stated that anyone observing them in that setting "would have been surprised to learn that they didn't feel emotionally close to each other."

Asked for their perceptions of the problems in their relationship, Ann complained of not having an equal say in decisions related to the family's functioning. For example, she did not feel that she was afforded equal input about where the family would spend vacations. Invariably "family vacations" were spent fishing and hiking at Gary's parents' cabin. Ann asserted that her suggestions about alternative locations for family vacations and/or entertainment frequently were vetoed by Gary. As a result, she had come to feel that her ideas were unappealing. After years of futile attempts to have her input considered, she stopped offering her ideas but harbored tremendous anger about not having a voice in that area of the family's decision making. Gary was visibly annoyed with Ann because of her disclosures. He retorted, "I thought you liked fishing. You always enjoyed going up to the cabin. You don't say that there are other things that you want to do."

Ann acknowledged, however, that with regard to the family's home, she, rather than Gary, was the principle decision maker in such areas as decorating and selecting the location in which they bought their home, which was close to the school she wanted the children to attend. She and Gary also shared in the family's financial decisions and in monitoring the finances at home and with the business. In the more mundane areas, such as grocery shopping or buying for the children, they shared decision making equitably and trusted each other's spending habits. Despite these positives, however, Ann was frustrated with the division of labor they had established. She felt that she was carrying too much of the workload at home and did not feel she had the financial freedom to hire a cleaning service.

At the end of the hour, I shared with the couple my belief that they were experiencing power inequities in their relationship because of structural and societal factors. Specifically, Gary was making considerably more money than Ann and in actuality was her "boss" at work. As a result, their lives were built around Gary's career; clearly his career contributions were seen as more important than her contributions. I speculated that their current division of labor and decision-making practices could be viewed as a power inequity and a significant contributor to their lack of intimacy. Ann and Gary agreed with this premise. Accordingly, I identified problem cycles in their relationship and normalized their presenting problem as a challenging struggle for many couples in our society. I informed them that it was not uncommon for couples to experience power inequities in their marital relationships because in the United States, traditional gender-role socialization teaches that men should have more power (and more say) than women in heterosexual relationships. I also provided information about research relevant to the importance of equity as a contributor to sustained intimacy and satisfaction in marital relationships, and I also presented some alternative models of marriage based on equality (Barnett and Rivers, 1996; Gottman, 1994; Rabin, 1996; Schwartz, 1994).

To help the couple to move toward gender equality, I shared with them information about the power equity guide (PEG), a therapeutic approach developed by my colleagues and myself (Haddock, Zimmerman, and MacPhee, 2000), and suggested that this approach might be helpful in their situation for several reasons. First, the PEG allows couples to assess and to determine if power inequity exists in their relationship; if it does, the PEG may be used to identify specific areas in which power needs to be balanced to increase marital satisfaction and intimacy. In addition, this assessment allows couples to identify and celebrate areas in which they already have achieved a balance of power. Second, the PEG can be used to educate couples about marital equity and to operationalize it in all aspects of their relationship.

Third, the PEG can be used to set specific goals after identifying the areas of functioning that were impeding closeness.

THERAPEUTIC SITUATION PRIOR
TO THE CRITICAL INCIDENT

Ann acknowledged and complimented Gary for being a good, involved, and caring father, especially with regard to the children's sports interests; Gary reciprocated and complimented Ann for being an excellent mother. However, Ann continued to complain of feeling shortchanged in the marriage. She believed that Gary expected her to be his secretary and solely to be responsible for the housework, including laundry, bills, budgets, and cooking, as well as meeting the children's morning, after-school, and weekend needs. She believed that Gary perceived his primary responsibilities to be the business, care of the lawn, and occasional home maintenance. Gary concurred with her assessment of their division of labor but maintained that since he worked full time it was a fair division. He further contended that if Ann would improve her time management skills, she would have sufficient time for all that she had to do. Ann became angry when Gary suggested that she lacked organizational skills. She perceived his statement as yet another example of his lack of appreciation and refusal to recognize her contributions to the family and the business.

Gary and Ann acknowledged that Gary's career had been their central focus and Ann's career had been to help Gary succeed in his career. Despite her complaints, Ann emphasized that she was happy with her career decision to work in the family business. She, however, wanted the business to be referred to as "Gary and Ann's business" instead of "Gary's business" because she had helped the business to flourish by working there part time and full time at home. She was upset that Gary seemed not to appreciate her contributions to his success or accord her much status in that area. She wanted either a salary or to have some part of the business attributed to her. Gary responded that he always had considered Ann to be his partner and expressed a willingness to explore ways in which he could help her feel more secure as an equal rather than a subordinate. This exploration included conversation about Ann having more equal access to finances (e.g., freedom to hire a cleaning service).

Although Ann was comfortable with her career decision to support Gary in his career, she was concerned that this pattern had spread to other areas of their lives. For example, Gary frequently coached his sons' baseball teams and played on adult softball teams himself. As a result, Ann often put aside her own needs and interests to cheer him on at games and enable him to spend time coaching. Ann was very interested in knitting and used to be quite good at it, but in recent years she had come to believe that "she did not have the time to pursue her hobby." Gary countered that Ann had neither identified or articulated her life's goals nor how he could be supportive of those goals; Ann admitted that she had not explicitly stated her personal goals.

Ann also shared her concerns about their sexual relationship. They both acknowledged that their sexual relationship had been unsatisfactory for several years. Ann credited her anger at Gary and sheer physical exhaustion for her disinterest in sex. Gary stated that as a result of Ann's lack of sexual interest, he felt rejected and had stopped initiating sex. Relatedly, he acknowledged his lack of attentiveness to the marital relationship in ways acceptable to Ann, especially with regards to emotional closeness and intimate conversation. Instead, he demonstrated attentiveness to Ann by giving her gifts, paying her compliments, and using humor with her.

Ann disclosed that in the earlier years of the marriage, she was particularly focused on "making their relationship work." To this end she gave Gary many greeting cards, read self-help books, and raised concerns that she believed needed to be addressed. Unfortunately, the more issues she raised, the less receptive Gary was to her suggestions. Gary asserted that Ann always made demands that were too difficult for him to meet. As a result, their discussions frequently resulted in Ann becoming angry at him and escalating her demands. He observed that "Ann is too emotional and holds unrealistic ideas of closeness." Ann countered that Gary frequently used sarcastic humor whenever she attempted to discuss a serious concern.

EVENTS LEADING TO THE CRITICAL INCIDENT

During Sessions 6 through 9, Ann and Gary were assigned homework to watch four videotapes—*The Power Dead Even Rule, Stale Roles and Tight Buns, Killing Us Softly,* and *Color of Fear*—that examine gender differences and inequities. They were assigned one video per week, and we discussed each video the next week in therapy. These videos examine gender differences in the workplace, male socialization (to be emotionally distant and unavailable), female socialization (to be objectified, passive, and dependent), and the subtle power of white male privilege, respectively. Concurrently, we continued to move step by step through the PEG. Together we assessed their relationship for power equity, looking for areas of strengths and areas for growth. Gary listened to Ann's ideas and thoughts in each of these areas and Ann was assertive and clear about what she wanted and needed from Gary, and about which issues she was angry. Interestingly, despite Ann and Gary's report that they had not had much success discussing these topics at home, they did a very good job of communicating with each other in therapy.

Gary responded openly to therapy and appeared to understand at an intellectual level how power differentials function in U.S. society. He also appeared to understand how men and women are socialized to accept these differentials and to behave accordingly. Ann became aware that much of her behavior and anger at Gary had been influenced by gender-role socialization (her own and Gary's) and that her frustration stemmed from her power inequities with Gary. As a result of viewing the videotapes, using the PEG assessment, and setting personal goals, Ann made many changes. For example, she began to attend a weekly knitting group at a local coffee shop and joined a book club in which mothers and their daughters read identical books. She and Leslie read Mary Pipher's (1994) *Reviving Ophelia: Saving the Selves of Adolescent Girls,* which reinforced for Ann the dangers of traditional gender-role socialization for Leslie. Ann also requested information from two places where she believed she wanted to spend the next year's summer vacation and began to make plans related to these upcoming trips.

Gary also took some positive steps by not resisting Ann's changes. Instead, he supported Ann's spending time in her new activities each week and requested to read *Reviving Ophelia* when Ann and Leslie had finished reading the book. Although he did not explicitly agree to go on the two vacations that Ann was planning, it was implicitly understood that he would do so.

Unfortunately, although Ann was making changes that contributed to her decreased anger and increased self-confidence, independence, and assertiveness, these changes had only a marginal impact on the couple's degree of intimacy. At this point therapy appeared to be moderately stuck, especially for Gary. He appeared to be agreeing politely with the importance of gender equity. He was not resisting Ann's changes and he was attentive to thinking about gender and power differently. However, beyond his verbal acknowledgment, he did not appear to be interested in initiating personal changes. At one level, I was impressed that each week Gary kept showing up in therapy, but I also was beginning to wonder how I might effectively engage and move him to a place of genuine change in his own behavior. Without Gary's equal investment in change, I doubted the couple would be able to achieve their goals of intimacy and closeness.

THE CRITICAL INCIDENT

Ann and Gary missed two weeks of therapy because Gary spent one week on a fishing trip with his cousins and sons. Two days after Gary returned from the fishing trip and he and Ann had seen a movie together, the couple returned to therapy. As they entered the room, I immediately observed that their interactions with each other appeared different. They were laughing more, touching each other, and overall appeared to be more connected with each other.

Gary explained that subsequent to the fishing trip, he was beginning "to see things differently" as a result of his new awareness about gender inequality. Everywhere he looked he was beginning to see gender inequities. The jokes at which he previously would have laughed (or even told) on the fishing trip now angered him when he thought of Ann and Leslie. He had come to realize that "those jokes poked fun at women and put down them." He was aware of the emotional distance between men, and between men and women. For example, although the men had fun and enjoyed the fishing, Gary became aware that the conversations were not intimate. He observed that in contrast to their husbands, the wives were more supportive of the men's goals. To this end, the wives had packed food, extra clothing, and even small gifts for the men to discover once they arrived at the cabin. Suddenly, he was hearing lyrics to music on the radio differently as he began to listen in terms of gender roles in relationships. Gary commented that on the fishing trip, the men willingly washed dishes and did housework-like chores that they were reluctant to do at home. He questioned why Derek and David were with him and Leslie was not; he wondered why he had set it up that way. He said that he felt sad and lonely during much of the fishing trip and thought about some changes he wanted to make in his own behavior. For the first time in many years, he could not wait to get home to Ann! Hearing Gary share all of this, Ann laughed, "If I'd known the fishing trip would be this powerful, I'd have sent him months ago!"

The night Gary returned home, Ann invited him to accompany her to see the film *Eyes Wide Shut*. Gary enthusiastically accepted the invitation and suggested dinner afterward. For several hours during dinner, Ann and Gary discussed the movie's meaning and implications in terms of gender-role socialization. Gary shared with Ann his awareness of gender inequity on the fishing trip and the feelings that had arisen in him. Their conversation was close and intimate—much different from their usual practice of blaming or criticizing each other or using sarcastic humor to avoid tough conversations. They also explored ways in which they wanted to modify their interactions with each other. They came to the realization that gender socialization permeates society and agreed that to effect change they needed to maintain a heightened awareness.

As they related their conversation, they both were very proud and emotional. However, Gary experienced difficulty translating his newfound awareness into behavioral change. He was clear that he did not want Ann to feel "second class" at work or to feel exhausted and overwhelmed and ultimately unattracted to him. He wanted her to "have her own goals and to speak up in terms of her own desires." However, despite Gary's expressed desire to make meaningful personal changes, he experienced some degree of difficulty in determining his role in effecting change. But compared to previous times, a key difference was Gary's desire to change. To that end he asked Ann and me to help him to identify ways in which he could behave differently. For the first time, he appeared genuinely motivated to *do* something different, rather than to just *think* something different.

THE AFTERMATH OF THE CRITICAL INCIDENT

Subsequent to the critical incident, the couple continued in therapy and focused on identifying and implementing behavioral changes for themselves. Accordingly, we revisited the power equity guide and collaboratively set small goals, looking for small consistent changes for Gary similar to those Ann had made prior to the fishing trip.

Following these discussions Gary committed to react with more enthusiasm to Ann's suggestions about alternative locations for family entertainment and/or vacations. He also agreed to assume responsibility for key household chores. For relationship maintenance, they contracted to go out as a couple to a movie, dinner, or just for coffee and discussion twice a month; each month one spouse would take responsibility for planning one of the dates. With regard to the children, they mutually agreed that household chores would be divided equitably between David, Derek, and Leslie based on need and ability rather than gender (e.g., the boys assigned outside work and Leslie assigned household work). They also changed their manner of communicating with each other to model for David and Derek ways to communicate more respectfully with Leslie. I commented to the couple that all changes, particularly the changes they were initiating, take time and would require that they be consistent as well as persistent in their efforts.

DISCUSSION

The Role of the Critical Incident in Getting Therapy Unstuck

Prior to the fishing trip, Gary was intellectually grasping gender-role socialization and its effect on him and on Ann, but he had not fully realized its power and impact at an emotional level until the fishing trip. My sense is that because the fishing trip was so steeped in traditional male language and behaviors, it suddenly stood out in sharp contrast to what Gary was learning in therapy. In therapy, he had gotten a glimpse of how gender-role socialization puts both men and women in "gender straitjackets," but he did not truly comprehend it until he saw how it restricted his behavior and that of his sons and cousins on the trip. In retrospect, this fishing trip (something I would have been unlikely to prescribe) was an excellent learning experience for Gary.

In the past, Gary returned home from these fishing trips "overgendered." This emotional state tended to heighten negative interactions between Gary and Ann. For example, previously upon returning home, Gary would toss his muddy boots and clothes in the laundry room, expecting Ann to clean them. However, this time, upon arriving home he cleaned and put away all of his gear and clothing and did not lament not still being out with the guys. This time he expressed a deep desire to be with Ann. In addition to presenting Gary with powerful examples of traditional male gender socialization, the critical incident also served as an opportunity for "absence to make the heart grow fonder" in a way that had not occurred previously. At some level, it appeared that the absence of intrinsic intimacy on the fishing trip contributed to Gary's yearning for greater intimacy in his daily life, especially in his relationship with Ann. Not only did Gary express his deep love for Ann, he also lamented that he had not had these insights and made changes years ago. He grieved for the intimacy that they could have had much earlier in their marriage.

With regard to her part in this solution cycle, Ann also made some significant behavioral changes. Whereas in the past Ann would ambush and immediately bombard Gary with anger upon his return from his fishing trips, this time she did not. She did not wait to ambush Gary and immediately pressure him to meet all of her needs. She invited him to a movie instead. She had moved out of her own gender straitjacket and was meeting her own needs in many ways. Consequently, Gary perceived her to be nonpunitive and more approachable.

The Implication of the Critical Incident for Therapy

Becoming aware of gender inequity in relationships is a quantum leap for most people, thus it was admirable that this couple could take another leap to set specific goals for creating power balance in their relationship and to invite each other to loosen his or her gender straitjacket. Clearly, Ann was able to make changes as a result of the therapeutic discussions about equity issues. However, for Gary, the leap came as a result of being with his male friends on a weeklong fishing trip. Although this trip ostensibly was much like other fishing trips taken before, this time, because of our therapeutic discussions, new insights were hidden in Gary's tackle box. On this trip Gary rediscovered his deep love for Ann and came to realize that he no longer wanted to treat her, although unwittingly and unintentionally, "one-down."

As a result of the fishing trip, Gary saw Ann as a much stronger woman than he previously had believed her to be. For her part, Ann discontinued many of her old patterns. For example, with regard Gary's softball games, she attended only those games that she felt she wanted to attend. Consequently, she no longer felt a need to express anger and resentment after attending Gary's softball games because she felt that she had to do so. Rather, she was taking care of herself; this was very freeing for Gary not to feel solely responsible for Ann's happiness. Thus he now viewed her more as a peer and fell in love with her more deeply.

Because Gary was being so vulnerable regarding his feelings and so willing to share equally the responsibility for maintaining the relationship, Ann experienced a resurgence in her love and affection for him. Oftentimes when anger and resentment has been built up in a relationship, as it had in Gary and Ann's, a couple can experience much difficulty in their attempts to recover intimacy. However, because therapy and the fishing trip had reinforced gender socialization as the problem, rather than focusing solely on Gary or Ann as the problem, the couple was less blaming of each other and in doing so were able to restore their original closeness fairly rapidly.

THE OUTCOME OF THERAPY

After the critical incident, I saw Ann and Gary bimonthly rather than weekly. During this period Gary was very cooperative and therapy focused primarily on their efforts to operationalize their goals. Gary and Ann were committed to each other and to relationship intimacy and were exploring different ways to achieve gender equality. Because Ann had been so over-responsible for the family's functioning for many years, Gary, by default, had become accustomed to being underresponsible for the family's functioning, especially with regard to household chores. We agreed that for Gary to begin to participate fully in household chores it was important that Ann relinquish responsibility for some of those tasks and to do so in a way that did not appear to manipulate or punish Gary. Ann came to realize that in the past her behaviors had been part of the problem and now needed to be part of the solution. To this end, I invited the couple to explore new schedules and divisions of labor. Accordingly, they developed new ways of budgeting to increase financial fairness, new divisions of labor specific to the children, and even newly stated sexual hopes with regard to ways to relate and connect as peers. I also invited them to focus more on the present and future possibilities with regard to their division of labor rather than to continuously dredge up the problems they had experienced in the past in negotiating equity.

Follow-Up

Following the termination of therapy I did not have any direct contact with Gary and Ann but heard of them via a cousin whom they had referred to me for therapy. The cousin informed me that the couple was doing great.

REFERENCES

Barnett, R.C. and Rivers, C. (1996). *She works, he works: How two-income families are happy, healthy, and thriving.* Cambridge, MA: Harvard University Press.

Gottman, J. (1994). *Why marriages succeed or fail and how you can make yours last.* New York: Fireside.

Haddock, S., Zimmerman, T.S., and MacPhee, D. (2000). The power equity guide: Attending to gender in family therapy. *Journal of Marital and Family Therapy,* 26(2), 153-170.

Pipher, M. (1994). *Reviving Ophelia: Saving the selves of adolescent girls.* New York: Ballantine Books.

Rabin, C. (1996). *Equal partners—good friends: Empowering couples through therapy.* New York: Routledge.

Schwartz, P. (1994). *Love between equals: How peer marriage really works.* New York: Free Press.

Commentary

Matching the Bait with the Catch

Charles Lee Cole

Commentator Background

Fifty-seven years old, Caucasian, male, PhD, twenty-nine years MFT practice.

Practice Setting

University-based MFT training program; limited private practice.

Theoretical Perspective

A collaborative couples therapy approach following the traditions of postmodern therapists such as Harlene Anderson (1997), Harlene Anderson and Harry Goolishian (1992), and Tom Anderson (1987) informs the perspective that I will use to comment on this case.

I appreciate Zimmerman's sensitivity to gender in her approach to therapy with Ann and Gary and also appreciate and identify with her use of the MRI and solution-focused approaches to working with the couple. Her focus on what she perceived to be the presenting problem is consistent with my belief that therapy needs to be driven by the client's description of the presenting problem. To that end I have found the techniques developed by the MRI and solution-focused models to be very useful in orchestrating the changes that the couple desires. Using these techniques, client couples are able to achieve the desired outcomes for which they sought therapy.

POINTS OF CONVERGENCE AND DIVERGENCE
WITH ZIMMERMAN

Based on Zimmerman's descriptions of this case, it is difficult to conclude that gender inequity appropriately describes the presenting problem from Ann and Gary's point of view. If indeed gender inequity is the presenting problem perceived by both individuals in the client couple, it appears on the surface that Zimmerman may be taking Ann's point of view and providing the voice that she has needed in communicating with Gary. I would argue that the traditional power differential of Gary having more power is as damaging to him as it is to Ann. Zimmerman used videotapes and oral presentations as therapeutic aids to teach this couple about gender inequities. However, based on her descriptions of therapy, Zimmerman does not address the negative impact of gender inequity upon Gary; only its negative impact upon Ann is described. Absent is any mention of the negative impact of gender inequity on Gary, I can only wonder how Gary, as a male, might have perceived the situation. Did he sometimes feel defensive during therapy because the emphasis was on how his power negatively impacted Ann? In addition to not recognizing that Gary also was impacted by gender inequity, Zimmerman does not say whether Gary was defensive or address how her model is designed to deal with defensiveness should it occur. Accordingly, I question how did the situation as defined—negatively affecting only Ann—affect Gary's willingness to think about and to make changes? Did the emphasis upon gender inequity's negative impact upon women in traditional marriage unbalance the relationship rather than balance it, or did it simply create entrenched positions? I would have preferred to discover the underlying values that the couple used to organize their relationship before I attributed meaning to the situation as described by the couple. The crucial process of gaining a fuller description of the marital situation that defines the problem from the perspective of the client is essential before embarking on a course of treatment. Any attempts to create change in the system without this vital information may be counterproductive. Accordingly, until I as the therapist have a fuller understanding of the couple's values, expectations, goals, etc., any movement and/or meaning that I might impose upon the couple's situation may contravene their value system. This is a central principle that governs/guides my work with couples and families. As a therapist I always have tried to respect the clients' value systems. This respect is grounded in the explicit expectation that what I personally might choose in my own life is not and cannot be what my clients would choose in their lives. Their marriage is not my marriage, and the life they live is not my life. Accordingly, I believe it is important that therapists appreciate the context of each couple's situation to obtain an adequate picture of their individual/collective situation as each spouse tells his or her stories. The context is embedded in values held by each respective spouse, and the values held by each spouse provide the filters used by the client couple in describing and evaluating their marriage.

Psychotherapy with couples often is complex because a couple's experiences with the marriage are shaped by not one but two separate value systems. Based on Zimmerman's description of Gary and Ann's marriage, it is unclear to me if either partner made the same assumptions about the nature of the organizational structure of their marital relationship as did Zimmerman.

At another level, clinical experiences with couples have taught me that some couples, regardless of social class, believe that husbands are the heads of the household. This preference for a traditional marriage system, which places a wife in a subservient position to her husband, may be counter to most marriage and family therapists' personal beliefs in the value of egalitarian relationships. This incongruous situation challenges us to remember that as therapists it is important that we respect such couples' beliefs regardless of our personal preferences.

AN ALTERNATIVE VIEW OF THE PRESENTING PROBLEM

Zimmerman's approach to therapy with Ann and Gary raises two concerns about the presenting problem. First, based on the brief case description, I can understand how Zimmerman might, from a feminist perspective, conceptualize the presenting problem as a gender-equity issue. Doing so is consistent with the line of questioning with which she initiates therapy. However, the available information does not present the actual process of how Zimmerman discovered and concluded that the central issue for this couple was gender inequity. Absent more details, I accept that a logic to Zimmerman's conceptual leap and her development of this line of questioning must have existed. It, however, would have been helpful if Zimmerman had provided more information about how the client couple perceived their marital situation from their own vantage point. Second, I wonder how the filters of Zimmerman's feminist lens shaped how she approached therapy as well as what she heard the client couple telling her. Because we as therapists can unwittingly superimpose our own assumptions onto our clients it is important that we empower/encourage clients to speak in their own voices and to resist imposing our definitions upon their presenting problems since doing so can alter the therapeutic process and its outcomes.

As an alternative to Zimmerman's description of the case, I would have framed the presenting problem differently. From my perspective, the couple's presenting problem principally is a problem of an interactional pattern organized around issues related to distance regulation. The patterning of these issues created distance and the polarization of positions. As the polarized positions began to crystallize, the couple became stuck in an interaction pattern that blocked interest in developing emotional closeness and intimacy. The more polar the spouses' positions became, the less either partner was desirous of or able to empathize with the other's position. The gender-equity issue, then, is a by-product of the polarization. From this vantage point, each spouse is focused only on self-interest and believes that the only solution for his or her problem would come from the other spouse; that is, "If only you would. . . ." Exaggerating the descriptions provided by Zimmerman, I can imagine that Ann, in part, perceives the problem to be "If only Gary would give me greater credit for my contributions, our marriage would be fine." Gary, on the other hand, might perceive the problem to be, "If only Ann would stop nagging and complaining about everything, our marriage would be fine." As long as the polarization continues to be exacerbated, the couple will remain stuck with little movement toward either achieving more intimacy and closeness or the many by-products of closeness and intimacy.

WHAT I MIGHT HAVE DONE DIFFERENTLY

Were I the therapist of record with Ann and Gary, my intervention strategy would have been to work collaboratively with the couple to create new spaces in their interactional pattern. The break in the cycle of polarization would emerge through the couple's dialogue. Based on my clinical experiences with couples in similar situations, I have found that by increasing empathy through couple dialogue collaboratively structured—to assure each partner comfort and safety in exploring the issues openly and honestly—I have been able to move couples away from their polarized positions. Using this approach, I assume the role of a master conversationalist who helps to open spaces in the couple's dialogue to help them to see the situation from a different perspective. Usually, this involves pacing and shifting the therapeutic focus by making punctuated transitions that reshape the contextual definitions of the couple's current social situation to anchor the problem description. At times this involves deconstructing meanings to loosen the stranglehold of polarized positions. At other points, the intervention may focus on collaboratively constructing new meanings that define the relationship in a context of shared definitions of reality.

THE CRITICAL INCIDENT

General Comments

My therapeutic work with couples is anchored in several underlying assumptions. One such assumption is that movement toward therapeutic change is a by-product of a critical incident which has changed the contextual meaning of the situation, which both produced and maintains the problem for which the couple is seeking therapy. I believe that some type of critical incident is necessary to motivate couples to change their relationships. However, the original motivational force that brings a couple to therapy may not be sufficient to propel them to the desired change. In many cases, the changes that occur throughout therapy mark therapeutic transitions that afford space to redefine the presenting problem. These changes often are typical of the types of critical incidents described in the treatment of Gary and Ann in which therapy had reached an impasse and needed some type of punctuated shift. The fishing trip served to break the cycle, thereby creating space for alternative meanings that redefined the situation. By opening up spaces in the couple's dialogue, the vicious cycle of unproductive interactional patterns is broken by the time interval shift of changing the structure of the therapy appointments.

Had I used a collaborative approach with this couple, I would have viewed the shift as redirecting the focus of therapy in light of the crucial information the client couple had given me through the critical incident. This type of client feedback specific to their immediate experiences in therapy is vital to create and maintain the collaboration between clients and therapists. Accordingly, when working therapeutically with couples, I periodically use brief ethnographic interviews to obtain feedback about each partner's perspective of the therapeutic process. Ethnographic interviews previously have been used by anthropologists and clinical sociologists to elicit respondents' experiences/perspectives about the culture in which they live (Spradley, 1979). In psychotherapy, especially MFT, ethnographic interviews are conducted by a person or persons other than the therapists of record. These persons elicit the clients' perceptions of the session at the end of the session. Here the conversation focuses on examining what the clients liked and did not like about the process that just concluded. From the clients' perspective, providing feedback in ethnographic interviews at the end of each session helps them to feel a co-ownership of the therapeutic process and sends a powerful message that their opinions are valued. As the therapist of record, the clients' feedback provides me with an informed approach to therapy that is firmly grounded in the client's experiences and evaluation of the therapeutic process. These periodic checks are gauges that let me know whether I am perceiving the therapeutic situation in the same manner as the clients. Based on this feedback, I can ascertain whether the line of questioning, pacing, and focus of therapy is consistent with what the clients want to achieve in therapy and are finding helpful. It also provides information about what clients want more and/or less of in subsequent sessions.

Specific Comments

The fishing trip provided an opportunity for Ann and Gary to reexamine their marriage in a different light. The time apart gave each partner the opportunity to see the other one's point of view and to gain insight with regards to what each one needed from the other specifically and from the marital relationship in general. In essence, the fishing trip provided space for each partner to shift from blaming the problem on the other partner and toward a more collaborative definition of the problem as "our problem," which made the crucial difference in moving together. The renewal of marital interaction after the fishing trip took on new meaning that emerged from the partners seeing each other in a different light. By opening up the spaces, Gary and Ann shifted from their polarized positions and genuinely moved toward each other. As the partners rediscovered each other, they both began to long for the intimacy that had been missing in their relationship for quite some time. This perspective represented a 180-degree turn (Lederer and Jackson, 1968) in the posturing of difference as threatening to each partner. With the reversal of polarized stances, the partners were able to empathize with each other and to move toward greater relationship depth (Mace, 1982). The increased empathy propelled the couple to desire greater closeness and intimacy on a new level, sharing the vulnerabilities that each one had masked with defensive posturing prior to the critical incident.

ETHICAL CONSIDERATIONS IN COUPLES THERAPY

When marriage and family therapists work with couples and families in therapy, it is important to be mindful of the many conundrums of the diversity of backgrounds and values that clients bring into therapy. The case of Ann and Gary's marriage illustrates a crucial dilemma regarding gender equity in the couple's division of labor, allotments of power and prestige in decision making, and family and business governance patterns. Accordingly, Doherty (1999, p. 4) observes, "Another example of ethical soul-searching for many family scientists is how to uphold the egalitarian ideals that most of us have for marriage in a society where many couples either do not aspire to an egalitarian marriage or find ways to rationalize not having one. When our own values and/or research findings get translated into family life [marriage] education or therapy, what ethical ground do we walk on when we decide to influence the couple's gender-based arrangements?"

CONCLUDING THOUGHTS

This commentary presents my alternative views regarding this couple's presenting problem. This view has shaped a different approach to therapy with Gary and Ann and persuaded me to try different bait. Doing so is illustrative of how as individuals and clinicians our selection of specific theoretical models that informs our practice can make the difference in the direction(s) in which therapy proceeds. Specifically, our choice(s) of therapeutic focus is, in part, a function/interaction of our training, personality, values, practice-setting context, and the contextual factors that the clients bring into therapy. Both perspectives—Zimmerman's and mine—are effective and illustrate that although the changes that occur in the client system may be stimulated and sparked by different therapeutic maneuvers based upon contrasting approaches to martial and family therapy, different approaches can be effective and need not be wrong or right, only different. Indeed, different ways exist to catch fish and do it well!

REFERENCES

Andersen, Thomas (1987). The reflecting team: Dialogue and meta-dialogue in clinical work. *Family Process, 26*(3), 415-428.

Anderson, Harlene (1997). *Conversation, language, and possibilities: A post-modern approach to therapy.* New York: Basic Books.

Anderson, Harlene and Goolishian, Harry A. (1992). The client is the expert: A not-knowing approach to therapy. In S. McNamee and K.J. Gergen (Eds.), *Therapy as social construction* (pp. 25-39). London: Sage.

Doherty, William J. (1999). Ethics, family science and family policy. *National Council on Family Relations Report* 44(4), 3-4.

Lederer, William J. and Jackson, Don D. (1968). *The mirages of marriage.* New York: W. W. Norton.

Mace, David R. (1982). *Close companions: The marriage enrichment handbook.* New York: Continuum.

Spradley, James (1979). *The ethnographic interview.* New York: Holt, Rinehart and Winston.

Commentary

Romancing the Gender Lens

Candyce S. Russell

Commentator Background

Fifty-two years old, WASP, female, PhD, twenty-seven years MFT Practice.

Practice Setting

University MFT clinic; limited private practice.

Theoretical Perspective

My work is primarily intergenerational (Bowen-informed) and structural with developmental and feminist overlays. When I see couples, I typically begin with an intergenerational lens; when I see a child-focused family I begin with a structural lens. The developmental overlay is a residual from my early training in family sociology. The feminist overlay is the most recent addition to my clinical armamentarium. A feminist perspective includes sensitivity to the privileges and limitations inherent in any "ecological" niche (Falicov, 1995). I consider men to be as limited as women by traditional gender-role socialization. Ethnicity, race, and the complexities that surround migration and dislocation also are becoming increasingly visible as a contextual frame for my work.

GENDER AS AN ORGANIZING THEME

A major strength of Zimmerman's work with this couple is her consistent focus on gender roles as a way to enter a marriage and to create change. In the early stage of therapy Zimmerman used the term "gender-role straitjacket" and thereafter used it effectively to link the middle stages of therapy to the early and later phases. Zimmerman also concretized the abstract concept of "gender equality" by using teaching videos and a pencil and paper inventory to help Ann and Gary to identify goals specific to gender-role equality within their relationship. Her familiarity with the research literature that documents the importance of equity in intimate relationships, and her own work in assessing and measuring power in marriage, enhanced therapy and allowed her to develop an effective strategy for her work with the couple. Her strategies included educating the couple and contracting with them for behavioral changes. She also taught the couple about gender, power, and marriage and helped them to negotiate new ways of being gendered persons in an intimate relationship.

Another strength of Zimmerman's work with this couple is her persistence. It is easy to give up and "try something else" in the middle phases of therapy when progress often is slow. Zimmerman may have felt like giving up at times but instead stuck with the frame of gender and power. In doing so, she provided a consistent framework for meaning and devised homework tasks to make the concepts concrete and usable. Consistent with her comment, "it takes a long time to learn new ways of being a couple," she patiently and artfully wove redundancy and reiteration into her approach.

WHAT I MIGHT HAVE DONE DIFFERENTLY

Frequently, couples in the middle years of life tend to feel sandwiched between generations, simultaneously aware that they still have time to make changes in their lives and curious to understand how they became the persons who they are today and who they may yet become. Were I the therapist of record with this couple, my strategy would have been to put words to the story that explains what Gary and Ann brought into the marriage from their families of origin and what of their own they added. In this regard, I would have helped them to identify patterns in their relationships with others and to focus on their contributions in maintaining those patterns. Specifically, I would have focused on how, as a couple and as individuals, they managed distance and closeness in a variety of relationships: at home, at work, and with friends, for example. Consistent with my intergenerational perspective, I would have asked Ann and Gary questions about their respective parents' marriages. For example, what do they know about their parents' marriages at this (middle) stage of the family life cycle? In what ways did they perceive their own marriage to be similar to and different from their parents' marriage in their (Ann and Gary's) ways of being middle-aged spouses? Would their parents be surprised that they were having relationship difficulties at this point in their lives? These questions would have been used to help Ann and Gary to depersonalize their struggles and to look to their respective extended families both as a resource and as a mirror from which to study self.

First, however, I would have asked them, "why now?" Specifically, what shifts had occurred in their emotional systems such that they are interested in therapy now? Ann and Gary entered therapy at a point in the family life cycle when their children were becoming less dependent upon them and their business was well established. Based on this, I might speculate that Gary and especially Ann now had the time and energy to invest in their relationship—something that they did not believe they had in the recent past. Despite this plausible speculation, I still would be curious to know *specifically* "why now?" What makes it possible and important to attend to the marriage now?

The answer to that question might come from their respective families of origin. For instance, the death of an elder in the family could create enough anxiety to destabilize the patterned relationship Ann and Gary had developed, especially if they were not talking about the loss (Cristofori, 1977). I also would have asked about recent marriages, divorces, deaths, and illnesses in the extended family as well as Ann and Gary's own health. Oftentimes it is easier to talk about dissatisfactions with a partner than it is to confront losses and potential losses that are beyond one's control. Were Ann and Gary members of a minority group or first- or second-generation immigrants, I would have asked them to talk about how comfortable they were feeling in their community and how they had decided which parts of the dominant culture to adopt and which parts to reject; I would have discussed the meaning of those decisions within the context of their families of origin.

The answer to "why now" could also relate to their business. Accordingly, I would have asked questions about their perceptions regarding their business in terms of its development, the changes it has gone through, and any changes that may be imminent.

DEVELOPING A CURIOSITY ABOUT SELF

In my clinical experience, couples typically enter therapy intent on getting their *partner* to change his or her behaviors. Having that awareness, would invite each partner to become curious about his or her own behavioral patterns and to be less focused on the other. Such a shift in perspective can reduce blame, disrupt cycles of pursuit and withdrawal, and enhance the development of a "self" that makes people more attractive to one another. For example, when Ann began to pursue her interest in knitting and attended Gary's ball games only when she felt like doing so, she was making decisions that helped her to define a "self." As a result, Gary began to see Ann in new ways and to feel less blamed by her. Here the key was the steps

Ann had taken to make her life better, regardless of Gary's reaction. By assessing equity in the couple's relationship Zimmerman helped Ann to be more focused on her "self" and less on Gary. Similar to Zimmerman, I might have arrived at a similar place with Ann by exploring with her the other relationships in her life in which she was accommodating in a like manner. I also might have suggested that Ann discuss with her mother or her sister their personal strategies for dealing with the pull to accommodate to others and what doing so has meant to their lives.

In U.S. culture, men, at some level, often are aware of missing significant connections in their lives, with their siblings, spouses, and/or children, and especially with their own fathers (Erickson, 1993). Accordingly, I might have explored with Gary his experiences of loneliness and used that to motivate him to become curious about "self" and his efforts to connect with others. I might talk with Gary about his relationship with his father and siblings and what it means to be a man in his family. Perhaps in his family there existed more than one way to be a man. How did he select his own pattern? If he were to make a change in his way of being a man, with whom would he first attempt a change? Would it be by risking more of his "self" with his father? Would it be by learning more about his father's life? Interestingly, Gary began to connect what he was learning about gender equity with his role as a father to his daughter before he learned to connect this knowledge with Ann. This is not unusual. Often it tends to be easier to "practice" a new way of being in relationships that are less intense than marriage.

At this point, therapy would look a bit like each partner listening to the other's individual therapy. Hopefully, the distance accorded that "spectator" seat would help each partner to reflect on the implications for self. Paradoxically, the more freedom that existed in Ann and Gary's relationship for each to be separate, the more they were attracted to each other. That sounds much like Murray Bowen telling us that "differentiation" is what makes intimacy possible.

MAKING USE OF THE CRITICAL INCIDENT

Zimmerman used herself as a teacher and as an observer of process. Perhaps most important, she waited for a shift in affect between Ann and Gary to teach them at a deeper level of affect. She was patient and receptive when Ann and Gary were ready to use her leadership in a new way. She also was respectful of the couple's accomplishments outside of the therapy room and willing to listen to their understanding of the fishing-trip weekend.

As Ann and Gary returned to therapy following the fishing weekend, I might have attempted to engage Gary in a more extended conversation about his understanding of the significance of the weekend and its meaning for his relationship with his wife, his daughter, and his sons. In this context, it might have been helpful to Ann to hear Gary retell the story of the past week and its meaning for him. In retelling the story Gary might have developed new understandings and implications for a broader range of relationships. This would be an opportunity to return to a focus on *relationship patterns*.

I also would have asked Ann to identify and discuss the personal changes she will need to make for her to relate to Gary's new ways of being a husband and father. For example, will she miss parts of the old patterns? Will she feel "displaced" in some of her roles as Gary steps up to share in the emotional work of the family? How has she dealt with previous changes in the relationship? How will she let Gary know what she appreciates about his changes and to what aspects of his changed behaviors she is having difficulty adjusting? How will she reinvest the emotional energy she previously used in her attempts to get Gary's attention? I also might have asked Ann and Gary as a couple to speculate about who they believe will notice the changes in their relationship; what do they feel their changes will mean to those people; and in what ways might others support or challenge their new ways of being a couple?

What If the Critical Incident Had Not Occurred?

With regard the critical incident, I have wondered how I might have used my personal experience with Ann and Gary if the "fishing epiphany" had not occurred—specifically, if weeks of therapy had passed and there was little more than superficial change in the relationship. Absent a naturally occurring event such as the fishing weekend, I might have commented on my personal experience of being with the couple in an effort to "turn up the therapeutic heat." Here I would be modeling with the couple an attempt at a new level of intimacy, hoping that Ann and Gary would take my lead and risk more intimacy with each other.

It may have been possible to move the couple to a new level in therapy by commenting on the feelings of sadness and loneliness I was experiencing as I sat with them in the room. Making such comments and being comfortable and willing to sit in silence for awhile might have opened the way for the couple to risk new affect. I can imagine such a scenario occurring during the period when Ann had made significant changes for herself, but Gary had not. Although turning up the emotional thermostat would be a decidedly "un-Bowen" thing to do, I firmly believe that change in therapy occurs at multiple levels. Consequently, a therapist can helpfully enter a system at cognitive, behavioral, *and* emotional levels (Christensen, et al., 1998).

It is difficult to avoid a sense of isolation and loneliness when one partner is socialized to be emotionally distant and unavailable and the other has been struggling to fill in the void. If I began to feel lonely myself as I sat with Ann and Gary, that would be my cue to comment on loneliness. Hopefully, by verbalizing my awareness, I would strike in Gary a responsive chord that would help him to engage in a new way. If I did this as a "technique" rather than as a genuine expression of my experience of the moment, I would expect Gary to retreat. However, if the comment emerged from our experience together, I believe that it might be helpful. I strongly believe that characteristically most clients appreciate honesty from a therapist, especially when they experience such honesty as the therapist's genuine care for them.

The Bottom Line

There always are multiple paths to any outcome. Zimmerman's path was informed by her scholarship and her belief that men and women are limited in unhelpful ways by traditional gender-role socialization. Her path is psychoeducational and includes careful plans for behavioral changes. The path I would have taken with Ann and Gary would have included elements of education as well. In that regard, I would have asked Ann and Gary to observe and to be aware of their behavioral patterns and would have involved them in a thoughtful, cognitive activity to help them to understand their roles in maintaining those patterns. I would have invited them to discuss how they planned to interact differently with each other and I also would have looked for opportunities to create change through affective paths. I would have done this either by highlighting the affect Ann and Gary brought into the room or by commenting upon my own experience of being with them as a couple. In working with this couple, Zimmerman neither emphasized affect nor commented on her personal experience of being with them. Despite not doing so, she was respectful of the couple's excitement after the fishing weekend and used it to motivate them to change.

CONCLUDING THOUGHTS

In her work with this couple, Zimmerman used a broad therapeutic lens that helped to heighten her awareness of the social context in which Gary and Ann are imbedded. The initial focus of my lens is narrower and emphasizes the intergenerational system. I would have introduced the issue of gender by asking each partner what it means to be a man or a woman in his or her respective family of origin and how each one would like his or her own family to be similar and different with respect to gender. Finally, it is important to point out that although I have suggested a different path for therapy with Ann and Gary, gender would have been a central feature in my work with this couple as it was for Zimmerman.

REFERENCES

Christensen, L.L., Russell, C.S., Miller, R.B., and Peterson, C.M. (1998). The process of change in couples therapy: A qualitative investigation. *Journal of Marital and Family Therapy,* 24(2):177-188.

Cristofori, R.H. (1977). Modification of loss in divorce: A report from clinical practice. *The Family,* 5(1):184-189.

Erickson, B.M. (1993). *Helping men change: The role of the female therapist.* New York: Sage.

Falicov, C. (1995). Training to think culturally: A multi-dimensional comparative framework. *Family Process,* 34(4):373-388.

CASE 8

Seeing Is Believing

William F. Northey Jr.

Therapist Background

Currently: Thirty-seven years old, white, male, PhD, nine years MFT practice. When I saw this family: twenty-four years old, a second-year MFT master's student, one year of prior clinical experience in an inpatient psychiatric hospital substance-abuse program.

Practice Setting

Currently: AAMFT's Professional Development/Research Specialist; limited private practice. When I saw this family: Practicum student, university's MFT clinic.

Client Characteristics

Al (age forty-eight), his wife Cheryl (age forty-nine), and their son Zach (age fourteen) were a Jewish-American family. Three older children, John (age twenty-one), Sharon (age nineteen), and Susan (age seventeen), completed the family. Only Al, Cheryl, and Zach participated in therapy; Zach was the IP. The family had been in therapy at the university's MFT clinic on two previous occasions over a two-year period. The therapists of record then were faculty members, and John, Sharon, and Susan respectively were the IPs; therapy focused on resolving issues specific to their academic difficulties, alcohol abuse, and violations of family rules. This time around, John and Sharon were attending college, Susan was a high school senior, and Zach was a freshman in high school. Al and Cheryl owned a small carpet-cleaning business.

Length of Treatment

Because of lengthy breaks, the family was seen on a variable schedule for approximately fifteen months. The critical incident occurred in Session 10 in the fourth month of therapy.

Theoretical Perspective

Initially, an eclectic approach was used in working with this family, later a MRI strategic approach. My MFT supervisor subscribed to a cognitive-behavioral approach.

PRESENTING PROBLEM

The family sought therapy because of behavioral difficulties with Zach. The parents complained that Zach neither followed parental directions at home nor did his homework or chores. In addition, his academic performance was poor; he got into trouble in school; and he was disrespectful toward his father at home.

THE THERAPEUTIC SITUATION PRIOR
TO THE CLINICAL INCIDENT

Al and Cheryl were loquacious and spent much of the early sessions telling and retelling about the "bad things" that Zach had done or heatedly arguing about other problems not directly related to the current presenting problem. As a result, during the first several sessions, I spent a significant amount of time attempting to slow down the process so that we might begin to prioritize and address the most pressing issues. Al and Cheryl expressed polar perceptions and opinions of identical events and often argued about inconsequential aspects of the events they reported. For example, although they agreed that Zach was late coming home or that he did not do his chores, they argued about how many minutes late he was coming home and on which specific day he did not do his chores.

Very early in therapy it became clear that Al was the stricter of the two parents and tended to overreact to Zach's behaviors. On the other hand, Cheryl assumed a protector's role vis-à-vis Zach's interaction with his father. In this regard, it was not unusual for Al to discipline Zach for some misbehavior and Cheryl to soften or altogether negate the sanctions Al sought to impose. Invariably, each parent rationalized and defended his or her actions as appropriate. Al believed that "Cheryl was babying Zach." To compensate for what he perceived to be "Cheryl's coddling," Al believed that he had to be tough on Zach. On the other hand, Cheryl believed that "Al was too tough on Zach." Consequently, she felt she had to protect Zach from Al's wrath. Compounding matters was Al's verbosity and his thunderous voice that amplified his speech and made his words seem even more fearful and caustic than they actually were or were intended to be.

For several sessions I attempted to negotiate an explicit parental agreement to establish identifiable, appropriate, and realistic consequences for Zach's misbehaviors. Unfortunately, Al and Cheryl disagreed about what was and what was not an appropriate consequence. For example, during our discussion Al would disqualify as "too lenient" a particular consequence Cheryl had identified and suggested. Cheryl would reciprocate and disqualify as "too stern" consequences that Al suggested. In support of her position, Cheryl would assert, "He's only fourteen!" Al would retort, "He's a young man!" Because the parents appeared unable to reach an agreement on the issue, i.e., appropriate consequences, I decided to employ a variation of the Milan groups "odd-even days" interventions to help them to move beyond the impasse (Selvini Palazzoli et al., 1978).

I told the parents that it was clear that they both cared very much for Zach and wanted the best for him. However, they tended to focus on different, albeit very important, lessons that he needed to learn: Al focused on Zach being responsible and Cheryl focused on Zach being a happy member of the family. Clearly, each one had privileged the lesson he or she wanted Zach to learn and as a result had failed to see the value in the other person's suggestions. "Accordingly, I am going to suggest something that will sound very crazy. The purpose of my suggestion is to help each of you to see the utility of the other one's point of view." That said, I then suggested that Al and Cheryl alternate days when each one would be the parent in charge. I emphasized that Zach's misbehaviors were not being corrected because while Mother and Dad were disagreeing, no one was paying attention to Zach's behaviors and he was getting away with proverbial "murder." "With the odd-even system, each of you will have an opportunity to emphasize his or her particular lesson without interference from the other one. For example, while Al might believe that Zach is getting away with bad behaviors on Cheryl's days, he would be able to ensure that Zach was being responsible on his days without fear that Cheryl would disqualify his sanctions against Zach."

Initially, Al was emphatic that the assignment "really was stupid;" Cheryl was equally as reluctant, albeit not as vocal. During additional discussion on the merits of the assignment, I extolled the benefit and the importance of seeing the value in each other's parenting style. With additional coaxing, I was able to persuade Al and Cheryl to commit to the assignment. That done, we selected the specific days on which each parent would be the parent in charge and discussed/clarified ways in which he or she might respond to the various situations that might arise. For example, what if Al was home with Zach on his day or on Cheryl's day and Zach misbehaved? As a neophyte therapist, I was oblivious to their lack of readiness to participate in this exercise. Had I been more experienced, I might have been acutely aware of their collective negative response and accepted that as an indication of their lack of readiness to participate. Blinded by inexperience, I overlooked the clue (which in retrospect seems obvious) and assigned the homework because I believed that it might help Al and Cheryl to be less extreme in their dealings with Zach.

Predictably, the homework assignment was unsuccessful. At the next session, Al began the hour complaining about the problems Zach had that week and his failure to do his chores and be respectful. I asked about the homework assignment and received a lukewarm response from the couple. They admitted that they each, but especially Al, experienced difficulty allowing the other to be fully responsible for his or her assigned days. More important, both parents asserted that the assignment lacked relevance for their situation. I iterated the belief that each parent had valuable lessons to teach Zach, but neither one would be successful until they each could see the value in the other one's perspective. Neither parent accepted my reframe.

The session immediately prior to the critical event was very chaotic; I felt that I was not making any progress with the family. The family again was arguing about minutiae; in the process, Zach tended to slip into the woodwork. This evasion protected Zach from his parents bickering and also allowed him to avoid responsibility for his behaviors. At this point I perceived therapy to be stuck. I was feeling stuck and therapeutically unable to help the family to move from conflict to resolution. Feeling stuck, I decided to present the case in my next group supervision meeting. At that meeting, one of my colleagues who had observed the family asked, "Is Al always that loud?" Both supervisors (who previously had worked with the family) and I replied, "Yes."

The supervision group observed that Zach was sitting back watching his parents argue about what he had done and how to discipline him. In light of this observation, various hypotheses were offered to explain why the family was behaving as it was. We hypothesized that Al and Cheryl "needed" to focus on one of the children to stay connected. Although this hypothesis was plausible, I pointed out that Al and Cheryl worked together in the family business and had ample opportunities to stay connected. Despite this, it could not be denied that all of their older children had been the focus of treatment; now it was Zach's turn. A counter hypothesis was that the parents were not disconnected; they really disagreed on how to parent. It also was suggested that perhaps Al and Cheryl did not fully understand the role that Zach's behaviors played in their interactions. Given this fairly benign frame, the supervision group recommended that at the next session, I should show the family the videotape of the therapy session the supervision group had seen. My purpose would be to point out to the parents how Zach was avoiding responsibility for his misbehaviors and was in some ways contributing to the process of their arguing.

THE CRITICAL INCIDENT

At the next session, I informed the family of the supervision group's suggestion and shared with them what I planned to do, then showed the videotape. I was hoping that the family would see on the videotape what the supervision group had seen, i.e., the manner in which Zach was able to avoid responsibility when his parents argued about how he should be parented. While the parents are focused on Zach, their bickering about how to parent him precludes an appropriate solution and keeps the family stuck. After the family had watched the tape for a few minutes, I stopped it. Al immediately asked, "Do I sound like that?" Cheryl, Zach, and I were taken aback by Al's question, but after we clarified what he was asking—was he really as loud as he sounded on the tape—we all responded "yes." I asked Al if he was aware that he spoke very loudly. He responded that he really was unaware that he spoke as loudly as he sounded on the tape. He then asked why no one had ever told him that he spoke in such high decibels. We discussed at length the negative impact of his thunderous voice not only in therapy but in the family and at his job. Cheryl also shared her perception of the ways in which Al's loudness affected her. She asserted that some people were afraid of Al because of the loudness with which he spoke. She also expressed the opinion that Al's loudness was his way to keep people, including Cheryl and the children, at a distance. Following this discussion, Al asked the family and me to tell him when he was speaking too loudly. We agreed to do so, but for the remainder of the family's time in treatment Al never spoke as loudly as he did prior to seeing the videotape.

THE AFTERMATH OF THE CRITICAL INCIDENT

Subsequent to the critical incident, Al and Cheryl continued to be focused on developing behavioral rules for Zach and appropriate consequences for their violation, as well as being more consistent in disciplining Zach. Approximately eight weeks after the critical incident, Zach stopped coming to therapy, and therapy became marital therapy explicitly because Al and Cheryl were unhappy with their marriage. They worked together in the family's business and spent a great deal of time together, but most of their time together was very stressful. In addition, neither one was involved in activities or relationships outside of the family or the family's business.

The Couple As Client

Following the change in the principle client, therapy now focused on marital issues such as intimacy and the renegotiation of the marital relationship during the couple's empty-nest phase of life. During this period, Cheryl was seen in an individual session. In that session, she expressed feeling trapped in the marriage, contemplating having an affair, and considering leaving Al. I thought it ironic that just as Al was becoming more vulnerable with Cheryl she was ready to leave the relationship. Whereas previously Al had been perceived to be the "bad guy," now when he was beginning to become a "good guy" Cheryl was not sure she wanted a relationship with him. Cheryl commented that even if Al did change, she did not feel that he could provide the level of emotional support she currently needed. We explored her options and her goals for herself.

I also met individually with Al and discussed his personal goals and what he wanted from his relationships. He was unaware of Cheryl's discontent and her concerns about the quality of their relationship. He asserted that the marriage was what he expected and although he believed that it could use some "tweaking," he generally was satisfied with the relationship. This session focused on heightening his awareness to Cheryl's concerns and assessing his willingness to address those issues.

I saw Al and Cheryl for one additional individual session each. The session with Cheryl explored two key issues: her need for experiences outside of the family and the business and her desire to leave the family business at some time in the future. Cheryl had come to the realization that she had limited her experiences to her family and the business and now felt a desire to expand her options. Consequently, we focused on and explored the viability of her options. Involvement in an extramarital relationship was one option that she considered but rejected. Instead, she elected to enroll in some university art classes.

Following the individual sessions the couple again was seen conjointly. The last few sessions with the couple focused on helping them to balance the need for intimacy and separation. Accordingly, we explored ways for them to create space that allowed each other to have parts of his or her life that were his or her own—apart from each other, the family, and the business. This was an alternative Cheryl had not considered during her individual sessions. Part of the limitation was pragmatic but most of it was self-imposed. Cheryl believed that Al would not allow it or she was not supposed to do it. Contrary to these perceptions, however, Al was quite supportive of her pursuing nonfamily/business-related experiences. He acknowledged that he currently was happy with his life but recognized that Cheryl might need other experiences to round out her life.

DISCUSSION

The Role of the Critical Incident in Getting Therapy Unstuck

Viewing the videotape profoundly affected Al because he genuinely was unaware of the high decibel level at which he spoke. As a result, the decrease in his verbal decibel level contributed to therapy becoming unstuck and to meaningful movement and change in the family relationships. That these changes are directly attributable to the critical incident is debatable. However, despite my questions about the contributions of the critical incident to these changes, it cannot be denied that it certainly created a ripple effect that affected a number of family issues.

The first of these was the presenting problem. By lowering his voice after the critical incident, Al's statements did not appear to others as harsh as they did prior to the critical incident and allowed others to "hear" his message rather than to defend against him. Specifically, his less imposing voice allowed Cheryl to be less reactive to his verbal disciplining of Zach. Although Al might not have been any less stern in dealing with Zach, his decreased decibel level did make his verbal statements more palatable to Cheryl and, to some degree, Zach. The lowering of Al's voice also allowed for more productive therapy sessions because family members could now concentrate on what he was saying rather than his angry-sounding voice. Previously when Al expressed himself verbally, the conversation usually came to a standstill. Now, after the critical incident, Al was perceived to be contributing to the discussion rather then laying down the law.

Al's lowered voice also contributed to Cheryl's willingness to accept his disciplining of Zach. This allowed the therapeutic conversation to focus directly on what was best for Zach and what was the best way for Al and Cheryl to achieve those goals. Accordingly, we spent the next several sessions developing explicit rules to guide Zach's behaviors and appropriate consequences for the violation of those rules. Therapy also focused on helping Al to be less reactive to Zach's violations of the rules. He perceived Zach's violations of the rules as a personal affront. From Al's point of view, Zach knew the rules; thus when he chose to violate the rules he was saying to Al, "Screw you, Dad." In keeping with the therapeutic goal to help Al to be less reactive to Zach's misbehaviors, I initially applied logic with a dash of adolescent development to persuade Al that Zach's behavior was benign—indeed, more mischievous then malicious. Al did not accept this perspective. He was convinced that because Zach knew the rules, breaking them was a clear affront to parental, especially Al's, authority. Since logic did not achieve the desired result, I reframed Zach's behaviors as an attempt to keep his parents engaged. Because Al and Cheryl were so busy with other parts of their lives, arguing over disciplining Zach had become a way for

Zach to keep his parents together. I assured the parents that Zach was probably not aware that he was doing this. Although I am not sure that Al completely believed the frame provided, he could not refute it entirely. Presenting Zach's behaviors as benevolent rather than malicious appeared to
lessen Al's reactivity to Zach and his behaviors.

Al's loud speech also negatively affected the degree to which he was included in the family's intimate daily occurrences. At one level Al's gruff-
ness gave him a (false) sense of control over others because people tended to
acquiesce to his demands, at least in his presence. However, because of the
family's fear of Al, they kept many secrets from him to avoid his wrath.
Cheryl was privy to those secrets and believed that although the secrets isolated Al from the rest of the family, they also protected the family from Al.
Consequently, while Al believed that he was in charge, in actuality he was
excluded from much of the intimate daily occurrences in the family. Cheryl
also expressed a belief that Al was emotionally crippled and could not deal
with some of the family issues and problems; he could deal only with anger.
As a result, the family treated him as emotionally crippled.

In a later session I raised this issue and asked Cheryl if she believed that
Al could not deal with problems in the family. She responded affirmatively.
I had suggested that one benefit in Al being viewed as such was that he was
not being required to deal with complex emotions in the family. I also explained that many men in U.S. culture experience difficulty dealing with
complex emotions, thus it was not uncommon for women to protect the men
in their lives. When asked directly for his perception of Cheryl's belief, Al
asserted that he could deal with a great many emotions and that he did not
need Cheryl to protect him. I accepted his response and asked him if he felt
the need to explore ways in which he could be more active in the family. He
responded that he would like to be more involved in the family. Al's request
for increased involvement in the family appeared to be the second turning
point in the therapeutic process. Prior to the critical incident, the family's
perception of Al as emotionally crippled made him an object of pity on one
hand and his loud voice made him an object to be feared on the other hand.
Now, however, after the critical incident, absent his imposing voice, his
needs were being heard and he had become a more involved member of the
family in need of emotional support from the family and deserving of respect.

Implications of the Critical Incident for Therapy

From my work with this family and the experience of the critical incident
I learned two important lessons. First, as therapists we never can predict the
kinds of impact our clinical interventions will have on clients. In my naïveté
I was certain that the Al and Cheryl would arrive at the same meanings of
the family's interaction as the therapists-in-training supervision group. How

could they see it any other way? In retrospect, I am reminded that therapists and their clients frequently hold differing perspectives of identical events (Sells et al., 1994; Smith, Sells, and Clevenger, 1994). Specifically, when therapists believed that the reflecting team was not helpful, the clients often did. When the therapist believed that no major problems were left to solve, the clients often did. Although a reflecting team is different from the viewing of a videotape, viewing the tape did provide the family, especially Al, with a new perspective on the problems being addressed. Furthermore, doing so placed the family's problems in a new perspective, which neither of their previous therapists had considered.

That therapists and clients often experience therapy differently may be disconcerting to some therapists, but it helps to remind me of the tentativeness of the human experience. It is important to remember that our ideas about systems are just as fluid as the systems themselves. Our theories, as well as our practices of therapy based on those theories, are intended as temporary lenses rather than as representations that conform to a social reality (Anderson and Goolishian, 1988). I also am comforted by the fact that although clients may not experience therapy in the same manner as their therapists, clients often are able to get what they need from therapy to improve their lives. "Therapists . . . will forever live in a twilight of partial truths. Real understanding of families is but an illusion or delusion that we carry as part of our work. . . . As a discipline, we understand very little about the people with whom we work" (Newfield et al., 1991, p. 306).

The second lesson pertains to the use of technology in therapy. Clearly, viewing the videotape provided Al with a new perspective; at the time Al was viewing the tape, he had never heard himself speak as others had heard him speak. His experience in viewing the tape is analogous to an out-of-body experience, i.e., standing outside of oneself and viewing oneself as others do. Probably a number of reasons exist for Al speaking the way he did; it seemed that everyone accepted his manner of speaking as "Just Al. That's the way he is." Viewing the tape allowed Al to change an aspect of his persona that most thought immutable.

THE OUTCOME OF THERAPY

At the end of the semester the family reported significant improvements in the marital as well as the parent-child relationships, especially with Zach. Life at home and at work had improved significantly. Cheryl now spent more time out of the office and was more productive when she was there. The improvements in the couple's relationship resonated with the rest of the family and they now jointly engaged in more pleasurable activities. I informed them that I was completing the final semester of my degree program; although they could continue for a few more sessions, I would not be able to continue with them. I offered them the option to terminate therapy at the semester's end or to transfer to another therapist in the clinic. I assured them that if they decided to terminate, they could return to therapy if needed. The next session Al and Cheryl informed me that they had decided to terminate because their relationship at home and work was "going well" such that they no longer needed therapy. Accordingly, we met for a few more sessions and then we terminated. The family expressed their gratitude for our work together; I credited their success to them.

Follow-Up

No follow-up with this family has occurred because I left the university following the termination of therapy.

REFERENCES

Anderson, H. and Goolishian, H. A. (1988). Human systems as linguistic systems: Preliminary and evolving ideas about the implications for clinical theory. *Family Process*, 27(4), 371-393.

Newfield, N. A., Joanning, H. P., Kuehl, B. P., and Quinn, W. H. (1991). We can tell you about "psychos" and "shrinks": An ethnography of the family therapy of adolescent drug abuse. In T. C. Todd and M. D. Selekman (Eds.), *Family therapy approaches with adolescent substance abusers* (pp. 275-310). Boston: Allyn & Bacon.

Sells, S. P., Smith, T. E., Coe, M. J., Yoshioka, M., and Robbins, J. (1994). An ethnography of couple and therapist experience in reflecting team practice. *Journal of Marital and Family Therapy*, 20(3), 247-266.

Selvini Palazzoli, M., Boscolo, L., Checchin, G. F., and Prata, G. (1978). A ritualized prescription in family therapy: Odd days and even days. *Journal of Marital and Family Therapy*, 4(3), 3-9.

Smith, T. E., Sells, S. P., and Clevenger, T. (1994). Ethnographic content analysis of couple and therapist experience in a reflecting team setting. *Journal of Marital and Family Therapy*, 20(3), 267-286.

Commentary

Finding One's Voice

Leigh A. Leslie

Commentator Background

Forty-seven years old, white, female, PhD, twenty-two years MFT practice.

Practice Setting

University MFT training clinic; limited private practice.

Theoretical Perspective

I used a feminist therapeutic perspective integrated with an interactional perspective to examine this case.

In this case report Northey provides an excellent example of a therapeutic situation experienced by many therapists: an unplanned intervention that significantly and positively affected the course of therapy. I approached this commentary with the recognition that commenting on such a case is paradoxical. It is at best awkward to discuss how I might have planned and conducted therapy differently than the therapist of record in a case in which the therapist's planning really was not the impetus for the turning point. Accordingly, my comments will address how I might have approached therapy with this couple prior to the critical incident. Then, recognizing that my therapeutic approach might not have led to the critical incident, I will discuss what I might have done differently subsequent to the critical incident.

GOOD POINTS ABOUT THE CASE

I like several aspects of Northey's approach to therapy with this couple. First, Northey began therapy with the simplest, most direct intervention in his attempts to get Al and Cheryl to agree on appropriate behavioral consequences for Zach. Based on a desire to respect clients' abilities and to empower them to assume responsibility for their treatment early in therapy, I believe it is important to begin therapy with the simplest interventions possible. Doing so potentially can free clients to take charge of their problems and make changes. Only when it is clear that such a direct, minimalist approach is not achieving the desired results do I believe it appropriate to move on to more distal causes for the problem. If difficulty in establishing appropriate consequences for Zach had been the only points of disagreement between Cheryl and Al, such an intervention would have quickly resolved their presenting problem. Second, I appreciate Northey's reframe of Al and Cheryl's impasse about disciplining Zach. Rather than offering an interactional interpretation that blamed one parent and could have potentially continued/escalated the spousal conflicts, Northey validated each parent's caring for and contributions to Zach ("Each parent had valuable lessons to teach").

WHAT I MIGHT HAVE DONE DIFFERENTLY

Prior to the Critical Incident

Given the background, the presenting problem, and the nature of the spousal interaction reported in the first session, I might have approached therapy with this couple differently. Specifically, I probably would have used primarily an interactional approach informed by feminist principles in my work with them. Using this approach, I would have explored the meanings or interpretations family members make of specific behaviors, the impact of specific behaviors on others, and the family's metacommunication—communication beyond what actually is said. As a feminist therapist, I also would want to be attuned to the significance of gender in the couple's interactions and communication. To that end, I would have used the feminist's concept of "voice" and how one finds and uses one's voice to explain this couple's interactions.

Once it was clear that Al and Cheryl's primary point of conflict was not simply their disagreements about appropriate behavioral consequences for Zach, I would have wanted to know what the couple was communicating through their arguments. As an alternative to the hypothesis posed by Northey's supervision group, I would have hypothesized that each parent was competing to be validated by the other. To examine that hypothesis I would have verbalized my confusion about whether the couple's arguments were about Zach's behaviors or about which parent was right. Continuing, I would have asked them momentarily to set aside their concerns about Zach and to tell me if the manner in which they argued about Zach is similar to the manner in which they argued about anything else; issues about their business, for example. If they answered in the affirmative (which would be my expectation), I then would have moved to illuminate what each spouse was attempting to achieve by arguing. At this point, the metaphor of "voice" becomes very relevant. Through our discussions I would hope to help each spouse to become aware that he or she was fighting/competing to be validated and to have his or her voice be heard. The consequences of feeling "unheard" would also be germane to our conversation.

Based on Northey's report, it is clear that Al becomes loud when he feels that he is not being heard. Cheryl's response to feeling not heard is less clear, although I would surmise that she becomes distant and withdraws. At this point, an examination of Al's vocal loudness and its effect on Cheryl might be beneficial. I tend to believe that when a client's interactional style (behavior) is well beyond the normal range such that most people overtly comment upon the behavior, it is appropriate to discuss the behavior in therapy. To that end the therapist can reflect to the client how he or she experiences the characteristic behavior (e.g., "I find myself wanting to pull back from you when you are so loud even though you are not talking to me directly"). Another useful strategy would be to ask other family members to share how the specific characteristic affects them. In addition, similar to Northey but for different reasons, I often find it helpful to show clients videotapes of their in-session interactions so that they might experience their behaviors as a spectator. Because I believe that what one believes about being heard and/or expressing oneself is a gendered experience, I also would have explored ways to introduce/integrate gender into the therapeutic discussion about "voice." For example, as a man, what does it mean to Al when he feels that he is not heard?

If, on the other hand, both Al and Cheryl agreed that their disagreement about disciplining Zach is the only issue about which they argue with such acerbity, I would have explored with them how they are attempting to use their voices on Zach's behalf. In particular, each parent had made statements that would suggest some type of gendered belief about Zach and perhaps about himself or herself as a father or mother, respectively. Accordingly, using Al's own words, I would have asked Al what it meant to him that Zach is a "young man." Such a question can lead to a rich examination of the meaning of manhood (both Zach's and Al's) and its attendant expectations. Similarly, I would have asked Cheryl what it meant to her that Zach "is only fourteen." Answers to this question may lead to a discussion of the youngest growing up, to Cheryl's role as a mother, and the meaning these things have in her life. The goal of these questions would be threefold: to change the way in which Al and Cheryl argue about Zach, to help each spouse to effectively "hear" the other, and to change the focus of the argument from Zach to focus upon whatever it is that is contributing to and maintaining the couple's combative style of interaction.

Following the Critical Incident

Seeing himself on the videotape and becoming aware of how loudly he spoke had a dramatic effect on Al's speech: he no longer "spoke as loudly." This change contributed to a more open discussion about Zach as well as other issues about which the couple fought. I support Northey's strategy to move the couple from a focus on Zach to a focus on their central issues and to provide each spouse the opportunity to express his or her needs for the marital relationship and for himself or herself as an individual. In particular, I concur with Northey's therapeutic strategy to reinforce Cheryl's need for some distance or separation in the marital relationship. In keeping with my earlier focus, I would have continued with the metaphor of "voice" and each spouse's need to be heard. In this regard, I would have punctuated how a reduction in Al's vocal level contributed to other family members' perception that Al was now more approachable. This change in perception enabled not only Al but Cheryl as well to be really heard.

As Cheryl considered her options for both "intimacy and separation," I would have spent more time with the couple exploring how Al might be able to provide some of the emotional support and intimacy Cheryl believed she was missing. Based on the case report, it appears that only Cheryl's needs for separation were addressed in therapy. Since Al appeared to be more accepting of the couple's current level of intimacy, he neither was asked to change his behavior with regard to marital intimacy nor did therapy address how intimacy might change in the couple's relationship. In short, because Al was content with the status quo, he was not asked to change his behaviors. Consequently, Cheryl's needs were not validated. Sadly, by not asking Al to respond to Cheryl's intimacy needs, Northey inadvertently may have sent a message that Al does not have to worry about Cheryl's emotional needs and/or that his emotional needs set the standard for the marriage. Proceeding from this premise, I would have asked, "What did Al believe Cheryl meant by wanting more intimacy? Did he believe he could provide such intimacy? Is he willing to do so for her?" To that end I would have asked Al to send Cheryl an unambiguous message that he is capable of providing her with some of her emotional needs. Doing so would let Cheryl know that he is sensitive to her needs and she does not have to do all the emotional work alone. However, if Al truly did not have a clue as to what Cheryl wanted with regards to intimacy, I would have invited the partners to discuss the issue with each other.

Finally, in light of Al's support of Cheryl's efforts to individuate, I also would have explored with Cheryl the source(s) of her gendered assumptions about Al's behaviors, e.g., "Al would not allow it" and that she was "not supposed to do it." The therapeutic discussion would then focus on Cheryl's other gendered assumptions that might be preventing her from having her intimacy needs met by Al. Here, I would have challenged Cheryl's beliefs that Al cannot meet her emotional needs. Whether her beliefs are based on some type of gendered thinking about men in general or a realistic past history with Al, her beliefs discount Al's human capacity for change and growth.

CONCERNS/ISSUES

This case also presents a clinical dilemma common to couples therapy, but Northey did not indicate how he dealt with it. Specifically, although it often is beneficial to alternate between seeing couples in conjoint and in individual sessions, doing so raises concerns about the confidentiality of the information that is shared in the individual sessions and if, when, and how that information will be introduced/incorporated into the conjoint sessions. Clearly, some information from Cheryl's individual session was shared with Al, but it is unclear if it was shared jointly by Cheryl and Northey or by Northey alone. Furthermore, it also is unclear if Cheryl was aware that the information would be shared. I believe that when individual sessions augment conjoint couple's sessions it is important that the therapist and the individual partners enter into an explicit agreement that specifies whether information from each partner's individual session will be shared in the conjoint sessions, how it will be shared, and who decides how it will be shared. I realize that Northey may have dealt with this concern in therapy but because of the space limitations of the case report it was not discussed.

A second concern is Northey's assertion that, "just as Al is becoming more vulnerable, Cheryl is talking about leaving." I found Northey's characterization of Al as vulnerable to be confusing and a veiled criticism of Cheryl. Based on my reading of the case report, Al became quieter than Cheryl during therapy and thus more accessible. I, however, do not equate "quiet" and "accessible" with being vulnerable. Perhaps Al's vulnerability may have been much more evident in session than in the case report. Northey also suggests that Cheryl was just beginning to consider leaving the marriage as Al was being more accessible (vulnerable). Alternatively, I would suggest that Cheryl had thought about leaving for a long time but now felt that she had a place to express her thoughts and someone (Northey) to listen. Consequently, to link Al's behavioral change to Cheryl thoughts about leaving the marriage discounts the history and quality of the relationship as each partner had been experiencing it for some time (especially since we know that the couple previously had been in therapy with their older children).

CONCLUDING THOUGHTS

This case ably demonstrates the clinical use of videotapes in helping families to see themselves differently. I believe, however, that as therapists, we tend to underutilize videotapes as a vehicle to provide families with a new perspective on themselves and their problems. Often, as was the case with this family, the changes that resulted from seeing the videotape were not planned by the therapist. Yet despite the serendipity of such situations, I often have found the outcome to be meaningful. In addition to helping clients to see their interactions with an "outsider's" eye, a videotape can be very informative for a therapist as he or she sees what clients consider to be important for themselves. Furthermore, videotapes can be useful to a therapist when he or she feels therapeutically stuck. Specifically, interactions that were missed in a session but now are visible on the videotape can tell a very important story and provide valuable information which would not have been available without the videotape. After-session videotapes can also be useful therapeutic tools that can help to open up a dialogue that can facilitate therapeutic movement subsequent to family members describing and interpreting what they see on a videotape. In short, incorporating this medium into therapy can be a useful tool for clients as well as therapists.

Commentary

Show Me One More Time

Terry S. Trepper

Commentator Background

Fifty years old, white, male, PhD, twenty-four years MFT practice.

Practice Setting

University family studies faculty; limited private practice.

Theoretical Perspective

My preferred theoretical perspectives include behavioral, structural, and solution focused. I used an eclectic and developmental perspective to comment on this case.

This is a very interesting case that exemplifies several truths about the practice of psychotherapy. Especially interesting to me is that Northey is presenting a case that he saw many years previously, when he was less experienced, and now has the benefit of hindsight to get a different view of the story than when he initially was a part of it.

GOOD POINTS ABOUT THE CASE

There are several points about this case and Northey's approach to therapy with this family that I like. First, Northey did a very nice, solid job of family therapy. He joined well with the clients, evidenced by their remaining in therapy for the long haul. He also received good supervision, made appropriate, timely interventions, and when his interventions did not lead to change he willingly modified his approach in the best interest of his clients. Northey seemed to learn from this family's lead and balanced moving at their pace and in their direction with leading them toward effective change. Looking from the perspective of a seasoned therapist, I was impressed with

the young Northey's enthusiasm and self-confidence to try a new intervention, his willingness to be flexible, and his presence of mind to recognize
when doing so was needed.

A Videotape Is Worth a Thousand Words

I believe that the critical incident—the showing of a videotape of a recent
therapy session—indeed was a serendipitous turning point in therapy. Showing
the family the videotape was an insight-oriented intervention presented in a
way that they could "hear." Alternatively, Northey might have said "Al, it
seems to me that your voice is so very loud that you may be intimidating
others in your family, which leads them to back off. Further, it seems that
this may be a way to actually remove you from the intimate connections
with your wife and children, rather than bringing you closer." However,
given the family's reaction to an earlier intervention—the odd-even days—
it was highly possible that they, especially Al, would have rejected that interpretation, also. Indeed, given the quality of the family's current relationship we might predict that, paradoxically, Al might have increased his decibel level to prove Northey wrong. Specifically, he might have raised his
voice in argument with Northey. More important, it is quite possible that had
Northey intervened verbally, Cheryl might have perceived his statement as
supporting her position and thus provided the justification for her to increase her anger and resentment of Al. After all, even the therapist said that
he was a loud, disconnected man. On the other hand, showing the videotape
had the positive effect of allowing Al to take a spectator's view of his behavior as he observed firsthand the results of his loud voice and scary demeanor.
How he reacted to the images on the videotape was under his own control.
He could decide for himself whether the images were accurate and if the
person he saw on the videotape was who he wanted to be. By not having
Northey interpret the video images *for* Al, this experience was made more
poignant and useful for him.

Videotapes Enhance the Spectator's Role

Showing clients a videotape of a previous session can be a powerful intervention even if it was not theoretically driven. Viewing a videotape can
accrue benefits similar to family sculpture and other nonverbal interventions. Such interventions permit people to see themselves as others see them
and can be illuminating, as was the case with Al. In family or couples therapy, after-session videotapes also can let people see how they affect others
in a way that is not possible during the in vivo interaction itself. The reality
of the current age of technology shared by most clients: an experience is
more powerful, more "valid," and ironically more "real" if it is seen on a
television screen. This may be particularly true for children and adoles-

cents, whose attention definitely will be far more focused when watching their family on a video monitor than it would be were it occurring "live." I have shown videotapes to clients on numerous occasions and have been pleased with the results most of the time. My favorite time to show video-tapes is in the final stage of therapy, during the period Mary Jo Barrett and I call "consolidation." During this period, we try to punctuate the changes clients have made as a way to help to solidify those changes. When, as spectators, clients see their interaction(s) from an earlier stage, that image can have a powerful, positive effect that usually makes them laugh at themselves and stays with them.

FAMILY THERAPY:
THE RELATIONSHIP IS THE THING

I was impressed by how systemic this systemic therapy was. Initially, therapy was focused on Zach and his problems but soon shifted to the couple's relationship. Then, in the middle phase of therapy, the focus was on the couple's individual growth and development, with emphasis on Cheryl. Finally, the family and Northey refocused on Zach with regard to the positive changes he had made. Of course, as family therapists, this all makes sense. We see individual problems as being influenced and maintained by the entire family system (as well as outside-the-family systemic influences). More individually oriented therapists might not have connected Zach's acting out with Cheryl's need for autonomy, but it certainly was there. These are the connections that our family therapy theorist forefathers proposed; they still are exciting today.

Northey also pointed out that a "ripple effect" was operating in this family. As family therapists we are able to see how change in one part of the system leads to change in another part. In this situation, watching a videotape of themselves led to other events. For example, Al began to listen more; his doing so, in turn, led to other events, such as Cheryl feeling stronger and more able to ask for what she needed emotionally. Of course, the "law of unintended consequences" has not been repealed. Therapists are delighted when an intervention, planned or unplanned, leads to changes in the direction desired by themselves and the client families. Conversely, however, we tend to be displeased when an intervention ripples negatively into a downward spiral, especially when we are not sure how or why it occurred. In this regard, this family could have watched the videotape, but Al could have instead believed/convinced himself that he acted appropriately; Cheryl could have told herself, "This is the last straw. If he doesn't even get it once he sees it, I am out of here." As a result, the outcome could have been very different. Given these possibilities, it is important that all therapists have a variety of clinical experiences and maintain ongoing clinical supervision of their work.

MFT Changed View of Clients' "Resistance"

Reading this case report I have come to appreciate how the attitudes of psychotherapists, but especially marriage and family therapists, have evolved with regard to clients not wanting to engage in an out-of-session assignment. In classic psychoanalysis, clients who do not accept an insight or suggestion from the therapist are perceived to be "resistant." Resistance was proof that they lacked insight and, tautologically also, was proof of their need for further treatment. During the 1970s, when I studied behavioral psychology at the University of Oregon in the heyday of behaviorism, it was accepted practice that clients who did not or would not complete their homework assignments were informed that they were "not ready to commit" to the program and were respectfully furloughed from therapy until they were agreeable to follow therapist suggestions. At that time doing so was considered a vast improvement compared to the pathologizing of resistance by psychoanalysts. Paradoxically, the outcome was not really much better. Psychotherapy and psychotherapists' current view of clients who do not complete their homework assignments was beautifully explicated by Northey when he stated: "The clients did not accept the reframe." From a narrative perspective, Northey and the family were unable to coconstruct a reality. Psychotherapy and psychotherapists certainly have come a long way with regard to the explicit respect we accord clients in our conceptualizations of their problems and their solutions. On the other hand, if we are honest, whether it was an insight that was not accepted or a behavioral homework assignment that was not completed or a reframe that was not accepted, the bottom line is: The intervention did not work!

CONCLUDING THOUGHTS

When a planned intervention does not work, that is precisely the time when therapists need to be creative and build from clients' experiences and solutions to create an environment that allows serendipity to flourish. A significant factor in the unfolding of this case is not the specific critical incident; rather, it was Northey's flexibility, openness, creativity, and humility. He appropriately sought supervision (despite his student status; many trainees may not have done so); he attempted new clinical maneuvers/strategies; he listened to the clients; and he molded all of that into a therapeutic mosaic, which ultimately was in the best interest of the family and helped them on their journey. I commend him for that and for his willingness to share his experience with colleagues.

CASE 9

My Children Are Not Liars

Harriet H. Roberts

Therapist Background

Currently: Sixty years old, black, female, PhD, twenty-six years MFT practice. Then: Fifty-six years old, twenty-three years MFT practice.

Practice Setting

Currently: Private practice. Then: The Houston-Galveston Institute.

Client Characteristics

The clients were Maria Garza (age thirty-eight), her husband Jessie (age forty), and their four children: twin daughters Marjorie and Odessa (age fourteen), son Sam (age twelve), and daughter Grace (age ten). Maria and the twins were referred for therapy by children's protective services because Mr. Garza had been accused of sexually abusing the twins. The children lived with their mother who recently had been released from prison. Mr. Garza, the children's primary caretaker during their mother's incarceration, now lived apart from his wife and children. Mrs. Garza was employed as a cook and Mr. Garza was employed as a construction worker. His primary language is Spanish; his use of English is limited. The twins were students in high school; Sam and Grace attended middle and elementary schools, respectively.

Length of Treatment

This family was seen for twenty concurrent family and individual sessions, August 1997 to February 1998. The family was referred by children's protective services and I consulted with the assigned CPS caseworker at least six times during the family's time in therapy. The critical incident occurred in Session 8.

Theoretical Perspective

A collaborative language systems approach was used in working with this family.

My work with this family is grounded in a collaborative language systems approach based on postmodern social constructionist theory (Anderson and Goolishian, 1988; Anderson, 1997). Using this approach, therapy focuses on creating a therapeutic context in which change can occur rather than on an accumulation of clinical techniques. This context is created through a commitment to provide nonpathological, nonhierarchical, nonpejorative, and nonjudgmental therapy to every part of the treatment system. Consequently, equal attention is paid to the views and concerns of each parent, each child, and other family members, as well as to the professionals from referring agencies, e.g., the courts, medical agencies, school professionals, and members of the family's social network. This approach allows families and their therapist(s) to define, from the families perspectives, the realities of the problems to be addressed and the goals to be accomplished.

PRESENTING PROBLEM

A caseworker called to refer the Garza family. She stated, "This family is being referred because Mr. Garza has been accused of sexually abusing his fourteen-year-old twin daughters, Marjorie and Odessa." The abuse allegedly occurred over a two-year period, while Mrs. Garza was incarcerated. She was released from prison approximately two months prior to the abuse being disclosed. Marjorie, Odessa, brother Sam, and sister Grace moved into their mother's home three weeks after children's protective services became involved. Mr. Garza denied sexually abusing his daughters.

Prior to meeting with the family, I met with the referring caseworker. During our meeting I asked about and developed an understanding of her assessment and goals for the family, their concerns, and their expectations for therapy. She requested therapy for the twins and their parents because she believed that Sam and Grace were minimally involved. In my initial contact with the caseworker, I was respectful of her expertise, opinions, concerns, and agenda, and invited/encouraged her collaboration.

During this conversation, she expressed the belief that Mr. Garza needed to be seen separately from Mrs. Garza and the twins. She believed that he needed concurrent individual and group therapy (a group for men who are legally charged with sexual abuse of a child). To that end, she officially referred (mandated) him to therapy.

THE THERAPEUTIC SITUATION PRIOR
TO THE CRITICAL INCIDENT

At the request of the caseworker an initial appointment was scheduled for Mrs. Garza, Marjorie, and Odessa. The caseworker had expressed the belief that the twins and their mother were the most distressed and needed therapy immediately. Interestingly, although I invited Mrs. Garza and the agency provided transportation for the family, she neither accompanied the twins to the initial appointment nor attended the first three sessions. Typically, on the day of each appointment, she called after the scheduled time or asked the twins to apologize for her not attending because of other commitments. I suggested to her that it was important that she participate in therapy to help me to learn about her family, her concerns for her daughters, her experiences with the agency, and her thoughts about what the judge and caseworker wanted for her family.

In this first session, Marjorie assumed the role of spokesperson for the twin sisters, but when they were talking, each girl seemed to seek the other's approval through eye contact or nonverbal cues. They provided detailed information about the abuse and were supportive of each other as they told their story. Their support and protection of each other were demonstrated in various ways. For example, they explained that on those occasions when their father would maneuver to have everyone except one of the twins to leave their home, the twins would create reasons to remain together. They feared their father would eventually force them to have sexual intercourse with him.

My primary goal in this session was to connect with the sisters, to put them at ease, and to reassure them that I was there to help the family to resolve its problems. They, in turn, expressed two primary concerns. First, they were concerned that their father continued to deny the abuse and, by implication, was accusing them of lying. Second, they asked that their father receive counseling. They described their father as "good" and "bad" and reported that his behavior with them was confusing. On one hand, he was described as a strict disciplinarian who made them attend church with him two or three times a week and who refused to allow them to listen to rap or rock music or to talk to boys. On the other hand, they said, "He would come into our room and touch us when he thought we were asleep."

They confided in each other and, after awhile, attempted to tell an aunt about their father's behavior but could not find the courage to do so. Whenever they attempted to tell their aunt, they were vague about what they were saying. They admitted that they were too embarrassed to tell anyone else. They eventually told their mother, several weeks following her release from prison; she immediately notified children's protective services. The girls also admitted that they were even embarrassed to tell me. However, my demonstration of sincere concern and empathy encouraged them to share their story. Grace attended the third session with Marjorie and Odessa. She had lived with another relative during her mother's absence but was aware of the situation involving her father and her sisters because the twins had shared with her details of their experiences with their father. She presented herself and behaved with a maturity beyond her chronological age and was very articulate and empathetic.

Mrs. Garza attended the fourth session along with the twins. She was very guarded and neither expressed her concerns freely nor talked about herself or the situation. However, in a later session, she disclosed that she disliked dealing with "people in authority" given her history of drug abuse; she blamed herself for failing to protect her daughters. She also expressed concern about the negative effects of the sexual abuse on the twins as well as the effects of her separation from all of the children. She questioned whether she should tell Mr. Garza's current fiancée about the allegations against him because the woman had two young daughters. After much thought, she decided to share the information with Mr. Garza's fiancée.

Grace, Sam, Mrs. Garza, and the twins attended Session 5. Sam appeared very uncomfortable during sessions. He appeared bashful and very uneasy, did not volunteer any information, and responded minimally to questions asked. Throughout the session, he covered his face often, especially when asked about his understanding about why the family was here. Mrs. Garza disclosed that Sam had not been told about the "situation" because he was too nervous. Despite his bashfulness, Sam did share what he knew about his sisters' problems. Much to his mother's surprise, he revealed that he was aware of the situation but had kept it a secret. Asked if his father had ever touched him, Sam refused to answer and showed signs of increased anxiety.

During Session 6, as in previous sessions, I acknowledged the complexities of the situation and the perceptible emotional pain shown by family members as they told their stories. Concurrently, I created a conversational space and process in which family members were free to express their thoughts and feelings and to expand on what had not been said (their private thoughts and feelings). Two new issues emerged in this session. First, Sam disclosed that he had been sexually abused by his father to a much greater extent than his two sisters. Second, Mrs. Garza and the children discussed her absence from them. The children disclosed that she actually had deserted them approximately one year prior to her incarceration. The children supported each other as they expressed to their mother the pain of having to explain to friends and relatives that their mother was not living with them and that they did not know why she left. Mrs. Garza did not offer any excuses for her behavior but rather touchingly expressed her grief for her children and asked for their forgiveness. The children were skeptically reassured, but the issue of trust remained paramount, as the children questioned their mother's current commitment to them.

EVENTS LEADING TO THE CRITICAL INCIDENT

Mr. Garza attended his own initial individual therapy session after his daughters had attended their second session. Despite the allegations and criminal charges against him, I treated Mr. Garza with respect, commended him for his efforts in keeping his family together and shared with him the praise that his children had given him. Because of my sensitivity to Mr. Garza's status as a court-mandated client, I was careful to minimize the possibility of an adversarial relationship developing between him and me. I wanted to help him to experience me as someone interested in him and in helping with what he defined as the problem. In his individual therapy, Mr. Garza continued to deny that he had sexually molested his daughters and that he needed therapy. He was calm but, because English is his second language, he experienced much difficulty expressing himself and became confused in response to specific questions or comments. Interestingly, when he was offered the opportunity to work with a Spanish-speaking therapist, he declined the offer. As might be expected, his active participation in group therapy was minimal; he insisted that he did not need to be in therapy but would comply only because of the court order. His group therapist reported that the other men in his treatment group labeled him as "hopeless" because he was in such denial about his situation. At this juncture, because of Mr. Garza's continued denial of the allegations of the sexual abuse and because of his need for therapy, therapy with the twins as well as his own individual and group therapy was stuck. Therapeutically, I felt unable to help the family to move from the position of anger, accusations, and blaming to a process of problem solution. The twins and Mrs. Garza expressed the belief that it was important that Mr. Garza admit his wrongdoing and tell the truth before therapy could progress and the emotional wounds of the abuse could begin to heal. Sam and Grace voiced similar sentiments.

THE CRITICAL INCIDENT

The turning point in therapy occurred in Session 8. I invited all family members, including Mr. Garza and his group therapist, to attend this session to address the family's problem. However, although each family member agreed to the meeting that was to include Mr. Garza, the caseworker initially would not authorize such a meeting. The caseworker had referred the family for family therapy but, from her theoretical perspective, family therapy in this case did not include the father. Unfortunately, prohibiting therapeutic contact between the accused and the abused in cases of child abuse is a common practice in many protective services agencies. Fortunately, following my discussions with the caseworker, Mr. Garza and his daughters were permitted to attend the session together. Accordingly, both parents, the children, and Mr. Garza's group therapist attended the session. The group therapist invited Mr. Garza to sit next to her so that she might offer support and, as needed, help to bridge the language barrier. The children sat in a random order and Mrs. Garza sat facing the circular arrangement but was not directly included in the therapy circle. I was aware of the need to avoid a physical confrontation between the parents and took every precaution to prevent such confrontation.

The session began with an iteration of the reasons for the conjoint family meeting. The children expressed a need to confront their father about his denial of the abuse; concurrently, they wanted to reassure him that they were not trying to get him into trouble. When he initially was questioned by the authorities, Mr. Garza had asserted his belief that Mrs. Garza had coached the children to lie about being abused to get him into trouble and to increase her chances of regaining custody of the children. Mr. Garza maintained that position in both group and individual therapy. The children openly expressed their thoughts and concerns to their father, but avoided eye contact with him. They were solemn and leaned over toward the floor, almost touching it with their faces as they mumbled among themselves.

Sensing the children's apprehension, I asked if it would be easier for them to talk with their father if they formed a "huddle," as in a football game. They readily agreed to do so and moved their chairs closer. Grace initiated the conversation and requested that Mr. Garza tell the truth about his abuse of the twins. Despite the children's sincerity, Mr. Garza maintained his innocence. Asked to describe the context in which the abuse had occurred, including time, place, and whereabouts of other family members, the twins were tearful and shared their feelings of frustration regarding their father's continued affirmation of his innocence. In that moment, the four children made a bold but serendipitous move. They challenged their father to tell the truth by reminding him that he had taught them to tell the truth regardless of the situation or the consequences. When asked to share his thoughts as to why his children would accuse him of abusing them if it were not true, Mr. Garza did not comment.

Recognizing that therapy was at an impasse, I verbalized the family's dilemma. If the children were telling the truth, a problem existed. If they were lying, a problem also existed. Given the dilemma, I wondered aloud to Mr. Garza about the children's motivation for taking such desperate measures. I shared with the family that an Hispanic colleague had told me that in the Hispanic culture of the Southwest, children, regardless to their ages, do not openly challenge their parents' "truth," especially in the presence of strangers. Such challenges are considered to be disrespectful. Mr. Graza visibly was affected by his children's emotional outpourings and chose to protect their integrity. He said, "If my children said that it is true, then it is true. My children are not liars." In that moment, therapy became unstuck as the children sighed a unified sigh of relief and Mrs. Garza expressed feeling relieved by Mr. Garza's circuitous admission that he had sexually molested the twins. Mrs. Garza did not excuse his behavior but rather attempted to make sense of the situation. She acknowledged that in her absence Mr. Garza had been under much stress in managing the dual roles of mother and father and that her behaviors may have influenced his actions.

DISCUSSION

The Role of the Critical Incident in Getting Therapy Unstuck

It is impossible to predict the course therapy might have taken if this family was not allowed to meet conjointly in therapy and the critical incident had not occurred. Clearly, the children's challenge to their father to tell the truth, using the same admonition he had used to teach them to tell the truth (no matter the situation), was the turning point for therapy. One might predict that had Mr. Garza not been challenged with the identical value he had taught his children, he might indefinitely have remained entrenched in his denial because of his intense feelings of shame. Indeed, he later acknowledged that he had experienced significant difficulty "admitting his disgraceful behaviors" even to himself. However, when challenged by his children he chose to publicly uphold their honor ("My children are not liars") and eventually admitted his wrongdoing, despite feeling guilty and ashamed. Until the occurrence of the critical incident, therapy was stuck; the family's "dueling realities" about the problem and its solution was entrenched. As a result, I felt therapeutically stuck and unable to find ways to address the family's truth and to help each member to begin a healing process.

The children's challenge of their father's denial (the critical incident) and his admission of wrongdoing during the session marked a turning point not only for therapy and for him but also for the redefinition of the children's relationship with both parents. The critical incident also contributed immensely to the beginning of the healing process for both the children and the adults. To this end, Mr. Garza took a significant step in his own healing process. In his next group session, he spontaneously admitted to the group that he had sexually abused his daughters.

Treatment of sexual abuse is a complicated and complex undertaking about which professional debate continues with regard to which is the most effective therapeutic approach. Accordingly, engaging families who have been involuntarily referred to therapy because of the sexual abuse of a minor is a complex matter. Frequently, such families tend to react to the referring source's implicit and often explicit messages that convey to them a feeling that they somehow are different or that they have done something wrong and are incurable bad people. As a result, these families often present for therapy with a considerable feeling of shame, guilt, and skepticism. In turn, these feelings often lead to early termination from therapy. For these families, initially no perceptible advantages to being involved in therapy exist; therapy often is perceived by family members as another form of social control (Roberts, 1990).

Implications of the Critical Incident for Therapy

The implications of the critical incident for therapy are remarkable. First, by insisting that therapy be stopped until her husband told the truth about his behaviors with the twins, Mrs. Garza unwittingly escalated and mobilized the children's challenge of their father's denial and the resultant critical incident. Her actions demonstrated to the children her ability and willingness to support and defend them despite having deserted them previously. Had she not insisted that the truth be told, Mr. Garza may have continued in his denial and the children's hurt and anger would have continued to alienate them emotionally from their father.

Second, for the children, their violation of cultural values—by creating the critical incident through their challenge of their father's "truth" ("I did not do it")—was rewarded by their father's upholding of the larger family value to tell the truth regardless of the consequences. The critical incident also helped to renew and strengthen the children's trust in both parents. Mother's action was evidence that she was a responsible parent who now could be trusted to protect them. Ultimately, their father could be depended upon and be trusted to uphold the values he had taught them. Father may have violated the incest taboo, but when the chips were down, he upheld and defended the values of truth and honesty.

A third implication is specific to the difficulty Mr. Garza experienced in verbally acknowledging his wrongdoing. He was painfully aware that he had violated at least two of his own values when he molested his daughters (the incest taboo) and lied about it (not telling the truth). As a responsible parent, he had taught his children always to tell the truth. Now, however, because he felt ashamed and feared the legal consequences of his actions (there was an imminent possibility that he could be incarcerated), he had violated the very values with which he had imbued his children. The critical incident provided him a way to regain his honor and his status as a responsible parent in the eyes of his children. Although he never directly said, "Yes, I did molest my daughters," he circuitously acknowledged his wrongdoing. In rising positively to the children's challenge, Mr. Garza reinforced the values he had taught his children. In doing so, he facilitated movement in the therapeutic process and helped the family to move from a stuck position of blaming, denying, and distrust to a place where healing could begin.

THE OUTCOME OF THERAPY

Subsequent to the critical incident, Mrs. Garza and the children remained in family and individual therapy for several more sessions. During this phase, therapy addressed issues specific to boundaries, guilt, shame, dependency, self-esteem, self-awareness, and self-agency. Mrs. Garza also continued in a drug-treatment group at another agency and developed an immensely strong relationship with her children. Mother and children attributed renewal of this bond to the reestablishment of mutual trust and open communication between them. She promised to protect the children from any risk of abuse as long as she remained drug free. Mr. Garza was sentenced to ten years of probation for his offense and continued in court-ordered therapy. He was granted supervised visitation by the court and continued to provide financial support for his children. He and his wife have focused on protecting the welfare of their children and continue to maintain a workable coparental relationship.

Follow-Up

Six months after terminating with the family, I contacted Mrs. Garza. She shared that she had custody of all the children. The children were attending school regularly; she was enrolled in a skills training program and continued to be employed as a cook. On the advise of the protective services' caseworker, she and the children were seen for awhile at a community mental health agency for follow-up. At the time of our contact, protective services no longer was involved with the family because the children no longer were considered at risk of being abused. Mr. Garza is employed, continues court-ordered therapy, and has regularly scheduled supervised visits with his children.

REFERENCES

Anderson, H. (1997). *Conversation, language, and possibilities: A postmodern approach to therapy.* New York: Basic Books.

Anderson, H. and Goolishian, H. (1988). *Changing thoughts on self, agency, questions, narrative and therapy.* Unpublished manuscript.

Roberts, H. (1990). *The experiences of black families who are involuntarily involved in family therapy treatment.* Unpublished manuscript.

Commentary

My Children's Good Example

Harvey Joanning
Patricia Keoughan

Commentator Backgrounds

Fifty-four years old, Caucasian, male, PhD, thirty-three years clinical practice, thirty-one years MFT practice.
Fifty-five years old, Caucasian, female, PhD, fourteen years MFT practice.

Practice Setting

University MFT program, limited MFT private practice.

Theoretical Perspective

We both are social constructionists and our clinical approach is integrative but influenced by collaborative language systems. The case study was analyzed in the same manner used in qualitative analysis of clinical data.

We long have been interested in collaborative language systems (CLS) (Anderson, 1997; Goolishian and Anderson, 1988). Consequently, having the opportunity to comment on a case in which the therapist used the CLS approach appealed to us as clinicians and theoreticians. We also have been impressed by the respectful and thoughtful manner in which Goolishian and Anderson (1988) have dealt with the families in the cases they presented at professional meetings. Clearly, Roberts has adopted a similar style. Based on our clinical experience, patience and respect always have proven to be an effective approach to therapy with sexual abusers. In our work with offenders, we have found that it is important to gain their trust through respectful collaboration if we hope to gain their confidence. Frequently, prior to entering therapy, offenders are treated harshly by the police and legal authorities. Such treatment is a major contributor to offenders' defensiveness, which clinicians have observed in therapy. In the case presented here, Mr. Garza, the offender, follows a similar pattern of defensiveness. We believe Roberts was wise not to confront him and, by doing so, compound his defensiveness. Her approach was much more elegant and productive.

We applaud Roberts's approach to therapy with Mr. Garza, but we emphatically do not condone sexual abuse. We believe abusers must cease to abuse, take responsibility for their actions, while the victims and potential victims must be protected. More important, we also believe that limiting sexual abuse is an act of social control best left to the legal and police systems. However, creating a context in which sexual abusers can confront themselves is the domain of therapy. Roberts created that domain in her approach to Mr. Garza and his family.

GOOD POINTS ABOUT THE CASE

The strengths of this case include the manner in which the sessions were conducted, who was involved, and the fact that Roberts allowed the critical incident to emerge rather than forcing it through some "clever clinical maneuver." Roberts's use of CLS, specifically her respectful encouragement of all stakeholders to voice their experiences, is the cornerstone of how this case was managed. Too frequently the offender silences the victims of abuse. Roberts was effective in countering that tendency. She countered forced silence by bringing all family members together in a relatively protected context, opened a space for conversation by modeling how to speak, and encouraged all parties to share their stories. Roberts waited for the elements of the story about the abuse to emerge much as cultural anthropologists would spend time with natives while studying their culture. In this case the natives revealed their culture in their own time and manner because Roberts encouraged them with her patient and attentive listening. She created a conversational space in which "family members were free to express their thoughts and feelings and to expand on what had not been said." This process is key to CLS and distinguishes it from other therapeutic approaches that tend to be more directive and confrontive. We doubt that Mr. Garza would have admitted his abuse had Roberts not provided the kind of conversational space inherent in her approach. Allowing the conversation to continue until the critical incident emerged was crucial to the success of this case.

Waiting for Context, Not Making Context

Many therapists would have pushed Mr. Garza to "fess up" and in doing so may have inadvertently prevented the therapeutic moment from occurring. Waiting for the appropriate contextual moment to emerge allowed the family an opportunity to tell their story in their own time and at their own pace and also provided Mr. Garza a face-saving way to admit his offense. As a result, he was able to admit a grievous abuse of his children because he was proud of the manner in which they conducted themselves. Although he had sexually abused his children, he had also taught them to be truthful. His children's bold display of ethical behavior encouraged Mr. Garza in turn to be ethical by admitting his offense.

Waiting for the contextual moment to occur also allowed healing to begin. This family had experienced horrible and long-term suffering. It is rare that families experiencing sexual abuse have an opportunity to tell their story fully and hear the perpetrator admit his offense. It is even rarer to have an opportunity for healing to begin. Often these families become fragmented and the wholeness of the family ceases to exist. As a result, they often become a collection of abusers and victims. Roberts' patient support of the contextual moment was instrumental in opening a space for the requisite healing to occur.

Roberts's suggestion that the children "huddle as in a football game" is an excellent example of how she created a conversational space. She intervened by shaping the context for conversation but did not directly shape the conversation. Unlike many therapists who would have "lead the clients" or "put words in their mouths," Roberts, again, assumes the role of an anthropologist. She encouraged a "cultural enactment" and observed how the natives conducted their business. By helping the children to collaborate, Roberts helped them to make "a bold but serendipitous move" that had a significant impact on the process of healing and the eventual outcome of therapy.

QUESTIONS FOR THE THERAPIST

Several questions emerged for us as we read the case. These questions are not meant as criticism of Roberts's work with this family. Rather, they result from our clinical curiosity.

1. How did Roberts view the social worker's behavior and attitudes about the case? Roberts was respectful of the social worker, but did she find the social worker respectful?
2. Did Roberts really want the social worker involved in therapy? What role might the social worker have played?
3. How might Roberts deal with the social worker's different view of family, specifically the desire to have the father excluded from therapy? In our experience, social workers often oppose having the abuser and victim(s) in the same room. What are Roberts's thoughts on the

subject? What might she share with the social worker about how CLS therapists view working with sexual abusers?

4. Is Roberts attempting to work with all parties of a "problem organized system?" We have seen Goolishian and Anderson (1988) do so and question whether this is what Roberts is attempting to do.

5. What aspects of the case would Roberts identify as illustrative of CLS?

6. Would Roberts agree with our choice of those aspects of the case that we have identified as examples of CLS in action? Many practitioners we have trained are interested in CLS and have asked, "What does CLS look like in action?" Roberts could help answer that question by identifying the key elements of CLS apparent in this case.

7. Why did Mr. Garza avoid using a Spanish-speaking therapist?

8. Roberts mentions that Sam also was sexually abused, but his abuse and attendant issues were not addressed as thoroughly as the abuse of his sisters. What were Roberts's thoughts on this difference? Was the difference due to the briefness of the case?

9. In the Implications section, Roberts reported that Mrs. Garza insisted that therapy be stopped until Mr. Garza told the truth about his abusive behaviors. This insistence was not clear earlier in the case. It would be interesting to have more information about how the desire to stop therapy was made manifest and how it shaped therapy.

CONCLUDING THOUGHTS

Overall, this case is both interesting and impressive. It is interesting because of the severity and intensity of the family's experience. It is impressive because Roberts was able to create a context for significant, perhaps even profound, change in the family system. Cases involving sexual abuse are tough. Roberts's approach was soft. The effect was profound. In sum, Roberts presents an excellent example of the effectiveness of collaborative language systems as an approach to therapy.

REFERENCES

Anderson, H. (1997). *Conversation, language and possibilities: A postmodern approach to therapy.* New York: Basic Books.

Goolishian, H. and Anderson, H. (1988). Human systems as linguistic systems: Preliminary and evolving ideas about the implications for clinical theory. *Family Process,* 27(4), 157-163.

Commentary

Safety Is Trust in Mother

Lynelle C. Yingling

Commentator Background

Fifty-eight years old, white, female, PhD, nineteen years MFT practice.

Practice Setting

Private practice.

Theoretical Orientation

My preferred theoretical orientation is integrative and includes elements of structural, strategic, and family-of-origin assessment and intervention techniques with a collaborative solution-focused style. I used a structural approach to examine this case.

This case presents several challenging issues: Paternal incest which is denied, mandated therapy, the mother's limited emotional strength consequent to drug-use history and related incarceration, cultural barriers to outsider knowledge of family functioning, and Mr. Garza's limited English-language fluency. All of these challenges seemed to be orchestrated harmomiously by Roberts with this family. Working first with the CPS system to establish a collaborative goal seemed critical to success. This relationship proved valuable when Roberts wanted to bring the entire family together later, despite the CPS caseworker's opposing preference. Without that joint family session, perhaps change would not have occurred and this family would have remained stuck indefinitely. Many families in the CPS system seem to be blocked from healing because of a caseworker's insistence on individual therapy rather than family therapy.

GOOD POINTS ABOUT THE CASE

Roberts's approach to therapy with this family resulted in many very positive outcomes. Looking at the case from a structural perspective, the siblings were encouraged to bond closely by the structuring of who attended sessions and by the use of a "huddle" during the confrontational session with Mr. Garza. Whether Roberts intended these strategies to be structural maneuvers, structural strengthening of the system was the result. I believe that this structural strengthening greatly contributed to and made possible the children's confrontation with Mr. Garza.

Another structural strengthening of the system occurred in Mrs. Garza as she discovered a safe place (the therapy room) that allowed her to feel valued and consequently to express her strengths by standing up to Mr. Garza. Her insistence that the truth must come out was the voice the children needed to hear. Perhaps the children's perception that Mom was competent to stand up to Dad after all gave them the courage to be strong and confrontational, knowing that now Mom would protect them.

Roberts's strategic message also was a contributing factor to the outcome of the confrontational session. In that regard, she used a combination of self-talk and thinking out aloud to externalize the family's impasse,

> Recognizing that therapy was at an impasse, I verbalized the family's dilemma. If the children were telling the truth, a problem existed. If they were lying, a problem also existed. Given the dilemma, I wondered aloud to Mr. Garza about the children's motivation for taking such desperate measures. I shared with the family that an Hispanic colleague had told me that in the Hispanic culture of the Southwest, children, regardless of their ages, do not openly challenge their parents' "truth," especially in the presence of strangers. Such challenges are considered to be disrespectful.

That double-bind message created a dilemma for Mr. Garza to sort out, which he did. His response, "If my children said that it is true, then it is true. My children are not liars" was perhaps as honest as he could be and still remain loyal to his culture. At least the family interpreted his statement as the admission for which they were waiting in order to again believe in their own reality and the essential parental hierarchy.

WHAT I MIGHT HAVE DONE DIFFERENTLY

Although the outcome of this collaborative nonhierarchical treatment plan produced positive results, I might have used a bit more structuring to protect the safety of the children above all else. One structured way to increase my knowledge of the family functioning would have been to use some self-report clinical assessment instruments, such as the SAFE (Yingling et al., 1998), at intake to allow each family member to provide confidential perspectives on how this family was functioning. The GARF Self-Assessment of Families instrument could also be used to plan measurable goals for change after the confrontational session.

Perhaps more individual coaching with Mrs. Garza prior to the confrontation session with Mr. Garza would have reduced the risk of danger. The case description did not mention any individual sessions with Mrs. Garza. Indeed, she appeared to be rather disengaged from the therapy process prior to the confrontational session. I would have felt uncomfortable not having a clearer understanding of Mrs. Garza's strengths. One possible intervention approach would have been to use the structured session psychoeducational approach described by Barrett (Trepper and Barrett, 1989). The metaphorical visual symbols of various family systems might also have been helpful in overcoming the language barrier with Mr. Garza.

When the family members came into the room for the confrontational session, I most likely would have required more structural seating (Minuchin and Fishman, 1981) to provide safety for the children while not isolating Mr. Garza. The family "huddle" was an excellent structural intervention used by Roberts to increase safety for the children. However, I would have been very conscious of the children feeling vulnerable and needing to feel protected by Mrs. Garza. Accordingly, I might have seated Mrs. Garza in a deliberate position as a "buffer" between the children and Mr. Garza. Not knowing how much individual work had been done with Sam and to what extend he was traumatized by Mr. Garza, I would have been especially sensitive to his reactions to this session.

In the sessions following the confrontational session, I would have included the extended family members to collaboratively develop a safety plan to prevent any future risks of harm to the children. If Mrs. Garza's extended family is too disengaged or too enmeshed, she risks failure in parenting.

WHAT ROBERTS MIGHT HAVE DONE DIFFERENTLY

The details of the therapy after the critical incident in the confrontation session are not available, but indications are that Mrs. Garza's hierarchy in the system was confirmed with the children such that they felt safer with her. Unfortunately, the specific techniques that were used to achieve that change within the family hierarchy remain speculation. However, Roberts could have used boundary-setting enactments in the sessions and at-home assignments to strengthen the parental hierarchy. Mrs. Garza's absence had resulted in the parentification of the teenage daughters and would have had to be realigned to create a healthy, safer family system for the children. Perhaps Roberts could also have explored with Mrs. Garza her family-of-origin patterns as a way to help her to break the destructive patterns of female submission and use of drugs to cope with depression. Communication skills training could also have been useful to break those patterns.

CONCERNS ABOUT SAFETY

My overall concern about the case description is that the confrontational session might have been premature without adequate preparation for the children or the parents. Given that Mrs. Garza was somewhat disengaged from the therapy process at that time, including Mr. Garza in a session with the children seemed to be risking harmful exposure of the children to his intimidation. Although I did not detect a good level of safety in the case description, I accept a priori that Roberts must have sensed a good level of safety prior to initiating that meeting with Mr. Garza. However, if the conjoint confrontational session had been premature, the harmful consequences for the children could have been devastating. For example, Mr. Garza could have intimidated the children into agreeing with him that they had lied. Mrs. Garza could have succumbed to his intimidation, the charges could have been dropped for lack of a witnesses, and the abuse could have continued as Mother returned to her drug escape. In a worse case scenario, subsequent to a divorce Mr. Garza is awarded joint custody and permitted frequent unsupervised access to the children, although he never admitted his incestuous behavior to be harmful and unacceptable. Indeed, he could likely have been awarded primary custodial parent with the right to establish domicile because of Mrs. Garza's drug history. Such a situation would have afforded him a significant degree of control over the children if he chose to move beyond the boundaries of Mrs. Garza's supervisory purview.

ETHICAL CONCERNS AND QUESTIONS

For me, therapy with incest families always creates substantial ethical tensions because so many misjudgments exist that easily can be made at all system levels. The consequences can be devastating for the victims, including the participating child, the observing nonparticipating children, the nonprotecting parent, and the participating parent. This case, using conjoint family therapy, illustrated how all of the family members are affected. No one, not Roberts, CPS, or the legal system, can absolutely protect families from becoming self-destructive. At some point, the abusing families have to be trusted to provide a safe environment for their children without further intervention. The question is when.

Based on the case report, Roberts's contact with Mr. Garza was limited to only two therapy sessions. Given the circumstances, I question whether that is enough family therapy to ensure a second-order change in the system. Absent Mr. Garza's direct apology to his victim daughters and son, is he repentant enough not to abuse again if given the opportunity? Perhaps extended family therapy with the entire system after his admission in his group therapy would have provided more assurance. Did therapy establish more backup systems within the extended family to monitor the safety of the children?

Outside the family system and the therapeutic system, the other threatening dimensions are the CPS system and the legal system. Roberts worked carefully with the CPS system to prevent reactivity that might have hindered the healing possibilities for this family. The legal consequences seemed to provide a chance for Mr. Garza to maintain some dignity and yet provide reasonable safety for the children. However, my clinical instincts question whether an adequate safety plan is in place. What might happen if Mrs. Garcia is not able to maintain sobriety and consequently fails to protect the children? Does the court have sufficient monitoring mechanisms in place to fill in that possible gap?

CONCLUDING THOUGHTS

For this family the therapeutic outcome was positive. Hopefully the Garza children will grow up to value and respect healthy boundaries in relationships as they observe their parents breaking the old patterns and substituting new ones.

REFERENCES

Minuchin, S. and Fishman, H.C. (1981). *Family therapy techniques.* Cambridge, Massachusetts: Harvard University Press.

Trepper, T.S. and Barrett, J.J. (1989). *Systemic treatment of incest: A therapeutic handbook.* New York: Brunner/Mazel.

Yingling, L.C., Miller, W. E., McDonald, A. L., and Galewaler, S.T. (1998). *GARF assessment source book: Using the DSM-IV global assessment of relational functioning.* Bristol, PA: Brunner/Mazel [Taylor and Francis].

CASE 10

A Young Man and a Penis Called Chipmunk

David A. Baptiste Jr.

Therapist Background

Currently: Sixty-one years old, black, male, PhD, thirty-two years in clinical practice, twenty-seven years MFT practice. When I saw this family: forty-four years old, PhD, ten years MFT practice.

Practice Setting

Currently: Private practice. When I saw this family: Full-time university counseling center but saw them in private practice

Client Characteristics

The Olsens, Dru (age fifty-eight), Eric (age sixty-one), and son, Ray (age twenty-six), were a white middle-class family. Three older sons, Eric Jr. (age forty-two) and twins Charles and Robert (age thirty-seven) and a daughter, Tammy (age forty-one), completed the family. Tammy and Amy, Ray's girlfriend, were present for one therapy session respectively. Dru was a lawyer with the federal civil service. Eric was an electrical engineer, employed as a manager at NASA's Southern New Mexico facility. Ray is an electrical/electronics engineer. He was unemployed and had been living with his parents for approximately three years. Eric Jr. and Tammy were lawyers in Chicago and Boston, respectively. Robert taught electrical engineering at a university and Charles was a high school science teacher.

Length of Treatment

The family was seen in concurrent family, individual, and couples sessions for approximately twenty sessions from April 1985 through the end of July 1985. The critical incident occurred in Session 9.

Theoretical Perspective

A strategic approach was used in working with this family in concurrent family, couples, and individual sessions.

Dru Olsen initially consulted me to "get some ideas about what I could do about my son who is having trouble leaving the nest." Three weeks earlier she and I spoke briefly at the conclusion of my presentation at a military mental health center. During that interaction, she jokingly said, "You sound like somebody I need to talk to." She asked for my business card and left. The next week she called. She said, "I think that you may be able to help me. My situation is getting out of hand and I think we all need help to sort things out." We scheduled an initial meeting for two weeks later; she was clear that she wanted information, not therapy. I agreed to see her alone initially and then decide where we would go from there.

PRESENTING PROBLEM

Dru disclosed that she had dissuaded Eric, her husband of forty-one years, from coming with her to this initial meeting because "I just was coming to talk to you to get some ideas about what to do about Ray." She, however, acknowledged that "Eric was not too happy with me coming alone. He told me not to prejudice you before he gets a chance to talk to you." Dru shared that Ray, her youngest son, is an electrical engineer but has worked for only six months since graduation. He now lived with her and Eric and was enrolled in graduate classes at the university. She and Eric—but especially Eric—want Ray to leave home and be independent like his siblings. She said, "I have tried everything, but nothing seems to work. He went to California but that too did not work out. We had to go and get him because he had problems, was depressed, and ended up in the hospital. The older ones invited him to live with them for awhile, but he refuses. After graduation, he did spend about two months with Tammy in Boston. Eric has been very patient with this situation, but now he is ready to blow a cork. He hasn't said so directly, but I know he believes that I am not as eager as he is to emancipate Ray; he thinks it is my fault that Ray would not, 'cut the apron strings.' Truth is, I too am worried about Ray; I want him to go out on his own. We raised them to be responsible and independent, but I am at a loss as to what I can do. I have tried everything, I think. That is why I am here: to get some ideas about what else or more I can do to get him to go out on his own. I just can't throw him out in the street. I know that Eric knows that, but I don't think he understands."

At the end of her narration, Dru asked, "So what do you think?" I shared my impression that she had a family, rather than a Dru, problem.

"Your family appears to have two interrelated problems. First, Ray is experiencing difficulty leaving home and Eric and you worry about him not being independent like the older children. It appears he is being compared to the older children rather than being seen as an individual with the same last name as the older ones. The second problem is a Dru and Eric problem. For forty-one years, you and Eric have been able to agree or at least compromise on matters affecting your family. Now, however, you two seem unable to do that. I question what has happened or is happening to make this long-standing decision-making partnership not work. You complain that Eric blames you for Ray staying at home. But you appear to have accepted Eric's way of defining the problem 'as the truth' and have accepted the problem as your own. At several points in your story, you made it clear that getting Ray to leave home is solely your responsibility. And coming here without Eric gives the impression that Dru alone rather than Eric and Dru jointly are responsible to find a solution to a problem that is bothering both of you."

Dru stared directly at me for awhile. Then said, "You don't mince words, do you?" I replied, "Those are my honest impressions. Did I misunderstand you?" She said, "No. I just didn't expect to hear that or have it put so cut and dried; you do have a way with words. I have to admit that you are right. Sometimes I do feel like it is my job to get Ray to leave home." She abruptly asked, "So, what do I do now?" I invited her to commit to family therapy and to invite Eric and Ray to join her for a family session to tell their stories and to provide their perspectives of the problem. She asked, "Is this a sort of psychologist discovery?" I replied, "Discovery plus some. Eric, Ray, and you are responsible for whatever problems exist within the family and I want to hear from everyone." She said, "I came to get some ideas to share with Eric, but now it looks like I am heading to therapy. I wanted to avoid that."

Dru was reluctant to commit to therapy because of previous negative experiences with other psychotherapists. She said, "The last time I went down this road, I got jumped on. I felt like the accused. Eric had to jump in before she would lay off me. That is something I will not forget." I commented, "Sounds like the family, but especially you, had a not so good experience with therapists." She shared that over the years the family had consulted at least twelve counselors/psychologists (75 percent female) for help with problems Tammy and later Ray had experienced while in high school. According to Dru, most of those therapists blamed the parents, primarily Dru, for the children's, especially Ray's, problems. One female therapist was very combative with Dru. "She jumped all over my ass; said I was more into my career than being a mother. That hurt! I was a lawyer by then. It took a long time to get over that. I told myself 'I'm never going through that again.' " That said, she said, "You seem straightforward and a lot more evenhanded. So far you haven't blamed or accused me of anything. I think I'll give it a shot." Asked if those experiences influenced her to ask for ideas rather than therapy this time, she said, "I didn't think of it at the time we talked, but yes, I was afraid to come here today, although I knew I should. I am still a little shaky but getting better. You match my way of doing things. You are direct and seem to know what you are doing. I think I can handle it. I will come back." Without further comment, we scheduled a family session for two weeks later. She also asked to be seen in my private practice although the counseling center's services were free to Ray as a part-time university student.

THE THERAPEUTIC SITUATION PRIOR
TO THE CRITICAL INCIDENT

At the second session, Dru, Eric, and Ray were present. I introduced myself to Eric and Ray and asked if Dru had shared with them any details of our meeting. Eric confirmed that, "Dru brought me up to speed on what you two talked about and said you look like a no-nonsense kind of a guy. That's good; she feels comfortable with you. You don't know this, but in Florida some shrinks gave her a real bad time. That left her with a bad feeling about shrinks. I am glad she feels good about you. Maybe now we can get Ray fixed and on his way for good." While Eric was speaking, Dru was using hand gestures and almost inaudible statements to interrupt him. Almost in a whisper, she said, "Eric, he knows." "Eric, I told him." "Eric, we only have one hour; let's talk about Ray." Eric did not immediately respond to Dru's subtle cues. She then shouted, "Eric, he knows!" At that point, Eric disengaged with a parting shot, "Well, I don't want a repeat of Florida." I thanked Eric for his concern and invited the family to tell me if at any point in working with me anyone felt that I was being unprofessional in dealing with him or her.

Ray was six feet, seven inches tall, a frail-looking young man, as thin as a proverbial rail. He appeared very unsure of himself and moderately depressed. I asked if Dru had shared with him the details of our meeting. He reported that she had not. More important, not until the night before this meeting was he informed that he was expected to come to the meeting. Dru anticipated my question and responded before I could ask it. She explained that she had planned to talk with Eric first but he was out of town. After he returned, "I got busy with work and other things and completely forgot until last night that I did not talk to Ray about coming here. I am sorry for that. But here we are, ready to go." Asked how he felt about coming to therapy on such short notice, Ray mumbled, "I guess it is for my benefit. But I've seen counselors for a long time now and I still can't get my life together. Mom said you look like you could help me this time."

I asked Eric and Ray respectively for their understanding of why the family was here. Eric saw Ray's current problems as a continuation of the difficulties he had experienced beginning in his sophomore year of high school. He believed that previous decisions he and Dru made about Ray's life "have been haunting us ever since." Dru interrupted to disagree with Eric's formulation of the problem. She chided him, "That has nothing to do with this. He really was sick. They wouldn't let him stay in the hospital all those months if he weren't sick!" Eric retorted, "I know what I know! You don't want to see a connection. They told us there is a connection and more and more I am beginning to believe it. I don't know what it is, but I hope this man can help us figure it out."

Following that exchange, I asked Ray for his understanding of the problem. He opened his mouth to speak but did not make a sound. Then in a quavering, angry voice he said, "I'm the family fuck-up! I just can't get my life together. I'm supposed to be smart and going places, but I'm going nowhere. I don't want to or like being sick, but I'm always sick and the doctors haven't figured out what's wrong with me." In unison, Dru and Eric attempted to reassure Ray that he was not the "family's fuck-up." Before either one said much, I gestured to them to be quiet and motioned for Ray to continue. He said, "I think I'm here so I can stop being sick, stop living with Mom and Dad, and get on with my life." He then addressed his parents directly, "I haven't told you this before, and maybe you don't want to hear it, but sometimes I just want to die. I don't like living like this. I just don't."

Dru and Eric's faces showed their collective surprise and disbelief in response to Ray's disclosure of suicidal ideation. Both stared intently at Ray. Dru began to cry. Eric hung his head and bit his lip intensely. They appeared to be searching for appropriate words to say, but neither one could find words. In the end, nothing was said. Ray broke the silence. He disclosed that since returning home he had thought of suicide only twice. I asked if there were times when he thought more about suicide. He replied, "Whenever I hear about friends who are doing good on the job or are getting married. I look at myself, see where I am, look at how my brothers and sister are doing, and it hits me, Ray, you are going nowhere. You are a fuck up. That's when I really feel like dying." I remarked, "Comparing yourself to your friends and your siblings, you see yourself as a failure and suicide as a solution for failure." Without hesitation, Ray replied, "Yes, something like that. I want to have a job, my own place, and maybe get married, but here I am still living with my parents. I don't think anybody understands how frustrated I feel; I'm twenty-six and still living at home. I graduated with honors and I haven't done a damn thing with my degree." I acknowledged and validated his feelings of frustration and asked for his ideas of what he believed may be stopping him from leaving home and how to overcome it. He admitted not having any ideas. He said, "If I knew what was holding me back, I'd be gone so fast it isn't funny. I'd be out there chasing wild women like Frank (Tammy's husband) said I should be doing."

Asked what might his siblings say about him still living at home, he replied, "I don't know what Eric thinks. I don't know him that well. Robert doesn't say much. We got along well when I was in college. Now he says I'm wasting my mind. Charles said Mom should have kicked my butt as much as she kicked his when he was growing up. Tammy thinks she is Miss Psychology, always telling me I'm not sick and I'm "faking" it to stay home. They all believe Mom babied me too much when I was little. Tammy and Charles told Dad to set a time for me to get my own place and get out." I commented that it appeared everyone except Ray had ideas about what is wrong with Ray. I asked, "Is there any merit to their belief and solutions for fixing what they believe is wrong?" He shook his head no. "I know they want to help me, but they really don't know what's wrong with me. I don't even know. I see life passing me by. I've never had a real girlfriend. I blow it every time. I fuck up everything except school. And a lot of good that did me."

Before I could respond, Dru screamed at Ray, "You are not a fuck-up. How could you believe that? We never told you that. Who told you that? None of my children is a failure. Your father and I are not failures. We pulled up ourselves from nothing. Not even our own parents gave us a fighting chance, but we made it and you all made it. You are not a fuck-up! I don't ever again want to hear you put yourself down." Dru began to cry in earnest. Eric moved closer to her, put his arm around her, and they both cried. In the lull that followed, no one spoke. I interrupted the quietness and asked Dru and Eric what was it about Ray's disclosure that elicited their strong reactions. Dru asserted, "I can't imagine any of my children killing themselves. That is unthinkable! That would say we didn't bring them up right. Eric and I started out at sixteen and nineteen, saw a lot of hard times, but never once thought of giving up or killing ourselves. We come from poor but strong Oklahoma folk and all my children have that strength in them." I commented to Dru that she sounded angry with Ray. She replied, "Yes, I am angry that he would put himself down and want to kill himself. We've always been there for him and will again. Wanting him to go out on his own don't mean we don't love him. We'll get him well. And I have the feeling you can help us do it." Asked for his reactions to Ray's disclosure, Eric shook his head and quietly said, "I can't talk now."

I asked Ray for his recollection of when life was good for him, when he did not feel like a 'fuck-up' or want to kill himself. He remembered his first year and fall of his second year of high school as good times. He said, "I guess just when I went to high school before I started getting sick was a good time. I played basketball then and everybody said I was good." He abruptly stopped playing basketball and withdrew from school because of illness. He could not recall a time as an adult when life was good for him. In college, he was not as sick but still was in the hospital a lot. Asked what he would do and how he would live his life if he were not sick, Ray's face lit up and he laughed with gusto. He said, "I would be working in California, making lots of money, and have a super girlfriend or be chasing lots of women." I commented that he came alive when sharing his vision of an illness-free adult life. Dru and Eric agreed; Dru coaxed him to, "Give your dream a try." Suddenly, his smiling face became a mask of intense fear. In a whimpering voice, he said, "I can't do that. I will get sick again. You don't understand how I feel." He then bolted from the room. Dru and Eric apologized for Ray's behavior, but I deflected their apologies and emphasized Ray's responsibility for his actions. Eric remarked, "You must have touched a nerve in him."

Dru and Eric confirmed that Ray's abrupt mood change was a new behavior for him. They both questioned whether he was deteriorating emotionally. Dru then asked, "What do we do now?" I shared with them that it may be a case of "the flesh is willing but the spirit is not ready. He believes he is not emotionally ready to go on his own. I do not believe the physical separation is the problem. Whatever is holding him back is emotional and may be unrelated to actually leaving home. I also have a hunch that in some way it may be related to high school because that appears to be when life began to go bad for him." I acknowledged my disagreement with Dru on this issue and asked her and Eric to tell me about Ray's difficulties in high school.

A Life Truncated

Dru dated Ray's difficulties to his sophomore year in high school. Prior to that time, "He was a normal, smart, outgoing kid who did well academically and played basketball." Midway through his sophomore year he abruptly withdrew from school, basketball, and friends and isolated himself at home. Concurrently, he began to complain of all manner of illness and rarely left the house except to see physicians and to be hospitalized. None of those consultations discovered any obvious medical reasons for his illness. After an exhaustive run of physicians and hospitalizations, the family physician recommended psychotherapy. As a result, the family consulted almost as many psychotherapists as physicians with little or no success. Ray would improve for awhile only to deteriorate later and be hospitalized. As a result, he was homeschooled by a private teacher assisted by his parents, particularly Dru. He graduated with his high school class and performed exceptionally well on the SAT (1500+) and ACT (32), college admission tests. During his first year of college he visited fewer physicians and never was hospitalized. His sophomore year his visits to physicians increased as did the number of hospital stays.

At this point, Eric interrupted Dru. He said, "Ray is the last kid and the only one home when he was in high school. Dru acted like he was her first child. The more she treated him with kid gloves, the sicker he got. I disagreed with her approach but lost that battle. Don't get me wrong; I love that kid. But we've been through a lot with him emotionally, not to mention the money. Until high school, and even after he started high school, he was a regular kid doing what kids do. Then wham, he was holed up in the house, sick, or in a hospital. Nobody could figure out what was wrong with him. He had surgery that the doctors said would fix the situation but that didn't work. For awhile in college he was doing fine and we thought it was over. Now we're back to square one!" As Eric ended his narration, Ray returned. He apologized for leaving. "I just couldn't take anymore."

At the end of this extended session I offered the family the hypothesis that, "physically, leaving home appeared not to be the substantive issue for Ray. That is too simple. If he really wanted to and you wanted him to leave home, you could rent him an apartment and, presto, he physically is out of the house. I believe it is more substantial. Whatever is hooking him is emotional and he has put it away so far he is having difficulty recalling it. He also is experiencing significant pressures to succeed like his older siblings and his parents. Much of that pressure is of his own doing but is tied into whatever is holding him to the only place he feels safe—home." I asked them to have a family meeting and to generate at least five ideas for getting Ray physically out of the home. I also asked them to discuss how they got along when Ray was healthy and what would Dru and Eric do if Ray was healthy and out of the home. I assigned each member a responsibility. Ray will take notes, Eric will be the convener/moderator, and Dru, the participant observer. We scheduled another session in two weeks.

Two days later, Dru requested an unscheduled individual session. At this meeting she was visibly anxious, fidgeted, and appeared much like a "cat on a hot tin roof." I asked if something critical or life threatening had occurred since our last meeting. In response, she shifted in her chair, crossed and uncrossed her legs, and with a deep sigh looked at the floor and said, "I have something to tell you but I don't know how you will take it or what you will think of me after I tell you. Eric and Ray don't know I am here, so please don't bring this up when they're here. Last time, you said that if we wanted Ray out of the house, we could easily rent him an apartment and that would be that. You are right. But when you asked us to think of ways to get Ray out of the house, it hit me that we have a loaded reason for not wanting him around. And I do feel like I am pushing him out, not for his sake but for our purpose." Looking directly at me, she said, "I guess there is no easy way to say this, so I will just come right out and say it. Eric and I are in a swinging-couples group that meets at members' homes. Since Ray's been home, we haven't hosted any or attended many group parties. So far, no one has complained, but I think it is just a matter time. So I sort of took on the job to help Ray leave home." She admitted feeling guilty about thinking about ways to get Ray out of the house but not guilty or ashamed about joining the group. She stressed that it was her idea, not Eric's, to join the group. "It was something different to do." She was clear that, "It's not something you tell kids, no matter how grown up they are."

At the end of her disclosure, I commented that it must have been difficult to share that part of her life. I assured her that my purpose was not to judge clients' behaviors, although I might comment on specific aspects of clients' behaviors as they relate to their presenting complaint. I asked if she saw a relationship between her private behavior, Ray's illness, and/or his difficulty in leaving home. Without hesitation she said, "No. But you did ask how Eric and I would spend our time if Ray was healthy and out of the house. Well, that's what we do and would do." I acknowledged my failure to make an initial connection between her disclosure and my homework assignment but assured her that I now understood her purpose in telling her story. Laughing, she said, "Here I am baring my soul and you didn't have a clue." I supported her belief that their swinging behavior appeared not to be related to Ray issues. I, however, wondered whether, given their lifestyle, she and Eric felt an urgency for Ray to leave home. She acknowledged there was an urgency but was very clear that they also wanted Ray to go out on his own for his own sake. More important, she felt that he was too old to be living with his parents. I remarked that having Ray at home must seem like unfinished business with regard to launching/emancipating adult children. Smiling broadly, she said, "You do understand!"

At the next session, Dru reported that the family meeting discussion was "Helpful but not much was accomplished. We all cried because none of us could see a clear way out of this situation." Ray had asked for time to "ease out of the home." To that end, he had begun to spend increasingly more time at a male friend's apartment and at his girlfriend's home; since the family meeting, he twice stayed overnight at Amy's home. Amy had invited him to move in with her, but he declined her invitation. He admitted that his refusal to move in with Amy was straining their relationship. "She thinks I'm not committing to the relationship." He denied he lacked commitment. He wanted the relationship as much as Amy did but still was uncomfortable living away from home. Paradoxically, he complained of feeling embarrassed living with his parents because, "I don't feel grown up." For Ray, not being at home full time was "a mixed bag." On one hand, it helped him to "be independent and get me ready to live on my own." However, his positive feelings were eclipsed by an uneasiness that, "Something bad is going to happen to me if I leave home for good." He did not know what the "bad thing" was.

Eric commented to Ray, "You're in a kind of a bind. You don't think you can make it on your own and don't like living with us." Ray replied, "Yes, but more. I really feel like something bad is going to happen to me when I am not living at home, and it really gets bad at Amy's." Again, he could not identify anything specific that contributed to his feelings of dread when at Amy's house. Asked what would have to happen for him to feel ready to leave home, Ray did not respond. Absent Ray's response, Dru looked directly at me and suggested that I meet with Ray individually to discover "what scares him when he is not home." Without revealing that she had preempted my thoughts, I agreed to meet with Ray individually. He asked that Amy be included because she had been asking to meet with him and me. Believing that Amy's presence in therapy could be of benefit, I consented to see her conjointly with Ray.

Three of four sessions I met with Ray individually; Amy was present for Session 4. Individual sessions focused on Ray's dread about living away from home permanently and how he would know when he is ready to leave permanently. During this time, his time away from home increased significantly. He alternated between a male friend's apartment and Amy's home. However, on at least four occasions when his friend was out of town, he elected to stay at a motel rather than with Amy or his parents. He explained that "Amy makes too many demands. I stay at a motel rather than fight with her." Neither Amy, his parents, nor his friend were aware that he was staying at a motel. Interestingly, now that he was spending time away from his parents' home, his feeling of dread was decreasing. He explained that he did not perceive his time away from home to be permanent. Consequently, because he knew he always could return home if he wanted to do so, his anxiety had decreased.

In all aspects, the three sessions were unproductive. Although Ray was spending more time out of the parental home and reported a significant decrease in his physical symptoms and anxiety, his efforts to "ease out of the home" were not achieving the desired results. He, however, continued to assure his parents, Amy, and me that leaving home permanently and living illness free were his highest priority. I shared with Ray my feelings that he appeared not to be internalizing behaviors that would sustain him when he did leave home permanently. Rather, he had developed a sense of a "safety net" that he could return home if the going got rough. I also expressed feeling therapeutically stuck and again shared with him my belief that physically leaving home appeared not to be the crux of his problems. "I am not sure what it is, but I feel strongly that it's related to whatever happened to you in high school." Ray listened attentively, did not ask any questions, but commented, "I wish to God I knew what's happening to my life. I don't know where its going." We scheduled to meet in one week.

EVENTS LEADING TO THE CRITICAL INCIDENT

Two days later, Ray called for an appointment because, "Amy and I may be breaking up. We want to talk to you." When we met, Amy vented much anger at Ray. She had learned from a friend, who worked at the motel, that Ray had stayed at the motel. She initially assumed he was seeing another woman. However, she erupted in a tirade when Ray explained that he stayed at the motel because,"You demand too much from me." Amy asked for evidence of her excessive demands. Initially, Ray was silent but, pressed by Amy, he said, "You always want to jump in the sack." That brought Amy to her feet. She faced Ray and screamed, "That's bullshit! You make it sound like that's all I think about because I want to have sex. I am normal. But something is wrong with you. You never want to have sex. You'd rather stay at a motel than have sex with me." Ray stared at Amy but said nothing. I invited the couple to talk about the problems in their relationship.

Amy shared that she and Ray had been dating for fifteen months and he spent many nights at her home "but we never have sex." She acknowledged that, "Ray was caring, loving, very romantic, and affectionate." However, whenever an amorous moment moved toward intercourse, "Ray always has a good excuse for not having sex." Previously, Ray never attributed his avoidance of sex to Amy. Now, however, she perceived him to be blaming her. She declared, "I know that you jerk off a lot; that makes me really mad that you would rather do that than have sex with me." Asked for his perception of the problem, Ray said, "It's not you, Amy. I want to go to bed with you, but something is holding me back." He, however, could not identify "the something." Asked if he stayed at the motel to avoid having sex with Amy, Ray replied, "I just didn't want to fight with her anymore. I know she doesn't understand. I don't." I invited him to help me understand what was contributing to him avoiding sex with Amy and how that behavior was related, if at all, to his difficulty in leaving home. He admitted not knowing if his avoidance of sex was related to leaving home and acknowledged that he was a virgin. He iterated, "It's not Amy." At that juncture, Amy stormed out of the room and Ray remarked, "I am so embarrassed." He then asked, "You must think that I'm really weird." I responded that I did not know what was weird. I, however, believed that whatever was troubling him was weighing heavily on his mind and was contributing to his decision to avoid sex. "I have a hunch that avoiding sex and avoiding leaving home are somehow related. We have to work to uncover how they are related." At the session's end, we scheduled a family session in two weeks.

THE CRITICAL INCIDENT

Three days before the scheduled family session, Dru called to tell me that Tammy would be in town and had requested to attend the session. Dru sounded unenthusiastic and her tone conveyed a veiled sense that she was expecting me to deny the request. I told her that I had no objections as long as it was OK with the other members. Three days later, the three regular members and Tammy were present. I introduced myself to Tammy and asked if her parents had shared any details of our meetings so far. She said, "Yes, some." I asked if she needed clarification or an explanation of anything that she was told. She dismissed my question with a curt "No" and said, "I just want to add my two cents." I assured her that I welcomed all perceptions of the problem and as Ray's sister she had a perception that I wanted to hear. Tammy was emphatic that her parents, especially Dru, had "babied Ray." He had a free ride and attended "almost private school" by being homeschooled. She believed that Ray was "faking it." She perceived Ray to "want to continue the good times" by continuing to be "sick" and to live at home with his parents. At this juncture, Dru hung her head and set her jaw but said nothing. Eric interrupted Tammy to inform me that Dru and Tammy "did not see eye to eye on much ever since Tammy was in high school." As a result, "I always have to get in the middle and referee." I assured Eric that he did not have to be a referee tonight because that was my job. I invited each member to express his or her feelings and promised an opportunity to clarify any misinformation. Ray and Dru attempted to challenge Tammy's formulation of the problem, but I gestured for them to be quiet and asked Tammy to continue. She said, "I know Mom doesn't want to hear this, but I believe that Ray is gay and afraid to admit it. When he stayed with me, I saw him always looking at or playing with his penis. He always was trying to look at Frank's penis and asked a lot of questions about the size of Frank's penis. Mom, you said that several times you saw him playing with his penis. If that is not signs of being gay, then I don't what is. I talked with some of my gay friends and they agree that he could be gay."

While Tammy was speaking, Ray looked at her scowlingly, Eric pounded one hand into the other, and Dru's face was beet red as she clinched her teeth. An awkward silence punctuated Tammy's comments. Ray spoke first. He admitted behaving in the manner Tammy described and in a very controlled voice told Tammy, "I'm not queer! I don't know why I did that, but I'm not queer." Dru's response to Tammy was explosive and caustic. She said, "When you told me that before I thought it was damn foolish then and I still think it is a heap of crap now. Why would you want to believe that about your own flesh and blood? He's got enough to worry about than to worry if he is gay. As long as I can remember you never liked how we raised Ray and never have anything good to say about me." Dru chastised me for allowing

Tammy to "spew her crap." I asserted that Tammy had a right to her opinion whether or not Dru agreed with her; it was important to hear that opinion. Asked if as an attorney she would exclude testimony because she disagreed with it, Dru dismissed my comparison. She said, "Here I'm not a lawyer; it's my son she's calling queer." I pointed out that regardless of her feelings about Tammy's hypothesis, we needed to consider it until we had a better one or could objectively reject it. Asked for his reactions to Tammy's hypothesis, Eric shook his head and quietly said, "I don't believe he's gay." I thanked Tammy for her input, invited the other members, especially Ray, to develop their own hypotheses about Ray's difficulty in leaving home, and agreed to meet in two weeks.

THE AFTERMATH OF THE CRITICAL INCIDENT

The next day, Ray came to see me at the counseling center. He began the hour questioning, "Do you think I'm queer?" and immediately declared, "I'm not queer!" I told him that I never know who is or is not gay until the person tells me. Now that he had told me that he was not gay, I would accept that as fact. He paused briefly and abruptly asked about the size of men's penises and if I thought women liked men with small penises. Before I answered one question, he asked another. His questions changed from general to specific. He said, "I want to ask you a personal question." Before I could say yes or no, he asked, "Do you ever think about the size of your dick?" Although surprised by the question, I told him that I did not usually do so. He responded, "I do. A lot." At this juncture, I asked, "What does that have to do with anything that is happening to you now?" He replied, "I'm not queer, but I think I figured it out." I waited for him to continue and when he did not, I asked, "You figured it out? Tell me!" Continuing, he replied, "Yes, I know why I don't want to have sex with Amy. I have a small dick and I know she will laugh at me if she sees my dick." I commented that his explanation made sense if he believed that he has a small penis. I asked, "Your dick is small compared to whose, and who said that your dick is small?" He replied, "All the guys said that my dick is little, like a chipmunk's dick." I asked, "Who are all the guys that told you that your dick is small?" He hung his head and revealed the secret that had kept him prisoner for approximately twelve years.

In high school, his basketball teammates frequently discussed the size of their penises. Compared to most of his teammates he was much frailer and shorter (approximately five feet seven inches) and frequently was the butt of their jokes and teasing about penis size. They nicknamed his penis Chipmunk and, by extension, called him Chipmunk. The teasing and jokes became a regular fare and soon moved beyond the basketball team. In time, his coach began to call him Chipmunk. He came to feel that everyone in the school knew that he had a "chipmunk's dick." As a result, he experienced tremendous stress and suffered in silence but never told his parents about being teased at school in part because he believed that they wanted him to be a basketball star like his brothers Charles and Robert, and in part because he genuinely liked school and excelled academically. In the fall of his sophomore year, he experienced a traumatic incident that changed his life. While showering after a practice, some of the boys restrained him while another took a Polaroid photograph of his penis and promised to hang copies throughout the school and also to give a copy to the girl in whom he had shown some interest. The coach came to the showers in response to his screams. He told Ray, "It's just a joke" and told the boys to leave Ray alone. The coach then joined the team in laughing at the "joke." As a result of that incident, Ray came to believe that everyone in school, indeed, the world, knew that he had a "chipmunk's dick." He never returned to school and for twelve years became "genuinely ill" to avoid being laughed at because he believed that his penis was small.

At the end of his outpouring, I empathized with him and acknowledged the emotional pain he had suffered for the past twelve years. He vented anger about the incident, about his coach who did not protect him, and about "the other counselors who wanted me to think that I'm queer and even gave me books to read about queers." When asked what had led to his recall after twelve years, he asserted, "Everybody thinks I'm queer. I'm not! I don't like Tammy calling me queer. That's just what those guys called me because I said I never had sex. Ralph [a teammate] always said that I did not have sex because my dick was too small." He abruptly asked, "Why don't you think I'm queer? You're the only counselor who didn't say I'm too tied up with Mom." I did not answer his question directly but commented, "Sounds as if that means a lot to you to have someone not label you as queer and to believe that the problem could be something else." He replied, "Yes, you didn't make us feel like we've done something wrong. Some of the other counselors were brutal with Mom." I shared with him that I never considered homosexuality to be a contributing factor in his illness or difficulty in leaving home. But I also did not believe that the problem simply was not being able to leave home. I was aware that something out there was frightening him. "What it was I did not know until now." Asked how he was feeling about leaving home now that he knew what was frightening him, he replied, "What I'm feeling is very, very angry as I was telling you. If I saw those guys now I don't know that I won't kick the shit out of them. One good thing is that I can tell Amy what I told you and maybe she will understand." I encouraged him to share his story with his parents and Amy and planned to see him and his parents the next week.

DISCUSSION

The Role of the Critical Incident in Getting Therapy Unstuck

In actuality, this case had been stuck for all of the twelve years that Ray had been ill and had been seeing other therapists. During that period, although he occasionally obtained some relief, it never was permanent and his illness persisted. Consequently, at the point at which the family came to see me, Ray and his parents still were stuck, unable to move on with their respective lives. Accordingly, although the critical incident facilitated/contributed to the uncovering of the source of Ray's illness, therapy remained moderately stuck because the attendant problem—Ray's difficulty in leaving the parental home—continued beyond the critical incident. The critical incident's central contribution to therapeutic movement in this case was as a cue that facilitated Ray's reintegration of a very negative affect—his teammates' assertion that he was gay and had a small penis—using Tammy's similar assertion—"Ray is gay" as the cue that facilitated Ray's recall. Clearly, Tammy's assertion that Ray was gay affected Ray in an identical manner as did his teammates' original assertions that he was gay ("I don't like Tammy calling me queer").

Given the simplicity of the event that led to Ray's recall, one might question whether he always knew the source of his problems and really was faking it, as Tammy believed. We may never know the answer to that question, but it is clear that although those negative memories were available to Ray, they may have been buried too deeply to be retrieved by an emotional impact of a lesser magnitude than Tammy's assertion. It also is possible that twelve years ago, Ray may have believed his teammates' pronouncement that he was gay and his penis was smaller than their penises. In this regard, concerns about sexuality is central to the adolescent experience. Consequently, as a fourteen-year-old without much reliable/objective information about sexuality, it is possible that the original negative assertions that he had a small penis may have been so overwhelming to Ray that he went into a twelve-year tailspin. However, now that he is older and has had several years of psychotherapy, hearing an identical assertion from Tammy ("Ray is gay") may have provided just the right magnitude of anger and emotional eruption sufficient to trigger the reintegration and recall of the original negative affect rather than to push him into another tailspin.

Implications of the Critical Incident for Therapy

Despite therapy not being fully unstuck, the implications of the critical incident are notable for therapy, for Dru and Eric, and especially for Ray. However, although I have credited Tammy's challenge of Ray's gender identity as the critical incident responsible for producing therapeutic movement, I now am less certain that only one critical incident occurred and not a summation of two similar incidents that contributed to Ray's recall. In a previous session, although not directly asserting that Ray might be gay, Amy had impugned his masculinity: "I'm normal. But something is wrong with you." Like Tammy, Amy was close to Ray and also had questioned his masculinity and indirectly his gender identity. Tammy's assertion that Ray was gay followed very closely Amy's challenge of Ray's masculinity. Consequently, it is possible that the two events may have summated and contributed to a significant emotional eruption that in turn led to Ray's reintegration and recall of that painful event.

Whether separate or summative, clearly the challenge to Ray's gender identity helped him to get in touch with an event that he had blocked out of his conscious awareness because of the pain and hurt attendant to it. However, hearing similar assertions from two persons so close to him may have helped to trigger Ray's recall of that event and helped him to react appropriately ("what I'm feeling is very, very angry") to it. Prior to Amy and Tammy's assertions, Ray experienced difficulty recalling the source of his illness, why he was afraid to leave home or to have sex with Amy. Post critical incident, following the recall of that painful event, he reported significant insight and understanding of his problem. This was freeing for him and by extension his parents.

THE OUTCOME OF THERAPY

I saw Ray and his parents for three more family sessions, saw Ray for two individual sessions, and saw Dru and Eric conjointly for five sessions. Family sessions focused on Ray's disclosure about the events twelve years earlier and his parents reactions to his story. Both parents expressed intense anger at the perpetrators of the "joke," especially the coach, for their respective roles in the event. They also expressed sadness for Ray for all he had suffered over the years as result of the "joke." Dru considered legal action against the coach if he still was at the school because, "his joke played havoc with all our lives all those years." She also promised to inform the school board about the event and to seek reimbursement "for all the money we spent on doctors and counselors."

The two sessions with Ray focused on helping him to further vent his feelings about what had happened to him and to help him to begin to heal. He reported that he and Amy were "talking again and would attempt to work things out." He did not say and I did not ask if they had or were planning to have sex. He also reported that he felt as if he was thawing after being frozen and for the first time he was feeling that he could be on his own. His immediate plans were to complete his master's degree at the university and then decide what he would do next.

The five couples sessions focused on a wide range of issues including Dru and Eric's feelings about "not having a clue that Ray had been treated so cruelly." They both felt that they had "let Ray down." Dru in particular chastised herself for "not putting it together sooner. I should have know that it was something like that because of the suddenness with which he just dropped school and everything to do with it. I know he suffered a lot!" We also focused on the strains in the mother-daughter relationship and the couple shared a family secret that was the antecedent of the conflict: Ray is Tammy's biological child born while she was in high school; Dru and Eric formally adopted Ray. Tammy requested that Ray be adopted outside of the family and was very upset that her parents had adopted Ray. As a result, she acted out in a variety of ways and the family sought therapy to cope with her behaviors. She sees Ray as a reminder of her "mistake." Since the adoption, the parent-daughter, especially mother-daughter, relationship has been strained. Ray does not know that he is adopted; that is a binding condition of the adoption. Dru described Tammy's relationship with Ray as strange. According to Eric, "They kind of get along, but I don't think they like one another." I suggested that the parents and Tammy consider a return to therapy to deal with the problem and to begin to mend the rift in their relationship. They expressed a willingness to do so but did not believe that Tammy would be open to it, especially because her husband does not know about her teenage pregnancy.

Follow-Up

Following termination of the family, I often saw Ray on campus but we only exchanged pleasantries. I twice saw Dru and Eric informally. On both occasions they reported that Ray was out of the house, still at the university, and their lives were peaceful. They lamented the continuing strained relationship with Tammy. Approximately five years later while in an airport, a young man holding a baby approached me; it was Ray. He introduced me to his wife (not Amy) and his daughter. He informed me that his parents had moved to Houston, Texas, and he was working in California and enjoying life. When he introduced his daughter, he said, "As you can see, I've changed."

Commentary

Sticks and Stones and Names Can Hurt You

Fred P. Piercy

Commentator Background

Fifty-four years old, male, Caucasian, PhD, twenty-seven years MFT experience.

Practice Setting

Currently: Head, Department of Human Development. Previously: Director, Marriage and Family Therapy Program, Purdue University; limited private practice.

Theoretical Perspective

I used an integrative theoretical approach to comment on this case.

I remember a fellow in college called Uno because he had only one testicle. I also had friends nicknamed Whale, Ox, and Buffy (short for Buffoon). Such names are funny in the abstract, but not if one must live with the ridicule behind them. I also remember Danny Fink. He hated his name so much that he legally changed it to Danny Dynamic. Our names *can* define us, and when our essence becomes reified in a name* it becomes more difficult to restory our lives. The present case is about the power of a name to suck a person's self-confidence, and a therapist's effort to help the person move beyond the limits of that name. Whoever said that "sticks and stones can break your bones but names can never hurt you" was flat wrong.

---

*A woman I once dated told me that "Fred" (my name) seemed more like a dog's name. Although I laughed at the time, I've kept track since then and can say definitively that I've met (slightly) more humans than dogs named Fred. (On the old TV show, *Barretta,* the star owned a parrot named Fred. I notice such things.)

SOME GOOD POINTS ABOUT THE CASE

It is clear that Baptiste is a fine therapist. He provides a trustworthy I-don't-take-sides stance with which even skeptical Dru feels comfortable. Baptiste does a good job of joining with family members and in redefining the parents' concerns about Ray as a *family* problem and not simply Ray's problem. This sets the stage for family therapy, which provides a larger context from which to understand Ray, and a sphere of influence to help him.

Baptiste believes that the breakthrough in therapy occurred when Tammy said that she thought Ray was gay. Tammy's statement reminded Ray of his experiences with similar accusations back in high school, as well as the cruel "jokes" played upon him because of his teammates' speculations about the size of his penis. This traumatic experience lead to Ray's subsequent withdrawal from school and his anxieties about dating and sex.

QUESTIONS AND SPECULATIONS ABOUT CHANGE

Most of my questions about this case revolve around Ray's subsequent improvement. Did Ray's insight about the link between his high school experience and his current anxiety bring about the change? I doubt that Baptiste, a strategic therapist, would say that insight alone made the difference. But what did lead to Ray's improvement? Perhaps it is good that Baptiste does not tell us since it provides an opportunity to speculate about what therapists from various theoretical orientations might do to help Ray.

Some strategic therapists might prescribe the symptom to break Ray out of his cycle of fear and withdrawal. For example, such therapists might instruct Ray to advertise his anxiety on dates. Other strategic therapists might attempt to reframe the problem. "Actually, there are some advantages to having a small penis, Ray," the therapist might say. "Women like to reassure men about such things. It sounds like a great come-on line." Yet another strategic therapist might even recommend that Ray conduct a series of interviews with women to discover what women actually believe about penis size. Such a task would serve to desensitize Ray to penis size and at the same time help him initiate more contact with women.

A cognitive therapist might ask for a "camera check" of what Ray is telling himself—"If 100 people were to see your penis, would all of them think it is small?"—and help him to identify his negative internal dialogue about penis size that keeps him fearful and frozen. The therapist would then work with Ray to develop alternative "self-talk" that would challenge his current negative self-statements. A cognitive therapist would also help Ray to examine his assumptions about having a small penis. "OK, if ninety percent of people who see your penis do agree that it is small, does that mean that the situation is terrible or that this would make you unattractive to women? After all, Howard Stern is always talking about his small penis, and claims women find him attractive."

Baptiste supported Ray in sharing his shame and hurt with family members. What resulted from that sharing is not unlike what occurs in emotionally focused couples therapy (Greenberg and Johnson, 1988) when a spouse elicits a supportive response from his or her partner by sharing a vulnerable feeling. When people show their vulnerability, others typically soften their anger toward them. Ray's show of vulnerability resulted in family members reaching out and supporting him. They also saw his current problems in a different light, one that actually cast him as a victim of cruel classmates and not as a lazy, aimless, or incompetent person unwilling to live on his own. When Ray shared his shame, he allowed his family members to see him as a potentially capable person who was hurt by cruel peers and an insensitive coach.

This case also appears to be a good fit for a narrative therapist, since Ray must ultimately write and live a more growth-enhancing story than the one defined by his former classmates. A first step would be for the narrative therapist to externalize the taunting and work with Ray on ways to overcome it. How has taunting or the name "Chipmunk" negatively affected Ray? More important, the therapist and Ray could explore times when Ray was not beaten by the taunting, times when he was more competent, more comfortable with women.

It also would be important to bring Amy into therapy, since her support of Ray would go a long way to reassure him. Could she say that penis size was not that important to her? Probably. Most women are more interested in a caring, giving, sensitive attitude than in the size of their partners' penises.

WHAT I MIGHT HAVE DONE DIFFERENTLY

If I were to have worked with Ray, I probably would have drawn from all the theoretical perspectives I mentioned above. I also would have felt it important to introduce facts into therapy. For example, at some point in therapy, I probably would have shared with Ray that while flaccid penises may differ in size somewhat, the differences are less when the penis is erect. It also is true that other men's penises look larger than ones own because of the angle of observation. (One typically sees other penises from the side while seeing one's own from above) (Annon, 1976).

And sometimes even the most commonsense advice helps. In *Jimmy the Bartender's Guide to Life* Kennedy and Boyles (1999) write that "there are two things men worry about: how much they make and how big they are. . . . Money won't make you a man. Neither will size" (p. 93). Jimmy the Bartender's advice is to "make love only to women you love and women who love you. Then you won't have to worry" (p. 93).

One unaddressed issue that I would have explored is what appears to be the rather hypersexual characteristics of this family. For example, since Eric and Dru like to swap sexual partners, I wonder what messages about sex they have given to their children. Also, Tammy revealed that Ray is "always looking at or playing with his penis." According to Tammy, Ray also tried to look at Frank's penis and asked a lot of questions about the size of Frank's penis. Ray even asked Baptiste if he ever thinks about the size of his penis. I wonder what messages about sex are present in this family and how they are affecting Ray.

CONCLUDING THOUGHTS

All of the critical events that Baptiste identifies could have occurred outside of therapy. For example, Amy shared her frustration with Ray outside of therapy. It is conceivable that Tammy could have reflected on whether Ray was gay outside of therapy. But without therapy, would these events have lead to Ray's remembering his high school teasing and brought about positive change on Ray's part? I doubt it. I believe that Ray's change was more likely with therapy as a catalyst. That is, therapy was the safe environment Ray needed to explore his trauma, his goals, and his sense of self. Luckily, Ray and his family found a sensitive, caring, competent therapist with whom to work.

AUTHOR'S POSTSCRIPT

In his commentary, Piercy speculates about what specifically I had done to help Ray with his problem. I did several things. I used a modified Gestalt two-chair technique and asked him to talk with his penis. The purpose was to make him aware that as he grew and became bigger (and taller) so too did his penis. Although there may have been some truth to his teammates' statements that at age fourteen his penis was small, at age twenty-seven, his penis, like his body, was no longer small. This was accomplished in six sessions.

Initially Ray experienced difficulty in moving beyond the pain of the traumatic event. He discovered that he had become attached to his status as a victim and was invested in playing out that role. It was not until I asked him to invite Amy to come in with him to provide her perception of the adequacy of his penis size (she had seen his penis but never commented pro or con about its size) that he showed a willingness to accept that his twenty-seven-year-old penis no longer was the small penis his teammates had seen at age fourteen. He was horrified just thinking about the prospect of Amy commenting about his penis.

Interestingly, after he made the connection between his physical size at age twenty-seven and the size of his penis at this age he was able to laugh at himself for believing that at twenty-seven his penis was still that of a fourteen-year-old.

REFERENCES

Annon, J. (1976). *The behavioral treatment of sexual problems: Brief therapy*. New York: Harper and Row.

Greenberg, L. and Johnson, S. (1988). *Emotionally focused therapy for couples.* New York: The Guilford Press.

Kennedy, J. and Boyles, D. (1999). *Jimmy the bartender's guide to life*. Emmaus, PA: Rodale Press.

Commentary

Somatizing Sexual Secrets

Susan H. McDaniel

Commentator Background

Fifty years old, female, Southern white Anglo-Saxon Protestant. Twenty-six years of practice as a family psychologist.

Practice Setting

University Departments of Psychiatry and Family Medicine; limited private practice.

Theoretical Perspective

Medical family therapy and transitional family therapy (blending a biopsychosocial approach with problem-solving and transgenerational eco-systemic psychotherapy).

"A Young Man and a Penis Called Chipmunk" is a fascinating story of identity confusion, family secrets, and a relatively short-term course of successful family therapy after years of unsuccessful individual and family treatments. Why was this therapy successful when others were not? That is a difficult question to answer definitively with a depressed, somatizing young man experiencing difficulty leaving home, but I would submit that much of the success is related to the stance of the therapist. Baptiste suspended judgment about all material disclosed during individual and family sessions: he accepted the family's secrets and the descriptions of what they thought was the problem. He did not move in with interpretations—minefields that had blown up in earlier therapies. He did not give into any temptation to blame the problem on an overprotective mother or on Ray's separation anxiety. Baptiste's accepting stance allowed the family to trust him. As a result, he was able to continue to gather information and to follow his sense that there was more to this situation than a typical leaving-home case. How right he was!

In this commentary, I will discuss the issues that I found compelling in this fascinating case: the technical decisions made by Baptiste, Ray's somatizing behaviors, and the secrets held by the family—their relevance to Ray's identity confusion and the issues that may face him in the future.

TECHNICAL ISSUES

I admire the clinical skills Baptiste brought to this case; the outcome is a testimony to his effectiveness. Much of what he did I hope I would have done in his place. In this section, I will describe what I believe were the technical elements that contributed to Baptiste's success. For the sake of discussion, I also will consider alternative ways in which my clinical approach might have differed from his, recognizing that my approach may not have been as successful or as appropriate if I actually were the therapist of record with this family.

Some of Baptiste's technical decisions were unusual, especially for family therapy in 1985, when he worked with this family. He readily combined individual, couple, and family sessions, and structured treatment based on client request. For example, he began with the mother, Dru, and saw her individually for the first session. In my clinical practice, I typically ask clients to identify the kind of problem(s) for which they want to see me. Accordingly, I believe that I would have asked to see both Dru and Eric in the first session once Dru had defined the problem as one involving parenting. However, I readily accept that more than one way exists to skin a cat (or a chipmunk), and Baptiste clearly used this session to accept Dru and her distress and then move to define the problem as a family, rather than individual, problem. In Baptiste's case report, Eric remained somewhat of a shadow figure; his distress was presented as much milder than Dru's and his perspective not as clear. I wonder: had he come in with Dru for the initial session, would that have been true? In a case in which a young man is experiencing difficulty moving out (of the parental home), a mother is the spokesperson for the family and accused of being overprotective, and the young man is having sexual identity concerns, the father's role in the family certainly is of interest. Later, Dru again was seen individually to tell the therapist of the couple's swinging pasttime and how it would increase in frequency if Ray were to leave home. Again, I wonder what Eric would have said about this disclosure. Dru insisted that both she and Eric were equally committed to this alternative lifestyle, but as a therapist I would have liked to hear Eric's point of view directly—a sense of why this choice was made by each of them and how it related to their relationship and their individual sense of themselves.

However, in spite of my curiosity about the dynamics underneath Dru's requests for individual sessions, it is clear that those sessions served as a foundation for a trusting psychotherapy that worked. Because Dru had been blamed by previous psychotherapists, it is likely that she needed to scope out this new therapist. Baptiste passed the test when he gave the public talk Dru attended. His straight talk in the first session proved to be an appropriate match for this attorney accustomed to confrontation. It also is possible that, in a family full of secrets, Dru sensed that Baptiste would be both sensitive and direct with her and the other family members when necessary. After so many failures, it must have been difficult for Dru to try psychotherapy again; it is a testimony to therapist-family fit and to Baptiste's joining skills that this time around the family, especially Ray, was successful.

Because of all the previous treatment failures, another important aspect of the early therapy was Baptiste's insistence that there was something more to Ray's difficulty leaving home; he was consistent in his belief that "this was not just a simple leaving-home case." His decision to explore the negative (and positive) aspects of Ray moving out was another technique that showed respect for the fact that if it were easy (for Ray to move out), it already would have occurred, given well-intentioned people and multiple psychotherapies. It was this technique that produced Dru's request for another individual session and her disclosure of the couple's swinging. Although Baptiste told Dru he did not feel that the couple's swinging was related to Ray's problems, it is interesting to consider what underlying dynamics might result in a son remaining frozen developmentally after episodes of sexual harassment by his peers, a daughter having a teenage pregnancy that was denied, and a couple who chose multiple sexual partners as a favorite, secret pasttime. Clearly, secrets and sexuality were part of this family's internal fabric.

In addition to the individual sessions with Dru, Baptiste's use of individual sessions with Ray to follow up on material generated in the sessions with Amy and with Tammy clearly contributed to the unfolding of this case. Such change of format (Gottlieb, 1995) is now more typical in family therapy but needs to be used thoughtfully and with a willingness by the therapist to deal with the secrets and boundary problems that frequently are a part of the patients we see.

WHAT I MIGHT HAVE DONE DIFFERENTLY

Because I am a medical family therapist (McDaniel, Hepworth, and Doherty, 1992, 1997), I likely would have spent time trying to understand more about Ray's illnesses. It is clear that Baptiste did get enough information to view these illnesses primarily as somatization or the somatic expression of emotional conflicts (McDaniel, 1995). I would have been interested in more specifics: What exactly were Ray's symptoms? What diagnoses were considered? How did the family respond to these diagnoses? Was there anyone else in the immediate or extended family who had similar symptoms? Finally, I typically construct a genogram in the first or second family session. In fact, I constructed one for myself as I was reading this case (see Figure 10.1). By the end of the therapy, the genogram had changed (see Figure 10.2). I wonder what would have been the effect on this family with secrets—Ray was the biological child of Tammy and her boyfriend, not of Eric and Dru—if a genogram had been constructed during a session? In addition, as soon as I drew a genogram, I saw that Dru was sixteen when Eric Jr. was born. Thus, Tammy repeated almost exactly her mother's pattern of having a child as a teenager; perhaps even getting pregnant at about the same age as Ray was when he was harassed by his peers. Trouble with sexuality during the high school years was a transgenerational pattern for this family—a pattern easier to see with the visual help of the genogram. Reworking the genogram in later couples sessions with Eric and Dru, when they revealed the secret of Ray's birth, would be another way of making the truth more acceptable, of helping them to view their family accurately, and of helping Ray with his identity confusion.

Somatizing Behaviors

Somatization is a process whereby a person expresses all feelings, whether physical or emotional, as somatic complaints. Sometimes it is an amplification of an organic disease process. Sometimes no organic problem can be found. Regardless, the symbolism or meaning given to whatever symptoms take place can be illuminating.

Typically, somatizing runs in families that are unable to express feelings directly (Griffith and Griffith, 1994; McDaniel, 1995, 1997). It is interesting to consider how Ray's family expressed difficult feelings and whether he had the space and support to, for example, tell a parent or a sibling about the harassment he experienced at the hands of his peers. Instead, his trauma went underground and he quickly developed physical symptoms about his physical concerns (i.e., the size) about his penis. Patients with physical complaints can be very difficult to treat in psychotherapy. If they could verbalize their emotions, they would not have somatization disorder! It is not surprising that Ray did not do well for many years in traditional psychotherapy. With regard to Ray's leaving-home problem, Baptiste told Dru and Eric that the flesh was willing but the spirit was not ready. Actually, with somatizing behavior, the flesh is not willing either. The body colludes with the spirit to protest some unresolved issue—in this case, Ray's history of sexual harassment. The connection between sexual trauma and somatization is well described (Katon, 1985) and always needs to be considered when somatizing behavior is prominent.

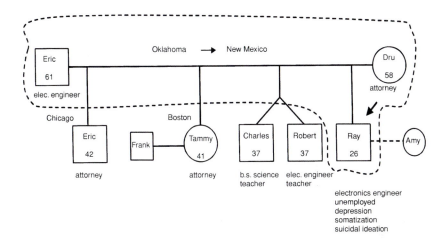

FIGURE 10.1. Olsen Family As Presented in Session 1

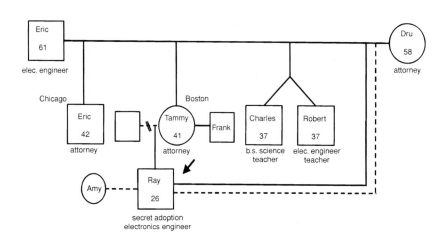

FIGURE 10.2. Olsen Family As Understood in Session 20

Family Secrets and Identity Confusion

Many secrets existed in the Olsen family: Ray's history of harassment and humiliation about the size of his penis, his parents' swinging pasttime, the real story of Ray's birth by his "sister," the identity of his biological father, and his adoption by his grandparents. All of these issues seem likely to have played a role in his identity confusion. But, until the story of the trauma of his high school years unfolded, he was frozen in time, unable to attend school, to deepen a relationship with a young woman for whom he cared, and to come to grips with his own behavior which he and others assumed to represent some hidden individual psychopathology. Unpacking this trauma, as Baptiste skillfully did, enabled Ray to reclaim his penis, his sexuality, and his life. Doing so also allowed him and his parents to depathologize his behaviors and to understand them as a reasonable response to a humiliating situation. As a result, his need to somatize lessened considerably. The question is whether he learned an emotional language to cope with his next emotional trauma.

What about the effect of the other secrets? It is not clear what the effects of Dru and Eric's commitment to swinging are. I, however, believe that the more relevant question is what kind of models they have provided for Ray in terms of his own sexual identity, his confidence as a man, and his ability to be successful and satisfied in life. What was the effect of Eric being his biological grandfather and his functional father? What about the tension between Tammy and Dru, and Tammy and Ray, that so clearly was related to her biological role (or absence of it) as Ray's mother? How might these issues emerge as Ray interacts with his own children? Has the therapy with Baptiste been substantial enough both to unlock the developmental process and to skirt these issues successfully, or will the issues become problems for Ray later in life?

Baptiste does not tell us much about the final five couple sessions with Eric and Dru. Ideally, I would have liked to know more about the quality of their marriage and how they came to decide to use the law to bind Tammy from revealing her true relationship with Ray. I'd also like to see at least a three- or four-generation genogram to learn more about this family's history of family secrets, male-female relationships, as well as sexuality. Although it is difficult to speculate about what we might find, such information always provides rich material for understanding and intervening in complex, stuck situations as was the case with this family.

CONCLUDING THOUGHTS

It is clear to me that Baptiste formed a highly successful and trusting relationship with Ray. Consequently, I hope that if a transition triggers another symptom, or if he or his family confronts another difficulty, Ray will not hesitate this time to seek psychotherapeutic assistance. I also hope that whichever therapist he sees contacts Baptiste. Doing so will save him or her a significant amount of work.

REFERENCES

Gottlieb, M. (1995). Ethical dilemmas in change of format and live supervision. In R. Mikesell, D. D. Lusterman, and S. H. McDaniel (Eds.), *Integrating family therapy: Handbook of family psychology and systems theory* (pp. 561-570). Washington DC: American Psychological Association.

Griffith, J. and Griffith, M. (1994). *The body speaks.* New York: Basic Books.

Katon, W. (1985) Somatization in primary care. *Journal of Family Practice,* 21(4):257-258.

McDaniel, S. H. (1995). Medical family therapy with somatizing patients: The co-creation of therapeutic stories. In R. Mikesell, D. D. Lusterman, and S. H. McDaniel (Eds.), *Integrating family therapy: Handbook of family psychology and systems theory* (pp. 377-388). Washington DC: American Psychological Association.

McDaniel, S. H. (1997). Trapped inside a body without a voice. In S. H. McDaniel, J. Hepworth, and W. J. Doherty (Eds.), *The shared experience of illness: Stories of patients, families, and their therapists* (pp. 274-290). New York: Basic Books.

McDaniel, S.H., Hepworth, J., and Doherty, W. J. (1992). *Medical family therapy: A biopsychosocial approach to families with health problems.* New York: Basic Books.

McDaniel, S. H., Hepworth, J., and Doherty, W. J. (1997). *The shared experience of illness: Stories of patients, families, and their therapists.* New York: Basic Books.

CASE 11

I Have No Problem

Andres Nazario Jr.

Therapist Background

Currently: Fifty-four years old, Latino, male, PhD, twenty-nine years MFT experience. When I saw this family: forty-eight years old, twenty-three years MFT experience.

Practice Setting

A combined COAMFTE training program, a private nonprofit clinic, and a private group practice.

Client Characteristics

This family consisted of Shanda Johnson (age thirty-two), a black, female, single parent and her three children: daughter Shakira (age thirteen) and two sons, James and Aquiles, ages nine and five, respectively. Shanda was employed as a food server at a large training institution. The children were students in high school and elementary school, respectively.

Length of Treatment

Ms. Johnson and her three children were seen for a total of eleven sessions over four months; she was seen individually for an initial session, in which the critical incident occurred.

Theoretical Perspective

An oppression-sensitive approach was used in working with this family.

Clients court-ordered to therapy and clients under the supervision of a state authority, such as parole and probation, more than any other clients, tend to elicit from me questions about the meaning of therapy and concerns about becoming an agent of social control. Confronted with such clients, I frequently question how I can work with them and maintain both my human and professional integrity. Do I hear their stories at face value? Do I have a moral responsibility to find a single truth? More important, who is my "true" client? Is it the individual, the couple or family in the office, the referring agency, or society? My work with Shanda Johnson and her children raised all of these questions for me as well as questions about oppression, social justice, and the role/impact of culture, ethnicity, race, class, gender, sexual orientation, socioeconomic status, religion/spirituality, and environment in the therapeutic arena, on the part of the therapist, the referring agency, and the client.

PRESENTING PROBLEM

Shanda Johnson was referred for therapy by her probation officer who contacted the office to inquire about an appointment for her. The probation officer reported that Shanda had contacted three other community mental health agencies but they had declined to work with her. I agreed to meet with Shanda to explore the possibility of working with her; later that day, she called and scheduled an individual appointment. Shanda arrived early for the initial interview; she appeared younger than her stated age. She reported that she had been arrested and charged by the police, tried, convicted, and sentenced to probation and mandatory counseling by a judge, but she was unclear about why she was treated in this manner. Despite her lack of clarity, she asserted her innocence of the offense for which she was mandated to therapy and was equally adamant that she did not have a problem.

THE THERAPEUTIC SITUATION PRIOR
TO THE CRITICAL INCIDENT

During the interview, Shanda was perceptibly anxious, spoke at a rapid rate, clutched her purse in her lap, and sat on the edge of her chair as though ready to bolt at any moment. As we discussed the specifics of her situation and her attempts to obtain counseling, her verbal tone expressed primarily frustration and a sense of injustice hung in the air. Concurrently, her body posture and her demeanor conveyed a sense of defensiveness. She told of feeling betrayed by her court-appointed public defender and of feeling overwhelmed by the situation that brought her to therapy. As a result, she had begun to feel like a victim and was invested in not being victimized further by having to acknowledge that she "had a problem." Shanda appeared not to understand that although she may not have had a mental health problem, the legal justice system perceived her as having a problem; now it *was* her problem whether or not she perceived herself as having a problem.

EVENTS LEADING TO THE CRITICAL INCIDENT

Clearly, Shanda was overwhelmed and angered by the events that brought her to therapy as well as having to be in therapy. At this juncture, in the absence of any negating factors, she had come to believe that the problem resided within her rather than with the legal system that had convicted her for an offense for which she continued to assert her innocence. I listened to Shanda's story with curiosity and respect and accepted her situation at face value and in the manner in which she defined it. In response, she began to look at her situation from a different perspective; for the first time since her arrest, she began to consider that the problem could be external to her. As a result, her tense muscles began to relax and together we attempted to help her make sense of her situation such that she could regain control of her self-worth.

THE CRITICAL INCIDENT

Shanda had been battered by the legal justice system, rejected by the mental health system, yet remained personally convinced of her innocence. Consequently, she neither perceived herself as having a problem nor being in of need therapy.

THERAPIST: So you were referred by your probation officer?

SHANDA: Uh-huh.

THERAPIST: What happened that you are here?

SHANDA: OK. I need to be counsel, but I don't know. The judge said . . .

THERAPIST: You don't know? The judge said you have to be counseled?

SHANDA: Yeah! He said I had to be counsel, but the other places said they don't do it like that. [Her tone sounded frustrated.]

THERAPIST: What do you mean, "they don't do it like that"?

SHANDA: They say you have to have a problem for—to get counsel, and you see, I don't have one. It is just that the judge ordered me to get counsel . . . and let me tell you what happened so you get the picture.

THERAPIST: OK.

SHANDA: OK. Me and my daughter was in a grocery store and there was a purse on the shelf and she picked it up. And so I told her "Let's take it to the front." So before we could get to the front—anyway, this man ran out there and grabbed at us and everything, so she ran in—she ran—she is thirteen, so she ran 'cause she was scared. And he knocked me down and whatever. So the whole thing got turned—it got all mixed up, whatever, saying that the purse was ours, but I just had my own one purse. So in other ways, they tried to make it like I had two purses because they said it was my purse, but it wasn't. So the thing boiled down to—they charged me and said they . . . they called strong robbery. I think it was that I robbed or shoplifted, whatever, and . . .

THERAPIST: That you robbed? Whom? Whom did you rob?

SHANDA: By picking up this pocketbook.

THERAPIST: Aha.

SHANDA: And they wanted to say it was mine so as I was . . .

THERAPIST: So you found a pocketbook . . .

SHANDA: On the shelf . . .

THERAPIST: . . . on the shelf.

SHANDA: . . . at the store.

THERAPIST: OK.

SHANDA: . . . and my daughter went and picked it up and so at the time we were going to get to the front because I was going to get a bag of ice. And she was going to the front to the cashier and I told her, "You can leave it there with the cashier by the front desk," but before we could get that far, off he ran and another man ran facing us and ran and knocked me down and my daughter—she got scared and ran. The whole thing boiled down that they said the pocketbook was mine, but I kept telling him it couldn't be mine because I had mine. It was like a joke. To me, it was like joking, but it was no joking matter for me! So it all boiled down to I went to jail and all of this. And when it was time to go to court, I didn't know exactly how this thing was—would go, so I asked [for a] public defendant. They gave me [one], which was the quickest way to get it over because by me going to work and back and forth I had to get—to get running back and forth, so he had me under the impression—he told me I could say "No contest" or whatever they call those words, so I thought—he got me believing that it did mean I didn't do it. But he didn't let me know that—that the judge would take it his way and just used it to say what he wanted, because he just automatically said guilty. And, see, if I knew that, I would have taken it to a jury, which is what I was first going to do, but I didn't know that's how it was going to go until I went to court that day and decided to say—because I didn't have that purse and it wasn't mine. So the judge ordered then that I get family counseling and put me on probation, and that's how I have the probation lady. And she called around to find out if there was somebody who could give me counseling now—from what I don't know. The rest is for you to decide.

THERAPIST: How is your daughter?

SHANDA: Oh! She is just fine; she is fine.

THERAPIST: She did not get in trouble?

SHANDA: No, that's what I said. They just said it's all me, so the probation officer said that she was carrying out what the judge said, and the judge said I need to get counseling. So she's been calling around to see if there is anyone that can give it to me. . . . And these places I've been to, they say they can't give it to me because they are for people that got problems they have to discuss. You know, they come to them to talk about it and not for trying to get counsel for people like me who do not have a problem. [Her voice expressed a sense of injustice that had not been validated.]

THERAPIST: So you don't think you have a problem?

SHANDA: Uh-uh!

THERAPIST: You got accused of something that you didn't do; you got stuck with the results of that; and you don't see that as a problem?

SHANDA: [For the first time she looks directly at me.] Yeah, that was a problem. Yeah, that was a problem! That is definitely a problem!

THERAPIST: Here is a woman saying that this is something that was put over me. I got stuck with going to court. I was sentenced to probation or whatever, and now they are saying I need to get counseling. That is a problem in itself.

SHANDA: [Sits back, relaxes her shoulders, puts her purse on the floor, softens her tone of voice.] Yeah, you are right. You are right. If you look at it that way, you are right. I have a problem. I couldn't believe it was happening to me. I have a problem!

THE AFTERMATH OF THE CRITICAL INCIDENT

My statement "You got accused of something that you didn't do; you got stuck with the results of that; and you don't see that as a problem?" seemed to have freed and energized Shanda to stand her ground that she was not going to be blamed or made to acknowledge a culpability that she knew was not hers. It also opened space for a new direction in therapy that focused not on her legal problems but on her life situation and some of her struggles as a single parent. She also discussed the death of her parents, both murdered at different times, and her maternal grandmother's suspicion that her father may have murdered her mother. She told of her grandmother, who raised her and whose death coincided with the birth of her first child; she dearly missed her grandmother. She cried as she spoke of her grandmother and disclosed that she felt isolated as a parent.

She described her teen years, during which she was involved in a few shoplifting incidents, but subsequently she distanced herself from any further illegal activities. In support of her claim of "going straight," she pointed to her five years of working as a food server without incident. Shanda speculated that the judge may have based his judgment of current culpability on her adolescent history. She discussed her concerns and hopes for her children and their future. Following this conversation, Shanda committed to continue in family therapy with her children to focus on some of the issues raised in this session. During that period, I worked with the family from an oppression-sensitive perspective (Early, Nazario, and Steier, 1994), which is grounded in a philosophy of inclusion.

The oppression-sensitive approach is a therapeutic modality developed at the Gainesville Family Institute and is appropriate for working with a variety of presenting problems and with diverse populations. It is influenced by the ideas of therapists such as HareMustin (1978); White and Epston (1990); Freedman and Combs (1996); Waldegrave and Tamasese (1994); and Hardy (1992). This approach emphasizes health rather than pathology, recognizes gender as an ever-present variable in psychotherapy, and supports and affirms diversity in sexual orientation as well as ethnic, racial, class, and cultural diversity.

DISCUSSION

The Role of the Critical Incident in Getting Therapy Unstuck

The critical incident in this case occurred in Session 1 and the event that crystallized it was simple rather than monumental. Although therapy was not stuck, Shanda and her perceptions of herself and her situation were stuck. Accordingly, it was not until she reflected on my simple statement of validation—"you got accused of something that you didn't do"—the moment of the critical incident, that she was able to look at her situation differently and to realize or at least consider that the problem could be external to her. Despite the change in Shanda's way of seeing her situation, the critical incident did not lead to therapy becoming unstuck. It did, however, contribute to and open space for Shanda to recognize the existence of a problem and to articulate the fact: "Yes, I have a problem!" Equally as important is the critical incident's contribution to Shanda's recognition that the legal justice system had imposed upon her life and had abused her and her family.

It is quite possible that because therapy was mandated, and Shanda was committed to fulfilling the court's requirement, any approach by a therapist willing to continue to work with her would have resulted in engagement.

However, I believe that each therapist brings to therapy his or her life experiences and these experiences influence the specific issues to which the therapist responds or chooses to illuminate. I recognize the danger of rendering other aspects of the conversation invisible as I illuminate that which connects with my own experiences. This danger is especially evident as we shift the therapeutic conversation from the "presenting problem" to attend to meaning systems, and to the relationship of certain domains of influence in the life of the family and each of its members and the issues they presented for discussion.

The Implications of the Critical Incident for Therapy

The implications of the critical incident for therapy are limited to its contribution in helping Shanda to see the situation differently and to acknowledge implicitly and explicitly that she did have a problem, although it was not of her own making. However, despite its limited effect, the critical incident made it possible for Shanda and me to engage in a conversation that allowed her to feel empowered, rather than abused and defeated as she had at the beginning of the hour. The change in Shanda's way of seeing her situation also contributed to her engaging in other conversations about family issues, the resolution of which strengthened her as a person and a parent as well as strengthened her relationship with her children. The critical incident may not have resolved Shanda's legal problem, but it helped her to identify and define the real problem and who was responsible to do something about the problem defined by the court.

THE OUTCOME OF THERAPY

Following the initiation of family therapy I met with Shanda and her children for ten additional sessions over a period of four months. During these sessions Shanda continued to assert her innocence and I continued to believe her. However, we chose not to focus on the legal issues that brought her to therapy or the impact of her probationary status on the family's life. Rather, therapy focused primarily on issues specific to race, gender, socioeconomic status, and spirituality as these related to Shanda and her children. For example, we explored whether Shanda's skin color impacted the manner in which she was treated at the store, arrested, and charged. Was the legal outcome influenced by her lack of financial resources to hire a personal attorney rather than a public defender? In what ways could the symbolic presence of her departed grandmother assist her in guiding her children in the manner in which she wanted? She expressed much concern about her children's future and was especially worried about raising her sons in a society in which young black males disproportionately are incarcerated or die at an early age due to violent acts.

Our discussions also opened space for the family to explore the multiple realities in which it existed. Both sons expressed a need for more contact with their peers; they were restricted from such activities because of Shanda's fear of the "bad influences" in the community. In addition, James expressed a desire for increased contact with his father, who lived in a nearby community. Responding to these needs, Shanda initiated a proactive approach to protect and assist her children to develop "tactics of survival," and sought community support for herself and her children. Currently, her life was centered around work and family and left very little time, if any, for herself. In this regard, she shared that as an adolescent she often missed age-appropriate activities because she had to care for her siblings after school until her mother arrived home. Clearly, caring for others was central to Shanda's definition of self. This discovery led to discussions about gender socialization and the role of women in black families. As a result, she sought support within an African-American mothers group working to decrease violence in elementary schools.

After ten family sessions, we mutually agreed to terminate because Shanda and her children felt that they no longer needed to continue in therapy; they were satisfied with their situation. Accordingly, with her permission I sent a letter to her probation officer attesting to her successful completion of therapy.

Follow-Up

I did not see Shanda or her children again after we terminated therapy. However, based on my interactions with her, I would expect that she will continue to be a strong woman and a strong mother for her children.

REFERENCES

Early, G., Nazario, A., and Steier, H. (1994). *Oppression sensitive family therapy: A health affirming model*. Washington, DC: American Orthopsychiatric Association.

Freedman, J. and Combs, G. (1996). *Narrative therapy: The social construction of preferred realities*. New York: W. W. Norton and Company.

Hardy, K. V. (1992). *Race, class and culture*. AAMFT 50th Annual Conference. Miami Beach, Florida, October 17.

HareMustin, R. (1978). A feminist approach to family therapy. *Family Process*, 17(2), 181-194.

Waldegrave, C. and Tamasese, K. (1994). Some central ideas in the "just therapy" approach. *The Family Journal: Counseling and Therapy for Couples and Families,* 2(3), 94 -103.

White, M. and Epston, D. (1990). *Narrative means to therapeutic ends.* New York: W. W. Norton and Company.

Commentary

Born a Problem?

Lisa Aronson Fontes

> We are the wrong people of the wrong skin on the multi cultural wrong
> continent and what in the hell is everybody being reasonable about?
>
> June Jordan, "Poem about my rights" (1989)

Commentator Background

Forty years old, bicultural, female, PhD, fifteen years practice and teaching.

Practice Setting

Currently teaching at a college; not practicing marriage and family therapy.

Theoretical Perspectives

My theoretical orientations are feminist and multicultural. I incorporated systemic perspectives in my comments on this case.

Shanda Johnson's luck had been bad. As a low-income African-American woman, Ms. Johnson was born "a problem" in a society that consistently fails to provide low-income people of her race and gender with adequate housing, protection from assault, health care, or a living wage. At age thirty-two, Ms. Johnson's history reflects more injustices than one person should have to endure in a lifetime: both her parents were murdered while she still was a child; she lost her mother figure, her grandmother, when she was only nineteen years old and pregnant. At the time of the therapy, she was a single parent raising three children without much support from their fathers or members of her extended family. As a teenager, she had been caught engaging in the rather common adolescent act of shoplifting, and fifteen years later was still stuck with this criminal record. As an impoverished single mother trying to hold down a job, she accepted a court-appointed lawyer and followed his advice without fully understanding the implications. In addition, she was rejected as a client by three community mental health agencies from whom she had sought services. Given this state of affairs, who could blame her, then, for entering the therapy room frustrated, confused, defeated, and determined to convince the therapist that she was innocent—that she was *not* a problem?

THE PROBLEM SHIFTS

Ms. Johnson was entitled to a little good luck, indeed, when Nazario welcomed her into his office. Nazario used a simple reframe in the first session to externalize Ms. Johnson's problem. He asserted that the problem was not in her head but rather in a system that had treated her unjustly. This premise enabled Ms. Johnson to relax her guard and to engage in action-oriented family therapy that helped her to learn to take control of those areas in which she *could* exert control—principally in her relationships with her children and her community.

Nazario's intervention is elegant in its simplicity; he points out some of the effects of his reframe. But I would like to highlight some of the effects of the reframe that Nazario did not address. Specifically, by accepting Ms. Johnson's story at face value and externalizing the problem, Nazario interrupted his implicit alliance with the system of control (i.e., police and probation) and realigned himself with the client and her family. Another realignment occurred over the course of therapy when Ms. Johnson chose to join a group of African-American mothers working to decrease violence in the elementary school. In doing so, she transformed herself from a criminal suspect to an agent for the reduction of criminal behavior. Presumably this would make her an ally of the police and vice versa—a striking shift.

Gender Problems

Nazario does not refer to the potential gender issues raised in this case. Specifically, all the men described by Ms. Johnson—the store detectives, judge, probation officer, court-appointed attorney, and even her father— were in roles in which they were supposed to have protected her. In fact, each one of these men not only failed to protect Ms. Johnson, they actively harmed her. Consequently, Ms. Johnson's contact with Nazario, a dedicated, concerned male professional, may have offered an important counterbalance to her disappointing history with male caretakers.

The Police Problem

It is difficult to comment on ten sessions of therapy so briefly described. However, the case report and Ms. Johnson's own story suggest that concerns about the police merit specific attention. For example, Ms. Johnson reported that her thirteen-year-old daughter fled when the police confronted her. Her behavior in that situation indicates that she may not have learned the best tactics needed to survive encounters with the police (Herbert, 2000). I hope Nazario worked with Ms. Johnson and her children to help them to develop survival strategies to minimize the likelihood of further disagreeable or dangerous encounters with the police. Perhaps this is one of the "tactics of survival" to which Nazario refers but does not elaborate.

Adjusting Alignments

Nazario begins his case report by expressing his uncertainty about who is his true client. Interestingly, however, the case description makes clear that from the inception Nazario decided that Ms. Johnson was his true client. He believed her story throughout the course of their work together and aligned with her powerfully. Through this alignment, he helped Ms. Johnson to write a new story about herself, a story in which she is not just rushing through life at a whirlwind pace but is a legitimate citizen who has been wronged. With Nazario's help, Ms. Johnson again shifts from being a passive victim to an active protector of her children and all children at school. Nazario also helped Ms. Johnson to establish a web of support for herself and her family.

Nazario insists that he believes in Ms. Johnson's innocence on the shoplifting charge. I cannot help wondering what would have been different for him if he had not been so certain. Would he have aligned with her less strongly? Confronted her more? Accepted more readily the role of agent of social control?

WHAT I MIGHT HAVE DONE DIFFERENTLY

Nazario's posttermination follow-up comments—no contact after termination—are somewhat disappointing, although not surprising given the current deplorable state of mental health in the United States; generally, clinicians are not reimbursed for phone contacts and are encouraged to close cases as soon as they can. If I were the family's therapist of record, I would have encouraged Ms. Johnson to check in periodically over a period of months after the therapy's formal termination. This contact might have helped Ms. Johnson conjure up the symbolic presence of the therapist, just as Nazario had suggested she conjure up the symbolic presence of her departed grandmother.

Is this kind of therapy enough? As an individual, would Ms. Johnson have benefitted also from a more intrapsychic approach that would have allowed her to confront her grief about her many losses and make a long-term plan for increased economic independence, among other possibilities? I have no doubt that she would have. But given the circumstances, the simple shift from a defensive problem denial to "there is a problem and it's not me" is a great start. In addition, Ms. Johnson and her children learned an important lesson: people who are charged with helping *can* sometimes be helpful. This bodes well for all the family members' future encounters with professional helpers.

CONCLUDING THOUGHTS

As June Jordan (1989) asserts in her poem quoted at the beginning of this commentary, any "reasonable" response to the oppression of African Americans in the United States is unreasonable. As therapists, we might easily be accused of colluding with the oppressors if our interventions are geared toward helping African-American clients to adjust to an unjust world. Nazario escapes this bind by helping Ms. Johnson to recognize her oppression, join with others, and develop effective tactics to survive. No problem.

REFERENCES

Herbert, B. (2000). A delicate balance. Editorial. *The New York Times.* March 9.
Jordan, J. (1989). *Naming our destiny: New and selected poems.* New York: Thunder's Mouth Press.

Commentary

The Problem Is a Problem

Kenneth V. Hardy

Commentator Background

Fifty years old, African-American, male, PhD, twenty-one years MFT practice.

Practice Setting

University MFT clinic; limited private practice.

Theoretical Perspective

My preferred theoretical perspective is integrative systemic. I used a multicultural perspective to examine this case.

Historically, the psychotherapy literature has been replete with unsubstantiated claims that racial and cultural "minorities do not believe in psychotherapy." Several advocates of such claims have been quick to point to the "documented facts" undergirding psychotherapy with such minorities. The "facts" that purportedly demonstrate minorities' reticence about entering psychotherapy or failure to remain actively engaged subsequent to beginning psychotherapy, often are cited as proof that they are recalcitrant and generally do not believe in psychotherapy.

GOOD POINTS ABOUT THE CASE

In this poignant account of therapy with Shanda Johnson, a single-parent, African-American woman and her children, Nazario skillfully and insightfully illustrates how this disbelieving woman began to believe in therapy once she was treated in a respectful, culturally honoring way. Clearly, Shanda, like many other members of oppressed groups, would neither invest herself nor believe in a process that prior to Nazario's work had failed to demonstrate that it believed in her. In an effectively powerful and subtle way, Nazario's refusal to engage Shanda in an ongoing game of "Tell the Truth," and/or "Truth or Consequences" was liberating for her. Throughout their time together, Nazario never once communicated to Shanda that he did not believe her or respect her as a human being.

Nazario's approach to therapy is grounded in a model predicated upon the notion that when people are oppressed their sense of dignity and self-worth are assaulted and damaged. Thus, as Nazario respectfully listened to Shanda and gathered "the facts," he also intervenes with laser-like accuracy. His interventions are simple and subtle, but potent. From the outset, he treats Shanda and responds to her in ways that enabled him to methodically restore and validate those pieces of her dignity that had been chiseled down by her daily encounters with the legal and mental health systems and, ultimately, society at large.

The Client versus the System: Whose Advocate Am I?

Given Nazario's therapeutic approach to Shanda and her problem, it is evident that he refuses to view her merely as a person mandated to therapy, i.e., as an emotionless, undignified other who is unwilling to take responsibility for her actions. Instead, his behavior is unusual, perhaps even radical, for the modern-day psychotherapist: he dares to see Shanda as a single-parent, African-American woman with meager economical resources. In Nazario's world view, these contextual variables have meaning, not just for Shanda's life, but for the lives of those persons who interact with her as well. It is this belief that ultimately gives birth to the critical incident—a pivotal moment in therapy. By daring to see Shanda in a more complex way, Nazario encourages her to do likewise. In so doing, Shanda is better able to appreciate that a problem exists, and the problem is infinitely more complex than the allegation that she stole a pocketbook. Through affirmation, acknowledgment, and validation Nazario invites Shanda to consider how some of her difficulties might have been attributable to ways in which her circumstances in the store were peppered with, if not discolored by, the finely interwoven threads of class, race, and gender.

A Simple and Parsimonious Approach

It would be very easy to comment on Nazario's approach with this family and to conclude that he did very little or that what he actually did counted for very little. Making the complex appear easy is the genius of Nazario's work and ultimately the essence of his oppression-sensitive approach to therapy. Using this approach, Nazario does not offer the family any long-winded, insight-laden, eloquently phrased, jargon-rich reflections, questions, or interpretations. As a result, at one level the session seems fairly naked. No sophisticated techniques or decentering strategies are employed. Instead, present only is Nazario's humanness and his authentic respect for a woman who has endured much and whose life force probably has been drowning in an incessant pool of disrespect since her youth. It is as though Nazario intuitively understands the most salient rule for working with members of marginalized populations: respect is everything and that being is doing! To that end, Nazario does not interrupt, challenge, or lecture Shanda; rather, he is able just to be. His doing so allows Shanda to do the same. A most compelling illustration of this experience occurred during the segment of the session in which Shanda provided a detailed and evocative account of her difficulties beginning with the day that she was arrested in the grocery store and concluding at the point at which therapy was mandated.

Reading Nazario's reiteration of Shanda's iteration of the "facts," many details begged closer scrutiny. I read with great anticipation, wondering how Nazario would gently shift from his stance of unequivocal respect to one that was slightly but diplomatically more challengingly inquisitive. To my surprise, he did not. His response was simple, empathic, and, above all, affirming. No classic and stereotypical queries were asked, such as . . . "Well, how come? . . . Well, help me understand why. . . . Do you *really* believe . . . ," etc. His simple and affirming response is "How is your daughter?" It is through these simple measures that Nazario rebuilt Shanda's trust and restored her dignity; these therapeutic goals are imperative when working with marginalized people.

QUESTIONS FOR NAZARIO

In general, I have a very high regard for Nazario's clinical work, but I have several questions/concerns subsequent to reading the case report. A majority of these concerns result from my curiosity about the specifics of Nazario's work. In this regard, I frequently asked myself, "How did he do this or what did he do?" Without an elaboration, Nazario's work appears to be so simple—at times, too simple! Over the years, I have worked with many clients similar to Shanda and, based on those experiences, it often is very difficult to establish trust or to successfully impact such clients' extant worldview. I do not doubt that Nazario was successful in reaching and connecting with Shanda. My guess is that the little things he did to facilitate a meaningful relationship and ultimately promote change may have been omitted from the case report for a good reason; space limitations, for example. Omission of a detailed description of some of the inside-the-session maneuvers that helped to create a respectful therapeutic milieu conducive to change constituted a major shortcoming of the case report. For example, in Nazario's description of the events leading to the critical incident, he notes, "I listened to Shanda's story with curiosity and respect, accepted her situation at face value and in the manner in which she defined it. In response she began to look at her situation from a different perspective and, for the first time since her arrest, she began to consider that the problem could be external to her." Although I believe it is often difficult for highly skilled and seasoned therapists to remain attuned to every minor subtlety they might execute that leads to a dramatic shift in a therapy session, it would have been helpful for Nazario to have given more critical thought to this aspect of his work. For instance, what else did he do or say, or did not do or say, that was instrumental in communicating to Shanda in such a convincing and unambiguous way that of the many "experts" she had encountered, he was one whom she could trust? Dramatic shifts occurred during several other points of therapy, but Nazario provided scant details and/or insight with regards to what facilitated those changes. It would have been most helpful to have known his process and the questions he asked. I wanted to know about the specifics of Nazario's approach not only because of my admiration for his approach to therapy but also because I believe a discussion of the "minor details" would potentially be instructive to other therapists working with a similar clinical population.

WHAT I MIGHT HAVE DONE DIFFERENTLY

After reviewing Nazario's stellar clinical work with this family, I have come to realize that considerable similarity exists in our approach to therapy with families. Much like Nazario, my clinical practice is also greatly influenced by the ideas that he calls oppression sensitive, and both he and I fervently believe in examining the critical interface between microlevel and macrolevel systemic issues. It is this core belief that encouraged Nazario, as it does me, to gently and respectfully broaden the context of Shanda's presenting problem to consider macrosystemic issues.

Despite the similarity of our clinical approach, however, I might have done some things therapeutically differently with this family. First, I would have discussed issues about race, class, and gender more overtly with Shanda. Although the integration of these dimensions of diversity was omnipresent in Nazario's clinical work with the family, I probably would have spent more time discussing these issues in a more overt and detailed manner with Shanda in particular. I believe that race, class, and gender, as well as a host of other dimensions of diversity, almost always are intricately interwoven into the fabric of our everyday experiences. Accordingly, I would have spent more time talking with Shanda about the impact, if any, that she perceived issues of race to have had on her life circumstances. I also would have explored the impact of gender and class. I would have initiated these "difficult therapeutic dialogues" with a discussion of race in the hopes that our shared racial background as African Americans would have provided a possible point of connection and safety. Obviously, no way exists of knowing with any certainty what meaning my identity as an African American would have held for Shanda. However, whether such discussions were facilitative or an impediment, it would have been an important dynamic for me to pursue clinically, because I believe that virtually all human interactions are shaped by the nuances of race, class, and gender. I believe this to be true even when "there is no problem."

CONCLUDING THOUGHTS

Clients mandated to therapy are among the most challenging clients that any therapist will encounter. Based on my clinical experiences with mandated clients, the complexity of such therapeutic encounters is heightened when the clients are members of socially devalued groups. In Shanda's case, she has a triple whammy: membership in three marginalized groups—African American, female, and poor. Since its inception, psychotherapy as it typically is conceived and practiced has been principally an upper- and middle-class endeavor and rarely has been designed with the oppressed/under-class in mind. Accordingly, therapists such as Nazario, who have spent a career working with oppressed populations, need to envision themselves as pioneers. However, it is important that such therapists remain mindful of the potential gaps which exist between that which is considered standard clinical practice and that which often is needed therapeutically by those who have been relegated to the margins of society. Thus, it is imperative for Nazario to expose other therapists to the many "little" (clinical) strategies/maneuvers that make a huge difference in the lives of oppressed people in therapy. Clearly he has a gift that if generously shared could affect the work of other therapists who strive to reach that hard-to-engage, mandated, oppressed client who "has no problem" but who often is perceived as "society's problem."

CASE 12

I'm Not Ready to Die!

Kenneth E. Newell
Gregory Brock

Therapist Backgrounds

Currently: Thirty-three years old, white, male, second-year MFT doctoral student, five-and-one-half years MFT experience. Then: twenty-nine years old, second-year MFT master's student, one year MFT experience.

Practice Setting

Currently: University mental health clinic. Then: Initially met in the guidance counselor's office at the child's school. Thereafter, university family therapy clinic. Clinical supervision (by Brock) was provided for this case.

Client Characteristics

The clients were a lower middle-class African-American mother, Ladare (age thirty-three), and her daughter, Michelle (age eleven), referred by the daughter's guidance counselor at the mother's request. The mother felt that her daughter was harming herself by withholding her feelings about the mother's illness. She believed that talking to a counselor would benefit her daughter. Because the guidance counselor felt ill prepared to provide therapy, she referred the family. Ladare was very active in school, church, and community affairs, had been divorced for approximately six months prior to entering therapy, and currently was unemployed. She was diagnosed with myasthenia gravis, a terminal illness. Michelle was an only child, an honor student in middle school, lived with her mother, and was the identified patient. Ladare had twelve brothers and sisters, all of whom lived within a seventy-mile radius of one another. None of the siblings attended any of the therapy sessions, but they played important adjunctive roles in the mother-daughter therapy.

Length of Treatment

The mother and daughter were seen for sixteen sessions over a seven-month period. The critical incident occurred in Session 9.

Theoretical Perspective

A psychoeducational approach informed by a structural theoretical perspective was used in working with this family. The goal was to maximize Ladare's emotional functioning and coping abilities in dealing with her illness and to improve Michelle's ability to cope with her mother's illness.

PRESENTING PROBLEM

Initially, I met with Ladare and Michelle in the guidance counselor's office at Michelle's school. However, because that office did not provide the required privacy, all other sessions were held at the university's family center. During our first meeting, Ladare appeared nervous and physically uncomfortable. In response to my probing about the source of her discomfort she disclosed that she was afflicted with a terminal illness. Ladare emphasized that *she* had accepted and dealt with her illness and that her immediate concern was not with herself or her illness but with her *daughter's* reaction to the illness. Ladare believed that because Michelle had never talked openly about the illness she was experiencing difficulty accepting the illness and was withholding her feelings. Not knowing the specific illness with which she was afflicted, I asked Ladare to identify her illness. After a long pause, she hesitatingly said, "Myasthenia gravis."

Ladare shared that her current symptoms were droopy eyelids, double vision, weak arms and legs, and difficulty swallowing. For her, the most frightening symptom was shortness of breath secondary to the weakening of her muscles. She intoned, "My lungs and heart are muscles and they may also weaken and therefore may one day quit working. If that happens, I may die." She believed her death to be imminent. The most difficult thing for her to accept was not death itself but not knowing when it would come. Her physicians were of little help; they equivocated. They told her that she might die in two weeks or twenty years. As if to reassure herself, she asserted that she had come to terms with her illness but that Michelle needed someone with whom to talk about the illness. Michelle was not reacting emotionally or showing any outward symptoms at this point.

THERAPEUTIC SITUATION PRIOR
TO THE CRITICAL INCIDENT

The first session in the family therapy center focused on Ladare's previous attempts to engage Michelle in a discussion about the illness. According to Ladare, those attempts were unsuccessful primarily because Michelle ignored her and appeared unaffected by the topic of conversation. In addition to Michelle's unresponsiveness, the setting for these mother-daughter after-school talks was a significant contributor to the lack of success. Ladare revealed that their conversations often were interrupted by distractions such as the television, visits from friends, and phone calls. Wanting to better understand the situation, I asked mother and daughter to role-play a typical conversation that would demonstrate a regular parent/teenager style of dialogue:

LADARE: The doctors have told me that I am very sick. Do you understand?
MICHELLE: Yes.
LADARE: Does my being sick scare you?
MICHELLE: No.

Observing Ladare and Michelle's communication, it was clear that, for different reasons, neither mother nor daughter really wanted to broach the topic. Their less-than-energetic attempt at communicating was perhaps their way of avoiding an unpleasant, unresolvable situation. Believing that a frank and open mother-daughter discussion of Ladare's illness was a necessary and important step toward Ladare eventually accepting her illness and toward Michelle's ability to cope with the illness, I encouraged the mother and daughter to role-play alternative ways to more effectively discuss Ladare's illness. My hope was that Michelle eventually would accept and cope with her mother's illness. This strategy was unsuccessful because Michelle continued to respond with single words to all of Ladare's comments and questions.

A genogram completed in this session revealed that Ladare had twelve brothers and sisters living in a close radius and that both parents still lived in the home in which she was raised. Ladare shared that she felt very close to her siblings and talked with each of them frequently but as yet had not shared information about her illness with any of them, despite having made several attempts to do so. She volunteered that she had not told her siblings about her illness because "I do not want to inconvenience them." I validated and supported her sense of independence that contributed to her not wanting to inconvenience her siblings yet emphasized to her the importance of familial support during times of illness. To help reveal her illness to her siblings, I role-played and rehearsed with her several telephone calls to her siblings in which she informed them of her condition. During the role-play situations, Ladare appeared comfortable and confident. Consequently, I asked her to initiate and complete a discussion about her illness with at least one sibling before our next session. At this point Michelle commented that she enjoyed visiting with her father and expressed a wish to do so more often. Ladare was the sole custodial parent and did not often allow Michelle to visit with her father. While Michelle discussed her wish for increased paternal contacts, she remarked that she was fearful that she may lose another parent. Michelle refused to elaborate when asked to do so. Interestingly, Ladare appeared not to be affected by Michelle's statement and elected not to probe further. Immediately prior to the session's end, I asked Ladare how *she* was coping with her illness. Ladare simply replied, "Fine."

The second session focused on Ladare's family of origin. She shared that her closest sibling relationship was with her oldest sister. They spoke with each other at least once a week. Despite these frequent conversations, Ladare did not complete the phone-call assignment from the previous session. To help her overcome her reluctance, I again role-played with her a phone conversation in which she disclosed her illness to her sister. Again, she was resistant to the prescription that she disclose her illness to her siblings; she did not want to inconvenience them. She said, "I do not want to inconvenience my sister because she is very busy with all her work." She offered an identical argument to support her decision not to disclose her illness to her other siblings. Because I believed that her siblings were an important and meaningful resource in her struggles with her illness, I encouraged her to invite all or some family members to attend future sessions. She rejected that invitation because "It would inconvenience them too much." At this point, Ladare appeared noticeably uncomfortable because she was the focus of the discussion. She immediately requested that the discussion focus return to Michelle. Concerned that her request to change the focus of the discussions was a deflection to avoid confronting painful issues, I continued to focus on Ladare and asked about other people, places, and things that might be helpful resources at that time. She identified her minister as the only human resource she could think of. However, she immediately disqualified him as a resource because "he is too busy to attend sessions."

To maximize Ladare's coping abilities as well as the number of resources available to her, I introduced the therapeutic goal of working with Ladare's friends and family members. Interestingly, Ladare deflected onto Michelle my intent to help her. She said, "Whatever will help with Michelle." The remainder of the session focused on joining with Michelle. This was a fairly easy task as I found her to be bright, energetic, and friendly. Our discussion focused on "fun" topics that allowed mother and daughter to laugh and play together.

At the beginning of Session 3, I focused on helping Michelle to discuss her feelings about her mother's illness. During this process Michelle appeared visibly uncomfortable, especially when asked to verbally express her feelings. To help Michelle feel more comfortable, I invited her to communicate nonverbally about the illness. To that end I asked her to use paper and pencil drawings and sand play to express her feelings. Michelle's artistic activities created "free time" for me to talk with Ladare. Unfortunately, Ladare elected to engage primarily in small talk with me and altogether avoided discussing any substantive issue related to the illness. Despite my prodding in previous sessions, Ladare still had not told anyone in her family about her illness. She continued to insist that she did not want to be a bother to her family. During this session Ladare displayed an ultrapositive coping attitude. However, contrary to her verbal reports and outward show of "doing fine," several signs showed that she was not coping as well as she wanted everyone to believe. For example, she continuously shifted the spotlight onto her daughter. Further attempts to help Ladare open up and address the difficulty she was experiencing with her illness were unsuccessful. Both mother and daughter used the same strategy to avoid the pain associated with the illness.

During the fourth session Michelle continued her drawings and sand play as her communication media. She reported, and my observation confirmed, that she enjoyed drawing her home, school, and friends and explaining her creations to her mother and me. Ladare responded approvingly to Michelle's creative expressions about her illness, her father, and even school. Because Ladare had developed a pattern of engaging only in small talk while deflecting the focus of the discussion onto Michelle and outright avoiding any discussion of her illness, engaging her was difficult. To engage her, I asked her to begin to keep a daily journal in which she could express her thoughts, feelings, fears, anger, or whatever she wanted to include. She appeared genuinely excited about doing so and promised to discuss her journal entries during our next session. Immediately prior to the session's end, she disclosed that she still had not asked any family member to participate with her in therapy. She continued in her refusal to have anyone other than Michelle join her in therapy. I continued to express concern about her unwillingness to discuss her own feelings and to encourage her to be more disclosing in future sessions.

Ladare began Session 5 with the declaration that she had not written in her journal because "the past week was difficult for me and I had trouble finding the time or energy to write." All week she had experienced difficulty with her vision: "My eyes were bothering me." She said she was embarrassed that her face was misshapen and her eyes appeared to be looking in two directions simultaneously. As a result, she wore sunglasses indoors and out, even in the presence of Michelle. She did decide, however, to share information about her illness with her oldest sister. She immediately downplayed the conversation because she did not want to burden her family with bad news.

Since Ladare had been avoiding any focus on her issues and had not kept her journal, engaging her continued to be difficult at best. In an attempt to engage her optimally I turned to an alternative means of communication. At the beginning of the session, I asked Michelle to act as a scribe and to write down Ladare's thoughts or to portray her thoughts in pictures. Ladare objected to that plan and requested that Michelle continue *her own* drawings and sand play. She was concerned that although Michelle had opened up a little in therapy, at home she continued to remain silent about what she was feeling. At this juncture, Ladare abruptly switched topics and requested that we focus on "Michelle's problem" for the remainder of the session.

Now that she again was the focus of the discussion, Michelle was visibly uncomfortable and elected not to communicate verbally. Instead, she chose to communicate her feelings through play. She used dolls to tell a story in which she was the main character, a turtle. The turtle usually spent all its time traveling around town watching the people and their families. Whenever the turtle became tired, sick, or scared, it retreated into its shell. Michelle wished that she had a shell to protect her from the world and that her mother had one just like it, only bigger. I perceived this story as a breakthrough for Michelle in that the story appeared to be communicating her wish that her mother had some protection against the disease. Ladare seemed to make a similar connection and validated Michelle for a creative story and for the thoughtfulness in wanting to protect her. Subsequent to her fantasy play, Michelle's manner, attitude, and overall in-therapy behaviors were markedly changed. She visibly was more comfortable in the sessions, volunteered more information, and responded willingly to direct questions and verbal probes regarding her feelings about her mother's illness. Ladare seemed pleased with the changes and progress Michelle had made and told her so.

Since the presenting problem—"Michelle's problem"—was approximately 95 percent resolved, I informed Ladare and Michelle that they were nearing the end of therapy and in the next couple of sessions they would begin preparing to terminate therapy. Ladare's reaction to this information was surprising. Somewhat angrily she expressed her displeasure at the decision to terminate and objected to the projected timetable for the termination of therapy. Ladare argued that despite the progress Michelle had made, she still needed more time in therapy. She believed that Michelle still had not fully vented *all* she was feeling about Ladare's illness and imminent death.

At this point I expressed confusion and feelings of being stuck. In previous sessions Ladare was adamant that sessions focus on addressing "Michelle's problem." Now that Michelle's problem was nearing resolution (Ladare acknowledged that it was), she was displeased that therapy was about to end and requested a continuation to address a problem that no longer existed. Despite her stated reasons for wanting therapy to continue, it was clear other unspoken personal reasons existed for her request. I was in a dilemma. Should therapy be continued under the guise of addressing only Michelle's problem, or should Ladare be challenged once again on the continued denial of her own issues? I reasoned that challenging her at this point would result in more defensiveness rather than cooperation. To test that speculation, I attempted to focus the discussion on how she was coping with her illness. Predictably she was not open to discussing her own issues. Such being the case, we agreed that therapy would continue and focus only on Michelle's problem.

Ladare began Session 6 venting her frustration with the state's social services department. She recently had been informed that her illness and its current symptoms—muscle weakness and double vision—did not qualify her for disability benefits. Despite her frustration and disappointment, she refused to be angry. Instead, she stoically accepted the department's decision. She said, "God will provide!" Realizing that she had focused attention on herself, she quickly switched the focus of the attention onto Michelle. She said, "Michelle wants to play with the puppets that I brought in for today's session." I decided not to challenge Ladare's transparent avoidance of her issues and accepted her suggestion to focus on Michelle. Ladare then handed Michelle the three puppets she had brought to the session. Michelle gave me a puppet she named Bad Witch. She kept a lion puppet and gave Ladare a rabbit puppet. I encouraged Michelle to guide the fantasy play so that limits were not placed on her creative expressions. She set the rules of the game. I could ask her questions, but if they were "bad questions" I had to use the Bad Witch puppet to ask them. The remainder of the session was spent trading the puppets among us. Everyone had the opportunity to ask direct questions about substantive issues, including Ladare's illness. For the first time, Ladare responded forthrightly to Michelle's questions without any attempt to deflect them. At session's end, I asked Michelle what she had learned from the session. She said she learned that it would be difficult for her to care for her mother without help. This observation was discussed further as the possibility of including family members in therapy was explored. Once again, I asked Ladare to invite her family members to attend therapy with her to help create a caring supportive group. Again she declined to do so.

During the next session, Michelle continued the theme of Session 6. She stated that her primary fear about her mother's illness was losing another parent. Ladare did not respond to Michelle's expressions of fear and loss and remained silent while Michelle discussed her fear of losing her mother. Michelle then asked Ladare with whom she would live if Ladare did pass away. All the possible options were discussed and focused mainly on her many aunts and uncles. Michelle asked if she could live with Ladare's oldest sister because Ladare was closest to that sister. Based on her nonverbal body language, this conversation was unsettling for Ladare. Such was her discomfort that she asked to leave the room for a short while. Upon her return, Ladare admitted that she still had not written in her journal nor talked about her illness with any other family members. She was not sure if her oldest sister had told any other siblings about their conversation. She continued to insist that she wanted to be an individual and "did not want to bother her family or put them out of place" by asking for their support. Interestingly, she blurted out that she was not using Michelle as a way to cope with her illness or as her only means of emotional support. I did not respond to this declaration, fully expecting her to elaborate; she did not.

In Session 8, I again proposed to terminate therapy because the therapeutic goals had been met and the presenting problem resolved. Ladare and I had agreed that because Michelle had been talking about her feelings openly for several weeks (since Session 5), the presenting problem had been resolved successfully. However, again, as in Session 5, Ladare requested that therapy be continued with the family. She now was less clear than in Session 5 about her reasons for wanting to continue in therapy. However, she remained adamant that therapy continue. Despite her lack of clarity about why she wanted to continue in therapy, I saw this as an opportunity to push Ladare to confront her illness. Accordingly, we agreed therapy would continue on the condition that Ladare focused on educating herself, Michelle, and her siblings about myasthenia gravis. Ladare agreed to teach her family everything she knew about her illness; she would focus primarily on the unpredictability of the disease and its most difficult aspects for her.

Ladare spent the remainder of the session discussing her current physical condition. She stated that on some days she woke up feeling fine; on other days she experienced much difficulty breathing or just getting out of bed. Those were the days that scared her the most because "I always feel that those may be my last days." For the first time in therapy, Ladare cried a little.

THE CRITICAL INCIDENT

Ladare had canceled what would have been our ninth session because she was feeling ill and Michelle had the flu. She asked to reschedule in three days rather than postpone to the following week. At Session 9 Ladare presented without Michelle. She said she and Michelle still were feeling sick, but she wanted to keep her appointment today. In the absence of Michelle, I was unsure how to proceed. In previous sessions, Ladare had made it clear that she was not interested in discussing her own issues; I harbored no illusions that today would be different. After a few minutes of silence in which both Ladare and I sat and gathered our thoughts, the critical incident occurred.

During those moments of reflections, I briefly considered canceling the session until Michelle could be present. However, before I could verbalize my thoughts, I observed that Ladare's face looked puzzled then scared. She then leaned forward suddenly and quietly whispered, "You know, we have been doing this all wrong. Michelle is doing fine with the news, but I am not. It's just that when I have to talk about it with you or my family, or even write it down on paper, it makes it real, and I'm not ready to die!"

I empathized with her feelings about the reality of her illness and her fears about dying, and invited her to share what she had been experiencing over the past months. She accepted my invitation to vent her feelings. For the remainder of the session she vented the emotions she had withheld, fought, sabotaged, and resisted disclosing and confronting for nine weeks. After forty-five minutes of venting, not only was she a most cooperative and hardworking client, she wanted to know more about other treatment options for myasthenia gravis and helped to develop her own treatment plan. She readily embraced the idea of strengthening her family support system and committed herself to tell all her siblings that she was ill and to educate them about myasthenia gravis.

The treatment plan that she and I developed required her to contact each of her twelve siblings and to update them about her illness. Despite a desire to contact her siblings, she concluded that phone calls were too expensive, too time consuming, too redundant, and too emotionally difficult. Consequently, we explored other options. These including visiting each sibling or announcing the facts about her illness at the next family gathering. In the end, she elected to send an identical letter to each sibling. The letter addressed four concerns: (1) Who will care for Michelle in a worst case scenario? (2) Will family members provide emotional support for her and Michelle while they are coping with her illness? (3) Will family members provide financial support for her? and (4) Will they understand myasthenia gravis and what it has been like for her? She also decided to write a separate letter to Michelle to explain in detail her feelings for her. Ladare knew that writing about her illness would be difficult especially because an early death was almost certain. I suggested she use time during our future sessions to write and discuss the letters. She accepted this offer openly. At session's end Ladare expressed a determination to no longer hide from her future and to make the best of the time she had left to live.

DISCUSSION

Characteristics of the Case Relevant to the Outcome

Looking back on this case, several characteristics specific to the family and to me are relevant to the outcome. The first of these occurred prior to the first session. Because the family presented with a medical symptom, I had chosen a psychoeducational perspective as the most viable therapeutic approach. The primary goal of this approach was to maximize the functioning and coping abilities of both the mother and daughter. This goal determined the structure of the sessions and kept me focused on involving the extended family and discussing the illness to a greater extent than would have been true had I chosen another approach.

Second, Ladare's explicit desire to direct the treatment focus on Michelle's problem to the exclusion of her own problems, despite the two being interrelated, was also significant to the outcome. Beginning with the initial session, I wanted to include Ladare's issues as an integral part of the therapeutic focus and made that clear on a number of occasions. However, an unintended consequence of Ladare's avoidance of her issues was the critical incident in Session 9. Her insistent focus on Michelle's problem prolonged therapy despite my awareness that clinically the presenting problem had been resolved. Ladare's insistence highlighted her unspoken needs and permitted me to be flexible with regard to the termination of therapy. I was confident that by a process of elimination Ladare would be forced to confront her own issues when we no longer had Michelle's problem upon which to focus.

A third characteristic is specific to me and to the psychoeducational approach I was using. Prior to the day of the critical incident I had spent hours researching myasthenia gravis and had every minute of the session planned. Consequently, when Michelle did not come with her mother, I became unsure of what to do. As a result, my slow reaction to the unplanned situation, as well as our momentary silence may have increased the tension and thus contributed to the development of the critical incident. Equally important was Ladare's moment of vulnerability. Her serendipitous disclosure that she, rather than Michelle, was more in need of therapeutic assistance changed the course of therapy.

Fourth, the unpredictability of the illness itself was a characteristic that affected the outcome of the case. Myasthenia gravis creates significant changes in the lifestyles of the affected persons and their families. The entire family system must contend with the illness and its complications, which include unpredictability, frustration, and muscular weakness. Even medicated patients are not free from future symptoms. Overwork and stress can contribute to future problems. Therapists as well as clients can be affected by these factors; the feelings of both parties need to be considered during each session. It was easy for me to think of Ladare as fragile and to rationalize that pushing her (even when I needed to do so) would overtire her or add unneeded stress. All of these factors permitted her to win the battle for structure (Napier and Whitaker, 1978).

Finally, because of the therapeutic approach I had chosen, I focused on involving Ladare's large family as a logical support group for her. Unfortunately, continued attempts to achieve this goal created a negative feedback loop that resulted in Ladare becoming scared and strengthened her resolve to deny/avoid the reality of her situation. This in turn contributed to me feeling therapeutically impotent and stuck perhaps because I may have been pushing Ladare to a place she was not ready to go, and at a pace at which she was not ready to move.

Role of the Critical Incident in Getting Therapy Unstuck

The critical incident was central to getting therapy unstuck. Clearly, Michelle's absence from the rescheduled Session 9 was a contributing factor. Throughout the nine sessions, because of her fears about the disease and of dying, Ladare had cast Michelle as her foil whom she had assigned the role of "designated griever" to avoid having to confront the reality of her illness. However, with Michelle absent and with no one upon whom she could deflect my questions and her feelings, she no longer could resist the opportunity to disclose herself. It also is possible that although Michelle was the IP, progress may have been achieved sooner had I seen Ladare individually earlier in therapy. Her refusal to confront her illness may have been for Michelle's benefit—being strong for Michelle's sake, not wanting Michelle to see her as vulnerable as she was in Session 9. With Michele absent, she could be vulnerable and "let it all hang out" without scaring Michelle. More important, the critical incident helped Ladare gain a different perspective with regard to who owned the problem. Previously she had presented the problem as Michelle's; now she accepted that as the affected person, she owned the problem; Michelle only externalized it. Accordingly, for the first time in nine sessions, she began her sentences with "I" rather than "Michelle wants" and focused the discussion on herself rather than on her daughter.

The critical incident also forced me to change as well. In later sessions, I became more patient with Ladare and focused on working at her level of comfort rather than being propelled by a particular goal that needed to be accomplished. Following the critical incident, each session began with us making small talk. This small talk appeared to calm Ladare's fears and helped to establish a working context that she seemed to appreciate. In addition, my focus also changed from trying to create support groups for Ladare's benefit to seeing the person rather than the disease—a person scared of waking up each day because she never could predict what her physical condition would be at day's end.

Implications of the Critical Incident for Therapy

As a result of the critical incident, the course of therapy changed. That incident was the catalyst that helped Ladare to confront the terrifying reality of her illness and possible imminent death. It also allowed her to acknowledge her possible avoidance behaviors and to admit to herself that she had been using her daughter to do her grief work. It is an axiom of life that one cannot face another person's serious illness or death without contemplating one's own illness or death. Consequently, although Michelle's illness was neither life threatening nor of the same magnitude as was Ladare's, it may have been just sufficient to push Ladare to contemplate her own illness and possible imminent death.

THE OUTCOME OF THERAPY

Ladare wrote the first three sections of the letter to her siblings during one therapy session and half of the fourth section in another session. The family's responses to her letters were immediate and very positive. She and Michelle were invited to spend one month with each relative. This plan allowed siblings to offer support as well as to spend quality time together with mother and daughter. Ladare was unsure about what would happen during these visits but was thrilled with the way her family had responded. Independent of me, and at home, Ladare wrote a two-part letter to Michelle and completed it before terminating therapy. One part was intended to be read immediately and the other part was intended to be read after Ladare's death. Ladare invited me to read Michelle's letter, but I chose not to do so believing that it was a special letter only for her daughter. I encouraged Ladare to give the letter to Michelle immediately and to set aside time to discuss it with her privately. Ladare savored the thought of having something that only she and Michelle would share. At the end of our sixteenth session, Ladare gave me a letter she had written the previous night. The letter expressed her heartfelt thanks and gratitude for my work with her and Michelle. Specifically, she was grateful for my patience that allowed her to come to terms with her illness in her own time and at her own pace. The conclusion of her letter informed me that her family would now be her therapist.

Follow-Up

At our final session Ladare and I agreed that there would be no follow-up sessions or scheduled contacts unless she deemed it very important or a crisis occurred. Three months following termination, Ladare contacted me to update me on her illness. She reported that she had experienced only a moderate physical decline (increased muscle weakness) but emotionally was doing wonderfully. She and Michelle were preparing to visit her fourth sibling and hoped that this visit would go as well as the earlier ones with other family members. She was hopeful that her emotional health would help overcome any physical weakness. Ladare also informed me that she had instructed her sister to contact me when the "worst" happened.

REFERENCE

Napier, A. and Whitaker, C. (1978). *The family crucible*. New York: Harper and Row.

Commentary

Living with Connection

Jeri Hepworth

Commentator Background

Forty-nine years old, white, female, PhD, twenty-one years MFT practice.

Practice Setting

Northeastern, inner-city, family medical health center.

Theoretical Perspective

This case is considered from the perspective of medical family therapy.

Newell describes a psychoeducational approach in his work with this family coping with illness, but he also has incorporated principles of medical family therapy (McDaniel, Hepworth, and Doherty, 1992) into his work. This commentary will consider treatment from the perspective of medical family therapy, will identify relevant principles of medical family therapy, and will note how I believe Newell incorporated these principles into his work. I also will indicate instances in which I might have utilized additional techniques or conceptualizations.

This family was lucky to have met and stayed with Newell. Luck may be an unusual word to describe a mother and daughter who are coping with a serious illness. But Newell clearly describes how the presence of illness can allow families to become closer and more thoughtful about their own lives. Through Newell's presence and "staying power," Ladare and Michelle were able to address their concerns with each other, particularly their fears, and incorporate others into their plans for the future. In the midst of uncertainty and fear, this family created a sense of joy and connection that eludes many families, regardless of their health status.

I do, however, have one significant disagreement with Newell's construction of the clinical events. Newell describes Ladare's moment of personal vulnerability as a serendipitous disclosure. From my perspective, the disclosure does not seem serendipitous or implausible; rather, it appears to be a response to the trusting relationship that Ladare and Newell had created. Yes, it was unexpected that Ladare had come to the session alone; therefore, Newell's careful plans for the session were of little use. However, it often is at those times when we as therapists are caught off guard that our clients become more vulnerable. Yet based on her behaviors in previous therapy sessions, it was clear that Ladare was a careful woman who would not disclose her concerns without being certain that it was safe to do so. I hope that Newell realizes his part in helping to create an environment that allowed for safety, trust, and truth.

A safe environment is a necessary backdrop for therapeutic work, including therapy with families who are coping with health crises. Newell's uncritical acceptance of the family as it presented itself, defenses and all, was pivotal in facilitating increased communication. In medical family therapy, the life and death issues require that therapists respect the clients' defenses and help them to normalize and acknowledge their unacceptable feelings. It was clear that the initial presenting problem of "Let's get Michelle to talk about my illness" was not initially an easy or even effective possibility. Newell recognized that individuals within a family have different tolerance levels for discussion about fears. Initiating and facilitating communication about those fears required Newell's ongoing monitoring of differing readiness and interests. This flexible communication can be enhanced with attention to the following specific characteristics of medical family therapy.

THE ILLNESS STORIES

Each illness event has multiple stories. Everyone involved with the illness, whether patient, family member, friend, or health provider has his or her own story. These stories reflect each person's education, culture, and beliefs about what constitutes illness and treatment (Wright, Watson, and Bell, 1996). In this case, Newell focused on Ladare's story and understanding of her illness and vainly attempted to obtain Michelle's story. Ladare knew her illness label, knew some of the symptoms, and feared that her life would end soon. But she had many unanswered questions about her illness and prognosis. For a majority of patients, this is usual and customary and is reflective of the uniqueness of each chronic illness.

Myasthenia gravis, as described by Newell, has a very unpredictable illness course. Newell accepted a priori that Ladare was "fragile," and that she believed that her "death could be imminent." Rather than accept these assumptions, it would have been very helpful in the beginning of therapy if Newell had attempted to learn more about how others understood Ladare's illness. In this regard, it would have been helpful if Newell had contacted

Ladare's physician, with Ladare's consent, to learn about the medical perspective of Ladare's condition. Facilitating communication among patients, families, and health providers allows the articulation of differences and the recognition of areas to address in future communication. More important, collaboration with medical providers can provide indispensable information and support for therapists as well as the family.

A component of illness stories is the family history of illness, loss, and caretaking experiences. Accordingly, I would have been interested in Ladare's other experiences with illness and possible loss. Given the lack of communication among her family members about her illness, it is likely that her family practices were to preserve privacy or focus on positive things rather than illness. But this is a clinical hypothesis in need of testing. Michelle had already experienced the social loss of her father and was fearful of losing both parents. Perhaps like most of us, she found it easier to ignore the whole issue. An alternative hypothesis is that Michelle did not have sufficient permission from her mother to talk about the illness, even though she wished to do so. Again, these hypotheses provide the basis for questions about meaning. By asking about how other family members have handled previous illnesses or loss, the emotional heat is taken off the present illness. Newell and the family hear the different ways that people have responded to illness and consider alternative ways to respond to the present crisis.

DEVELOPMENTAL ISSUES

Ladare knew that this was not the time in her life that she was supposed to deal with her own mortality. Chronic illness in middle adulthood is a crisis—in part because it is developmentally unexpected. Children are even less prepared to cope with illness and loss. In a just world, Michelle should not have to worry about her mother's health and certainly she should not have to worry about how she as an eleven-year-old might have to care for her mother. Illness disrupts the family developmental life cycle; it can be reassuring to families when therapists openly discuss such disruptions with them. For example, early in therapy, Ladare seemed to want Michelle to talk about her illness in an adult manner and experienced frustration when Michelle was unable to do so. Many families find it helpful to be reminded that people of different ages do respond differently to illness. A young adolescent, for example, might be viewed as selfish because he or she may focus on friends instead of an ill parent. Helping families to verbalize and to maintain developmental distinctions, while also recognizing the changes that illness creates, can be helpful; doing so requires a delicate balance. In this regard, had Newell met with Ladare in an individual session early in therapy, she might have been more open to focus on Michelle's needs as a child. As Newell ultimately realized, pushing Michelle to talk about her feelings did little to make her feel more cared for. Helping Ladare to feel empowered as a parent who could arrange care for her daughter is a therapeutic goal that arises from developmental concerns.

AGENCY

Agency, a core principle of medical family therapy, describes an active involvement in and commitment to one's own care. Although we cannot control our health, we can make personal choices about how we deal with illness and the health care system. As therapists we can help clients to move from being passive recipients of health care to knowledgeable participants and partners.

Information facilitates agency. As a therapist, I might have helped Ladare to identify what she knew about her illness and what she did not know. Based on her response, we could then, with the help of medical colleagues, determine whether ways existed to obtain more information, what other resources could be utilized, and how much the patient wants to know about her illness. When we help our clients to identify and to ask their questions, they tend to feel more informed and increasingly are able to make better informed choices. Facilitating choice and agency is a mutually reinforcing process, such that when a patient feels better about negotiating his or her care with a physician, for example, he or she is more likely to be willing to discuss future care plans with family members.

Agency can be facilitated by "putting the illness in its place." Caring for a family member during a health crisis requires a balance of focus on the illness and on other dimensions of life. Putting the illness in its place means allowing enough emotional and physical energy for caretaking but not allowing the illness to sap all of the family's strength such that no reserves are left for other activities.

Some families benefit from rating, on a scale of 1 to 10, how much of their lives are consumed by the illness. When the family agrees that the illness is a 9 in their lives, but they would like it to be a 4, it is important that the therapist helps them to discuss how they could realistically make it only a 6, for example. Discussion can then focus on what the family can do to initiate more nonillness fun and incorporate such activities into their daily living. For example, questions can be asked regarding how family members enjoyed themselves before the onset of the illness. What has been neglected or postponed? For many families, laughter or joy often are replaced with sorrow and worry. In this regard, Ladare and Michelle might have benefitted from brainstorming about activities that might have distracted them temporarily from the illness but also would bring them closer. Helping families make plans for activities that previously were enjoyable or activities in which they always wanted to participate is a creative and very satisfactory part of medical family therapy.

COMMUNION

Communion, a second core principle of medical family therapy, refers to the enhancement of the emotional bonds that often are frayed by illness. People with illness frequently respond as Ladare did, who did not want to burden her many siblings with her worries about her illness. Illness can be isolating, as patients feel less able to enjoy their previous activities but continue to believe that they should not complain or bother others. A cycle of separation and noncommunication may occur such that those with illness can come to feel increasingly isolated just when they require more support from others.

Communion can be enhanced with social support of many kinds; Newell utilized this throughout the treatment. For example, in addition to attempting to facilitate deeper connection among Ladare and her sisters, Newell also encouraged Ladare to talk with her pastor. This is a place in therapy for consideration of larger systems—of social support groups, religious communities, friends, and extended family, as well as immediate family like Michelle. Communion also is enhanced when patients and families feel support from and have satisfactory communication with the medical community. Effective collaboration between patient, family, therapist, and medical providers facilitates this process.

A clinical technique may have been useful to foster communion. Newell could have asked Ladare to pretend that one of her sisters was sick and asked her what she would have wanted to do. Invariably, Ladare would have said that she wanted to help her sister. If pushed a little further, clients like Ladare readily admit that the sister whom they are trying to "protect" is someone who, if asked, would want to be included. When clients understand that others want to help, they also can come to understand that allowing themselves to be helped by others may be a gift to that person rather than a burden. This simple discussion often helps clients with illness to realize how their reluctance to share their concerns may have impeded communion.

ADDITIONAL SYSTEMIC IMPLICATIONS

Independent of the specific techniques or questions used, medical family therapy includes attention to larger system issues among providers and family members. Similar to a medical provider, therapists become a part of the treatment system; they become part of the problem as well as potential solutions. Countertransference issues for therapists working with chronically ill clients are significant, because illness and loss are inevitable parts of the lives of therapists as well as clients (McDaniel, Hepworth, and Doherty, 1997).

Systems theory also equips us to notice the shifting responsibilities and roles among family members. The term "designated griever" describes how one member may assume specific roles for the entire system. Early in the family treatment, Ladare may have been denying her own feelings while focusing on how Michelle should acknowledge her grief. Michelle, however, was not willing to assume that role solely. Her refusal to do so challenged Ladere to begin to recognize her own grief. As a result, a more equitable sharing of grief as well as joy occurred in this family.

CONCLUDING THOUGHTS

Although the principles of medical family therapy were not explicitly articulated by Newell, the principles of communion and agency were substantially addressed in this therapy. As a result, Michelle and Ladare felt much more connected to each other and to the extended family, who made themselves available to help care for both of them. As mother and daughter made the connections between themselves and with others, they were able to develop new ideas for initiating and facilitating contact with others and for having more fun together in their life. With some plans made for the future, they were freer to enjoy their present. Newell also moved from feeling a sense of responsibility for the clients to "accept" their illness, to being a partner who could help Ladare and Michelle feel less alone and enjoy their life together. There is no good luck when serious illness occurs. The luck and good fortune is found in our responses to one another as we respond to health crises.

REFERENCES

McDaniel, S., Hepworth, J., and Doherty, W. (1992). *Medical family therapy: A biopsychosocial approach to families with health problems.* New York: Basic Books.
McDaniel, S., Hepworth, J., and Doherty, W. (1997). *The shared experience of illness: Stories of patients, families and their therapists.* New York: Basic Books.
Wright, L., Watson, W., and Bell, J. (1996). *Beliefs: The heart of healing in families and illness.* New York: Basic Books.

Commentary

I'm Not Ready to Talk

Karl Tomm

Commentator Background

Sixty-two years old, white, male, MD, psychiatrist, thirty-two years family therapy practice.

Practice Setting

Family therapy program, University of Calgary, Calgary, Alberta, Canada; private practice.

Theoretical Perspective

A bringforthist, second-order, systemic view of family and therapeutic systems. This approach focuses on patterns of interaction and emphasizes the clinician's responsibility for the distinctions he or she brings forth in his or her awareness and uses to orient himself or herself in the clinical situation.

In commenting on Newell's report of therapy with Ladare and her daughter Michelle, I acknowledge and applaud the wonderful therapeutic outcome. Stricken with myasthenia gravis, Ladare was in an extremely difficult life situation. She was faced with progressive deterioration in her physical health and the probability of premature death. Accordingly, she recognized the need to prepare her daughter for future difficulties. Given that Michelle had refused to talk to her mother about her feelings regarding the illness, Ladare appropriately took the initiative to obtain professional help to facilitate a conversation with Michelle about the illness. Happily, by the end of therapy mother and daughter achieved a remarkable degree of openness on the issue, not only between themselves, but also between them and members of their extended family (who probably would have to assume Michelle's care). Therapy facilitated this shift toward greater openness and sharing in the mother-daughter relationship and with the extended family. I suspect that even in the face of further deterioration of her physical status Ladare would readily acknowledge that therapy had significantly enhanced the quality of her life. This would be a very gratifying result for any therapist.

CENTRAL ISSUES

With regards to this commentary, I take the relevant questions to be: Which therapeutic events and therapist behaviors contributed to, or restrained, the process of change toward this increased openness? How did this occur? To answer these questions I will use an interpretive lens that is systemic, second order, and bringforthist. This approach is systemic in that I focus on patterns of interaction. I do so in both the family system and in the therapeutic system. It is second order in that, as a therapist, I observe my looking to see what I am seeing and to see how seeing things in different ways enables different therapeutic approaches. Similarly, I look at the observing and seeing of family members and the therapist in this case. It is of utmost importance that I take responsibility for the distinctions that I bring forth in my awareness and use to orient myself in these reflections. I also invite family members and therapists to take responsibility for the descriptions that they bring forth. Finally, I acknowledge my position of privilege as a white male therapist in an academic setting in being able to offer these comments. Newell has placed himself in a vulnerable position by openly sharing his work, his thoughts about it, and inviting comment. I hope my comments, while differing from his perspective, will respect his vulnerability, yet provide some useful differences.

The Problem As I See It

The family presented as a mother-daughter dyad within which the mother insisted that the daughter talk about her feelings about the mother's illness. I suspect that the more Ladare requested that Michelle be open about her feelings, the more Michelle refused to talk and maintained her silence. Michelle's refusal to talk in turn probably fueled Ladare's concerns and triggered further demands to open up. Thus, from a systemic perspective, the core clinical problem here could be described as the reciprocal interaction pattern of requests and demands coupled with avoidance and refusals. It is created by the coupling of two types of behaviors that become mutual "invitations" which foster recurrence and stability in the pattern as a component of the relationship. Repeated requests invite avoidance; persistent avoidance invites further requests to respond. When the intensity of this kind of interaction increases it might more aptly be described as: demands invite refusals and refusals invite demands. Thus, the presenting problem as I see it lies in the interaction pattern that exists in the interpersonal space between the mother and daughter, not within either one of them. In other words, it is primarily a systems problem, not an individual problem.

I acknowledge, however, that the effects of this pattern on the interactants would be to pathologize each of them as individuals. Ladare probably felt very disappointed and frustrated with Michelle, possibly even angry or exasperated. Michelle probably felt somewhat confused, anxious, guilty, possibly afraid, or angry as well. Both undoubtedly felt very miserable when they were interacting in the grip of this pattern. It is because of these secondary negative effects that I label this a pathologizing interpersonal pattern. The behaviors in the pattern tend to be repetitive and become coupled. Hence, the pattern may be seen as circular. The circularity of the pattern does not necessarily mean that the participants have equal strength or responsibility in the maintenance of the pattern. Indeed, this particular pattern is probably somewhat hierarchical in that demands have relatively more power than refusals in activating and perpetuating the pattern.

Therapeutic Assumptions

At a theoretical level I assume that any relationship system that has any significant duration over time (history) will elaborate a wide repertoire of recurrent patterns of interaction. Indeed, human relationships are very complex and usually are quite rich with possibilities for alternative patterns of interaction. Some of these patterns are problematic; many others are not. In fact, I assume that the repertoire of patterns in an ongoing relationship will always include healing patterns and wellness patterns as well as pathologizing patterns. The difference between a healthy relationship and a problematic relationship has to do with the degree of flexibility in movement among these different interaction patterns and the amount of time that the persons involved live in healing and wellness patterns as opposed to pathologizing patterns. When a pathologizing pattern becomes an established way of relating, it can become a central aspect of the relationship and eventually dominate the behavior of the individuals in that relationship. This often makes it extremely difficult to get out of the pattern. My task as a therapist, then, is to be attentive to the potential for healing and wellness patterns and attempt to bring them forth to displace the pathologizing pattern. This potential was evident throughout therapy with Ladare and Michelle. Eventually, the healing pattern of open disclosure of painful experiences coupled with appreciation and respect for openness emerged quite strongly. This pattern of openness coupled with appreciation became increasingly dominant toward the end of therapy.

A possibility for this healing pattern emerged in the first session when Michelle disclosed her fear that she might lose another parent. Unfortunately, Newell's response to this openness was a request for more elaboration rather than appreciation and respect for the disclosure. My sense is that his request probably was experienced by Michelle as another demand (like her mother's) and triggered further avoidance. As a result, the pattern of demands coupled with refusals resumed its dominance at that moment. Sustained therapeutic efforts to move out of the dominant pathologizing pattern occurred when Newell encouraged Michelle to express herself through play. The focus on play decreased the demand to talk and created greater opportunities for change to occur. In my opinion, a critical incident also occurred during the fifth session when Newell and Ladare listened appreciatively to Michelle's story about the turtle. Indeed, the story itself is an open disclosure of Michelle's understanding of the pattern of avoidance coupled with threats. At that juncture, Ladare praised Michelle for her creativity and thoughtfulness. This response contributed significantly to the healing pattern of openness coupled with appreciation that later became strong enough for the subsequent therapeutic breakthrough.

SOME GOOD POINTS ABOUT THE CASE

I concur with Newell's report that multiple factors contributed to the critical incident described in the ninth session when Ladare suddenly opened up and shared her painful experiences. Fortunately, on this occasion, Newell responded to Ladare's openness with empathy, respect, and appreciation. His response contributed enormously to the further emergence and endurance of the healing pattern. Undoubtedly, Newell's work in preparing for the ninth session by researching medical information about Ladare's illness contributed to his readiness to respond empathetically in that moment. The illness of both Ladare and Michelle just prior to session nine probably heightened Ladare's fears, which, in turn, probably intensified her vulnerability and willingness to take the risk to become more open and disclosing.

Although serendipity may have played a part, a strong readiness for change in both Ladare and Newell during that session appears to have existed. I believe that the sudden absence of any requests, demands, or pressure from Newell (i.e., to follow his prepared agenda at the beginning of the session) contributed significantly to Ladare's dramatic openness. Caught off guard when Michelle did not attend, Newell was faced with Ladare alone, and he became genuinely uncertain. This therapeutic uncertainty expressed itself in silence. As a result, much more space became available for Ladare to bring forth her concerns spontaneously. Although Michelle's absence from the session may have been a contributing factor in Ladare's increased openness, I suspect it was the shift in Newell's stance from confident directiveness to hesitant uncertainty that made it possible for Ladare to shift her stance to complement Newell, who was already primed to receive and to support her increased openness. Once the healing pattern became established in the ninth session, the remaining therapy appears to have proceeded very smoothly. As noted earlier, this healing pattern had emerged for awhile in the fifth session as well. Unfortunately, the struggle over termination toward the end of that session reestablished the pathologizing pattern as dominant. But, fortunately, a transitional pattern toward wellness emerged at the very end. Ladare's demands to continue therapy were eventually met with concession by Newell, rather than refusal. His shift toward acceptance made it possible for the therapeutic process to continue to unfold and contributed to conditions for a reemergence of the healing pattern in subsequent sessions.

SOME NOT-SO-GOOD POINTS ABOUT THE CASE

A common family systems phenomenon is for family members to automatically invite others, including therapists, to view things the same way they do. This often inadvertently recruits therapists to participate in the same problematic interaction patterns in which family members are embedded. This recruitment process inevitably slows the progress of therapy and may stabilize or even aggravate the problem. In this case, Newell refused to join Ladare in seeing and accepting Michelle's refusal to talk as the primary problem. His refusal made it difficult to covertly join with Michelle and to support her end of the pathologizing pattern of interaction. However, he went farther to actually join in with the problematic pattern. Newell's major initiative in the clinical situation was to demand that Ladare open up about her feelings about her illness by speaking to him and to members of her family of origin. Predictably, this approach failed. Michelle was not ready to talk under pressure, so it is not surprising that Ladare was not ready to talk about herself. The more Newell demanded that Ladare reveal the specifics of her illness experience, the more she resisted his demands and deflected the focus onto Michelle. In effect, the pathologizing interaction pattern spread from the family system into the therapeutic system. The demands for openness coupled with avoidance of openness generalized from the mother-daughter relationship to the therapist-mother relationship. I doubt that Newell was aware of this at the time. Had he clearly distinguished the dominant pathologizing pattern between Ladare and Michelle and brought it forth in the therapeutic conversation, the possibility of him becoming aware of how he also had slipped into it would have increased. Similarly, if his supervisor could have distinguished this pattern and openly shared it with Newell, I suspect Newell would have received the input with appreciation, and the enactment of the healing pattern in the supervisory relationship could have enabled its generalization into the therapeutic and family relationships.

Empathy for the Therapist

I concur with Newell that adopting a structural theoretical perspective and a psychoeducational approach predisposed him to join the family in a way that was problematic. The structural perspective favors a stance of objectivity. The therapist assumes that he or she will remain outside the system and can diagnose and trust its structural problems. The assumption of distinct separateness between the therapist and the family makes it more difficult for the therapist to recognize problems in the therapeutic system. The psychoeducational approach further supports the therapist's entitlement to adopt a directive stance to correct the problems he or she sees in the objectified family members or their relationships. Thus, in this particular case, because of Newell's predicative assumptions, he began with a great deal of directiveness. For example, he directed the mother and daughter to play certain roles; he directed them in exercises designed to clarify the presenting problem; he instructed Ladare to contact her family of origin; and he repeatedly requested that Ladare speak about her experience of her illness when she was worried about Michelle. Quite possibly these directives may have been experienced by Ladare as unwanted demands. Thus, the structural and psychoeducational models increased Newell's vulnerability to drift toward the pathologizing pattern.

We are immersed in a culture with a strong tradition of individualism. It is difficult to recognize the degree to which we are influenced by it. I struggle against it when I become aware of it but slip back again and again. Even in commenting on Newell's behavior, I find myself drifting back toward individualistic descriptions of him while I try to maintain a systemic focus on the family. Clearly, Newell used a predominantly individual lens to view this family and its concerns. He perceived Ladare to be avoidant and demanding. I suspect he also construed her to be a domineering mother who was tyrannizing Michelle with her worries. These perceptions would predispose him to become directive in trying to get her to change her behavior. Unfortunately, the directiveness fed the pattern and brought forth more resistance, which simply served to frustrate Newell's good intentions.

Ethical Concerns: Issues of Gender, Race, and Male Dominance

In keeping with the dominant pathologizing pattern, Ladare was inclined to resist and avoid complying with Newell's demands. I suspect that issues of gender and race may covertly have contributed to the strengthening of this pathologizing pattern in the therapeutic system. The family members were female and black; the therapist was male and white. Male dominance and white privilege would support Newell's nonconscious entitlement to be directive and make demands of the family. Fortunately in this family, considerable strength existed to resist patterns of white male dominance. Unfortunately, the resistance usually took the form of silence, avoidance, and refusal to comply, rather than open protest. This passive form of resistance actively fed into the problematic pattern. In my opinion, Newell's reference to Whitaker's "battle for structure" is a seriously problematic metaphor in this situation. This metaphor tends to strengthen the therapist's presumed entitlement to dominance and hence supports his participation in this kind of pathologizing pattern. In contrast, a metaphor that emphasized liberation from oppression would probably have been much more helpful here. Indeed, what was needed for healing and wellness was liberation from the oppressive demands for openness in the family along with liberation from the demands for concession to professional authority, male dominance, and white superiority of knowledge. A stronger commitment to liberation by therapists in general would guide them to bring forth more space for those who are marginalized and have less power to speak their experiences and be heard.

A bringforthist perspective invites the therapist to pay attention to what he or she brings forth in his or her distinctions that organize his or her responses. For instance, in this case, Newell initially brought forth (defined) Ladare as avoidant. Doing so served to justify his directiveness and confrontation. If, instead, he had distinguished (perceived) her as being under the influence of oppressive demands, he would have taken steps to minimize his demands, to honor and appreciate any constructive initiative that she took, no matter how small, and to maximize her space to speak her experiences easily and freely.

WHAT I MIGHT HAVE DONE DIFFERENTLY

As noted earlier, my preference is to see the primary problem in the systemic interaction and not within the persons interacting. Thus, I seek opportunities to draw distinctions of behavioral couplings. I ask myself: what class of behaviors in this relationship typically triggers what other class of behaviors? Then I put these behaviors together as interaction patterns. I choose to see the pattern as recruiting the persons involved to participate in it by selecting the relevant problematic behaviors from their repertoire of behavioral possibilities. In bringing forth the core problem in my awareness as a pathologizing interpersonal pattern, I am more liable to maintain a systemic perspective and reduce the inevitable cultural drift toward an individualistic view. Doing so also enhances my ability to hold a stronger disposition of compassion toward the persons involved, since I tend to see the participants as unfortunate victims caught in the web of the pathologizing pattern in the system.

Having identified a pathologizing pattern, the next step would be to conceive of possible healing patterns that could constitute antidotes to the pathologizing pattern. I assume that some aspects of the healing pattern already exist in their repertoire. My interventions then entail a process of opening space for the healing patterns to emerge, perhaps even enacting parts of them myself in my own interaction with the family. For instance, one intervention I would have considered to open space for change would have been to acknowledge openly my position of privilege as a professional and my position of dominance as a white male and commit myself to minimize this and to maximize the knowledge and authority of family members with regards to their own experiences. In other words, I would try to find ways to enact authentic openness which would probably be appreciated and, in so doing, initiate a healing pattern in the therapeutic system. More important, I would be sure to appreciate their spontaneous openness and their appreciation of each other's openness as a way to support the emergence of the pattern in their relationship.

With regards to specialized techniques, I would have considered using an internalized other interview. Here, I would have interviewed Michelle as an internalized other within her mother as a way to open space for Ladare to appreciate Michelle's experiences more fully and also to give Michelle an opportunity to hear some possible descriptions of her experience through the voice of her mother. To interview Ladare in this way would have taken the pressure off Michelle to respond while at the same time honored the mother's desire to focus on Michelle's experience. I would have asked the internalized other carefully formulated questions framed to demonstrate an appreciation for Ladare's openness (in responding to my questions) and respect for the internalized daughter (for sharing her experience) so that the preferred healing pattern could emerge more readily and become established in the therapeutic system as well as in the family system.

CONCLUDING THOUGHTS

That said, I applaud Newell for his flexibility in finding alternative ways of responding to this family as the therapy unfolded. He became progressively less directive, less demanding, and more open to uncertainty. I deeply appreciate his willingness to share his therapeutic work with this family with me and a public audience of readers who could benefit from his experience. I also appreciate his openness to collegial comment. Once again, I acknowledge my position of privilege as another white male in being given the opportunity to comment on this case. I hope that my reflections will be heard as an offering from an alternative perspective rather than a demand for agreement, submission, or change from Newell or any other professionals. I genuinely endorse equifinality and accept that many different ways exist to enable therapeutic change. The perspective expressed in this commentary, then, is only one point of view and is based on my selective interpretation of

Newell's case report. In being open to offer, but not impose, what I perceive to be potentially useful ways of thinking and practicing, I too am trying to remain consistent with my preferred therapeutic stance and accept what works for families and for other therapists.

REFERENCE

Napier, A. and Whitaker, C. (1978). *The family crucible*. New York: Harper and Row.

CASE 13

Visiting All the Monsters

Margaret K. Keiley

Therapist Background

Currently: Fifty-seven years old, white, female, EdD, twelve years MFT practice. When I saw this family: Fifty-three years old, EdD, eight years MFT practice.

Practice Setting

Currently: University MFT clinic, limited private practice. When I saw this family: Family therapy consultant to an HMO in a large metropolitan community.

Client Characteristics

Alan (age thirty-five) and Janice (age thirty), a common-law immigrant couple (both from the Caribbean country of Trinidad and Tobago), and their two sons, Edgar (age eleven) and James (age nine), were referred for therapy by the Department of Social Services in a large metropolitan community. Alan and Janice were crack addicts and unemployed. Edgar and James were students in elementary school; Edgar was afflicted with sickle-cell anemia. Martha (age fifty-three), Janice's mother, owned and shared the two-story building with Alan, Janice, and their sons. Edgar, James, and Martha were not directly involved in therapy.

Length of Treatment

The family was seen for ten sessions of home-based family therapy beginning in the spring of 1996 through the summer of 1996. A serendipitous happening occurred in Session 5. The resulting critical incident occurred in Session 6.

Theoretical Perspective

A narrative, feminist, and emotion-focused approach was used with this family.

INTRODUCTION

My invitation to become a part of this couple's battle with their "monsters" was a chance happening. I was invited into this family's life as a witness to this conflict on a day when the "monsters" of drug addiction were raging. Because I accepted this invitation, I had the opportunity to witness the drug "monsters'" power and my clients' fear as they tried to decide if they were willing and able to vanquish these enemies. Up to this point in the therapy, I had been mired in a battle with the couple *about* their drug addictions. In this critical incident, the couple and I became collaborators in a struggle *against* their addictions.

PRESENTING PROBLEM

Janice, Alan, and their two children were referred to a health management organization (HMO) through their local Department of Social Services (DSS). This family had been receiving services from DSS for two years. Because they presented with severe and multiple problems, they were referred to the HMO to be part of the project with which I was associated. I was assigned to see this family in their home (home-based therapy) for a total of fourteen sessions.

The limited referral information I received stated that Janice and Alan were common-law spouses, drug addicts, and had two sons. One son, Edgar, had sickle-cell anemia and the DSS had removed both children from the parental home several times because the parents had been arrested for domestic violence. The family lived on the first floor of a two-story house in a very low-income neighborhood. The house was owned by Martha, Janice's mother, who lived upstairs.

I experienced several problems gaining entry into the DSS system and into the family's system. This case was being managed by the DSS of a large metropolitan community, thus the task of establishing contact with the overworked social worker and the supervisor assigned to the case was formidable. Similarly, my efforts to schedule an appointment with Janice and Alan were problematic. The project's funding agency required that I meet with the family every week for fourteen weeks. However, it was fully three weeks before I was able to schedule a meeting with Janice, Alan, and the DSS worker.

THE THERAPEUTIC SITUATION PRIOR
TO THE CRITICAL INCIDENT

Janice and Alan's apartment was quite dark because the window shades were drawn. The furniture was old and threadbare. Janice immediately apologized for the appearance of their home. Because of the DSS's involvement with this family, a DSS worker was assigned to introduce me to the family. While we waited for the DSS caseworker to arrive, Janice and Alan told me about Edgar's difficulties with sickle-cell anemia.

Following the DSS worker's arrival, she, the couple, and I spent one and one-half hours discussing the problems Janice and Alan might want to address in family therapy. The discussion was chaotic; Alan and Janice talked very loudly at each other and at the same time. Each recounted the wrongs the other had done in his or her life and each asserted that if only the other spouse would change all their problems would disappear. Fortunately, the spouse's iteration of the other's presenting problems did not escalate. During these "conversations," I had difficulty getting their attention. When I finally was able to outshout them, I commented that it must be difficult for them to hear each other. They smiled and agreed that this was true. They seemed to recognize this pattern of conversation. Both Janice and Alan seemed somehow comforted by their conversations; however, as an outsider, I understood very little of the spousal interchanges.

Returning to the question of problem identification, Alan disclosed that drug abuse was a major problem for him. He had been a crack-cocaine addict for nearly twenty years with few periods of abstinence. He had spent some time in the Army and had been trained as a medic. Since leaving the army, he had been gainfully employed sporadically but not recently. Janice complained that her basic problem was lack of financial support from Alan who was always around, like superglue. She said, "Just seeing Alan sitting in front of the television is enough to make me angry." When asked if lack of financial support was her only problem, Janice admitted that perhaps her drug use also got in her way. She said, "I would be clean [drug-free] for awhile, but when I couldn't see any positive results from staying clean, I would get discouraged and return to using drugs."

The DSS worker introduced the issues of domestic violence and neglect of the children as two other presenting problems. She interjected that three times in the past two years the children had been removed from the parental home and placed temporarily with relatives because Alan and Janice were in jail on domestic violence charges. At this point, Janice and Alan recounted their most recent incident of domestic violence, which occurred one month prior to our meeting. For her part in that incident, Janice spent a week in jail. She had threatened Alan with a knife. In all of the incidents of violence, both parents had been using cocaine. They agreed that Alan last hit Janice about two years prior to that incident. Now they mutually abused each other verbally; physical abuse was directed at the furniture and/or the walls.

In light of this information, the couple, the DSS worker, and I decided that the first major problem to be addressed should be Janice and Alan's drug addictions. Because the couple had stated that they had been drug free for the past two weeks and the children appeared to be doing quite well emotionally, we agreed to focus on the couple's addictions and relationship before we included the children in therapy. We jointly decided that Alan would enter an inpatient drug-rehabilitation facility and Janice would attend a community drug program. Interestingly, despite participating in the decision-making process, Alan and Janice objected to the terms of the final plan. Alan said he was afraid to enter treatment away from his home city because he believed that Janice would return to using crack cocaine while he was away. Janice countered that she could never get clean while Alan was around because he was a bad influence: "He is always inviting his dope-smoking friends over to the house." Because Janice and Alan claimed to have been drug free for two weeks, the requirement for formal drug treatment was deferred conditioned on Janice and Alan committing to weekly family therapy with me. Neither spouse had ever been involved in therapy of any kind, but each was willing to give it a try; perhaps it would be useful. The DSS worker confirmed that the current plan would be fine for now, but the couple's progress in staying drug free would be monitored by DSS.

At the end of the session, Edgar and James came home. They appeared to be outgoing, well dressed, and friendly. They also seemed to care a great deal for their parents. They ran to them and hugged them. They did not appear to have any fear of them at all. Janice acknowledged that the children usually go to Alan for comfort and help with schoolwork; they tend to come to her for more concrete things, like lunch. She questioned whether she was a good parent. In support of her concern, she shared that Alan was the parent responsible for administering Edgar's daily medication for sickle-cell anemia. Alan was emphatic that his children were the most important part of his life and that he had to be with them. Janice and Alan agreed that their relationships with the children were quite loving and warm, but that their relationship with each other had not been close for a long time.

EVENTS LEADING TO BEING STUCK

During the next session, Janice, Alan, and I began deconstructing their differing views of each other and unpacking the moments in their relationship that had led to drug use and violence. Janice described herself as fearful and lazy because of her drug addiction. Interestingly, Alan described her as brave but not always in a "good" way. According to Alan, Janice's bravery and energy were qualities that initially attracted him to her, but these qualities also made her "go out and do" drugs. Janice described Alan as shy and sensitive—qualities that allowed him to be a good parent to the children. As Alan agreed with that description, Janice added that Alan was also selfish, arrogant, and an animal.

In response to my questions about times when they felt warm and caring toward each other, they described a pattern—a sort of dance—that they have been unable to change. In this dance, Alan moves toward Janice, but she pulls away from him because she resents his inability to take care of her financially. She perceives his approach to her as his attempt to take advantage of her. When she pulls away, Alan feels rejected, snaps back at her, and then they are off and running, becoming verbally abusive with each other. They agreed that they cared for each other, but their history seems to get in their way constantly and separates them. They both admitted that when they are physically separated, they feel incomplete. When asked if they wished to remain together, they were clear that they could not leave each other.

Janice and Alan had spent many of their years together dealing with financial uncertainty, living with broken furniture, and having little food while they struggled to find and afford drugs and alcohol. Each one felt that the other was to be blamed for their current life conditions. Neither Janice nor Alan had many marketable skills at the time that I saw them. Janice hoped that Alan would support her financially, but he liked to stay at home with the children. Alan hoped that Janice would allow him to be closer to her, but she wanted to go out and get a job. In the meantime, because both of them had no saleable skills and were actively addicted to cocaine, life remained unchanged.

As we talked about their addictions, Janice, unrehearsed, assumed the role of a quasi narrative cotherapist. She likened her drug addiction to a "monster" constantly wanting her to use cocaine or to drink. Because she already had externalized the problem, I asked her to think about what this monster said to her to entice her to use drugs. She shared that this monster told her that she could do drugs in a controlled way: "If Alan would just leave me alone, I could find that perfect 'high' that is out there waiting for me." Janice admitted knowing that this monster was lying to her and that she had to say no to it, but she was afraid she was not ready to do that. I asked her what was keeping her from saying no. She said that maybe she did not really think the monster was lying to her. She really did think that the monster might be right and a perfect high did exist.

I asked Janice if she could tell when her monster was beginning to talk to her. She said that when her body was craving drugs she felt pinpricks and pain, as if the monster was trying to get her attention. At this point in our conversation, Janice expressed her fear that talking about her monster was going to get her into trouble with DSS and that she might possibly lose her children. I assured her that she would not get into trouble; having a desire to use drugs was not the same as using drugs.

Taking a cue from Janice, Alan began to talk about his own monster. His monster beckoned him to follow Janice. For example, when Janice would leave the house to get high, Alan's monster would say, "OK, let's just go along with this." The two of them would eventually get high and perform a dance similar to the one described earlier. The movements of the dance unfold in the following manner: Alan issues an invitation to dance; Janice refuses to dance with him; Janice dances with her monster; Alan counters by dancing with his monster. When exacerbated by drugs, this dance quickly escalates into violence because their respective monsters are dancing also. I asked them to pay attention to what the monsters were saying to each of them and to the times that each were able to refuse to listen to his or her monster's calls and were able to dance with each other instead.

The third session was integral in our fight with their monsters and my eventual visit with them. During this session, I met with Janice alone and she shared with me her personal history and her family's history. Her mother and father immigrated from the Caribbean to the United States when Janice was five years old. She described her upbringing as "quite strict." Her parents did not physically discipline her, but the rules were strict and she knew she had to follow them. She was her father's favorite; but the father-daughter relationship was filled with "sparks." When asked to tell me about the "sparks," she declined to answer.

Her mother is Trinidadian and her father is Tobagan. Interestingly, she identifies herself as a Tobagan rather than a Trinidadian (although twin islands, the country is formally known as Trinidad). A few years ago her father returned to Tobago. Janice declined to visit her father for fear that he would treat her like a child and inadvertently she would insult him in some way. Her two older brothers also had returned to Tobago; one brother was deported because of criminal activity. Her older sister had moved to Los Angeles several years earlier and was working for the LAPD. This sister is married, has two children, never became involved with illicit drugs, and is doing quite well in all spheres of her life.

Janice next shared with me more about her drug monster and its effects on her life and her view of herself. By this session, I had read Janice's DSS file. I commented to her that as I read her file I had become upset by how long she had been fighting her monster. She said that for a very long time she felt like she had been in between "darkness and light, behaving like a lion or a tiger, yet always victimized like a lamb." She revealed that the drug monster was not the only thing that abused her. Many of the people around her victimized her as well. In fact, she felt that she was in some kind of spiritual danger. She was afraid that her mother might have put a voodoo curse or spell on her. The physical sensations of drug craving that she previously had described—the signals to her that the drug monster was near—she also felt when certain people such as her mother or Alan were too close to her.

As Janice described her spiritual life to me, taking care to distinguish it from a religious life, she shared some of her writings that she kept hidden from others. We looked through the papers and Janice talked again about the physical sensations she experienced when she was craving drugs. She said that the writing seemed to help with these sensations; it kept the monsters at bay. Janice expressed concern that all this might make her sound crazy to other people. I assured her that she did not sound crazy to me. She stressed that she knew it was going to be up to her to defeat her monster and break the spell. I promised to stay with her throughout her fight; she did not have to do it alone. By the end of this session, I felt very close to Janice, who appeared quite vulnerable. I was impressed with her imagination, creativity, and honesty.

Later that week, at a case consultation held to review the various HMO cases, several of the other therapists suggested that Janice might be experiencing some psychiatric difficulties, such as hallucinations or paranoia, among others. I agreed that this might be possible and suggested that perhaps a psychological evaluation was in order. I also cautioned that some of what Janice was experiencing might well be the long-term effects of drug withdrawal and/or a "spiritual" sickness. The consensus of the consultation was to recommend to Janice that she take a battery of psychological tests. However, should she refuse to be tested, we were willing to stick with her in her fight to defeat her monster and break the spell.

After the third session, Janice avoided meeting with me. She scheduled and canceled three sessions. I believed that Janice felt that she had exposed a bit too much of herself during our last session. I also was afraid and sad for Janice that she was attempting to defeat her monster alone. Meanwhile, in phone conversations with Alan, he reported that he had found a job and was working three days a week. Based on his reports, he appeared to be having some success in resisting his own monster's invitations to follow Janice around like "superglue." As a result, he was spending more time outside of the house in gainful employment and not using drugs. He hinted to me that Janice had gone out a few times to do battle with her drug monster.

I persuaded Janice and Alan to meet with me for a fourth session. I also invited the DSS worker to be present at this session in case Janice and Alan had returned to using drugs. At this session, the DSS worker cautioned the couple that if they currently were using drugs their children would be taken from them. She also reminded them of their commitment to meet with me each week to deal with their drug addictions. Alan reconfirmed his willingness to meet with me. Janice complained that I had been of no help to her, but she would meet with me anyway. She requested more tangible help. For example, she wanted a pair of earrings she could wear to job interviews, or maybe a certificate at the end of our time together as an indication that she had gotten something from spending time with me (my cotherapist surfaces again!). I assured her that I certainly would give her a certificate.

Compared to Janice, Alan appeared to be getting his life in order; he continued to work three days a week. Janice reported that she was spending most of her time in the house. Paradoxically, she appeared to be a bit forlorn now that Alan was giving her the space she craved.

Several times during this session, Alan and Janice enacted their dance with each other—talking loudly and simultaneously. This time, however, they added a step. Each spouse shuffled through separate piles of "important" personal papers while yelling at the other. This was a duel of sorts and I was not sure who was winning. I knew I was not winning! Since I had become their family therapist, Janice appeared to be escalating her problem behaviors, and both spouses were adding to their repertoire of nonproductive "conversations."

STUCK

At this juncture, therapy appeared to be stalled and I was beginning to feel quite defeated. Although on one level I was not surprised by Janice's complaint about my uselessness, I did find myself struggling with my own monster here. I was angry, sad, and scared. I was angry because I felt that I was being rejected, and most likely I was being rejected for drugs. I was sad because I knew what the consequences of this reattachment to drugs might be for Janice and Alan. My fear was that Janice was listening to her monster in the hope of finding that perfect high and that soon Alan was going to listen to his monster and follow Janice once more. I allowed myself to have these appropriate feelings, but I could feel them pulling me away from my connection with Janice and Alan.

A SERENDIPITOUS HAPPENING

At the end of that fourth session, Janice and Alan recommitted to therapy with me. However, despite their verbal commitment, scheduling a meeting was no easy task. Typically, we would schedule an appointment, but on the day of the appointment when I called to tell them that I was on my way,

Janice would ask to reschedule because she was on her way to a job interview or off to see the dentist, or Alan was just leaving for work. As a countermeasure, I stopped calling Janice and Alan prior to visiting them. I reasoned that if I did not call before our scheduled appointment, they could not cancel. At the time I made this decision, I had no idea that showing up unannounced at the appointed time would mean that I actually would meet the monsters and experience the curses, but that is exactly what happened. When I did visit with all the monsters, therapy became unstuck.

Using this strategy of just showing up at the couple's door, I woke up Janice when I arrived at her home for the fifth session. I told her that I had been feeling sad about not talking with her the past week. I commented that during Session 3 when we spoke about the spiritual dangers she was confronting, I felt close to her and hoped we might continue getting to know each other. She acknowledged that she had been more honest and open with me during that session than she had been with anyone previously; she, too, felt disconnected since then. I emphasized that I was interested in finding ways to help her to defeat the monster that dogged her heels. She said that she knew it was going to be up to her to do that; she needed to do it on her own. I agreed that it was her fight, but that I could be with her while she tried to do battle with her monster and perhaps my being with her would help. Janice said she was not sure how that would be useful to her.

Alan came downstairs with Martha, Janice's mother. He told me that Martha wanted to meet me. Martha brought with her a number of mementos she wanted to show me. She showed me pictures of her wedding in Trinidad, a picture of her during her early days in the United States, greeting cards given to her upon her retirement from the hospital in which she had worked for twenty-five years, and testimonials to her good work. Martha suggested to me that Janice needed someone to take charge of her life. I remarked that I thought Janice already had begun to take charge of her life by agreeing to meet with me. Martha was unimpressed by this. At this point, Janice began talking about the forces that were against her and moved to the couch to sit next to me. She stated that if these forces would just leave her alone, she would be able to get her life together. Then Martha and Janice began talking simultaneously and loudly. I looked for Alan; he was across the room, smiling. Sitting between mother and daughter as they continued to speak in this fashion, I began to feel an undercurrent. I was not sure what it was, but I just sat there until I felt it subside.

Martha then told me that she thought the DSS workers had been "taken in" by Janice's stories; Martha believed that Janice never told the DSS workers the truth. According to Martha, "the real story occurs after the DSS worker leaves the house." I assured her that I did not feel that I was being "taken in." In fact, Janice had been quite truthful with me about many different things; I trusted her not only to tell the truth but to take charge of defeating the forces that were threatening to derail her progress. During this part of the conversation, Janice sat by my side and said nothing. I wondered if I had experienced one of the "evil curses" that Janice had described.

THE CRITICAL INCIDENT

As I had done for Session 5, I showed up for Session 6 without calling ahead. Janice was hesitant to open the door, but she finally let me into her home. She complained that her face looked really awful. She appeared quite agitated. When I walked into the living room, Alan came out of the bedroom and warned me, "Now you will see the worst." At that moment, Janice lifted her shirt and a knife fell out of her pocket. Alan picked it up and took it away. I was scared. I knew that the smart thing to do would be to leave, but I also felt I needed to stay. I quietly questioned: why had they answered the door? They knew what would be the consequences of doing so. If they were caught using drugs, a likelihood existed that they might lose their children. They allowed me to enter for a reason; I was sure of that.

I attempted to talk with Janice; because she was high, her conversation was difficult to follow. Alan cried as he listened to us talking. When Alan attempted to talk with Janice, she unleashed a verbal tirade. Most of what she said made little sense to me and she seemed unable to control her outbursts. Suddenly, she threw onto the floor in front of me the papers she had showed me in Session 3. She then knelt down, grabbed my hands, and lurched forward into my face. I just held her hands while she cried. Still kneeling, she asked for help. I promised her that I would try to help her to find help. We stayed together in the room—Alan and Janice crying, I holding Janice's hands.

After awhile, Janice and Alan calmed themselves and we talked about the meaning of this incident. At this point, I told them that, as we had agreed, I would have to report their drug use to DSS. Alan said that it was good that I could see what it was like when the monsters won, but he was afraid that DSS would take the children away. I told him that no matter what happened with DSS, together we could find a way to defeat these monsters. Dealing with the monsters was the most pressing battle to fight. Other battles could be fought later.

By this session, I had met all the monsters, including my own, and experienced the curses. Janice and Alan had trusted me enough to let me into their house when the monsters were raging. Now I knew the worst, but I also had seen some of the best. I had seen bravery, sensitivity, honesty, and resolve. I called DSS and talked with the assigned caseworker. She promised to check on Alan and Janice later in the day when the children came home. I told her I would call the "screening" division and report the drug use.

THE AFTERMATH OF THE CRITICAL INCIDENT

The next day, I saw Janice and Alan; they both reported doing better. We talked about the events of the last two days. They shared that the dance with the monsters had begun when Alan brought home a six-pack of beer after work. His father had recently died; he was feeling sad and felt that a few beers might help to ease his grief. Janice then suggested that they buy a bottle of whiskey. She was so insistent that Alan eventually bought the whiskey. A few hours later, Janice left the house, pursuing her monster's promise of the perfect high. Alan stayed home and took care of the children. He put them to bed that night and got them up the next day for school. Alan had been able to silence his monster. He stayed home and did not follow Janice. For Alan, staying home was an important step. Doing so allowed him to take charge of his life and to defeat his own monster who always insisted that he must follow Janice.

Despite being in the midst of a battle with her monster, Janice had let me into her house that morning only a short time after arriving home following her search for the perfect high. In doing so, she allowed me to see how badly her monster treated her and how deceitful its message really was. Although Janice may have been too high to be fully cognizant of why she had let me into her house, it is possible that having a witness to this destruction challenged her to acknowledge at a deeper level what she had always known but had been hoping never to have to acknowledge consciously—the drug monster was a liar and had little to offer her. I had been with her through some difficult times, had witnessed her struggles with some rather enticing monsters and some rather irritating curses. In fact, I had seen her at her "worst" and had not abandoned her. I had stayed connected and willing to help. I felt I had become a compassionate and protective compatriot as Janice grappled with her monster and curses.

As Janice and Alan described how their battles with their monsters had progressed over the past two days, they both acknowledged how important it was to them that I had been willing to stay with them during the last part of the battle. Perhaps even more important, they said, was the fact that I had come back to continue to work with them. Even though I had seen the worst in them, I had not given up on them.

Implications of the Critical Incident

The critical incident proved to be a significant turning point for this couple. They discovered that although I had seen them at their worst, I still cared about them and believed them to be worthy of respect and continued support. For me, the significance of this incident was the realization that the attachment bond is important in all therapeutic situations, even those in which therapists have to struggle to stay attached to their clients because of their own fears and judgments. As a result of this critical incident, my clients and I were able to begin to map out strategies for their campaign to defeat their monsters.

My work with this particular family affected me profoundly. Certainly, a critical incident and a serendipitous turning point were a part of this story. I have reflected upon the serendipitous turning point, my decision after Session 4 not to call Alan and Janice before I showed up for our appointments. I'd like to believe that my reasons for doing so were based on considerations of respect and accountability. That is, I had been questioning if by calling the couple to remind them of every scheduled appointment I was infantalizing them and reinforcing an unspoken belief that they were incapable of remembering appointments. In retrospect, I believe that my own sense of powerlessness might have influenced my decision as well. Feeling powerless and stuck at that point, I just made my way to Alan and Janice's door. Perhaps my own feelings of despair were similar to the feelings of despair that Alan and Janice were experiencing. Consequently, my feeling powerless and arriving unannounced for the scheduled appointment allowed me to experience a situation somewhat similar to that of my clients and to feel reconnected with them. During Session 5 and, more important, in Session 6, I learned a great deal about the power of being present with clients, even protecting them at times, while they struggle to defeat their monsters, or get out from under curses they believe were placed upon them. This is a story about such struggles: Alan and Janice's struggles to overcome their drug addictions and to stop their domestic abuse, and my struggles to stay with them in a critical situation that some might have considered dangerous.

THE OUTCOME OF THERAPY

The Department of Social Services did not remove the children from the home, but the agency insisted that Janice and Alan comply with mandatory drug screens. Over the last few sessions, we spent time devising ways through which Janice and Alan could continue to defeat the monsters that had beckoned them for so long. For example, when Janice felt the cravings for drugs, she would write some poetry to drown out the monster's voice with her own voice. At those times when writing did not work, she would eat something sweet. She acknowledged that she could not continue using drugs and drinking. Alan was still working and was planning to enter a medic retraining program in the fall. He felt that to defeat his monster he had to listen to himself and find something other than Janice to follow.

At the last meeting with the entire family, Janice and Alan reported that they continued to be drug and alcohol free and discovered that they were getting along better as individuals and as a couple. They also reported that the children were relating to them in a different way and that the four of them had been engaging in more family-related activities, e.g., talking with each other, taking walks together, and going on picnics. The youngest son, James, expressed his pride at being promoted to the next grade. He had been in danger of being held back, but in the final weeks of the semester he had improved his grades sufficiently to be promoted.

During this meeting, I was struck by the changes that had occurred in such a short time. When I read the DSS file before the third session, I felt quite depressed about how long these spirals of drug addiction, violence, and blaming had been occurring. The complaints Janice and Alan had reported to me in our first session were the identical complaints recorded in the DSS files by the DSS workers two years prior to my entry into the case. I had begun therapy with this family feeling very powerless. Now, the bickering between Janice and Alan had ceased. They were working together in their conversations, not fighting with each other. They both commented about the difference being sober and drug free was making in their relationship and in their relationships with their sons. We spent some time reviewing the strategies for defeating monsters, but for the time being, those monsters were gone.

POSTSCRIPT

After I terminated with this family, I moved to another part of the country and did not maintain contact with them. However, during the few months that I still was in contact with the HMO, I learned that the family was continuing to do well and that Alan and Janice in particular were continuing to defeat their monsters.

Commentary

Trading Monsters for Dreams

Eric E. McCollum

> But I, being poor, have only my dreams
> I have spread my dreams under your feet;
> Tread softly because you tread on my dreams.
>
> W. B. Yeats

Commentator Background

Fifty years old, European-American, male, PhD, twenty-five years MFT practice.

Practice Setting

University MFT clinic; limited private practice.

Theoretical Perspective

Primarily influenced by the common factors models.

As I read Keiley's description of her work with Alan, Janice, Edgar, and James, I wondered what could I say about it. Admiration, not comment, seemed most appropriate. Keiley visited the country of monsters and came away the victor, as did her clients. I am not sure that all of us could do so. To understand how Keiley was able to help Alan and Janice, I have used the lens of the four common factors that contribute to therapeutic outcome—client contributions, the therapeutic relationship, hope and expectancy, and theory and technique. Lambert and Bergin (1994) first described these factors in their review of decades of psychotherapy outcome research. When I encountered this approach to understanding therapy outcome through the work of Miller, Duncan, and Hubble (1997), I felt that I had found the missing piece in my understanding of what makes a difference in therapy. Ironically, the factors we as therapists spend most of our time thinking and talking about, and teaching our students—theory and technique—makes the least demonstrable contribution to therapy outcome. The therapist's theory and technique accounts for only about 15 percent of the variance in outcome in psychotherapy outcome studies. Although this sounds a bit discouraging, it certainly fits my experience. How many times have I worked with a family in which the presenting problem was positively resolved through reasons that I could not identify when I looked only through the framework of the various theoretical models with which I was familiar. No structure was changed; no insight had been gained; no paradoxes were delivered; and no intergenerational connections had been made, yet the clients made significant changes and thanked me for my help. More frustrating were the situations in which I had worked within the bounds of a specific theoretical approach, delivering the right interventions at the right time according to the model, yet nothing happened. Obviously, by focusing only on the model I was using, I was missing something important. I recalled that feeling as I read Keiley's case study. We would miss too many of the important things she did if we look only at her critical incident as some deviation from a therapeutic model.

CLIENT CONTRIBUTIONS AND CHANCE EVENTS

Client contributions and chance events have been identified as the factors that makes the biggest difference in therapy outcome. Fully 40 percent of the variance in outcome is explained by the strengths and motivations clients bring to treatment, naturally occurring exceptions to the problem, and chance events that lead to change. Obviously, as therapists we have little direct control over these things. We cannot create a chance event in the therapy room like we can orchestrate an enactment. But we can be mindful of the importance of such things and punctuate them as they find their way into therapy. Keiley did a masterful job of bringing to light Janice and Alan's strengths and competencies despite the overwhelming problems that brought them to therapy. Each time it would have been easy to assume the worst about this couple, Keiley chose to believe the best. For example, during the third session when Janice described some experiences that would be easy to regard as symptoms of a psychiatric disorder (e.g., her mother putting a curse on her), Keiley instead sees aspects of Janice's spiritual beliefs. Although not disagreeing with the treatment team's recommendation that Janice be evaluated psychologically, Keiley reminds the team that what Janice described might just as well be the result of a spiritual sickness. Not only is Keiley's stance respectful of Janice's West Indian heritage, it also demonstrates her willingness to assume the best.

Obviously, the incident that Keiley has identified as a turning point in therapy—her unannounced arrival at Alan and Janice's home while Janice was high—represents a chance event that led to change. What is interesting is how Keiley had the courage to use this event and to help Janice use it, too. Common clinical wisdom proscribes conducting therapy with an intoxicated client. Some clinicians contend that doing so will condone drug use. Others assert that no productive work can be done with an intoxicated client. Encountering Janice while she was high with a knife falling out of her pocket must have been a very frightening experience indeed. It would have been easy for Keiley to get back into her car and leave. Despite her fears, however, Keiley chose to stay. By doing so, she not only saw firsthand Janice's monsters, she also communicated in a very tangible way her belief that Janice could tame them. She did not do so naively. She was clear that she had to report Janice's drug use to DSS with the attendant risk that Edgar and James might be removed from the home. I believe that Keiley's belief in her clients allowed her to take this stand yet not lose her relationship with them in the process.

THERAPEUTIC RELATIONSHIP

The client-therapist relationship accounts for approximately 30 percent of outcome variance. Although this is more familiar ground for therapists—Carl Rogers (1951), after all, made an identical observation approximately fifty-one years ago—we often pass over it quickly as if it were a given in therapy. Doing so may be a mistake. Research has found that the quality of the therapeutic relationship is a strong predictor of outcome in drug treatment (Conners et al., 1997), family therapy (Quinn, Dotson, and Jordan, 1997), and even when medication is the only treatment given for depression (Krupnick et al., 1996). It is something we can directly affect because it is a relationship of which we are a part. According to Miller, Duncan, and Hubble (1997), the ingredients of a strong therapeutic alliance include: accommodating treatment to the clients' level of motivation, accommodating clients' goals for therapy and their ideas about intervention, and Carl Rogers' core conditions of helping—accurate empathy, respect, and genuineness. Plenty of evidence for these ingredients exists in Keiley's therapy with Alan and Janice.

To my mind, the incident that set the stage for such good work occurred in the first session, not the fifth. When Keiley accepted Alan and Janice's refusal to enter the drug treatment programs that she and the DSS worker felt would be most helpful, she clearly was accommodating treatment to her clients' level of motivation as well as their own goals and ideas for how therapy should proceed. Two weeks of being clean is not much of a track record on which to hang one's therapeutic hat with clients such as Janice and Alan, whose addictions are long-standing; the possibility of relapse is always eminent. Yet despite the odds against her, Keiley decided not to battle Janice and Alan over their need for more intensive treatment. Instead, she agreed to try their plan with the caveat that any further drug use would result in removal of the children from the home. Was Keiley simply siding with her clients' denial? Would a more confrontive approach have worked better? At least one study suggests not. Miller, Benefield, and Tonigan (1993) found that a directive-confrontational therapist style in alcohol-abuse treatment was associated with more drinking, not less, one year posttreatment, compared to a client-centered approach. Given the follow-up information Keiley provides in her case report, it appears that her decision to follow Alan and Janice's plan was justified.

Rogers' core conditions for the therapeutic relationship are also evident in Keiley's case study. Her efforts to understand the inner lives of her clients were not only effective, they were heroic, culminating in the actual meeting with Janice's monster. Her empathy isn't naive, however. Keiley is candid about her own fears as well as her sense of being stuck and failure when therapy stalled.

HOPE AND EXPECTANCY

Hope is fostered in treatment when therapists believe that solutions can be found and they communicate this to their clients. It also is fostered when therapists find and highlight strengths that they see in their clients, and when they help to separate the problem from the person. Keiley did all of these things in her work with Alan and Janice. She consistently found ways to communicate her vision of their strengths to them. For example, in the first session, despite having been told about the family's myriad problems, Keiley helps the couple to talk about an area in which they felt competent—parenting their two sons, one of whom has sickle-cell disease. With Janice's help, Keiley also works to separate the problem from the person, labeling the problems the family faces as monsters who have invaded their lives rather than as evidence of personality defects or character flaws. By doing so, she allows her clients to keep intact a vision of themselves as able to triumph over the difficulties that bring them to therapy. One of my first supervisors told me that sometimes the therapist's job is to carry the hope for our clients when they become dispirited. Keiley did this actively throughout her work with this family, and I believe that it was Janice and Alan's understanding of Keiley's hope for them that contributed to them opening the door to her the day she arrived to find Janice high and Alan in tears.

THEORY AND TECHNIQUE

The last of the four common factors—theory and technique—account for 15 percent of the variance in outcome. Therapy models do not serve us well as inviolate blueprints for how to conduct therapy with everyone. Instead, they provide a set of tools we can use to tailor our actions to our clients' needs and expectations. In her case study, Keiley makes good use of the narrative model to do exactly that. I am left to wonder whether Keiley began her work with Alan and Janice knowing that she would externalize something or whether Janice's reference to monsters called forth an externalizing frame. I suspect, based on my own experience as a therapist, it was the latter. Good therapists enter the work with curiosity about what is their clients' worldview and how theory can guide them to join helpfully with that worldview, not with the conviction that they must impose a preselected theoretical framework on the problems their clients bring to them. Keiley pays careful attention to Alan and Janice's monsters, to the strong emotions she finds in the family, and to the dilemmas of joining with clients while simultaneously taking a stand about the importance of protecting their children.

CONCLUDING THOUGHTS

Although I believe that the common factors model helps us understand what worked so well in Keiley's work with Alan and Janice and their family, no purely intellectual analysis can capture what makes good therapy good. I recalled Yeats's words—quoted at the beginning of my commentary—the first time I read Keiley's case study. Coming uninvited into a poor family's home, her presence alone an emblem of their failure in the eyes of society, Keiley was in a perfect position to trample the dreams to which Alan and Janice struggled to hang on. I have seen it happen many times. The press of severe problems, funding limits, pressure from other service providers, and the therapist's own vulnerabilities all propel us toward quick fixes that tidy things up on the surface but never touch the dreams of the clients we serve. Keiley somehow avoided that trap with Alan and Janice and found ways to step lightly in her work with them. As a result, they left therapy closer to realizing their dreams, not being pulled away from them. Perhaps respect for dreams is the intangible factor in good therapy—the part that is essential yet eludes explanation by any model.

REFERENCES

Conners, G. J., Carroll, K. M., DiClemente, C. C., Longabaugh, R., and Donovan, D. M. (1997). The therapeutic alliance and its relationship to alcoholism treatment participation and outcome. *Journal of Consulting and Clinical Psychology,* 65(4), 588-598.

Krupnick, J. L., Sotsky, S. M., Simmens, S., Moyer, J., Elkin, I., Watkins, J., and Pilkonis, P. A. (1996). The role of the therapeutic alliance in psychotherapy and pharmacotherapy outcome: Findings in the National Institute of Mental Health Treatment of Depression Collaborative Research Program. *Journal of Consulting and Clinical Psychology,* 64(3), 532-539.

Lambert, M. J. and Bergin, A. E. (1994). The effectiveness of psychotherapy. In A. E. Bergin and S. L. Garfield (Eds.), *Handbook of psychotherapy and behavior change,* Fourth edition (pp. 143-189). New York: Wiley.

Miller, S. D., Duncan, B. L., and Hubble, M. A. (1997). *Escape from Babel: Toward a unifying language for psychotherapy practice.* New York: Norton.

Miller, W. R., Benefield, R. G., and Tonigan, J. S. (1993). Enhancing motivation for change in problem drinking: A controlled comparison of two therapist styles. *Journal of Consulting and Clinical Psychology,* 61(3), 455-461.

Quinn, W. H., Dotson, D., and Jordan, K. (1997). Dimensions of therapeutic alliance and their associations with outcome in family therapy. *Psychotherapy Research,* 7(4), 429-438.

Rogers, C. (1951). *Client centered therapy: Its current practice, theory and implications.* Chicago, IL: Houghton Mifflin.

Commentary

Embracing Monsters

Leslie L. Feinauer

Commentator Background

Fifty-two years old, Caucasian, female, PhD, twenty-two years MFT practice.

Practice Setting

University MFT clinic and limited private practice.

Theoretical Perspective

Psychodynamic approach with strong experiential and systems focus was used to examine this case.

Janice and Alan's presenting problem focuses on drugs and alcohol as the monsters, but clearly symptoms of a deeper problem that has inflicted serious injury to Janice's core sense of self exist. From a system's perspective, an interaction in the responses and defenses of Janice and Alan has maintained their relationship in its disturbed state. Although Janice appeared to be the focus of therapy, evidence suggests that a change in one part of the system (Janice) created problems in and reverberated through the rest of the system, including Janice's husband, their two sons, and, by extension, her mother.

Consistently, the therapeutic experiences Keiley described revolved around what I perceive to be transference issues. I believe awareness of and responsiveness to these issues are critical for therapeutic experiences to be effective. Janice's levels of shame and transference in part explain her intense positive and terrified feelings toward Keiley. As early childhood issues specific to trust and dependency surfaced, Janice transferred the unresolved issues she had with her parents and significant others onto the Keiley. In cases such as this one, I believe it is important that therapists understand that their clients' transference of feelings and associated behaviors are unconscious productions. Effectiveness with such clients requires that therapists establish and set limits and boundaries while staying "with" the clients and affirming their ability to move through the unmastered stages of development (dependency through interdependency). I believe that when clients are able to move beyond their shame, they are able to make different choices, be more in themselves, and create lives unfettered by the burdens of their past.

WHAT I LIKED ABOUT THE CASE

In working with this couple, Keiley was spontaneous in her use of herself to provide neutrality, abstinence, and empathy. In her interactions with them, she provided experience rather than explanations or content. Although nothing can undo this couple's past, Janice and Alan "cleverly" selected serious monsters that allowed them to reexperience the severe abuse and alienation they had experienced earlier in life. Keiley was unable to undo or remove the emotional scars left behind but was able to create a context in which the couple experienced their environment differently. To that end, they were able to change the meaning they made of their interactions and experimented with different ways of coping with life.

During the period of treatment, Janice's sense of self was very weak and needed to be strengthened. Recognizing this need, Keiley was supportive, accepting, helpful, and provided structure that strengthened both Janice and Alan. Had Keiley not behaved as she did, the choice might have been to elect an intervention (e.g., hospitalization) that would have increased chaos and potentially resulted in psychosis. In working with families that present with chaos, I take the position that empathy and supportive interactions invite transference to occur. These can mobilize the repressed and unconscious needs that contribute to the expectations that clients place on their therapists and in turn shape the transference. Concurrently, it is important that therapists set limits or boundaries that provide clients with a sense of safety; clients often feel out of control and very vulnerable. However, although safety exists in stability and predictability, boundaries often may invite negative as well as positive transference. The goal for the therapist is to provide structure that is genuine, authentic, supportive, safe, and based in reality. The client(s) will then respond with either a negative or positive transference. The experience of having an effective source of authority (parent, therapist, system) with whom to interact provides the opportunity to sort out and experiment with new and different behaviors. In her work with this family, Keiley did provide them with a structure that was safe, genuine, authentic, supportive, and anchored in reality. She instinctively knew what she wanted to do in the relationship and accomplished it through introspection, thoughtfulness, and working collaboratively with the family to make decisions about the direction of treatment.

Keiley's intuitive approach in addressing Janice's issues contributed significantly to the outcome of this case. In doing so, it seems that she behaved therapeutically different with Janice and her family than she might have in other therapeutic situations. This approach may have been a reflection of her unconscious awareness of Janice's delayed emotional development. However, despite this awareness, Keiley appeared to have intrinsically believed and explicitly conveyed to Janice that she was capable of emotional growth and development. To this end, she allowed Janice to be dependent without fostering dependency. An example of this was calling to remind Janice of scheduled appointments. During the appointments, Keiley invited Janice to talk about herself, her fears, and her past. Keiley was not afraid of Janice's emotions. Keiley punctuated Janice's expressions and needs without shaming her. Then, when she determined that the timing was right, she required Janice to assume greater autonomy by expecting Janice to assume the responsibility for remembering or being accountable for her scheduled appointments.

It is very likely that Janice's receptivity to Keiley's approach contributed immensely to her transferring to Keiley her expectations that Keiley's response to her would traumatically shame her. Her past experiences had shown that shaming her tended to be the most frequent response from significant others. During the process of engagement as she expressed her feelings (fears, expectations, beliefs, ways she made sense of life, etc.), Janice experienced her "present" with Keiley very differently than she expected it to be. Most significant, Keiley was willing to expose herself in a way that allowed her to talk with Janice about the meaning they each made of the situations. Janice was then able to undo experientially the distortions from the past as she applied them to the present realities.

I believe that experiential learning is important to the therapeutic process. Based on her work with this couple, Keiley appears to share a similar belief. I also believe it is critical that clinicians understand that insight cannot substitute for reexperience. Indeed, specific insight into the meaning of each event is not necessary for growth and change to occur in therapy. However, new experiences in the face of old expectations and beliefs that provide new understandings, meaning, and patterns are critical emotionally for growth and change.

Another important factor in this experiential process occurred as Keiley validated Janice's unmet needs and her affect when she was in the situation or the experience. As Janice was able to express her emotions and experience her unmet needs in the present, Keiley was able to help Janice to confront the irrational and erroneous beliefs that supported and maintained her behaviors and manipulations. The places, situations, and relationships in which these issues, needs, and responses manifested themselves in Janice's life began to emerge. At that point, Janice could begin to identify when she was in the destructive processes. In the scenario Keiley presented, this was the point at which the story ended (or began). With support and continuing reality testing provided by Keiley, Janice's ability to uncover and release the negative response helped her to bridge the shame, pain, and losses connected to family and other significant relationships.

As Janice became cognizant that her automatic responses were destructive She became equally aware that a different life script was possible. Accordingly, she began to develop new behaviors and to alter her relationships with others, including her husband and children. Keiley's mere presence required Janice to do some reality testing. When Keiley did not respond in the "usual" manner that Janice had come to expect others would respond to her, Janice was challenged to develop alternative ways of making meaning and behaving. Keiley demonstrated in her actions that she believed (therapeutic expectations) that Janice's new ways of behaving would have fewer costs and greater benefits in actually getting her needs met. Consequently, as Janice stabilized and her larger support system reinforced new patterns of learning and reality testing, she behaved in more appropriate and assertive ways.

With complicated cases such as this, a team approach may be more effective than relying on a sole practitioner. Without a therapeutic support system, therapists can become stuck in the clients' system and become lost or mired. However, on occasion, therapeutic support systems can be counterproductive. Keiley used her therapeutic support systems—the DSS caseworker and the HMO case conference—appropriately and productively. In this regard, because of the DSS's specific involvement with the couple, Keiley was able to access the agency's resources to positively influence the family. For example, in the fourth session it was very helpful to Keiley to have the DSS caseworker present to caution the couple about the possibility of the children being removed from the home rather than having to do so herself. This allowed the transference to remain undisturbed, made everyone aware of the requirements of therapy, and established limits and boundaries for safety.

WHAT I MIGHT HAVE DONE DIFFERENTLY

From my theoretical perspective, one potential problem I perceived was that Keiley had not consciously conceptualized as transference the interactions between her and the family. As a result, Keiley's actions might have reinforced Janice's defenses. Without Keiley's honest, supportive, trustworthy attitude that conveyed a sense of advocacy toward the family, individual members might also have increased their resistance and distrust because they had experienced the environment as detached, unresponsive, and uncaring. In such situations I believe it is essential that therapists provide acceptance without joining clients in all of their judgments. Although this may seem intuitive and common sense, the degree of chaos and destructive testing done by some clients like Janice exerts a great deal of pressure on therapists and require that they stay out of their own countertransference. This is not easily done. Some indication exists that Keiley may have been confused or distressed by Janice's irrational rejection of her for drugs. Had Keiley conceptualized the interactions as transference, doing so would have depersonalized them, and made them conscious in the therapeutic conversations, interactions, and therapy in general.

Often, the transference is disrupted when a therapist fails to provide the "perfect" empathy or sensitivity expected by clients. For example, in the third session, Keiley said something insightful, correctly interpreting a situation or confronting an issue Janice had with her spiritual sickness. However, at that point Janice became upset that Keiley was not completely tuned into her. Although Keiley intended to be compassionate and understanding, Janice interpreted her comment as "too close to home" and pulled away. Based on her past experiences with significant others, Janice may have expected Keiley to discount her experiences and perceptions. This expectation contributed to Janice's fear that Keiley would represent her to others as crazy. Given Janice's fear, it was important that Keiley affirm Janice's impressions as real, accurate, and present. Keiley also needed to be very clear with Janice about what she would say regarding the revelations that Janice had shared with her. For example, how would Keiley represent Janice to DSS? What would be done now that Janice had revealed the secrets? Once Janice believed that Keiley understood and validated her experiences, she could be more open to looking at them and confronting her monsters.

In the fourth session, Janice experienced some disruptions in the transference. This disruption contributed to Janice's temporary regression to previous modes of dealing with relationships and resulted in her defensively distorted and exaggerated demands upon Keiley. When that manipulation was ineffective, Janice defensively distanced, withdrew, and complained that Keiley was useless. In doing so she set in motion a "rejection dance" (Wollf, 1988). Such disruptions in transference can lead to a need for the therapist to restore the transference through interpretation. At that point I would have descriptively confronted the issue and interpreted the closeness in some way. For example, I might have expressed appreciation for their willingness to trust me and to allow me to see their relationship being stuck or seeing their terror. Keiley did not discuss how she moved from being stuck to the couple's recommitting to therapy. Rather, she intervened in ways that addressed the transition and succeeded in reestablishing the transference. Generally, the therapist will search for clues that explain the breach in the relationship and communicate understanding and caring to the client. Keiley did just that. She conveyed to Janice the sense that she was important and that Keiley was taking her seriously.

Healing experiences in psychoanalytic treatment require: (1) a feeling of being understood by another and (2) a sense of one's own efficacy regarding the other (Wolff, 1988). Accordingly, Keiley examined the function of Janice's emotions and the manner in which they were expressed, and enabled Janice and the family to have an "authentic relationship." For example, when Janice felt and acted helpless, she may have been protecting Alan so that he could feel helpful and powerful. This enabled him to avoid feeling and expressing helplessness or anger toward himself and her. During the critical incident, Keiley was true to herself and to Janice. During this interaction, Janice was able to experience her own efficacy in eliciting an attuned response, of having made a dent, of being somebody—a confirmed self.

Because of her history of emotional difficulties, Janice was at risk at several levels. She had not been able to contain the chaos surrounding her life. As a result, she chose to cope with her stresses in ways that released her anxiety or protected her from experiencing it. In dealing with such clients I believe it is important that therapists evaluate the danger to their clients based on an accurate history. If the ability to create safety is limited and resources are scarce, it is appropriate to focus therapy on solving problems until safety is possible. In this regard, it is an important maxim of psychotherapy that the manner in which clients have handled previous trauma is predictive of how well they might handle future problems.

REVIEW OF THE CRITICAL INCIDENT

Janice was in the throes of dealing with her unmet needs in her usual manner (self-medicating with drugs and alcohol or other mood modifiers). Although she may not have consciously expected Keiley to appear (at her home) as scheduled, the transference was present; Janice may have harbored at least an unconscious expectation that Keiley (as parent) would play out her role. The possibilities were that (1) Keiley would be accountable, caring, supportive, responsible, and arrive at the house or (2) Keiley would not fulfill her responsibilities and promises about coming at the appointed time. Based on Janice's past experiences, and especially in light of the events of that day, Janice predicted that a much greater probability existed of the latter expectation occurring. At this point, Janice unconsciously set up the circumstances to open an opportunity for her to make new meaning of old events. Because Janice had a positive transference to Keiley and Keiley had been calling to remind her of future appointments, Janice tested Keiley to see if she really was the caring, responsible, and committed individual that she appeared to be. She was attempting to ascertain whether Keiley was deserving of her trust.

When Keiley was invited into Janice's home, Janice was willing to reveal the extent of the unmet needs she was experiencing. She may have been responding to the confidence Keiley showed in her (e.g., showing up at the house unannounced). Keiley's demonstration of confidence in Janice challenged Janice to confront her expectations about relationships and to confront the consequences of her behaviors. Keiley's approach provided Janice an opportunity to look at her issues, needs, and responses in the presence of a safe relationship. Doing so provided Janice new reality testing that revealed new limits and boundaries which increased her own sense of safety (as well as for her whole family). In the presence of the "safe" therapeutic relationship with Keiley, Janice faced herself in the present and discovered that her old schemas for relationships were not applicable to her relationship with Keiley. As a result, Janice was able to ask for and get her needs met in alternative ways.

In this critical event, the issues of accountability, dependency, and intimacy were all present in a positive and healthy way. Hope existed that the problems in Janice's past relationships were more about significant others (e.g., mother, father) than about herself. In Janice's relationship with Keiley hope existed that she might be cared about (by Keiley) whether or not she took care of Keiley. Hope also existed that she could be dependent yet not be rejected as she felt she was by her significant others (by her mother, for example). Janice had presented to Keiley a history of times when she felt that injustice occurred in her life. She also had provided Keiley with a picture of her unconscious through her dreams. Keiley had witnessed and respected Janice's world and responded to her in a positive, appropriate way while still holding her accountable for her choices. This was a new and very healing experience for Janice.

CONCLUDING THOUGHTS

Clients do us the great honor of trusting us with their innermost secrets and terrors. Often they are unable to articulate their issues and usually act them out instead. Healing begins when such clients are able to reexperience the trauma of their lives in a safe and contained setting. As therapists, when we are able to provide clients the kinds of therapeutic environments and relationships that can help to facilitate their restructuring, growth and change occur. This case of Janice and Allen and their assorted monsters poignantly demonstrates the power of reexperience—transference of feelings and expectations onto a safe, caring, trustworthy individual who responds (even in the face of anger, rejection, and antagonism) in ways that are accepting, responsible, genuine, and kind. A kinder, gentler response!

REFERENCE

Wollf, C. (1988). *Treating the self.* New York: The Guilford Press.

CASE 14

Therapist or Firefighter?

Marc N. Barney
Janie K. Long
Adi Granit

Therapist Backgrounds

Thirty-one years old, Caucasian, male, MA, six years MFT practice.
Forty-six years old, Caucasian, female, PhD, sixteen years MFT practice.
Thirty years old, Israeli, female, MA, six years MFT practice.

Practice Setting

University family therapy clinic.

Client Characteristics

Steve (mid-forties), his wife Mary (mid-forties), and their two sons, Derek (age sixteen) and Peter (age fourteen), were a white middle-class family; Peter was the IP. Steve was a business man and Mary an educator completing an EdD in educational administration. Derek was a high school junior with above-average grades and was a class officer; Peter was a high school sophomore. The family came to therapy because Peter was disrespectful of his parents and teachers, in trouble with the law, doing poorly in school, and being contentious at home. As a younger child Peter had excelled in sports. Compared to some of his peers, Peter was late entering puberty. Mary and Steve believed that Peter's delayed development was a significant contributor to his behavioral difficulties.

Length of Treatment

The family was seen over an eighteen-month period in two separate phases of therapy for a total of twenty-five concurrent individual, couple, and family sessions beginning in the fall of 1997. The critical incident occurred in Session 4 of the second phase of therapy (the tenth session overall).

Therapeutic Models

We used an integrative approach in working with this family; our therapeutic techniques were culled from several models, including Haley's strategic, Satir's experiential, Minuchin's structural, reflecting team, and MRI brief.

PRESENTING PROBLEM

The family initially presented for therapy because of home- and school-related behavioral difficulties with Peter. Mary was seen for two individual sessions in which she expressed concern that Peter was "beginning to move down a path toward greater difficulties." Specifically, he behaved impulsively, had been diagnosed as "hyperactive," had been prescribed Ritalin, and was susceptible to negative peer pressures. In addition, three years earlier, Peter had been placed on two years' probation for stealing. Asked about the therapeutic outcome she wanted, Mary identified cessation of Peter's swearing, being less impulsive, and learning to "check himself before he acts," as reasonable outcomes for the family. Mary also identified Peter's poor grades, lack of respect for authority (especially his parents), difficulty getting out of bed in the mornings, and swearing at others, especially Mary, as additional concerns.

THE FIRST PHASE OF THERAPY

In the first two individual sessions with Mary, the assigned therapist (Barney) approached therapy from the MRI brief-therapy perspective and, as a result, did not believe it was necessary to meet with the identified patient. Treatment focused on Mary and her concerns; at that juncture, she appeared to be the family member most upset with Peter's behaviors and most prepared to do something about it.

After the second session, it was clear that seeing Mary and Steve conjointly would be important to gain an understanding and an assessment of the strengths of their parental subsystem. At this juncture, I considered including elements of strategic therapy (Haley, 1980) in working with this family. Steve and Mary were both present for the third session, during which we explored the dynamics of the parental subsystem. Interestingly, although

Mary and Steve reported unanimity in dealing with Peter's behaviors, I silently questioned whether this couple's in-session show of unanimity was concealing what actually occurred at home in dealing with Peter's behaviors or whether they truly were unified in disciplining their son.

Mary and Steve did not report any conflict in their marital relationship. Consequently, I explored with them their attempted solutions to Peter's behavioral problems, with special attention to what was attempted to extinguish the offending behaviors and what had not worked. The parents reported that they had grounded Peter, reasoned with him, and on occasion Steve physically shook him. They revealed that of all the sanctions, shaking Peter appeared to be most effective in curbing his behaviors. Steve was emphatic that shaking Peter was not something he liked to do; he did not like to use physical force. Concerned that shaking Peter might constitute physical abuse, I asked in-depth questions about how shaking worked, in what contexts it occurred, and the duration of it. The parents' answers persuaded me that the shaking did not constitute physical abuse. I then asked Mary and Steve to provide an example of a typical situation in which Peter's misbehavior occurred. In a typical situation, Derek would say something and Peter would be offended. Peter then would verbally attack Derek. Mary would intervene to attempt to calm them down, but her efforts frequently were futile. At that juncture, Steve would intervene; occasionally, his efforts would result in calming down the boys.

At the end of this session, I normalized the situation. I told Mary and Steve that Peter was a teenager in a "transition phase" and was attempting to establish his own identity by exploring how he could be different from the family. The challenge for them as parents was to develop appropriate behavioral boundaries for Peter while concurrently allowing him to begin to spread his wings. I offered to join them and form a team to help them to get more of what they wanted from Peter while allowing him the freedom to develop into an adult. They accepted my offer. Despite their assent, the couple canceled the next session and promised to reschedule. After several unsuccessful attempts to reschedule the couple, I closed the file without knowing the status of the family's problems.

A few months after closing the case, I met Mary while shopping. She informed me that the family's situation had improved moderately; she, however, wanted to return to therapy. She said that she was very busy because she had begun to work on an EdD. Accordingly, she would reschedule another therapy session when time permitted. A few months later, I met Mary again. She said that she had been meaning to contact me to schedule another session. I informed her that I would be continuing at the university for my PhD, and she promised to call me soon to reschedule. In October 1998, Mary called to schedule an appointment. I decided that this time I would approach the family's problems from a different theoretical perspective and

I would involve the entire family rather than only the adults. As I began the second phase of therapy with this family, I worked as a part of a treatment team and incorporated elements of various treatment models including experiential, strategic, structural, reflecting team, and MRI.

THE THERAPEUTIC SITUATION PRIOR
TO THE CRITICAL INCIDENT

In this second phase of treatment, the team speculated that the marital relationship may not be as strong as it had been portrayed. Based on that assumption, we requested that each family member prepare a list of what he or she would like to see changed in the family. Members were instructed not to share their completed lists with one another at home. Instead, each list would be discussed at the next session in the presence of the therapist.

At the next session Mary was absent, but the other members shared their individual wishes about what each wanted to see changed in the family. Derek began the exercise and expressed a wish to see more collective familial decision making, to see all family members earn their keep and not expect anything without working for it. He also wished that family members would not act without a good reason and that the home environment would be less hostile and emotionally warmer. Derek's first wish—increased unity between parents and siblings—was unclear to the team. Asked whether he meant that the parents should have more unity with each other or that the children should have more unity with their parents, he quickly said, "Both." In response, Peter shouted, "Shut up, Derek. There's no problem between Mom and Dad." The team viewed this transaction as very important to the family dynamics but did not comment.

Peter shared his list next. He wished for more equality among family members, greater acceptance of and less focus on past mistakes, more respect and validation; he also wished for his parents to keep the promises they made to him. Steve shared next and wished for increased respect among family members, for family members to take pride in their home, and for a greater focus on positives. Although Mary did not attend this session, she provided her list of what she wished to change in the family. She wanted to see more (emotional) warmth in the family, more (family) unity, and better (intra-familial) communication. Interestingly, Derek rather than Steve was the bearer of Mary's list. That Mary entrusted her list to her son rather than to her husband heightened the team's suspicion that the marital relationship may be experiencing strains, contrary to how it initially was portrayed. The team also speculated that Derek might have usurped Steve's husband/father position in the family.

At the end of the session, I processed the contents of the four lists with the team and invited Steve and his sons to listen to the team's discussion of the session that had just ended. I sat in the observation room with the family and observed them as they listened to the team's discussion. The team noted that the family appeared to be polarized: Mary and Derek had a very strong relationship and Steve and Derek had a good relationship. They also observed that the relationship between Steve and Derek did not appear to be as strong as the relationship between Mary and Derek. Not unexpectedly, Peter's relationship with all family members appeared to be strained. Given all that had transpired to this point, the team questioned whether the marital relationship between Mary and Steve was viable. When the team disclosed that Derek had wished for greater unity between his parents, Peter verbally attacked Derek. He said, "See, Derek, you should not have gone there! You know they don't want others—" Before Peter could complete his sentence, Derek cut him off: "Be quiet!" Steve observed the interaction but said nothing. I speculated that Mary and Steve were the "they" to whom the boys were referring, and Peter, being cognizant that Derek might have exposed the possible strains or distance in the marital relationship, was attempting to protect his parents. Unfortunately, the hour ended and the team was unable to follow through with this speculation. During the follow-up processing of the session, the team decided that in the next session we would ask the family which member had briefed Mary about the events of the session. Our collective prediction was Derek. Accordingly, during the next session, one of the first questions asked of the family was which member briefed Mary about the events of the session; as predicted, it was Derek. Again, the team was struck with the dynamic which clearly placed Derek in the husband/father position in the family and placed Steve in a peripheral position.

EVENTS LEADING TO THE CRITICAL INCIDENT

A few months prior to returning to therapy, Mary had entered a doctoral degree program in addition to her full-time job as a teacher in the same high school attended by Derek and Peter. These two activities consumed a significant portion of Mary's time and energies. As a result, time spent with other family members was limited. In this regard, Peter often complained in therapy that his mother, "was never around anymore." Because Mary worked in the same high school her sons attended she was aware of the other teachers' complaints about Peter's behaviors and also was an available target for Peter's in-school misbehavior and tantrums; she admitted feeling embarrassed at work as a result of Peter's misbehavior.

During this period, Steve lost his job and experienced much difficulty securing a new position. When he did find a new job, he worked hard to establish his value to keep the new job. As a team, we wondered about the effects of Steve's job loss on his relationship with Mary. We also wondered if anyone else in the family other than Peter was concerned about the amount of time that Mary's activities demanded.

While Mary and Steve were making important career decisions, Derek entered his senior year in high school and was preparing to graduate and eventually attend college. In addition, perhaps because of his parents' difficulty in managing Peter's behaviors, Derek increasingly assumed a parent-like role with Peter. On several occasions, in the presence of his parents, Derek asserted that he knew a better way to parent Peter than did his parents. Predictably, Peter resented Derek's parental role in his life. Initially Mary and Steve did not discourage Derek's parenting of Peter or his parental position in relation to them. They—especially Steve—were doubtful that they could change the situation on their own. The team continued to speculate that an emotional distance might exist between Mary and Steve, evidenced by their in-session behaviors. Specifically, their eye contact with each other was poor, and Steve often sat with his body turned away from Mary and the therapist. In addition, they rarely sat next to each other and were not affectionate with each other. Given this situation, therapy appeared to be stuck, and I was beginning to feel stuck because of the lack of therapeutic progress with the family. In response to this situation, the team formulated the idea that I should sculpt the family to uncover some of the covert family dynamics. We hoped that in doing so Derek's parental position and the emotional distance between the parents would surface. We were uncertain whether the family would respond but believed that whatever happened would give us new information with which to work. This was the primary therapist's (Barney) first sculpting exercise; as a result, the supervisor actively coached him via the phone from behind the mirror.

THE CRITICAL INCIDENT

To get the family involved in the sculpting experience, I placed each member in a pose that represented how the team experienced the family. Derek was posed standing on a chair with his mother to his left and his father to the right. I placed his hands on his parents' shoulders. Peter was posed in front of the other three family members a short distance away and facing them. This placement had a profound effect on the family evidenced by Mary's tears, Steve's perceptible discomfort, and Peter's hunching of his shoulders and later crouching in the corner on the floor. I asked each family member how he or she felt to be in the position that he or she occupied in the sculpture. Mary became very emotional and stated that she wanted Peter to be with the rest of the family and for Derek not to be up on the chair. She also said that she felt very sad about what the sculpture represented. Next, Steve revealed that he felt helpless in his position. His body was turned slightly away from the rest of the group, and he appeared very uncomfortable and distant. Derek said he did not like being up in the chair; he wanted to be on more equal terms with the rest of the family. Despite his objections, the team perceived Derek to be the most comfortable in his sculpted position. Peter said he did not care one way or another about his position in the corner. However, although he verbally protested that he did not care, his body language betrayed his feelings; he was as upset with the sculpted portrayal of the family as were his brother and parents.

Our intent was to have individual members refashion the family as each would like to have seen it. Unfortunately, only Mary had time to present her portrayal of the family. She had Steve stand to her right and she held his hand. Derek was to her left and was kneeling on one knee. Peter was to his father's right and also on one knee. The family was arranged in a circle, and Mary instructed all members to hold hands. Interestingly, Steve appeared to experience the most difficulty holding hands. He looked very awkward and uncomfortable holding his wife's hand and leaned away from his sons. Derek stated that he did not want to have to "parent" his brother but that at times he had to do so because his father was not there. Despite Derek's expressed wish to resign his parental role, he responded in a parental fashion to a remark Peter made immediately following the sculpting exercise.

THE AFTERMATH OF THE CRITICAL INCIDENT

The team had intended to show the family a videotape of this session at our next meeting, but Steve did not attend that session. The team wondered about the meaning of Steve's absence. We may have read too much into his absence, but it was interesting that following such an intense session the family member who appeared to be most upset by the sculpting was absent. Following that session, I changed supervisors, returned to using an MRI brief model, and worked with the family without the benefit of a reflecting team. This change proved to be therapeutically ineffective with this family, and I again felt frustrated that the family and I were not making any progress in therapy. Rather, I now felt like a firefighter putting out the new fires that the family brought into each session. I believed that I should go in whatever direction the family took me despite my hunch that the fires really were smoke screens that the family was using to distract me from the substantive issues: the emotional distance between Mary and Steve and its impact upon the family's functioning. I continued in my efforts to extinguish the fires as they were brought to therapy. After a few sessions, I felt like I was becoming the family's homeostatic mechanism keeping them functioning just enough to stay together while they avoided the core problems.

Three months later, I changed supervisors and began working again with the reflecting team and using a structural approach with the family. During this phase of therapy, the team's concerns about the quality of the marital relationship remained high despite Mary and Steve's refusal to acknowledge that possibility and confront the issues. Instead, the parents persisted in their belief that Peter was the problem. However, the couple's in-session behaviors, e.g., poor eye contact and limited communication, belied their verbal disqualification about the strains in the marital relationship.

DISCUSSION

The Role of the Critical Incident in Getting Therapy Unstuck

At the time the family participated in the sculpting exercise, neither the impact nor long-term consequences of the activities that occurred within the session were immediately evident or comprehensible. However, as therapy continued, it became evident that the most meaningful work with the family occurred when I was able to reference information culled from the sculpting session. Although the critical incident neither fully unstuck therapy nor had that immediate "miracle" effect representative of a critical incident, it was a turning point in the therapeutic process and a catalyst that created small but substantive changes and a significant ripple effect for the parent-child, sibling, and spousal relationships. The effects of the critical incident were also obviously interrupted by the change of supervisors and the loss of the reflecting team in the middle of therapy. Clearly, the critical incident did percolate the family's system and contribute to the eventual removal of emotional restrictions and barriers to meaningful changes and relationships in this family.

Whereas previously the parents and Derek were mired in a nonproductive undeclared battle for the right to parent Peter, and Peter appeared to have been invested in exhibiting as many maladaptive behaviors as he could conjure up, post critical incident the parents, Derek, and Peter were able to resolve their issues by using information referenced from the session in which the critical incident occurred. I was then able to resign my position as the family's firefighter and return to being a therapist who helped the family, specifically the parents, to revitalize their marital relationship, reclaim their rightful parental authority over their sons, especially Peter, and help Derek to return to being a typical teenager rather than being Peter's surrogate parent.

The Implications of the Critical Incident for Therapy

The effects of the critical incident on therapy were more a whisper than a bang. Although limited and not immediate, the critical incident was important as a catalyst that contributed immensely to the eventual changes in this family. The events of the sculpting session provided the team and me with some validation that our collective hunches were correct or at least plausible; the marital relationship may not have been as solid as the couple had portrayed it to be. The critical incident also provided a glimpse at the coalition between Mary and Derek. More important, the critical incident pushed family members to confront their feelings about the family's functioning despite the adults' denial about any rifts in their marital relationship. Clearly, each member's needs were not effectively being met, and they all wanted the family to be more responsive to their individual needs. However, in the absence of parental leadership, both Derek and Peter behaved in their own unique way—Peter misbehaving; Derek believing that he had to step in for parents who may have been immobilized by their own relationship problems.

THE OUTCOME OF THERAPY

Following the critical incident, therapy was minimally unstuck. But the issue that brought the family to therapy, i.e., Peter's maladaptive behaviors, remained unchanged. As a result, the family continued in therapy for approximately eighteen more sessions after the critical incident and addressed issues specific to Peter's maladaptive behaviors, Derek usurpation of parental authority in attempting to parent Peter, the breakdown of the parental executive system, and difficulties in Mary and Steve's marital relationship.

During this period, because Mary and Steve continued not to acknowledge existence of a marital problem yet elected to see Peter as the problem, I accepted their definition of the problem as well as the team's definition that all may not be well with the marital relationship. Accordingly, I agreed with Mary and Steve that Peter was on the road to self-destruction and suggested that they needed to unite in disciplining Peter. Subsequent to my acceptance of Mary and Steve's definition of the problem, they became less resistant. I was then able to help them to pool their individual strengths and to use that strength as a resource to strengthen their parental executive system, present a more united front to their sons, and actively disrupt Derek's parenting of Peter.

Later in therapy, in response to a challenge by Peter that Mary needed to divorce Steve, Mary circuitously acknowledged that the marital relationship could have been experiencing strains. Because she was not explicit in her admission, I used information from the sculpting session to further emphasize the impact of the strained marital relationship on Derek and Peter's perceptions that the parental relationship was in trouble. I reasoned that whether or not Mary and Steve perceived their relationship to be strained, if Derek and Peter believed it was, their behaviors may have been maladaptive attempts to keep their parents together. Framing Derek and Peter's behaviors as benevolent rather than malevolent provided Mary and Steve with a different way to see the problem and also gave them explicit permission to confront the strains in their marital relationship and to do something about it. Accordingly, I suggested that the couple begin to spend more time together at home and to go out on dates. As a result, they began to talk with each other in front of their sons, went on a date, and later went away for the weekend without their sons. Derek appeared very excited about the date; this reaction both surprised and pleased his parents.

As time went on, the parents became increasingly more affectionate with each other in sessions, had more eye contact, and communicated directly with each other. Concurrently, as their relationship improved, they observed small but perceptible positive changes in Peter's behaviors. Mary and Steve expressed the belief that these changes were perhaps the result of Derek graduating and being at home less. They also reasoned that Peter was trying harder to change his behaviors because he wanted to get his driver's license and a car. Despite not crediting their changed relationship for the improvements, they never fully denied that the changes might have been due to their improved marital relationship.

The Termination of Therapy

Barney's last session in the clinic was the final session of therapy. In that session, Steve and Mary sat closely next to each other and often touched each other. They reported that life was much quieter at home and credited Peter's improved behaviors as a contributor. They were emphatic that therapy had been helpful for them and acknowledged that their relationship was now stronger. They also recognized that their improved relationship had helped to restore balance in their home.

Follow-Up

Neither the couple nor the family were contacted following Barney's departure. In the final session the couple was told that another team member would be happy to meet with them if the need arose. However, based on their reports at the terminating session and having had no further communication with them, we accept that the quality of life for all family members continues to be satisfactory.

REFERENCE

Haley, J. (1980). *Leaving home: The therapy of disturbed young people*. New York: McGraw-Hill.

Commentary

Farmer, Naturalist, Environmentalist

Suzanne Midori Hanna

Commentator Background

Fifty-one years old, Asian, female, PhD, twenty-five years MFT practice.

Practice Settings

University-based family therapy training program; limited private practice.

Theoretical Perspective

I practice from an integrative family therapy approach but my preferred therapeutic model is developmental-interactional and combines maps of relationships and transitions (visual time lines and genograms) with structural-strategic-intergenerational interventions. My interventions also are informed by Ericksonian and social construction modes of thought.

This case presents an excellent example of a therapist who openly shared his working hypotheses with a family then provided an opportunity for family members to respond. As is typical for clinical cases, the earlier stages of the therapeutic process set the stage for the most important work to evolve. Consequently, beginning with the sculpting process, Barney broke new ground, dug up the dirt, turned it over, planted seeds, and then let the field settle to produce a new crop of changes.

QUESTIONS FOR THE THERAPISTS

My questions are specific to the first phase of therapy and focus upon the process by which Steve became involved in the therapeutic process. We hear the voice of Barney, but little is said about how either Mary or Steve felt about the therapeutic process. How was Steve invited? Why did he come?

What were his intentions, thoughts, and feelings? If Mary was the customer, how did she feel about including Steve? Was Steve a customer for something and did Barney discover the root of Steve's customership? These questions remain unanswered because of the limited information provided in the case report. I, however, believe that such questions are worth asking to discover what was this family's, but especially the couple's, experience of therapy at that time.

I also have questions about Barney's nonverbal and verbal messages to the family. It appears that Barney preferred to emphasize interpretations of the nonverbal messages. However, doing so can be problematic because reality is constructed solely upon assumptions. For example, with regards to Derek, the assumptive statement was made that, "Despite his objections, the team perceived Derek to be the most comfortable of any family member." With regards to Peter, it was stated, "although he verbally protested that he did not care, his body language betrayed his feelings." Interestingly, the reflecting team appeared to have privileged one message level and not the other with greater validity. I can only wonder why one message level is considered more "real" than another. Is it possible that discrepancies between message levels are genuine dilemmas between which family members are torn in two directions? In my clinical experiences, I have found the presence of dilemmas to be a powerful influence on clients' freedom to move toward or away from change. This may explain the effectiveness of strategies such as split opinions, some paradoxical interventions, and Greek choruses. When constructed to address the actual dilemma of a person as he or she experiences it, these interventions are the highest form of "systemic empathy" we can achieve (Hanna, 1995).

Given the strengths of this case, I found myself wondering about Barney's tone in describing the process. I interpreted his tone as one of disappointment because he made a series of references to the couple's behaviors which are interpreted as a strained marital relationship and resistance. It is unfortunate that Barney appeared to be so discounting of the process that resulted in such a positive outcome. I wonder where he developed such expectations? Could it be that although many roads lead to Rome, Barney was disappointed that his preferred road, i.e., addressing the marital relationship directly, was not the one the family had chosen? Or was it because an immediate change in the family's approach to the presenting problem did not occur? Based on my reading of the case report up to that point, I did not expect a positive outcome because Barney appeared to be apologizing for the absence of a "miracle" and the couple's resistance to addressing the marital relationship.

THE THERAPEUTIC RELATIONSHIP:
CRUX OF THE PROCESS

Barney stated that "Mary and Steve did not report any conflict in their marital relationship." Despite this, however, he had unasked questions about the quality of their marital relationship. What was the perspective from which those questions arose? What influenced those lingering questions? Unlike Barney, I was less interested in the couple's marital relationship and more interested in the therapist-client relationship and in knowing more about Mary and Steve as people. For example, what did the couple think of Barney as a therapist? Could they detect his unasked questions? What was this couple like as human beings? What were their hopes, fears, and dilemmas?

With regards to the client-therapist relationship, one answer came in the second phase of treatment when the family elected to return to therapy with Barney. I believe that when clients reenter therapy with a previous therapist of record, their doing so is a credit to the previous client-therapist relationship. From a reader's perspective, the case report understated the events of the first phase of treatment. Clearly, something was positive, hopeful, and comfortable about the family's initial experience with Barney, although he may not have perceived the experience as such since he did not report any progress in the first phase. I wonder whether the normalizing process at the end of the first phase helped Mary to lessen her anxieties about Peter. Perhaps this normalizing process also was validating from Steve's perspective and the couple actually relaxed. Conversely, I also wondered if something did not fit for this couple. Barney's proposal that Mary and Steve work as a team may have been too big a leap for the couple if they already were emotionally disengaged. However, I believe that the positive relationship with Barney won out and the couple returned to therapy more willing to risk another round.

The second phase of therapy immediately made room for multiple voices, especially the voices of the males members of the family. If Mary had been the customer in the first phase, Steve, Derek, and Peter were engaged in expanded possibilities during the second phase. From a gender perspective, the engagement of the males felt liberating and equalizing to me. By adding their voices to Mary's, the men in the family also were explicitly assuming some active responsibility for the well-being of the family.

THE CRITICAL INCIDENT

General Observations

During the turning-point session, the sculpting intervention appears to have accomplished two ends. First, it enabled Barney to express his working hypotheses about the family's organization. In this regard, Breunlin, Schwartz, and MacKune-Karrer (1997) have suggested that organization is the family's leadership, balance, and harmony. However, contrary to Barney, I do not believe that the sculpting exercise uncovered the family's covert dynamics. Instead, I believe that by participating in the sculpting, the family had an opportunity to know Barney's thoughts and to respond to them. The nonverbal sleuthing on the part of the reflecting team was over. The family could now directly validate or refute Barney's hypotheses.

Barney reports that "despite Derek's expressed wish to resign his parental role, he continued to respond in a parental fashion. Barney could have manifested "systemic empathy" for Derek's dilemma by commenting upon the difficulty attendant to resigning his parental role and the negative side effects that can accompany such a change. Typically role shifts are not discrete events; they usually are gradual transformations. Consequently, I did not expect Derek to change his behavior simply because he said he wanted to do so. Accordingly, I would want to explore the pros and cons of a possible role shift and to help Derek to develop a plan for how he might cope with the adjustment to it all. Doing so would have allowed me to honor Derek's verbal message, and I also would have been able to test my interpretation of his nonverbal behavior. How he responded to exploring the pros and cons would help me validate or disqualify my hypothesis about his nonverbal behavior.

Similar assumptions about Mary and Steve's nonverbal behavior stimulated my thinking. Was this a stage for them? Had it always been this way? When did things between them change? What kept Barney from exploring the team's assumptions about the couple's nonverbal behaviors and from letting the couple validate or clarify the meaning of their behaviors? The key to these conversations is having a supportive relationship that allows Barney to be curious and hopeful. The case can be made that the solution to this problem may lie in a rediscovery of Mary and Steve's previous problem-solving patterns. Oftentimes when clients are confronted with difficulties they tend to focus on the negative of the situation and forget about successful strategies they had employed in the past to overcome other life problems.

Serendipitous or Deliberate Intervention

My commentary of this case uses the editor's definition of a critical incident as a "serendipitous turning point" or "unplanned occurrence," and I looked for the surprises in the case instead of the deliberate interventions. Accordingly, I see the sculpting of the family as a planned intervention rather than as a critical incident. Thus I was not surprised by the family's response to the sculpting exercise because of the many indications that they were uncomfortable about addressing conflict directly.

On the other hand, however, I consider other therapeutic occurrences to be significant and unplanned. The first of these occurred in an earlier session from which Mary was absent and Derek shared his perceptions about the parental marriage. During that session, Steve, Derek, and Peter were listening to the reflecting team when Peter blurted out his thoughts and feelings in protection of his parents' dilemmas. I believe that intervention had a major effect upon the therapeutic process and might not have occurred if Mary had been present. Each son presented a different side of the family dilemma, but Barney did not focus on either Derek and Peter's comments. At that juncture, it would have been an opportune time to address the quality of the parental marriage from both Derek and Peter's perspectives. For example, both Derek and Peter could have been asked, "Has it always seemed this way to you?" If not, "When did your perceptions begin to form?" The following week, Mary could have been briefed about what had transpired in that session and then included in the process.

I perceived Steve's absence from the session immediately following the sculpting exercise as another unplanned occurrence. In that session the team speculated about the meaning of Steve's absence, but the case report is silent about how the absence was addressed or explored. If it was not addressed, why not? Again, I believe that that occurrence could also have been a springboard for meaningful therapeutic conversations.

WHAT I MIGHT HAVE DONE DIFFERENTLY

Since Derek and Peter had acknowledged the presence of parental marital discord, I would have explored the meaning of their comments with the team behind the mirror. If need be, I would have respected the couple's desire to avoid the topic by acknowledging their hesitance and exploring other aspects of their relationship, such as some of their best times together. Doing so would have allowed me to talk about the couple's marital strain without directly addressing it. To that end I would have initiated the conversation by examining a different and positive time in the couple's relationship. I would have asked when things changed in the relationship and explored specific events that influenced those changes. I also would have explored the couple's fears regarding what would happen if they talked openly about their marital strains. Doing so would be predicated upon my belief that if the problem is situational, a review of the past would help the couple to gain perspective. If the problem was historical or chronic, a review of the past would help the couple to identify the foundational time period or the specific relational task that never was completed.

THE AFTERMATH OF THERAPY:
GENERAL COMMENTS

It seemed a shame that Mary, the customer, was afforded the first (and only) opportunity to present her wishes for the family. In my clinical work, when I have identified the customer, I try to discover what the noncustomers want and work to engage them until they are equally invested in defining the direction and goals of our work. Brooks (1998) makes some compelling arguments in his summary of "Why Traditional Men Hate Psychotherapy." He traces the social construction of masculinity and notes how the practices of psychotherapy are disempowering to women yet also drive men away. He also argues that the culture of men and what fits for them in psychotherapy is different from what fits for women.

If we hypothesize that Steve was uncomfortable with a feminized construction of the family and the therapeutic process, we might see evidence in later sessions that the pragmatic, indirect approach to the couple's relationship suited Steve well. Bravo! The executive branch of the family held out in a united front until therapy suited their unique needs. I enjoy cases like this in which we can see how the family helps us as therapists to honor their individuality. Erickson and Rossi (1979) have stated that resistance is merely an expression of the client's uniqueness. Bravo again! Barney was flexible enough to fit with the family's developmental needs. He simultaneously and unconditionally accepted Mary and Steve's as well as the team's definition of the problem. This is a "both/and" approach, which fits well in this situation. He also addresses the parents' concerns and waits for an indirect opportunity for the team's concerns to be addressed. That time arrived when Peter challenged his parents about their marriage. By waiting until a family member raised the issue, Barney maintained a meta position toward the problem instead of entering into a power struggle with Mary and Steve about the definition of the problem. The latter would have been an example of the solution becoming the problem. Barney wisely kept Mary and Steve's reality in focus until it was time for them to address Peter's perceptions.

Defining the Problem: Accepting Clients Where They Are

In his discussion about the outcome of therapy, Barny addresses several critical parts to the therapeutic process. For me, this sequence appeared to be the most critical of all the incidents. Here Barney takes an important step by unconditionally accepting Mary and Steve's definition of the problem. Based on the preceding commentary, Barney's doing so appeared to be an unplanned turning point. The result? The couple "became less resistant and I [Barney] was able to help them to pool their individual strengths." Again, Barney's unconditional acceptance led to yet another unplanned occurrence when Peter suggested that Mary needed to divorce Steve. At that juncture,

Barney responded to Peter's comments by addressing the "appearance" of the marital relationship. More important, Barney did not share the team's observations about Mary and Steve's marriage. Instead, he asked the couple directly about their sons' perceptions of the parental marriage. That was the perfect angle. Barney's doing so was acceptable to Mary and Steve and addressed all family members' dilemmas without assigning blame. His framing of Derek and Peter's behaviors as "benevolent" also is a good example of Stanton's (1981) notion of "ascribing noble intentions." Rather than viewing this framing of Derek and Peter's behaviors as a technique, I consider it an important validation of the dilemmas that are inherent in the family's presenting problem. The misbehaving child (Peter) is in a bind and is attempting to solve a problem. The therapist's task is to determine and to understand what the specific problem is that the attempted solution is addressing and to help all family members to address it appropriately and effectively in a face-saving way.

From my perspective, this latter sequence is the real critical incident of this case. Despite my earlier speculations about what might have happened if Derek and Peter's perceptions were addressed sooner, this sequence seemed timely because Barney had come full circle in his approach to the definition of the problem and, ironically, Peter had shifted his position from protecting his parents' dilemmas to confronting his own dilemma; he appeared ready for Mary to confront Steve directly.

CONCLUDING THOUGHTS

This case report raises important questions about the influence of one therapeutic model or another upon the outcome of therapy. With this case, the process shifted from solution-focused and brief interventions to an integrative model, back to an MRI brief model, and back to an integrative mode of structural family therapy with a reflecting team. When Barney discusses feeling like a firefighter, he does so as if firefighting is not a legitimate role for a therapist. Given my earlier remarks about traditional men and psychotherapy, I would not rule out the usefulness of pragmatic approaches to problem solving (Hanna and Hargrave, 1997). Such approaches may lay the very groundwork needed for a client who is dealing with more sensitive issues to trust his or her therapist. In hindsight, I believe it is important to explore how each stage may have influenced the eventual therapeutic outcome. In deciding what is the "real" work of therapy, I would have conducted an ethnographic interview with Mary and Steve about the different stages and of the therapeutic road as they individually and collectively walked it.

Clearly this family recognized Barney's humanity and trusted him enough to return to him for a second round of therapy. Barney demonstrated flexibility in his use of different approaches, his inclusion of multiple voices, and his willingness to raise some difficult issues. He also demonstrated patience and respect for the family through his acceptance of its agenda. More important, in a critical incident, he seized the moment to facilitate a new direction that respected all family members' dilemmas. Consequently, rather than questioning whether he was a therapist or firefighter, I would characterize him as farmer, naturalist, and an environmentalist. He accepted natural process, understood the potential for growth in the elements, perceived the connections between them, and nurtured them along until just the right time to prune, trim, or harvest. His doing so resulted in a therapeutic outcome that produced a bang, in my opinion, rather than the whisper Barney reported it to be.

REFERENCES

Breunlin, D.C., Schwartz, R. C., and MacKune-Karrer, M.B. (1997). *Metaframeworks: Transcending the models of family therapy.* San Fransciso: Jossey-Bass.

Brooks, G. R. (1998). Why traditional men hate psychotherapy. *Psychotherapy Bulletin,* Summer, 33(3):45-49.

Erickson, M. and Rossi, E. (1979). *Hypnotherapy: An exploratory casebook.* New York: Irvington.

Hanna, S.M. (1995). On paradox: Empathy before strategy. *Journal of Family Psychotherapy,* 6(1), 85-88.

Hanna, S.M. and Hargrave, T.D. (1997). Integrating the process of aging and family therapy. In T.D. Hargrave and S.M. Hanna (Eds.), *The aging family: New visions in theory, practice and reality* (pp. 19-38). New York: Brunner/Mazel.

Stanton, M.D. (1981). Strategic approaches to family therapy. In A.S. Gurman and D.P. Kniskern (Eds.), *Handbook of family therapy* (pp. 361-402). New York: Brunner/Mazel.

ADDITIONAL READINGS

Hanna, S.M. (1997). A developmental-interactional model. In T.D. Hargrave and S.M. Hanna (Eds.), *The aging family: New visions in theory, practice and reality* (pp. 101-130). New York: Brunner/Mazel.

Hanna, S.M. and Brown, J. H. (1999). *The practice of family therapy: Key elements across models,* Second edition. Belmont, California: Brooks/Cole.

Hargrave, T.D. and Hanna, S.M. (1997). Aging: A primer for family therapists. In T.D. Hargrave and S.M. Hanna (Eds.), *The aging family: New visions in theory, practice and reality* (pp. 39-60). New York: Brunner/Mazel.

Commentary

Firefighters Need Teamwork

Thomas A. Smith

Commentator Background

Forty-seven years old, Caucasian, male, PhD, twenty-four years MFT Practice.

Practice Setting

University family therapy clinic; limited private practice.

Theoretical Perspective

My preferred theoretical approach to therapy is systemic integrative and includes elements of solution-focused, structural, Haley's strategic, and MRI. I used structural and solution-focused perspectives from which to comment on this case.

This case is representative of a "great training case" that any university MFT clinic would love to have come through its doors; it is also very representative of the kind of cases I have supervised in the child and family unit of a community mental health center for which I provide professional training. As a commentator, I acknowledge I have the advantage of hindsight which Barney did not have when he worked with this family and I also acknowledge that it is much more difficult to conduct therapy than to comment on someone else's conduct of therapy after the fact. My thanks to Barney, his colleagues, and the editor for inviting my comments on this case.

In this commentary I discuss Barney's technical decisions with regard to the clinical techniques and approaches he used with this family and also will present my alternative perspectives and approach. I, however, recognize that my approach may not have been as successful, effective, or appropriate as Barney if I were the actual therapist for this family.

GOOD POINTS ABOUT THIS CASE

I admire the clinical skills that Barney brought to this case; certainly the outcome is testimony to his effectiveness with this family. I also commend him for his overall therapeutic effort, clarity of presentation, and spirit of exploration with this family. In the first three sessions with the family, his approach to therapy is consistent with Haley's strategic approach. He met individually with Mary and Steve respectively for one session but did not meet with the identified patient (IP), Peter, or his brother Derek. He also accepted Mary and Steve's definition of Peter's misbehaviors as the presenting problem, dealt with Mary and Steve at a parental level, identified appropriate goals for therapy, developed a therapeutic contract with Mary and Steve to pursue the identified goals, and appropriately explored Steve's self-reported physical shaking of Peter to determine if that behavior rose to the level of child abuse. In addition, although he initially saw Mary individually, he later involved all family members based on his appropriate hypothesis that Mary and Steve's marital relationship might be troubled.

NOT-SO-GOOD POINTS ABOUT THIS CASE

In his initial meeting with Mary and Steve, Barney dealt with them as parents of the IP rather than as a couple experiencing relationship difficulties. His language in that meeting suggests that he attempted to normalize the situation with regard to Peter as one in which an adolescent was in need of both space and structure. However, although his statements to Mary and Steve were about parenting, seeing them without the children may not have sufficiently resonated to commit them to parenting issues as a therapeutic goal. Had he succeeded in persuading Mary and Steve of the importance of focusing on parenting issues, subsequent meetings with them to discuss parenting goals might have had more of a "ring of truth." Barney may well have done so but did not indicate that he did.

Barney shares his silent speculations that a schism might exist in Mary and Steve's relationship. Unfortunately, Barney's ruminations may have been betrayed by his clinical actions when he moved quickly to encourage the couple. His doing so detracted from his attempts to hypothesize and to discuss the couple's relationship difficulty and provided them with an excuse not to confront the issue.

WHAT I MIGHT HAVE DONE DIFFERENTLY

The First Phase of Therapy

In my clinical practice I also have used Haley's strategic approach in working with many families. However, I always have experienced significant disagreement with that aspect of the strategic approach that permits clients who present individually to be accepted for family/marital (relationship) therapy, as was the case with Mary. As a structurally oriented therapist, I would have asked that all family members be present for the initial meeting because I believe that it is important to physically see in therapy as many of the family members as possible. Seeing the family together allows me to assess its structure and transactional patterns so that therapeutic interventions can create the desired changes that would help to reorganize the family into healthier patterns of interaction. When an adolescent is the family's IP, I believe that it is much more important to meet together with all family members. This is especially true when the therapeutic emphasis is on forging a balance between supporting the adolescent's need to develop autonomy and identity with the parents' need for him or her to function within a defined family structure. For that reason, I believe that it would have been prudent for assessment purposes to see Peter and perhaps Derek, respectively, in individual sessions. Accordingly, subsequent to the initial conjoint family session, I typically would have scheduled at least one therapy session with the adolescent IP (Peter). Doing so would have emphasized my intention to treat the adolescent as moving toward adulthood. More important, seeing Peter individually would have sent a clear message, at all levels of communication, that I was attending to the problem as the family presented it. I believe that Barney missed many opportunities to address issues relevant to the family as a unit because the entire family was not convened. For example, Mary and Steve's described an interactional sequence that involved a disagreement between Derek and Peter that culminated in Mary and Steve mediating the escalating patterns. Had the entire family been present in the room, the described sequence would have provided a golden opportunity for an enactment with all members rather than Barney discussing the situation with the parents alone. Enactment is one of the cornerstone techniques of the structural approach and is used to assess and restructure family interactional patterns.

Another element of the structural approach that I believe might well have made a difference in this case is Barney joining with the clients. He may have done so, but joining with clients is not an emphasis of Haley's strategic approach. Had Barney been successful in effectively connecting with Mary and Steve, he may have helped them to experience his caring and commitment to them and their situation, which may have been an important element in gaining and maintaining their commitment to therapy.

What Barney Might Have Done Differently

In his initial individual meeting with Mary, Barney used a strategic approach. Had he used a solution-focused approach concurrently with the strategic approach, he might have been more effective in moving Mary from her focus on Peter as the problem to the family, and especially the marital relationship, as the problem. Using a solution-focused approach, Barney could have seen Mary individually and asked her to recite the "litany of sins" she perceived Peter to have committed. Subsequent to her recitation, she then could have been encouraged to reformulate her view of Peter. Barney could have suggested that Mary focus on how she wished Peter would be and share her thoughts about living with Peter as she wished him to be. Doing so might have helped her to reconsider how she viewed Peter and his behaviors. The intent would have been to help Mary to reformulate her negative goals for Peter—i.e., *not* swearing and being *less* impulsive—into positive goals focused on what Peter would do instead of swearing and being impulsive. Subsequent to her identifying positive goals for Peter, she could then have identified exceptions and on-track behaviors that Peter was exhibiting already. In addition, it would have been helpful if Barney had inquired further about Peter's early athletic prowess/success. Doing so might well have provided for exceptions or a direction. Barney's decision to meet with Steve subsequent to meeting with Mary shows that he already was moving in a positive direction that might well have led to a different outcome.

Barney's discussion with Steve about him physically shaking Peter presented a golden opportunity to raise the therapeutic intensity. Barney could have strongly empathized with Steve about the out-of-control feelings that contributed to him shaking Peter. By amplifying those feelings, Barney might well have provided the edge necessary to push Mary and Steve more strongly toward a meaningful commitment to treatment. Coupled with the information that might have been gained from sessions with Derek and Peter, the overall effectiveness of the therapeutic bargain could have been sharpened. In this regard, Minuchin and Fishman (1981), from a structural perspective, emphasize the importance of taking a "middle of the road" position when treating adolescent IPs. Sells (1998), also from a structural perspective, emphasized the importance of binding parents to work with the therapist—i.e., being ready to "go to the mat"—as a key to success in working with difficult adolescents. Had Barney done so, he might have moved Mary and Steve toward a higher level of commitment to treatment.

The Second Phase of Therapy

Viewed from a structural perspective, Mary's involvement in doctoral studies and Steve's unemployment presented an opportunity ripe for some relationship restructuring. Because of their particular circumstance, Mary was involved less with the family and Steve had become more involved. Previous to being unemployed, Steve was reported to be peripherally involved with Peter and Derek while Mary tended to be overinvolved, especially with Derek. Barney could have used Mary and Steve's changed circumstance intentionally to involve Steve more with both sons, thus involving him more in the child-rearing/parenting aspects of the family. This restructuring could have been framed to emphasize the importance of adolescent boys having a meaningful, mentor-like relationship with a loving male role model. Doing so might have motivated Steve to become more actively involved with his sons. In addition, Steve's increased involvement with his sons might have reinforced his fathering role and boosted his self-esteem, especially since he was unemployed and probably needed a boost to his self-esteem. Capitalizing on Steve's new status as "valuable parent," Barney could then have emphasized the importance of Steve and Mary spending time together, e.g., for parental coordination/reporting reasons. His doing so might have been a more effective means of addressing the marital issues metaphorically.

What a Difference a Team Makes

That the family returned for a second round of therapy with Barney certainly is an indication that he had made a successful connection with Mary and Steve, or at least Mary, in the first phase of therapy, despite his subjective feelings that nothing substantial had occurred in that phase. Clearly Barney learned from his earlier experiences with the family; this time around, he involved all family members in treatment. During this phase, Barney used an integrative approach that included elements of five therapeutic perspectives. He also continued in his belief that Mary and Steve's marriage was at best "shaky" and that the couple continued not to acknowledge that fact. With the support of a reflecting team he focused directly on the couple's marital relationship. Here therapy focused on challenging Mary and Steve's marriage and Peter and Derek's active protection of their parents. Although Barney does not indicate that Mary and Steve responded to his challenge of their position in any meaningful way, the outcome of therapy tends to confirm his hypothesis.

THE CRITICAL INCIDENT

Family sculpting is an experiential therapeutic technique (Duhl, Kantor, and Duhl, 1973) that is consistent with the structural tradition and focuses on in-session action and intensity of experience to catalyze a therapeutic break-through. In contrast to Barney, most therapists who use family sculpture in clinical practice do not begin with their own sculpt, because a prevailing be-lief exists that doing so might constrain the family's creativity. The more common practice with family sculpting is to have each family member, in turn, sculpt the family and then react to each other's representations. For ex-ample, initially each family member might sculpt how he or she sees the family and later, time permitting, offer "goal" sculpture based on how each member would like the family to be. Using this model, the therapist then functions as a director who keeps the action going and sustains discussion among family members.

In contrast to the more traditional approach to sculpting, when therapists use a reflecting team they tend to begin with their own sculpt. Doing so tends to be consistent with the therapeutic perspective of reflecting team as intervention. Based on the case report, it appears that the reflecting team's intent was to involve family members by inviting them to conceptualize and present goal sculptures of how the team wished the family could be. This ap-proach to family sculpting is a creative adaptation to a reflecting/solution-focused perspective. The intent of this approach appeared to have been two-fold: first, to capitalize on the impact of Barney's or the reflecting team's sculpt to initiate new directions; second, to use another medium to present the reflecting team's ongoing concern about the couple's emotional distance and Derek and Peter's respective helpful responses to that process.

Unfortunately, Barney's choice of style of the initial sculpture did not al-low opportunity for the unencumbered dramatic display of individual fam-ily member's current perceptions of the family. In my clinical experiences, I have found that the opportunity to be informed of each family member's perceptions of the family greatly enhances the assessment/hypothesizing possibilities for the therapist. For example, such perceptions are helpful in developing metaphors for action and direction. More important, the some-times profound, often jolting impact of the spacial/physical experience that sculpting can provide for family members can be heightened and tends to be more meaningful when its genesis is *from within the family*, rather than from an outsider such as a therapist or a reflecting team. Unfortunately, because only Mary actually was able to sculpt the family, I view the sculpting exer-cise as incomplete. I feel that it would have been important for Barney to seize the opportunity to follow up more fully with sculpting opportunities for Steve and his sons.

Despite my comments about Barney's nonstandard sculpting practice, I am aware that the sculpting exercise had a profound effect on this family. The sculpting experience appeared to be of such intensity that Steve elected to distance himself and not attend the session immediately following the sculpting exercise. Clearly Barney/the team's sculpt reinforced/emphasized their questioning about the quality of Mary and Steve's marital relationship. I applaud Barney's creativity in using multiple methods to alert Mary and Steve to the schism in their marital relationship. However, I question the wisdom of doing so in such a relentless manner since several indications existed along the way that the couple was resistant to confronting the issue. More important, the direct approach was not achieving the desired therapeutic end.

MFT CLINICAL TRAINING:
SOME UNINTENDED CONSEQUENCES

This case highlights two worrisome issues that are characteristic of university-based MFT training and are a challenge to effective treatment. Students in university-based MFT clinical training programs are exposed to clinical practice from a variety of therapeutic modalities as a means of providing an integrated theoretical approach. Unfortunately, rather than being integrative, the broad-based approach tends to be similar to therapy described in this case report. Treatment often tends to be disruptively tied to the academic term and the particular case supervisor rather than being dictated primarily by the evaluation of the client's progress based on the treatment provided. In addition, the logistics of supervisor change, also typical in MFT training settings, tends to disrupt the flow of therapy as was the case, with this family, and resulted in what Barney described as an "ineffective period." In this case, the mandatory change of supervisors and the supervisor's initiated change from a reflecting team approach contributed to what Barney referred to as a "firefighter period" during which he appeared to be floundering therapeutically.

Happily, the next supervisory shift reinstated the reflecting team and allowed for more effective possibilities to utilize data obtained during the sculpting exercise. The consequences of these practices, as illustrated by this case, are a cogent argument for either longer, cross-term case assignment to one supervisor or more focused efforts to be truly integrative by matching the techniques used with the data on progress. Had this occurred with this case, the more structural/reflecting team process would have dominated.

DEFINING THE PROBLEM:
WHOSE PRESENTING PROBLEM IS IT ANYWAY?

I always have been impressed by Haley's (1987) strategy of accepting as valid a client's initial presenting problem. He believes that accepting clients where they are comfortable offers therapists the best place from which to initiate a therapeutic relationship, although a therapist may, if indicated, attempt to shift the therapeutic focus to another problem. Early in my own clinical training, after having lost many clients because I attempted to switch to a second-level presenting problem too early in the therapy process, I learned the benefit of initially accepting clients' presenting problems in the manner in which they presented and defined it. In this regard, Barney's comment that Mary and Steve were less resistant when he finally accepted their definition/framing of their problem that it was Peter, not their marriage, that needed help was a striking acknowledgment. Interestingly, with regard to the outcome of this family's treatment, Barney points out that after he switched positions the couple finally addressed some couple issues. Based on the case report, it is clear that Barney's eventual acceptance of this couple's presenting problem in the manner in which they defined it resulted in positive changes for both the couple and their sons. Had Barney followed Haley's dictum sooner, he may have been able to restructure the family by capitalizing upon naturally occurring events that could have moved metaphorically to couple issues in parenting as well as parent-child and possibly sibling relations. To his credit, Barney was able to allow the couple to attribute the positive changes reported at termination in a manner in which they could best accept them. His doing so was most effective in leaving the door open for this family to return to treatment in the future.

CONCLUDING THOUGHTS

Many elements in family therapy are represented in this case, but it seems to me that the case highlights four issues:

1. the efficacy/superiority of one theoretical approach compared to the many other approaches. Barney initiated therapy with a solution-focused and brief therapy approach, moved to an integrative approach, then to returned to an MRI brief approach, and then recycled to a structural approach. Despite all of the theoretical meandering, it is unclear that any one approach was superior to the others or was responsible for the positive outcome for the family. Perhaps the most significant variables here were the quality of the client-therapist relationship, Barney's te-

nacity, and the family's trust in him that allowed them to return to therapy with him;

2. the importance of involving the entire family in therapy sessions as opposed to seeing family members individually;
3. accepting clients' presenting problems as the client defines/frames it rather that entering into a power struggle with the clients to persuade them to accept the therapist's definition of the problem; and
4. for student clinicians but especially for clients, the oftentimes frustrating problem of working within the limits of the university's schedule and required supervisory changes. It is quite possible that had Barney stayed with the original supervisor and the reflecting team he and the family may have made better therapeutic progress. It is a credit to his and to the family's tenacity that despite all the twists and turns the outcome was positive.

REFERENCES

Duhl, F., Kantor, D., and Duhl, B. (1973). Learning, space, and action in family therapy: A primer of sculpture. In D. Bloch (Ed.), *Techniques of Family Psychotherapy* (pp. 47-63). New York: Grunne and Stratton.

Haley, J. (1987). *Problem-solving therapy*, Second edition. San Francisco: Jossey-Bass.

Minuchin, S. and Fishman, C. (1981). *Family therapy techniques*. Cambridge, MA: Harvard University Press.

Sells, S. (1998). *Treating the tough adolescent*. New York: The Guilford Press.

CASE 15

Jimmy the Flying Reindeer
and the Two Mothers

Carolyn I. Wright
Linda Stone-Fish

Therapist Backgrounds

Currently: (CW) Fifty-four years old, white, female, PhD, ten years MFT practice. When I saw this family: MA, five years MFT practice.

Currently: (LSF) Forty-six years old, white, female, PhD, twenty-four years MFT practice.

Practice Setting

Hospital outpatient clinic.

Client Characteristics

The clients are members of a lower socioeconomic white family consisting of Shirley (age twenty-six), her husband Joe (age thirty-five), her sister, Joan (age thirty-six), and three children: Kyle (age seven), Clark (age two), and Jimmy (age six). Kyle and Clark are Joe and Shirley's biological children. Jimmy is Joan's son but lives with Shirley's family because Joan temporarily and voluntarily relinquished custody of Jimmy to Shirley. Joe is employed full time in a fast-food restaurant; Shirley is a full-time homemaker. Joan is trained as a dental hygienist but was unemployed and receiving SSI benefits; she is a lesbian in a long-term relationship with her partner, Anna. Kyle and Jimmy are in first grade. Jimmy's pediatrician had referred Jimmy and Shirley to therapy after Jimmy had moved in with Shirley and Joe.

Length of Treatment

The family was seen for fourteen therapy sessions over six months. The critical incident occurred in the first individual session with Jimmy.

Theoretical Perspective

A feminist theoretical approach was used in working with Jimmy and his family.

PRESENTING PROBLEM

Jimmy's pediatrician had referred Jimmy and Shirley to therapy because Shirley was concerned that Jimmy might have been neglected and abused by his mother, Joan. At the time of the interview, Jimmy was living with Shirley and her family; Shirley was his legal and physical guardian. Consequently, she was eager to make Jimmy's adjustment to her family as uneventful as possible for him. Approximately six months earlier, Jimmy's mother, Joan, a single parent, had voluntarily relinquished custody of him to Shirley. Joan had been clinically depressed for approximately one year; while an outpatient at a state psychiatric facility, she arranged for Jimmy to live temporarily with Shirley but retained reasonable visitation with Jimmy. Accordingly, Jimmy usually spent weekends with Joan in the country unless she felt "too stressed" to care for him. Shirley had scheduled the appointment for the family and believed that a session with Joan would be useful. She, however, was doubtful that Joan, already engaged in individual therapy, had the energy also to engage in family therapy.

THE INITIAL SESSION

Shirley, Joe, Kyle, Clark, and Jimmy were present for the initial family session. For this session, Wright, the first author, was the therapist of record and the second author, Stone-Fish, was a consultant. During this initial session, Jimmy was talkative and friendly but apologized frequently to Shirley and the therapist for any and all of his actions. Shirley referred to him as the "little mayor" and lamented that he "knew too much big people stuff." In this meeting, Shirley tearfully said, "I want my kids to have normalcy. I want them to know they're loved. I want them to be respected and to know that they're respected. I also want them to know that no matter what they do, where they go, their parents are there for them." The three boys appeared appropriately connected, alternately teasing and sharing with each other and showing an unusual level of physical affection and attention to each other. Jimmy appeared especially close to Clark, who was talkative in the session.

Kyle actively played with the dollhouse when not asking to go to the bathroom. Jimmy eagerly bounced from sitting next to one family member to another and appeared to be comfortable with Joe, whom he lovingly called "Uncle Sam." Each member of the family comfortably discussed what was "difficult" and what was "nice" or "helpful" about having Jimmy residing with the family.

Joe and Shirley presented different and conflicting goals for Jimmy's stay with their family. Joe's goal was to adopt Jimmy ultimately to end his inconsistent weekend visits with his mother; he believed those visits confused Jimmy. My clinical intuition told me that Joe wanted to terminate Shirley's relations with Joan because he believed that Joan often upset Shirley. Unlike Joe, Shirley's primary goal for Jimmy was eventually to return him to his mother's custody. A secondary goal was to inform Joan that she, Shirley, was doing a good job parenting Jimmy while he was in her care. Shirley expressed concern that Jimmy was presenting to Joan an unjustifiably negative picture of his life with her. She said, "He always tells her the bad stuff, not the good stuff."

Joe noted that for the first time in Jimmy's six years of life, he was living within a brotherhood of males. Joe was proud that he had helped Jimmy to learn how to protect and defend himself "like a man" instead of making faces "like a girl" when he was angry. Like his cousins, Jimmy now had his own collection of miniature hot rods and was learning to hold his own in the male world into which he had entered.

During this session Shirley constantly monitored the children's movements and repeatedly questioned whether the quality of her parenting was adequate. I (CW) commented that I was exhausted just observing her interactions with the children. As though in response to me, Joe expressed his admiration for Shirley's mothering abilities; he, however, did not take an active role in physically parenting the children. While Shirley chased the boys, Joe, an obese man who frequently was short of breath, sat and talked with them. He acknowledged his physical limitations in dealing with the children. He said, "I couldn't do it." He, however, was supportive of Shirley and felt connected and comfortable with the children. Shirley's parental hypervigilance also was apparent in her relationship with Jimmy. She appeared to be more protective of Jimmy than of her own sons. She said that she did not want Jimmy to experience a childhood similar to the one she and her siblings had experienced. (As adolescents Shirley and her siblings experienced many out-of-home placements including foster homes and a reform school; the resulting separations were devastating for the siblings.) I silently wondered how much of Shirley's "protection" of Jimmy was actually for his sake and how much of it actually was her intrinsic need to protect. As if reading my thoughts, Shirley verbalized her own awareness of and ambivalence about the extent of her protectiveness of Jimmy.

THE THERAPEUTIC SITUATION
PRIOR TO THE CRITICAL INCIDENT

From December 1994 to May 1995, I met with various combinations of family members. In the fifth session, Joan joined us for the first time; thereafter she and Shirley were seen intermittently for conjoint sessions. Occasionally, I met with Joan, Jimmy, and Shirley together, and Jimmy often shared his therapy hour with Joan and Shirley. Since this was an extended family system with multiple issues, we developed several initial goals to guide therapy with them. However, the major goals were specific to Jimmy's triangulation and divided loyalty to his two families.

Accordingly, therapy focused on helping Jimmy to learn to love and to receive love from both families without feeling disloyal to either one. Therapy also focused on: (1) helping Jimmy to reconnect emotionally with his mother whether or not he would return to live full time with her, and (2) helping Shirley to feel "good enough" as a parent by helping her to heal her emotional wounds, which resulted from her childhood experiences with inadequate parenting. I believed that if she could feel competent as a parent, she would be able to support Jimmy with her love and nurturance and later let him go without feeling that she was abandoning him. As a result of her negative childhood experiences, she had come to equate love with abandonment. Despite those negative experiences, Shirley was a strong woman and presented as very capable of nurturing her children in positive ways that her own mother did not provide.

In a family session Shirley expressed concern about Jimmy being troubled but not being able to express his feelings about being troubled or about what was troubling him. Although Jimmy engaged with her family, Shirley perceived him to be an outsider looking in. Shirley identified this concern as her own projection but still expressed deeply felt concerns about the meaning(s) of Jimmy's silence. I also was concerned about Jimmy's silence. Although Jimmy appeared to be satisfied, he also appeared to be worried about his mother and somewhat confused about where he belonged with regard to the two households and the two "mothers." Shirley and Jimmy appeared to be in parallel processes: each one needed to find his or her own voice and to recognize and take responsibility for what he or she was feeling. This included their respective sadness and anger.

THE CRITICAL INCIDENT

In the first individual session with Jimmy, I asked him to draw a picture of his family. My goal was twofold: to join with Jimmy to experience his family and his experience of his role in his family, and also to let him know that I valued his perspective. It was the end of January, but Christmas still played heavily on his mind as he drew his grandfather, Poppy, as Santa in a sleigh. Uncle Sam (Joe) was the closest reindeer to grandfather ("because they were men and they did things together"), and Kyle, with a large red nose, was the lead reindeer. Shirley and Clark were also represented as reindeers flying around the family house Jimmy had created. Jimmy drew Shirley as the largest reindeer of the family group and showed her hovering over the three boys. Interestingly, he drew his mother as a human on the ground saying "Hi" rather than as a reindeer stationary or in flight.

The reindeers, except for Kyle, who was appropriately reined in by his father, appeared to be free floating, as if flying by the spread of their antlers. Jimmy confirmed that the antlers were used like wings for flying. He also informed me that reindeers ate food, like oatmeal, that was covered with magical sprinkles that helped them to fly. "Blitzer" was having some trouble flying, and Jimmy asserted that compliments from others helped him to fly better. I silently wondered if it was my compliments that were needed. Accordingly, I spread my arms and waved them as if they were wings and I was in flight. In response, Jimmy raised his arms and pretended to fly around the room. I complimented him on his "flying" and he appeared to fly to greater heights.

Jimmy did not represent himself in the picture he had drawn. I asked, "Where are you?" He replied, "Upstairs in the house, in the dark, in a room with the windows shut, so you can't see me." He was not sure why he was in the dark room. I asked Jimmy how would I know that his completed picture was a picture of his family? In response, he quickly labeled the picture "Jimmy's family" then added "with the red hair." I told him that I still was confused and asked, "How would I know it is your family?" He did not immediately reply. However, as we began to pack up the crayons, he stopped abruptly. In a moment of intense concentration, he asked if I wanted him to insert himself into the picture. I told him that it was his picture, therefore it was his choice whether he inserted himself. He then drew himself as the tiniest reindeer, standing, feet on the ground, next to his mother. He said he was four. This depiction was a turning point in Jimmy's therapy. His spontaneous drawing of a reindeer was a tangible metaphor that expanded my perception of him and also provided me with new information about his feelings toward his mother—his loyalty to her as well as his fears. What he truly wanted was to be with his mother, even if she could not fly.

At the end of this session, Shirley came to pick up Jimmy. As Jimmy and I walked into the waiting area, Shirley was at the front desk loudly complaining that Jimmy had told his mother some negative things about her. Sarcastically, Shirley asked me if Jimmy had said anything good about her in our session. I was concerned about how Jimmy might be experiencing her question. Was he feeling pressured or disloyal? At that moment, I felt the presence of the large, powerful, anxious reindeer hovering overhead and understood firsthand why Jimmy represented Shirley as the largest and perhaps the most powerful reindeer in his family picture. Although I understood the need for her hypervigilance, I told Shirley that we would talk about her concerns in our next session.

THE AFTERMATH OF THE CRITICAL INCIDENT

In subsequent individual sessions with Jimmy following the critical incident, I used play therapy to enhance our therapeutic relationship and was able to accomplish a great deal in therapy while playing. I also used feminist-informed approaches to help him to identify and act upon his needs. To this end, in one session Jimmy used play dough to sculpt a green man whom he named "Spike." We spontaneously collaborated on a song and a poem about Spike. We sang the song to a rapper's beat and snapped our fingers and slapped our thighs. In our moments of levity, Jimmy described his likes and dislikes about an assortment of topics, such as food and his mother's partners; for the first time he talked about his older half sister who was surrendered for adoption at birth. His mother had told him about his sister, but he never had met her. Spike helped Jimmy and me to talk more easily about angry and sad feelings. Spike also enabled Jimmy to tell me directly that hugs and compliments helped him to feel better. Accordingly, he spontaneously hugged me at the end of the session and did so again at the end of each session thereafter; I reciprocated by complimenting him more.

Concurrently, I also used puppets as my "cotherapists" to help Jimmy to find his voice. Each puppet had its own projective personality and helped me to develop "group therapy sessions" for Jimmy. Jimmy chose a baby dinosaur, still in its egg, as the puppet with whom he identified. He named this dinosaur "T. Rex." I chose a rooster, whom I named "Cluck Cluck," as a coach for Jimmy. Cluck Cluck was somewhat loud, boisterous, and direct. He taught T. Rex how to crow "from the diaphragm" and also helped me to play and to coach Jimmy from a new perspective. As a result, I developed an approach that was both supportive and directly confrontational yet allowed me to be the safe therapist I always had been for him. We did not talk about play; we played. The play transformed our process. Over the course of therapy, T. Rex gained power and oftentimes asserted his power. For example, he told Cluck Cluck to "lock your jaws" when Cluck Cluck's directness became too intense. I complicated T. Rex for asserting himself and Cluck Cluck affirmed for Jimmy that he had become assertive. Through this play, Jimmy was able to verbalize his angry feelings about his absent father and his older half sister, as well as his mother's need to take care of herself to be able to better care for him.

As part of our therapeutic menu, Jimmy and I also played checkers and I helped him to understand that different rules existed for different games, just as different rules existed for different families. I also helped him to understand that by learning the specific rules for each situation he could hold his own and possibly even succeed in the game. During this period of play, Jimmy was able to identify his pattern of indirect expression of anger. He often experienced difficulty in expressing his anger directly to his aunt. I commented to him that his fear of expressing anger directly may prevent him from getting what he wanted; it certainly could prevent his voice from being heard. I invited him to think of his anger as a gift he could share with his aunt. I said, "Right now you are giving your anger to your mother to hold or to express for you." He replied, "No, I give it to Anna." This was new information that allowed me to better understand the importance of Anna (Joan's partner) in Jimmy's life.

During this period, Jimmy also felt safe enough to explore issues that had been bothering him but were not expressed previously. One such issue was his beliefs about men. Accordingly, we discussed his ideas about men after I experienced much difficulty in holding his full attention in a session and observed him playing with a male figure from the dollhouse. During our discussion, Jimmy shared his belief that, "They [men] make rules. Mothers are always trying to get them out of the house, and they don't work." When asked who was like the men he had described, he replied, "My father." Cueing on his response, we briefly talked about his father and his half sister and I encouraged him to share his musings with his mother. He shrugged his shoulders and appeared uninterested in my suggestion. However, despite his initial show of indifference, he later changed his mind.

At session's end, I walked Jimmy to the waiting area. While I spoke with his mother, he suddenly yelled, "Mom, I've been talking to my therapist and I have a question I want to ask you." Then, looking much like the "little mayor"—head down and hands clasped behind his back—he walked in circles around me and between his mother and me. Talking directly to his mother, he asked, "What does my sister look like?" Joan replied that she had baby pictures of his sister at home and asked, "Would you like to see them?" He nodded his head affirmatively but kept walking around me as though he was engaged in a ritual dance. I then prompted, "Was there something else, Jimmy?" Stammering, he asked, "What does my father look like?" Joan answered immediately, "He had red hair." Jimmy stopped his questioning and immediately hugged his mother tightly. I watched them standing there, holding each other silently until Joan looked at me and said, "The love of my life stands before me." I quietly said, "I know. I can see that. You are such a good mother."

DISCUSSION

The Role of the Critical Incident in Getting Therapy Unstuck

Therapy with Jimmy and his "two mothers" was difficult and stymied rather than stuck. However, although the critical incident did not lead to therapy becoming unstuck, it did become a building block for therapy. By his own admission, Jimmy began therapy hidden in a dark room where no one could see him. After he placed himself in his picture, he began the process of defining himself. He learned how to be a male, a son, a nephew, and a brother. He also learned to trust his thoughts and feelings as he learned to trust others. More important, he learned to trust his voice. In the midst of his struggle were two mothers, both of whom loved him and inadvertently contributed to him feeling divided in his loyalty and confused as to whom he needed to listen and whom it was important to please.

Joan and Shirley had experienced parental deprivation as children and feared that Jimmy would experience the same fate. As a result, they were determined to provide for him a loving, reliable family, which is something they themselves never knew. Their efforts were successful and resulted in Jimmy feeling loved. In parenting Jimmy, Joan and Shirley's childhood pain was exposed.

Shirley recognized that Jimmy's vulnerability reminded her of her own vulnerability when her parents had placed her in foster care. She recognized and acknowledged her helplessness, her anger, and feelings of not being appreciated as the custodial mother. She saw in Jimmy all of her own abandonment issues that she could not experience through her own children because she and Joe were competent and stable parents. Jimmy, however, was not a product of Joe and Shirley. Rather, he was a product of Joan and Shirley: a double dose of their family of origin. I perceived both Joan and Shirley to be Jimmy's actual parents. Similar to children of separated and remarried parents, Jimmy often was triangulated into Joan and Shirley's adult issues.

Implications of the Critical Incident for Therapy

The family was struggling with relationships on two levels. Jimmy was struggling with the feeling to be loyal to two mothers, and Shirley and Joan were struggling in their sororal relationship specific to their mothering roles with Jimmy. Jimmy's picture had provided me with a great deal of information about his invisible loyalties. Aunt Shirley was by far the largest reindeer hovering over the boys, all of whom were looking straight at Jimmy, a reindeer himself, yet he stood close to his smiling mother, whom he drew as a human rather than a reindeer. Although Jimmy enjoyed "playing" as a reindeer, he still was his mother's son. Jimmy's metaphor allowed me to talk to

Shirley in a very different way about some of Jimmy's behaviors that she found to be quite disturbing.

On another level, the critical incident also helped Joan and Shirley to clarify their mothering roles with regards to Jimmy. Shirley was experiencing much difficulty as she contemplated relinquishing her temporary custody of Jimmy. As a result of the critical incident, I was able to talk openly with everyone involved about Shirley's ambivalence. Shirley worked very hard to let go of "fixing things" for Jimmy and his mother and to clarify boundaries while acknowledging how difficult it was to do so. One such clarification was that Shirley needed to tell Jimmy that he would be visiting his mother every weekend as planned rather than to keep him wondering if he would be doing so. If Joan did not want to have Jimmy with her for the weekend, it would be her responsibility, rather than Shirley's responsibility, to tell Jimmy so. Shirley's protective maneuver of "wait and see" had created undue anxiety for Jimmy. I reframed nurturing as creating safety through structure. This reframe allowed Shirley to expand the definition, nurture herself by setting limits on her responsibilities as a surrogate mother, and to work on her expressions of anger. I also encouraged Shirley to share her feelings and thoughts about parenting in general, while I affirmed her parenting skills. She eventually internalized her "good parenting" skills and came to believe and to accept that she was more than "just an adequate parent."

THE OUTCOME OF THERAPY

During the period that the family was in therapy, Shirley had become pregnant again. She stopped being a "mother" to Jimmy and permitted herself to be his aunt. Consequently, Joan and Shirley learned to collaborate as sisters in parenting Jimmy rather than continue to compete as maternal rivals for his loyalty. To that end, each sister learned to care for Jimmy during the times he was in her respective care, unconcerned about his loyalty when he was not with her. Joan and Shirley also worked on their own self-issues, such as interdependency and connectedness, and began to stabilize their personal relationships. Because they both were aware that their respective spouses might feel threatened by their new closeness and increased communication, they used therapy to help them to learn to communicate the importance of their sibling and coparenting relationships to their spouses.

Jimmy also made changes in his life as a result of therapy. During school vacations, he spent up to ten days at a time with his mother. He began to give Anna less anger to hold; instead, he took a risk and now shared his anger directly with his aunt. Jimmy also expressed a desire to share equally all of his in-session drawings with both Shirley and Joan. Accordingly, we copied each drawing to facilitate him doing so. Concurrently, he began to clarify for himself who was his "real mother." To this end, he asserted that Shirley was not his mother, although she did "mother-like things" for him. Similarly, Theresa, Joan's new partner, was not his mother; she was a friend. However, Anna, whom he asserted "is married to my mother," was also his mother. From his perspective, the nice part about having two mothers is "there is always one around."

Follow-Up

One year following the termination of therapy, Jimmy was living permanently with his mother but continued to see Shirley and Joe weekly. Joan and Shirley remained close as loving sisters and friends, but Anna ended her relationship with Joan. Joan reported that initially Jimmy missed Anna but now sees her on weekends; he now accepts Theresa as his second mother. Shirley informed me that she, Joan, and her brothers were planning a family reunion. This reunion would be the first time in twenty-five years that all the siblings would be together; she thought I would like to know.

Commentary

Where Are the Fathers?

Marcia E. Lasswell

Commentator Background

Sixty-seven years old, female, Caucasian, MA, forty-two years MFT practice.

Practice Setting

Private practice, COAMFTE-accredited training program supervisor.

Theoretical Perspective

Integrative/systems approach. I used a cognitive, psychodynamic, and psychoeducational approaches to examine this case.

It is easy to comment positively on a case that has been handled by competent therapists, especially when the outcome is successful. As I read and reacted to the case report, I became aware that I was slipping into my supervisor's mode as I began to make notes in the margins detailing questions that I would have liked to ask the therapists. This is what I would have done were I listening to a supervisee tell me about this family. This, however, is neither a criticism of Wright nor is intended to offer a better approach. Rather, in the spirit of postmodern supervision, I longed for a dialogue with Wright to make sure that I understood what I would need to know if I were the therapist of record for this family.

SOME GOOD POINTS ABOUT THE CASE

I applaud Wright's decision to involve the family in family therapy as the preferred mode of treatment and to include Joan in therapy, since restructuring the relationship between Joan, Jimmy, and Shirley appeared to be a primary goal for therapy. It is unclear, however, how many of the fourteen sessions had elapsed before Jimmy was seen alone and when in time the critical incident occurred. I also liked Wright's creative use of play therapy which appeared to restructure the immediate family to be more comfortable for the sisters. If Joan can stay on a steady path, perhaps Jimmy will be all right. He certainly appears to be a resilient child. I wonder if plans exist for continuing therapy for Joan who, based on her past problems, is likely to have psychological ups and downs in the future.

ALTERNATIVE VIEWS

Jimmy As IP: Real or Constructed?

Although the family was in family therapy, it is clear in the first session that Jimmy became the sole IP as each family member discussed what was "difficult," what was "nice," and what was "helpful" about having Jimmy living with the family. At one point, Shirley commented that she experienced Jimmy as "an outsider looking in" (at the family). The first session's discussion of the impact of Jimmy's presence in the family underscored his outsider status. Interestingly, when Jimmy drew his family portrait, he also underscored his "otherness" by omitting himself from the picture. When questioned, he explained that he was shut away in darkness. I question Wright's decision in the first session to begin by structuring Jimmy as an outsider and the IP. Perhaps she did so because that is the way it was in reality, but it would have helped my understanding of this family's dynamics had Wright explained that decision.

Questions for the Therapist

Subsequent to reading the case report, many questions remain that I would have liked to ask Wright. My need to question in these areas results from a desire for answers that would ease my concerns about Joan's stability and Jimmy's welfare. The first of these are about Jimmy's pediatrician's referral of the family to therapy because he was alarmed by Shirley's concern that Jimmy may have been abused and neglected by his mother. I realize that Joan had been hospitalized for depression and had legally and physically relinquished custody of Jimmy, but the reported details do not support Shirley's fears of abuse and neglect. Because ultimately one of the goals of therapy was to reunite Jimmy with Joan, it would have helped to know whether any evidence existed to Shirley's misgivings about Joan's parenting or whether Shirley had unduly alarmed her physician. Several clues about Shirley's own mistreatment as a child and her maternal overprotectiveness support the latter assumption. However, the case report is unclear about what might have led the pediatrician to make such a referral.

Several other questions result from concerns about which I wish Wright had elaborated. In particular, I am interested in the fact that Jimmy has an older half sister who was given up for adoption at birth. Was that adoption necessary because of Joan's depressive state? Were earlier circumstances in her life relevant to whether Joan would be able to sustain a stable home for Jimmy if they were reunited? When Jimmy hugged his mother and she spoke of her love for him, Wright commented, "You are such a good mother." Up to this point, it appeared that Joan had not been sterling, if reliability is a criterion. I can only wonder about Wright's decision to affirm Joan in this manner rather than to stop with the first sentence which spoke directly to Joan's statement of love.

Wright minimally mentions Theresa, Joan's new partner. Her doing so left unanswered many questions about Joan's parting with Anna and what appeared to be an almost immediate recoupling. At the posttermination one-year follow-up, Jimmy was living with his mother. She had ended her relationship with her partner, Anna, whom Jimmy saw on a somewhat regular basis but still missed. Jimmy had referred to Anna as his "mother," believing that she and his mother were married. Clearly Anna was another loss in Jimmy's family structure that too quickly was filled by Joan's new love, Theresa. When Joan changed partners, I wonder how the impact of that change on Jimmy was considered. Although in actuality Joan's change of partner may not have been as impulsive as it sounds, it nevertheless raises some concern for me about whether Joan is extremely dependent or even given to manic phases. Might she be bipolar? An unintended consequence of Joan's change of partners is that Jimmy was left to figure out his relationship to Theresa and perhaps wonder how long she will be a part of his "family."

Points of Convergence and Divergence with Wright

Wright states that she used a feminist approach with this family. However, as I read the case report, I question which of her strategies were examples of feminist therapy. Aside from working to strengthen Joan and Shirley's relationship and to help them to clarify their identities vis-à-vis each other and Jimmy, it is unclear to me what specific feminist therapeutic principles were used with this family. Certainly the males in this family received minimal therapeutic attention. I hope that the minimal attention to the males in the family was not intentional to allow for maximum attention to the females. My understanding of feminist therapy is that, among other things, men are encouraged to play an active but nonsexist role in raising children so that mothers are not held solely responsible for caretaking and for how their children are raised. Accordingly, my title of this commentary, "Where Are the Fathers?", is indicative of my puzzlement over the issues with Joe ("Uncle Sam") and Jimmy's absent father who, despite his absence, nonetheless appeared to be very important to Jimmy. Interestingly,

Wright appears to applaud and encourage Joe to define for Jimmy a very sexist definition of being male, although that definition seemed to preclude identifying with the women in his family.

I concur with Wright's hypothesis that Joan and Shirley had serious personal problems overlaid and intertwined with many residual issues from their family of origin and indirectly were using Jimmy to solve those problems. I, however, was troubled by Wright's perception of "two mothers" and her statement that Jimmy was a "product" of Joan and Shirley while neglecting Joe's role in the family drama. If, as Wright asserted, Jimmy needed to learn "how to be a male, a son, a nephew, and a brother," then more nonsexist discussion of the important males in his life would have been helpful. Absent such a discussion, therapy with this family has a decidedly sexist ring to it and does not appear to be representative of a feminist therapeutic approach as I understand it.

Early in the case report, Joe was described as a man with whom Jimmy was comfortable and loving. Joe wanted to adopt Jimmy, which was at odds with Shirley's intentions. On the other hand, Joe appeared supportive of Shirley's everyday parenting behaviors, although he often backed off as though she did enough for both of them. Other than a brief mention in Jimmy's family picture and a passing comment that Shirley was pregnant again, presumably by Joe, Joe was omitted from the later sections of the case report.

One of the first questions Jimmy asked his mother was about his father. He hugged his mother when she said that his father had red hair. When Jimmy drew his family picture and, upon prodding by Wright, labeled it "Jimmy's family," he quickly added "with the red hair." Did Jimmy have red hair and identify with his father when told that his father also had red hair? If not, what was the significance of red hair? In one session, Jimmy commented that mothers always were trying to get men out of the house and the men, like his father, do not work. This appeared to be a very fruitful area to be pursued in therapy rather than merely urging him to share these thoughts with his mother.

WHAT I MIGHT HAVE DONE DIFFERENTLY

The ending to therapy with this family appears to be a happy one. Accordingly, I hesitate to say whether I would have done anything significantly different. However, given my questions about Wright's therapeutic approach and my questions/assumptions about Joan's emotional state, I would have approached therapy with this family differently based on my clinical experiences and theoretical orientation. First, contrary to Wright, I would have included the males more and in a less genderized way than she has. Second, consistent with my systemic orientation, I would not have cast Joe, in particular, as a minor character. Third, I would not have placed Jimmy in the IP role at all—certainly not in the first session. Next, I would have looked at Joan's history of partner changes, depressive episodes, and parenting attitudes as likely to be problematic in the future unless she continues therapy as she, Jimmy, and Theresa establish still another family unit. These new family units are major changes for all of them. My sense is that Joan expected Jimmy to adjust to the roller-coaster existence of her life rather than expecting that she and the other adults would give forethought to how to make life easier for Jimmy. Finally, I probably would not have seen Jimmy in as many individual sessions as did Wright. Alternatively, I would have used play therapy, picture drawing, "Cluck Cluck and T. Rex," or whatever my variations might have been, but I would have had family members present as observers or even participants. Everything that emerged during those activities could have been eye-openers for the others in a much more powerful way than usually is possible by simply reporting to them what had occurred between Jimmy and his therapist.

CONCLUDING THOUGHTS

It is difficult to quarrel with a good therapeutic outcome. This family was fortunate to have had experienced therapists who were able to understand their needs and to help them to put all of the pieces together in the best interest of Jimmy. It takes courage to put one's clinical skills and especially a critical incident on display and invite colleagues to comment. These therapists confronted a difficult situation and, to their credit, not only did a very good job but followed up posttermination to see how their treatment was being utilized. They are to be commended. That said, it is important to point out that although I might have taken a different therapeutic approach with this family, that does not mean I would have done anything better, only different. Taking a different approach serves only to remind me of the many different therapeutic paths there are to the common goals that we all share as marriage and family therapists.

Commentary

Mediating Solomon's Mothers in the Best Interest of the Child

Earl F. Merritt

Commentator Background

Fifty-three years old, African American, male, MA, twenty-six years MFT experience.

Practice Setting

Limited private practice.

Theoretical Perspective

Systemic-developmental augmented with intergenerational concepts. I used a systemic-developmental perspective to examine this case.

Compliments to Wright and Stone-Fish for their Solomon-like approach in dealing with the two sisters, Joan and Shirley, who perhaps unaware and unintentionally were attempting, through Jimmy, to resolve some of their childhood losses with regards to parenting. The satisfactory outcome of this case is testimony that the therapists' efforts were effective and successful in helping the sisters to resolve their maternal rivalry in the best interest of Jimmy, whom they both care about and love. Bravo!

GOOD POINTS ABOUT THE CASE

The therapeutic team of Wright and Stone-Fish found ways to help this family in spite of itself when it appeared that the sisters' maternal needs were overshadowing Jimmy's needs. Rather than dictating to Joan and Shirley what they already knew (Joan is Jimmy's biological parent; Shirley is his aunt), Wright and Stone-Fish, by "making the obvious explicit," allowed the sisters to come to terms with the obvious, to feel comfortable with that fact, and to continue to care about Jimmy.

Wright's decision to include Joan in the therapeutic process rather than restricting involvement to Shirley's family is commendable. Also commendable is the "multimedia" approach she used (art, draw a family; movement/music, a spontaneous composition about Spike; play therapy, checkers; and use of a "virtual" group with Cluck Cluck, T. Rex, and Jimmy) to help Jimmy to emerge from the darkened upstairs room in which he had closed himself to attenuate the strains of the loyalty issues attendant to dealing with the great reindeer surrogate mother and the reluctant (often "fairweather") biological mother. Throughout her work with the family, Wright kept her focus on Jimmy as the central figure and did not allow herself to be distracted by the several sororal/maternal issues of Joan and Shirley. Doing so was in itself quite a feat given the complexity and intensity of the sisters' issues as well as the expanse of their collective needs.

POINTS OF DEPARTURE WITH WRIGHT

Wright asserts that one of the positives of Jimmy living with his aunt's family is his initiation into "maleness:" "he learned to be a male, a son, a nephew, and a brother." Despite this and Joe's observation about Jimmy's maleness, "for the first time in Jimmy's six years of life, he was living within a brotherhood of males," Wright did not explicitly or even tangentially address issues specific to Jimmy's maleness. Indeed, throughout her work with the family, Wright paid scant attention to issues specific to the male members. Throughout the case report Joe's role in the unfolding family drama is given fleeting mention despite his significant input in writing the family's script. For example, Joe's vision of a resolution to Jimmy's stay with his family is diametrical to Shirley's (Joe wanted to adopt Jimmy "to save him from Joan's inconsistency;" Shirley wanted to return him to his mother) and Joe was concerned that Joan's interactions with Shirley "were upsetting to Shirley" (and by extension to him and their sons). These feeling/issues never were explored to discover how they fit into and/or contributed to Shirley's angst about her sister's competence to parent Jimmy and her own need to prove to Joan (and perhaps herself) that she was a quality parent and was doing a good job of parenting Jimmy while he was in her care. In addition, Jimmy and Wright discussed Jimmy's understanding of males and Jimmy shared the view that "men do not work and mothers always are trying to get them out of the house." Given that Joe spent much time at home because of the nature of his job, it would have been helpful if Wright had explored with Jimmy whether his unflattering view of males included Joe as well, since Joe was initiating Jimmy into "maleness." If Jimmy perceived Joe to fit his view of males, how comfortable was Jimmy in learning to be the kind of male that he held in such low regard? Surrounded as he was by women who seem not to have a particularly high regard for males, would Jimmy experience conflict in learning his male roles from Joe?

POINTS OF AGREEMENT WITH WRIGHT

Although my therapeutic approach with families is different from Wright's approach, I would like to believe that I would have done some of the same things that she did in working with Jimmy and his two mothers. Specifically, I also would have taken a cue from Jimmy's family portrait (in which he represented his mother as a grounded human next to whom he stood) and helped him to reconnect emotionally with his mother as her son rather than as an occasional weekend visitor. The reconnection occasioned by the family portrait was positive for both Jimmy and Joan, who came to realize that in spite of her many life difficulties, she could be Jimmy's mother even if she could not fly as high as her sister.

Similar to Wright, I also would have encouraged Jimmy to seek information from his mother about the half sister whom he had only heard about. His doing so strengthened the connection between him and his mother and perhaps gave Joan an opportunity to confront an event (the adoption) that may have been a very difficult experience in her life.

WHAT I MIGHT HAVE DONE DIFFERENTLY

It is always difficult to second-guess a therapist of record's approach to a particular case based only on a case report. That said, I might have done at least four things differently in working with this family because of my different theoretical orientation and clinical experiences. First, in her first individual session with Jimmy, Wright used the draw-a-family technique to join with him and to understand his family relationships. Interestingly, given that it was the first individual session with Jimmy, there seemed to be no foundation for the use of that technique. Rather than using that technique in the first session, I would have used that time to get to know and to understand Jimmy as an individual (he previously had been seen as a part of the family group) in context and would have used the draw-a-family technique after we had established a client-therapist connection and rapport. Second, since Jimmy was being seen in family therapy, I would have seen him for fewer individual sessions and would have included Joe much more in the process as a major character than Wright did.

Third, Jimmy explained that he was absent from the family picture because he was "upstairs in a dark room where no one could see me," but

Wright did not explore with him the meaning/reason for his symbolic presence in the room. As a result, his being in the room and the meaning he attached to being there remain a mystery. I believe that had Wright probed Jimmy about the meaning of putting himself in a dark room (as she had done about him omitting himself from the family picture), her doing so would have contributed to a fuller understanding of how Jimmy was perceiving himself in his dual family.

Fourth, subsequent to the critical incident, Wright and Jimmy briefly discussed his concerns about his biological father. However, rather than allowing Jimmy to fully express his concerns, Wright deferred further discussion of the issue to his mother: "I encouraged him to share his musings with his mother." Given Wright's earlier recognition that Jimmy needed to learn to be male, I would have spent more time (even if it required an extended session) further exploring his feelings and concerns about his father before asking Joan to fill in the missing pieces. I would have used the substance of my discussion with Jimmy to provide both a point of departure for Joan and information that she could have used to guide her at-home discussion with Jimmy about his father.

A Comment on Perspective

Wright identified as "feminist" the favored theoretical approach she used in working with this family. Beyond this declaration, however, I found nothing in her clinical approach that fits my understanding of the application of a feminist theoretical approach to therapy. Indeed, I am hard-pressed to identify any techniques used with this family that are based specifically on a feminist theoretical perspective. Instead of a feminist approach, I find that much of her clinical approach is best described as systemic integrative.

CONCLUDING THOUGHTS

Clearly, therapy with this family was not a walk in the park for Wright perhaps because, as she points out, the family was experiencing difficulties on multiple levels. It therefore is a testimony to her clinical skills (and Stone-Fish's supervisory skills) that the outcome was positive for all parties involved, especially Jimmy. Under usual circumstances, it is at best difficult to mediate issues of maternal "rights/competence" between two (of more) nonsanguine claimants. But when the claimants are sisters who bring tremendous emotional baggage to the situation, therapy is that much more difficult. In that regard, despite the points of disagreement I have raised about Wright's clinical approach with this family, it cannot be denied that the family was well served. Each sister accepted her appropriate place/role—as mother or aunt—in Jimmy's life and continued to be friends and to love Jimmy no less.

It is important to emphasize that although I have suggested alternative ways to approach therapy with this family, my approach may not have been any better or more effective than Wright's, only different. I am aware that it is easy to sit outside someone else's therapy room and to offer suggestions or condemnation, but conducting the actual therapy is the difficult part; Wright has done that and Jimmy and his family are better off because of her efforts.

CASE 16

It's All About the Dog

William H. Watson
Judith Landau
J. Steven Lamberti

Therapist Backgrounds

Lamberti, primary therapist (JSL): Thirty years old, white, male, MD, psychiatry resident.

Landau, case consultant/senior family therapist (JL): Forty-five years old, white, female, MB, ChB, psychiatrist, twenty-two years MFT experience.

Watson, clincial team member, forty-seven years old, white, male, psychologist, family therapist, and AAMFT-approved supervisor, fourteen years MFT experience.

Practice Setting

The family and marriage outpatient clinic, department of psychiatry, university medical center.

Client Characteristics

The clients, Virginia (age twenty-nine), Eddie (age thirty-two), and their daughter, Rachael (age eighteen months), are a lower middle-class white family; Virginia is the IP. Virginia's stepfather, her mother, Mary, her maternal grandmother and grandfather, her brother Jeremy (an alcohol and drug abuser age twenty-seven), and his girlfriend were also involved in therapy at various points. Virginia is a registered nurse with several years of work experience but is currently unemployed; Eddie is unemployed.

Length of Treatment

Virginia was seen for approximately fourteen couples, individual, and family sessions (often including the baby) throughout the year. The extended family was seen by both therapists for four sessions over four months in 1980. All sessions were supervised by Dr. Landau. The critical incident occurred in the fourth extended family session. For two and a half years prior to the family consultation, Virginia had been in individual therapy with a psychiatrist.

Theoretical Perspective

A transitional family therapy approach that integrates biopsychosocial, ecosystemic, and intergenerational perspectives was used in working with this couple and the extended family.

Virginia was the first outpatient client of the primary therapist, Dr. Lamberti, a second-year psychiatry resident. Her chronic depressive symptoms had not responded to any of the conventional psychiatric treatments in which she had been involved over several years. After six months of unproductive individual therapy with Virginia, Lamberti decided, as a desperate last measure, to seek a family therapy consultation with Dr. Landau.

Virginia had consulted Lamberti for treatment because her psychiatrist of eighteen months had left the area. She initially had sought treatment because of severe depression and low back pain. Her many complaints and symptoms resulted in her having to terminate a successful job. During the eighteen months of individual therapy with her previous psychiatrist, she also was hospitalized twice and treated with multiple antidepressants and electroconvulsive therapy (ECT). Despite these efforts, she remained severely depressed, struggled with suicidal ideation, and was dysfunctional in her daily life. She constantly complained of back pain and at times was virtually unable to walk. She, however, spent much of her time and energy "doctor shopping" in the hope of obtaining pain relief and/or compensation from her employer for her back injury. Over time, she required narcotics to control her pain. As a result of her pain and depression, she was unable to parent her young daughter and angrily rejected her as well as her own family. Over a relatively short period, Virginia had deteriorated from a functional and responsible professional to a highly dysfunctional, regressed, and needy individual.

THE THERAPEUTIC SITUATION PRIOR
TO THE CRITICAL INCIDENT

Virginia temporarily was unable to work because of her back injury and was still feeling the negative effects of the breakup of her secret extramarital affair. As a result, she became depressed and anxious. In December, she saw a psychiatrist and was prescribed an antidepressant but reported no relief. As a result, her symptoms worsened and she was hospitalized for ten days and treated with another antidepressant, with equivocal response. Antipsychotics were added to address her agitation and some loosening of her thoughts. At discharge, she was diagnosed with major depression, single episode, and borderline personality disorder. Within a week of her discharge she relapsed and was rehospitalized from January through March. Again, antidepressants appeared to have a minimal effect on her depression. Her treatment was complicated by back pain, irritable bowel syndrome, and migraine headaches, all of which appeared to worsen during hospitalization. She eventually required narcotics for pain control. Since Virginia did not respond to antidepressants, ECT was begun. This treatment was moderately effective, but after six treatments she refused to continue.

Virginia returned to live with Eddie, her husband. Because she feared that he might not let her stay, she "allowed" herself to become pregnant. She continued in individual therapy with her psychiatrist but did not continue pharmacotherapy because of her pregnancy. She also continued to complain of depression, anxiety, back pain, and muscle weakness, and spent much of her time and energy seeking compensation for her back injury. Fifteen months after her discharge from the hospital, her psychiatrist left and Virginia was transferred to Lamberti, who saw her weekly for individual psychotherapy. She spent the first few sessions grieving the loss of her first therapist who, she felt, understood her well. It is notable, however, that she and her family reported that she had made no perceptible improvement in the eighteen months she had worked with that therapist.

Over the next several months she expressed intense feelings of rage toward her parents for abandoning her and lamented her difficulty in parenting her daughter who was born shortly before the transfer to Lamberti. She also expressed her need for nurturing and complained that Eddie was not giving her enough. She stated that she felt stuck with Eddie but had never shared her feelings with him. She constantly complained about back pain and how it prevented her from "bonding" with her daughter and from working. In an attempt to obtain pain relief, she contacted several other health professionals and had several work-ups; all were negative. She also continued to complain of depression and considerable anxiety. Despite receiving therapy and medication, she appeared to be deteriorating emotionally. Unable to sleep at night, she ruminated for hours. She also began to eat poorly and became suicidal. As a result, she was initiated on yet another antidepressant, which helped with the most intense of her depressive symptoms, but she continued to complain of depression, to be preoccupied with back pain and its impact on her life, and to ventilate anger about her family.

Because of Virginia's general lack of progress after two years of individual therapy and her intense and unresolved feelings about her family, Lamberti suggested a course of family therapy. She initially resisted because of her fear that "family therapy might make things worse." However, she was curious about the idea of meeting with her family to work on issues and eventually agreed to give it a try. A contract for four family consultation sessions was established. Prior to beginning family therapy Virginia shared with Lamberti her family history and its contributions to her anger toward her mother and her extended family.

Virginia's Story

Virginia is the oldest of four children that included: a brother, Jeremy (age twenty-seven), a sister, Emily (age twenty-five), and a brother, Michael (age twenty-three). Virginia described her earliest memories as happy ones. She remembered being close to her father, an alcoholic, and distant from her mother, whom she described as being irritable and moody. When she was in kindergarten, her happy memories were replaced by frightening ones after her father's personality changed following a work-related head injury. Subsequent to his injury, his drinking increased and he became violent, frequently beating his wife and children. Virginia remembers hiding to avoid being beaten whenever her father came home. Her mother, then undergoing psychiatric treatment for depression, decided to file for divorce. She gained custody of the children but felt she could not care for them properly as she was depressed and unemployed. Upon the advice of her psychiatrist, she sent the children to her own parents in Missouri. Virginia clearly recalls that at approximately age five or six years she lived with her grandparents. She had believed that she was going to visit for only "a little while." In fact, she remained with her grandparents for ten years and did not return to her mother; the children saw her mother for brief visits only when she visited her parents.

Virginia was one of six people who lived in a small mobile home with her grandparents. She did not have a curfew and received minimal adult supervision. She recalled that her grandmother was emotionally distant and unaffectionate yet intrusive, with mood swings, a low tolerance for frustration, and periods of euphoria. Her grandfather was disabled due to several strokes. He frequently was agitated and emotionally and physically abusive to family members. Despite his abusiveness, Virginia felt close to him. During this time, she grew very close to her younger siblings, all of whom looked to her for support and encouragement.

As an adolescent, Virginia often felt anxious and depressed. She also felt abandoned by her own parents and unwanted by her grandparents, especially her grandmother. During this period, she yearned for love, attention, and structure. She often stayed out late and began experimenting with drugs and alcohol; she made several suicidal gestures. When she told her grandparents that she felt life was not worth living or that she had taken an overdose of aspirin, they either punished or ignored her. Despite these difficulties, she was academically successful in high school and popular with her peers.

Throughout high school, Virginia dreamed of becoming a nurse and taking care of people. Upon graduation from high school, she returned to her hometown to attend nursing school. During her first semester in nursing school, she met Eddie and they began to live together. While attending nursing school, she also reinitiated contact with her mother and discovered that she was depressed and needy. Virginia and her mother, Mary, spoke very little about the reasons Virginia was sent to live with her grandparents; discussion of the topic tended to exacerbate Mary's depression.

Four years later, Virginia graduated from nursing school and began working at a local hospital. Although the work was difficult, she was quite successful, evident by her promotion to a level II nurse and head of various work-related committees. Virginia's family soon perceived her as its most educated and able member. As a result, Mary called Virginia daily for support and encouraged her to provide nursing care for her ailing grandparents who had moved to their area because of their failing health.

At age twenty-five, approximately about four years before beginning family therapy, Virginia experienced a series of family catastrophes, including her maternal grandmother's hospitalization because of gastrointestinal bleeding; her mother's hospitalization because of a heart attack; and her brother Jeremy's hospitalization following a car accident in which he had been charged with drunken driving. Virginia helped to arrange each hospitalization and took time off from work to help each family member. At this time she was living with Eddie but was having an affair with a medical resident at work. That relationship ended badly and Virginia felt crushed and guilty. She continued to be the major support of her family until she injured her back while lifting a heavy patient at work. Virginia's psychiatric difficulties began subsequent to her back injury.

EVENTS LEADING TO THE CRITICAL INCIDENT

Virginia, Jeremy, Mary, and Drs. Lamberti and Landau were present at the first family therapy session. In this session, Mary shared that, as an adolescent, Virginia's father learned that the person he had believed to be his uncle while growing up was in actuality his older brother. He had never understood why his mother was so attentive to his "uncle." One day, in a drunken, jealous rage, he attempted to kill his mother by crashing the car in which she was a passenger. After his divorce from Mary, he became an alcoholic. He now is disabled and lives in a VA hospital; his uncle/brother died of alcoholism. Mary explained that this information never before had been discussed in the family. Disclosure of family secrets continued in this session as Virginia revealed to Mary her continuing anger and hurt that she had abandoned her (to her grandparents) when she was a young child. She was clear that she had not gotten over her feelings of hurt, although at one level she knew that her mother had reasons for her decision. With much feeling, Mary explained that she felt she had no choice but to behave as she did. She further explained that her psychiatrist had advised her to move the oldest two children out of the home to protect them from their alcoholic father's drunken beatings. Her plan was to get him into addiction treatment and to obtain a divorce. She took the children by bus to her parents in Missouri. Because she could afford only one ticket, both children rode on her lap. Jeremy appeared to be in shock; he never before had heard this story. Virginia listened attentively but appeared to be unmoved by her mother's story. At session's end, the therapists suggested including other family members in this conversation to broaden its impact and to amplify the resources and competencies of this family who had been beaten down by their experiences and was prone to see themselves as incompetent and inadequate despite surviving extremely difficult circumstances.

At the second family session, Virginia, Eddie, and their daughter as well as Mary, her husband, and Jeremy and his girlfriend were present. Virginia returned to the theme of maternal abandonment and its contributions to her continuing hurt and anger. In response, Mary tearfully exclaimed, "You don't know what it was like having to leave you kids!" For the first time she shared with Virginia and Jeremy how she had worked long hours and extra jobs on weekends and took no time for herself as she struggled to provide money regularly for their upkeep. She also told them that she had missed them and constantly thought about them. During that period, Mary's mother neither permitted her extended visits with the children nor allowed her to parent her children while visiting. When Mary complained, her mother told her to "shut up and leave." Virginia and Jeremy appeared to be overwhelmed by Mary's story. They repeatedly said, "We did not know." For the first time, they began to show recognition that they fully understood what Mary had experienced during that period. The therapists worked to assist Virginia to "hear" and to "believe" that her mother loved her and was committed to her. They also worked to help Mary to "hear" and to "empathize" with Virginia's pain related to her feelings of being abandoned. This time Virginia appeared to be perceptibly touched by her mother's story and began to modify her inner sense of worthlessness related to feeling abandoned by Mary. She and Jeremy had grown up believing that their mother had left them because she did not care about them. However, now that they heard her story they began to reconsider their interpretation of those events.

At the third family session, Virginia again expressed rage and fury that her mother had abandoned her. The therapists were puzzled by Virginia's reactions. Stories that had been buried for years were being revealed; as a result, family members were reconnecting and bridging cutoffs that had isolated them from each other and fostered resentment. However, despite the disclosures in the previous session and Virginia's "understanding" of the conditions that contributed to Mary's decision to send the children to Missouri, the central dynamic of Virginia's depression continued unabated. Interestingly, although Virginia appeared to be stuck, efforts in the third session to continue to bridge the cutoffs were helpful to Jeremy. For the first time in his life, he allowed himself to believe that his mother loved him. Accordingly, he began to give serious thought to confronting his alcoholism and drug abuse after many years of denial. He and the family decided that it would benefit all parties for him to move back home thus allowing his mother and stepfather to parent him, an opportunity they had been denied in his formative years. Hopefully, by going home to be reparented he would be able to "leave home by going home." While Jeremy appeared to be letting go of his hurt and was focused on restructuring his life, Virginia continued to be moody and depressed and to complain of back pain and exhaustion. Something was not connecting and the therapists felt stuck. Accordingly, following Sluzki's, (1979) dictum, "When stuck, expand the system," Virginia's maternal grandparents were invited to attend the next session.

THE CRITICAL INCIDENT

In the fourth family session, Virginia and Mary explained to Virginia's grandmother that she was struggling with feelings of abandonment because, as a little girl, she was sent to live with her grandparents. In response, her grandmother remarked, "Well, Mary had problems, and I guess that was how she solved them." (It was easy to understand how Virginia had grown up with the impression that her mother had blithely dumped her at her grandparent's home.) Mary protested that her actions went well beyond merely solving a problem she had. She then engaged in a lengthy discussion with her mother about other long-standing disagreements/tensions between the two of them. Chief among these was Mary's cutoff from her brother Max (Uncle Max) and his wife, Celia. Mary asked her mother, "Can you explain to me why I'm not allowed over at Max and Celia's?"

MOTHER: You know why.

MARY: No, I don't.

MOTHER: Yes, you do. It's about your dog.

MARY: The last story you said it was the sofa; now it's my dog?

MOTHER [shouting]: Well, you let your dog on the sofa, probably. It was the same as with my dog, Rusty. Celia said it was the time you brought your dog over to her house and it gave fleas to her dog.

Virginia was skeptical of the explanation. She asked, *"That's* why she won't speak to Mom? It's gotta be something else!" Her grandmother assured her that it was not; she said, "No, it's because of the dog," With increased tension in her voice, Virginia asked, "Celia forbade Mom to come to her home or to see her children or her own brother anymore because of the dog? I don't understand." The therapists also listened in disbelief; they did not understand. It was clear, however, that something momentous was happening beneath this mystifying interchange. The intensity of the cut-off between Mary and Max was too intense to be reduced simply to "just fleas." Even a beginning therapist would agree that Mary could have visited without her dog. To capitalize on the intensity created by this bizarre explanation, the therapists ended the final contracted family session and scheduled an appointment with Virginia and Eddie for the following week.

THE AFTERMATH OF THE CRITICAL INCIDENT

Two days following Session 4, Virginia called for an unscheduled appointment; she was in the midst of an acute, suicidal depression and asked to be seen immediately and alone. After a consultation, the therapists agreed to see Virginia for an emergency session but requested that Eddie and both therapists be present. The therapists were concerned about not playing into a pattern of maintaining secrets in the context of a system rife with secrets and cut-offs. They also believed that Virginia was in need of support from those who loved her most. More important, they were impressed with Eddie's supportive and sensitive expressions of concern for Virginia in the family meetings and were equally persuaded that his participation in the session would be a tremendous resource for Virginia. Virginia was assured that she would be seen alone by Dr. Lamberti if the situation became too stressful for her. Fueled by the discussion of Uncle Max in the previous family session, this session proved to be a critical one in Virginia's treatment. Virginia struggled intensely trying to decide whether it was safe, in the presence of Eddie, to reveal what was troubling her. Sensing her conflict, the therapists left the room and gave Virginia and Eddie time alone to talk.

Left alone with Virginia, Eddie was supportive of her and responded with sensitivity as she melted into his arms and sobbed heavily. He comforted her quietly. Responding to Eddie's tenderness, Virginia disclosed to him that her uncle Max had repeatedly and regularly molested her beginning when she was a young girl. Max eventually was caught molesting another child. She never had told anyone until years later. Unfortunately, when she told her grandmother, Virginia was criticized for not telling her earlier, and her grandmother defended Max. When Virginia was an adolescent, Mary had asked her if Max had molested her. When told that he had, Mary "dropped it." Her doing so conveyed to Virginia the impression that Mary was more concerned about Max than she was about Virginia. Virginia said that she was infuriated that no one had protected her. These feelings had sustained her rage and self-loathing and had contributed directly to her refusal to forgive her mother for abandoning her. Eddie listened attentively and talked with Virginia for a long time about how she had been treated by Max and about how other family members had reacted to her disclosure about the molestation. The family secrets buried for years were now revealed and no longer in control. Following that disclosure, Virginia appeared to experience a new level of openness and trust with Eddie. This openness provided her a new freedom and perspective from which to deal with her family and herself specific to these painful stories.

DISCUSSION

The Role of the Critical Incident in Getting Therapy Unstuck

Clearly the critical incident was pivotal in getting therapy and Virginia unstuck (if only temporarily). The critical incident was the beginning of the end of the secrecy and denial that had held Virginia (and the extended family) in its grip for years. At the time the critical incident occurred the therapists were not clear what it meant, but it clearly meant something important with regard to a turning point in Virginia's therapy. Until Virginia was confronted by her grandmother's absurd explanation for her mother being cut off by Uncle Max's family, she was mired in a cycle of secrets, isolation, anger, rage, and despair that kept her in the role of patient. This was manifested through many self-defeating behaviors and especially a depression that was resistant to multiple psychotropic medications, which kept both therapy and Virginia stuck. However, as the entire family assembled for the fourth session, the extent of the false mythologies and mystification (Laing, 1965) they had used to maintain the secrets and to protect the family became evident. As they shared their stories and revealed their secrets, these mystifications that had bound them together and kept them apart finally broke down. This was the fundamental impact of the critical incident in unsticking therapy. Grandmother's insistence that the dog was to be blamed now fell well outside of the ability of anyone's willed suspension of disbelief. It was too much; this was the trigger. Finally, Virginia had to speak. She did so at the very next session and revealed a major family secret.

Implications of the Critical Incident for Therapy

Although Virginia did not maintain her therapeutic gains over time, the critical incident was an explicit catalyst that contributed to the exposure of family secrets, the repair of cut offs, and the creation of new channels of contact and communications in the family. These changes were set into motion by the critical incident for Virginia and her family years later, evidenced by the success of other family members in dealing with addiction (e.g., Jeremy), isolation (e.g., Mary), and the family's continued involvement in Virginia's life benefitted (stepfather and Jeremy were more emotionally supportive of Virginia) in her treatment in subsequent years.

The critical incident also impacted Virginia's therapy in at least two significant ways. The discussion about Uncle Max in Session 4 was the cue that impelled Virginia to disclose the secret (of being molested) that she had held for all those years. Second, Virginia's disclosure of the secret to Eddie and his comforting and compassionate manner of accepting and dealing with Virginia and her secret signaled a change in their relationship. For Eddie, Virginia's disclosure resulting from the critical incident in the previous session was a clarifying event. Finally, much of Virginia's behaviors, including her depression and anger toward her mother made sense for the first time— she was molested by her uncle, criticized by her grandmother, and ignored (and from her perspective even doubted) by her mother. In this context, her self-loathing and her rage toward her mother began to make more sense. For Virginia, Eddie's acceptance of her was an indication that perhaps all was not lost in their relationship. She could trust Eddie not to reject her for telling the secret; he might even protect her. This was something she felt her sanguine family had not done. Now she could stop focusing on pathology, including her individual role as "patient" and her family roles as "rescuer" and overfunctioning caretaker (providing care for her grandparents) who exhausted herself by focusing on the needs of others to the exclusion of herself. Now she could also focus on her strengths and accomplishments (she earned a bachelor's degree and was a competent nurse) and was free to be a parent to her daughter and a wife to Eddie. The changes set into motion by the critical incident also freed Virginia and her family in other ways. The exposure of the secret reasons that family members left each other (and home) allowed for the recreation of continuity in the transitional pathway of the family (Landau-Stanton, 1982). Now family members were free to leave home in a healthy way. Removing the shroud of mystery and mystification regarding the family's history allowed family members to rewrite the story grounded in a more complete sharing of family members' realities and the context in which events occurred and in contrast to the constriction, secrecy, and cutoffs of the past. For example, Mary did not, as her children had imagined, go off and live a happy life after leaving them; Celia really was not banishing the dog but was in a real sense protecting her husband; father's "uncle" was, after all, really his brother; family members abused alcohol, attempted murder, had abortions—all in an effort to cope with the real struggles and challenges that life presented to them and not out of fundamental malice. As Virginia, Jeremy, and the family understood and accepted this new perspective on the family's story, forgiveness grew, family members reconnected, and trust was reborn.

THE OUTCOME OF THERAPY

Virginia's disclosure was the turning point of her therapy. However, much working through remained to be done, but now the course was clearly set. Virginia continued to struggle with deep depression and within two months of Session 5 she was rehospitalized and initiated on a trial of lithium with adequate results. Unlike previous periods of decompensation, this time her recovery was more rapid. Upon discharge from hospital she observably was less depressed, had significantly decreased her "doctor-shopping" to obtain medication for her back pain, spent more time with her family, and was more open and accepting of their support in later family meetings. As a part of her aftercare, she was seen for two monthly follow-up meetings with her family. At these meetings she reported feeling much less depression, having increased energy, and enjoying more satisfying relationships with Eddie and her family. As a result, her antidepressants were tapered and the therapist agreed that further meetings were not necessary at this time. Accordingly, a follow-up appointment was scheduled for six months. Virginia returned within four months complaining of depression, hypomania, and marital conflicts. In response to an increasingly clear pattern of bipolar mood swings over the course of her treatment, she was reinitiated on lithium, and she and Eddie were seen in biweekly couples therapy for the next eight months until the end of Dr. Lamberti's residency. Lithium effectively controlled her hypomanic episodes. However, she periodically was noncompliant with her medication and as a result decompensated.

Although Virginia was not yet out of the woods, she now appeared to be making progress. Her response to the family and couples therapy had been remarkable; no longer was she cyclically rehashing her feelings of anger and bitterness at her mother. Her connection with her family was now much more solid and stable and involved frequent contact and satisfying mutual support. Jeremy was referred for alcoholism treatment and has remained sober. As a result he needed less attention, and became more of a support for Virginia. Their stepfather assumed a more active role as a father figure for both Virginia and Jeremy. Mary has assumed more responsibility for her parents' health care, thus freeing Virginia from that responsibility and its attendant pressures. Freed of those responsibilities, Virginia was better able to parent her own daughter. Although she had not yet returned to work, she had become increasingly well organized and motivated at home and also had been serving as a community volunteer.

POSTSCRIPT

We would like to be able to report that Virginia's life after this point in her therapy went increasingly well, that her depression abated, that she returned to work, and is living a productive and fully recovered life. Unfortunately, such has not been the case. Virginia's depression did not abate. She has continued in treatment for at least nine years with intermittent complaints of depression, suicidal ideation, multiple somatic symptoms, and hypomanic episodes. As a result, she has been unable to return to work and continues to be on disability. She also complains of feeling frustrated with Eddie and threatens to leave him; in the interim, she has been involved in a few extramarital relationships. Despite her many complaints and symptoms, she had remained out of the hospital for four years after terminating with Lamberti. Within the next four years, her grandfather died, her therapist of two years (Lamberti) left, and Eddie agreed to a divorce. Each of these life events led to Virginia being admitted to a psychiatric hospital. She also participated in the psychiatric hospital's day treatment program on two occasions and is receiving aftercare treatment in the hospital's continuing treatment program for patients with persistent emotional disorders.

Despite the continuation of severe difficulties in Virginia's life, it bears noting that a family systems approach promises significant benefit. The course of Virginia's ongoing depression appears closely related to issues of abandonment and closeness, with decompensations often triggered by losses and with storminess in her relationship with her husband often erupting after periods of harmony and warmth—issues that would suggest relational therapy as a treatment of choice. Unfortunately, according to her treatment records, the psychiatric residents who worked with Virginia after Dr. Lamberti's departure pursued the more traditional psychiatric regimen of individual and pharmacotherapy rather than couples or family therapy. Her equivocal response to this is consistent with the limited benefit she derived from her initial two years of individual therapy. It is of further note that discharge summaries from her various subsequent hospital admissions make particular mention of her positive responses to couples and family sessions as well as the dramatic positive effect on her of emphasizing her strengths and successes. We find it especially interesting that her day treatment therapist writes of her erratic attendance to the program, except on the days when family therapy sessions are scheduled. We can only wonder what difference it might have made if they had continued to be included all along.

REFERENCES

Laing, R.D. (1965). Mystification, confusion, and conflict. In I. Boszormenyi-Nagy and J. Framo (Eds.), *Intensive family therapy* (pp. 343-363). New York: Harper and Row.

Landau-Stanton, J. (1982). Therapy with families in cultural transition. In M. McGoldrick, J.K. Pearce, and J. Giordano (Eds.), *Ethnicity and family therapy* (pp. 552-572). New York: The Guilford Press.

Sluzki, C.E. (1979). Migration and family conflict. *Family Process*, 18(4), 379-390.

ADDITIONAL READINGS

Horwitz, S. (1997). Treating families with traumatic loss: Transitional family therapy. In C. Figley, B. Bride, and N. Mazza (Eds.), *Death and trauma: The traumatology of grieving* (pp. 211-231). New York: Taylor and Francis.

Landau-Stanton, J. (1986). Competence, impermanence, and transitional mapping: A model for systems consultation. In L.C. Wynne, S.H. McDaniel, and T.T. Weber (Eds.), *Systems consultation: A new perspective for family therapy* (pp. 253-269). New York: The Guilford Press.

Watson, W.H. and McDaniel, S.H. (1998). Assessment in transitional family therapy: The importance of context. In J.W. Barron (Ed.), *Making diagnosis meaningful: New psychological perspectives* (pp. 161-195). Washington, DC: American Psychological Association.

Commentary

Never Too Old to Learn New Tricks

Thomas C. Jewell

Commentator Background

Thity-one years old, Caucasian, male, PhD in clinical psychology, ten years family therapy practice with severely and persistently mentally ill clients.

Practice Setting

University of Rochester Medical Center, Department of Psychiatry's Strong Ties Community Support Program (outpatient).

Theoretical Perspective

A psychoeducational, family skills building approach was used to examine this case.

The case of Virginia exemplifies the impact of severe and persistent mental illness on people who are afflicted as well as their loved ones. It is well documented that psychiatric illness impacts virtually all aspects of an affected person's life, including but not limited to work, self-esteem, family relationships, daily functioning and interpersonal interactions, quality of life, and hopes and fears for the future. Often, people with psychiatric histories similar to Virginia (e.g., multiple psychiatric hospitalizations, chronic mood disorder symptoms, unsuccessful psychopharmacologic management of symptoms, ECT, and a sharp decline in independent living skills compared with premorbid functioning) are treated in isolation from their family members or primary support systems. It therefore is commendable that Lamberti and his colleagues courageously engaged the entire family in treatment in the best interest of Virginia.

GOOD POINTS ABOUT THE CASE

In their efforts to help Virginia to salvage her life, Lamberti and his colleagues sensitively and appropriately expanded the family intervention to include Virginia's spouse, brother, and other extended family members. Lamberti is to be commended for his continued endorsement of family therapy as the primary mode of treatment despite Virginia's initial fears that such treatment could make things worse. His decision to expand the system even further by including the maternal grandparents after the second family session is an excellent example of translating theory into action per Sluzki's dictum "when stuck, expand the system." Since only a few published clinical reports exist (e.g., Gamache, 2000; Wasow, 1995) that directly include grandparents of clients with serious and persistent mental illness in the treatment of those clients, Lamberti's willingness to do so is remarkable.

Despite the confusing nature of the critical incident that initially baffled both Virginia and Lamberti, he successfully created a safe environment for Virginia at a point in treatment when she really needed to feel safe. Nowhere is this more apparent than during the aftermath of the revelation about the dog when Virginia disclosed to Eddie that she had been sexually abused by Uncle Max. Indeed, it is a testimony to Lamberti's clinical skills in dealing with Virginia during this period that she neither had a relapse nor required rehospitalization for four years following family and couples treatment.

A NOT-SO-GOOD POINT ABOUT THE CASE

The manner in which psychiatric treatment was provided to Virginia subsequent to Lamberti's departure raises some important and practical issues regarding the transfer of care from one provider to another. Based on the case report, Virginia's psychiatric care was transferred, with very little "live" discussion among providers, to a new psychiatric resident who was unfamiliar with her and her circumstances. The new provider treated Virginia with a traditional psychiatric regimen of individual and pharmacotherapy rather than couples and family/relational therapy to which she had responded well. This change was initiated in spite of the awareness (per the hospital's discharge summaries) that Virginia had responded more positively to couples and family sessions than to individual treatment, and the day treatment program therapist observations that Virginia's attendance in the program was erratic except on those days when family therapy was scheduled. Although Lamberti's team was not involved with Virginia during this period, this shift in treatment modality does raise some concerns with regard to the continuity of care for Virginia and the quality of that care. Clearly, the continuity of care for Virginia post Lamberti was less than optimal and certainly may have contributed to her floundering and relapses during that period.

Given all that was known about Virginia, her circumstances, her work with Lamberti, and the progress she had made when treated from a family therapy perspective, the change to a new, inexperienced, individual-oriented provider does not appear to be appropriately indicated. Even if Virginia was assigned to a new therapist it would have been prudent either to keep Dr. Landau involved in Virginia's treatment as a supervisor of the resident because of her familiarity with Virginia's case or to assign Lamberti to meet jointly with Virginia and the new resident to familiarize him or her with Virginia's circumstances; the case report is silent about what specific actions, if any, were taken. To not continue with the family therapy approach that netted the best response and benefits for Virginia is to not provide the best quality of service to clients. In this case, although the change in provider and modality and the circumstances under which it was done may not be wholly unethical, it certainly is questionable.

WHAT I MIGHT HAVE DONE SIMILARLY

Although my therapeutic approach with families (psychoeducational) differs from Lamberti's approach (transitional), I would like to believe that I would have done some of the same things that he did in working with Virginia and her family. Specifically, I also would have moved from an individual (as was the case with her previous psychiatrist) to a family approach to capitalize upon the family members as a resource and support for Virginia. In this era of managed care and limited resources, I deem it very important to reach out to family members of clients—especially clients with severe mental illness—to benefit the clients, build a therapeutic partnership with family members, and offer them compassionate services. I also would have expanded the system per Sluzki's dictum especially since, as it turned out, doing so was instrumental in helping to uncover long-standing severe problems between Virginia's mother and her grandmother, and provided the impetus that contributed to Virginia's disclosure of her sexual abuse.

WHAT I MIGHT HAVE DONE DIFFERENTLY

Generally, it is difficult to second-guess a therapist of record having read only a distilled case report. However, because of my different theoretical orientation and clinical experiences, I might have done some things differently in working with this family. I believe that the individual and family treatment of persistent mental illness is a complex undertaking. Therefore, following the critical incident, I would have offered the family, especially

Virginia, suggestions about where to obtain adjunctive assistance to therapy. Specifically, I would have continued to mobilize for Virginia the professional talents/resources within the marriage and family clinic and also would have incorporated and recommended adjunct supports/resources for her (e.g., educational resources, family psychoeducation, National Alliance for the Mentally Ill [NAMI] support and coping skills groups, and relapse prevention courses) as well as specific supports for Eddie, which can be found in many U.S. communities. The goal of this "package" of meaningful professional and community supports would have been fourfold: (1) to help Virginia to maintain control over her symptoms and succeed in preventing future relapses, (2) to achieve a greater level of autonomy and vocational functioning, (3) to deepen her family and marital relationships, and (4) to improve her overall acceptance and treatment of her psychiatric illness.

In addition, I would have explored at length with Virginia her apparent parentified child syndrome (Brown, 1989). Often clients who willingly or unwillingly adopt such a posture tend to: experience high levels of stress, feel responsible for the problems in their respective family systems, and experience guilt when "pulling away" from those systems. In this regard, Virginia was functioning under burden of the many expectations placed upon her by her family such that she became their major support and the primary "go to" person for a variety of relatives who sought her assistance. I believe that if Virginia had been helped to understand this dynamic and had been taught appropriate limit-setting strategies, she might have been better able to reduce her environmental stresses and forestall relapse. Her doing so also may have helped her to escape from the cycle of family demands and interrupted the homeostasis of meeting those demands at the sacrifice of her own mental and emotional well-being. To Lamberti's credit, many of his interventions with Virginia were designed to "free" her from her many family responsibilities and to allow her to make progress in reclaiming her life.

Other interventions might have included bibliotherapy for Virginia. Here, I would have recommended Eva Marian Brown's (1989) book *My Parent's Keeper: Adult Children of the Emotionally Disturbed,* especially the section that presents recommendations and advice from people with emotionally disturbed parents—a way for people who have "been there" to speak to the reader. Although no one in Virginia's family currently was diagnosed as mentally ill or was in treatment (Mary received psychiatric treatment some years previously and Jeremy needed to be in treatment for his alcoholism), the family's history of trauma, paternal substance abuse, poor boundaries maintenance, and inappropriate communications and expectations extended back for several generations and certainly contributed to Virginia's psychiatric condition. Hopefully, Virginia would have garnered insights from the book about her family and advice about how to better interact with them.

Given Eddie's role as the spouse of a mentally ill person, I would have used a spouse-focused approach in working with him as a part of Virginia's support system. Spouses such as Eddie have a unique perspective and experience of mental illness that is unlike that of parents, siblings, or offspring of people with mental illness (Mannion and Meisel, 1993). Such spouses also tend to have a significant need for a thorough, ongoing, and compassionate education about severe mental illness, treatments, and community resources specific to their partners who are suffering from mental illness. To help Eddie to alleviate any unnecessary additional suffering, I might have referred him to a peer-led coping skills workshop that is conducted by local NAMI chapters. Such workshops provide up-to-date information, education, and support related to mental illness and allow family members to interact in an educational and positive environment. The goal of such a workshop would be to increase Eddie's coping effectiveness and to help him to reduce stress in the environment; it is one strategy for extending the reach of the family therapist into Virginia's home environment and to indirectly assist her.

Similarly, I would have engaged Eddie in psychoeducational family-focused treatment (FFT) designed specifically for families with a member experiencing mood disorders (Miklowitz and Goldstein, 1997). I also would have recommended to Eddie that he enroll in a relapse prevention course (Amenson, 1998) designed to teach him to recognize and respond to early warning signs of mood disorders. The goal of this recommendation would have been to extend the reach of family therapists. Although the critical incident helped Eddie to "make sense" of Virginia's behaviors and attitudes for the first time, I believe that his new level of understanding could have been enhanced by providing him with concrete tools (e.g., a customized warning signs checklists for mania and depression) with which to assist Virginia. These resources would have helped him to demystify Virginia's mental illness and provide him with concrete approaches of how to help her.

A Question About Clarity

While reading the case report, I longed for more details about the biweekly couples therapy that continued for eight months after a follow-up appointment in which Virginia complained of depression, hypomania, and marital conflicts. I assume that these sessions contributed to Virginia's four years without a psychiatric hospitalization. However, absent any details, I question whether it was the biweekly couples sessions or something else that actually made a difference in Virginia's four-year remission of symptoms.

CONCLUDING THOUGHTS

This case demonstrates the impact and effectiveness of a family therapy approach to working with clients with serious and persistent mental illness. I commend Lamberti and his colleagues for their insightful and sensitive work with Virginia and her family. By joining together with family members, spouse, parents, grandparents, siblings, and offspring, Lamberti has shown that family therapists can extend their therapeutic reach to better serve seriously mentally ill clients about whom both they and family members are concerned. Perhaps relapse prevention and recovery work for Virginia would have progressed even farther had Lamberti made use of some of the community resources mentioned in this commentary and had the new therapist (resident) continued Lamberti's good work by adding adjunctive family interventions to the treatment plan. We may never know, but it is a viable hypothesis.

REFERENCES

Amenson, C. S. (1998). *Family skills for relapse prevention*. Pasadena, CA: Pacific Clinics Institute.

Brown, E. M. (1989). *My parent's keeper: Adult children of the emotionally disturbed*. Oakland, CA: New Harbinger.

Gamache, G. (2000). Grandparents caring for grandchildren: When parents have mental illness. *The Journal of NAMI California*, 11(2), 32-33.

Mannion, E. and Meisel, M. (1993). *Teaching manual for spouse coping skills workshops*. Philadelphia, PA: The Training and Education Center Network, c/o Mental Health Association of Southeastern Pennsylvania.

Miklowitz, D. J. and Goldstein, M. J. (1997). *Bipolar disorder: A family-focused treatment approach*. New York: The Guilford Press.

Wasow, M. (1995). *The skipping stone: Ripples effects of mental illness on the family*. Palo Alto, CA: Science and Behavior Books, Inc.

Commentary

Wagging the Dog

Nancy B. Ruddy

Commentator Background

Thirty-seven years old, female, Caucasian, PhD, child and family psychologist, eleven years in practice.

Practice Setting

Currently full-time private practice.

Theoretical Perspective

I used a transitional family therapy perspective to examine this case.

This case report presents a good example of transitional therapy and highlights many of the salient features of the transitional therapeutic approach to working with clients and their families. It also highlights some of the challenges family therapists face when their interventions are seen as "a last resort" rather than a regular part of treatment.

GOOD POINTS ABOUT THE CASE

At least five points about this case bear comment. The first of these is Lamberti's emphasis on working with this family from a perspective of strengths rather than dysfunction. Despite the seemingly intractable difficulties of Virginia and her family, Lamberti proceeded from the premise that families do the best they can given their limitations and circumstances. Accordingly, he searched for and found ways to emphasize the family's strengths rather than labeling its members "dysfunctional" with "no executive subsystem." Further, he encouraged the involvement of extended family members to help Virginia to understand the family's history and to support her efforts to change. In addition, he also constructed a list of the family's strengths to help it redefine itself from a standpoint of "functioning but stressed" rather than "dysfunctional." In doing so, he helped Virginia to see that she had the support and love of her family and to understand that many extenuating circumstances existed, past and present, that affected her family's functioning.

Second, throughout his work with Virginia and her family, Lamberti focused on building bridges to create emotional support between family members. Prior to family therapy, this family evidenced a very low level of emotional connection and trust. Prior to working with Lamberti, Virginia clearly felt burdened (e.g., responsibility for grandparents' health care) rather than supported by her family. She was the family caregiver and felt that she received very little or no recognition from other family members. This felt lack of recognition and her memory of being molested by her uncle Max, as well as the ending of the extramarital relationship with the medical resident, contributed to Virginia's difficulty in trusting others. Given that situation, it is to Lamberti's credit that he was able to help Virginia to reconnect emotionally with her family and to begin to trust again. Jeremy's decision to attempt sobriety may have been a first step toward Virginia developing trust in others. Eddie's sensitive responses also helped Virginia to realize that she was not completely alone. It is quite possible that the family acted on Lamberti's assumption that it could help and support Virginia. It also is possible that perhaps the support had always been there, but Virginia was unable to access it prior to her involvement in family therapy.

Third, Lamberti helped Virginia to reexamine her understanding of the relationship cutoffs in her family. Lamberti's work with this family demonstrates that examining a family's "lore" about the cause of a cutoff is likely to unearth a painful secret such as substance abuse, domestic violence, or, in Virginia's case, sexual abuse. In this case, because "the story" was so perplexing and so ridiculous, Virginia was forced to reexamine her assumptions about her family. Lamberti's earlier work with Virginia about the "lore" of her being "abandoned" by her mother laid the groundwork for Virginia to be more open and to recognize that perhaps her version of the family's history was not the only way to understand her family. Empowered by that new knowledge, Virginia was able to challenge the "lore" surrounding the family cutoffs.

Fourth, Virginia's disclosure is a testimony to Lamberti's ability to create a safe environment for Virginia. His doing so allowed her to challenge her old perceptions of her family and to share the revelation of the sexual abuse. Prior to beginning therapy with Lamberti, many factors prevented Virginia from revealing her secret. She was terrified, mirroring the terror about the secret that had kept everyone silent. Her grandmother had rebuffed her childhood attempts to get help, and her mother had not been able to help her when, as an adolescent, she told her about the abuse. As an adult, she was not sure her husband would support her if she revealed her secret. She needed to feel that some place existed in which she could disclose the molestation without being rebuffed. During her work with Lamberti, Virginia observed his respectful responses to the multiple perspectives of her family members. This respectful stance may have led Virginia to believe that she had finally found someone who would believe her.

Fifth, Lamberti's emphasis on strengths contextualized Virginia's past to make sense of her present. One of the most healing aspects of Lamberti's work was his ability to understand the context of Virginia's multifaceted problems and the various perspectives of each of her family members. As a child psychologist, I am aware that young children tend to assume responsibility for much of what happens to them. Children also tend to believe that situations would improve "if only" they were "better" children. Accordingly, it is easy to understand how this conceptualization of family problems results in a sense of worthlessness and negative worldview, such as that experienced by a young Virginia. On the other hand, when adults begin to understand their parents' shortcomings in the context of the parents' own issues and circumstances, they come to understand that much of what was challenging in their family was not only beyond their control but also beyond the control of their parents. As a consequence, it becomes more difficult to be angry and rejecting of a parent once his or her story is known. Being informed not only helps the aggrieved person understand and appreciate his or her parents, but also himself or herself. In Virginia's case, she came to realize that her mother had made sacrifices for her. She also realized that her mother's decision to leave her with her grandparents was not cavalier, and although it had been painful for her as a child, it also had been very painful for her mother. Virginia's challenge of those rigid assumptions about her parents (some were planted by her grandparents) set the stage for her to begin to challenge other "verities" she had held about her family and herself.

A NOT-SO-GOOD POINT ABOUT THIS CASE

Based on the case report, very few family sessions were held after the critical incident. It is unclear from the case report why more family sessions were not held. Although it is impossible to know with any certainty, it appears that Virginia would have benefited from further family therapy. The critical incident that occurred during a family session set the stage for Virginia's disclosure of sexual abuse and also revealed that Virginia was struggling with intense individual issues related to the molestation and current familial relational stress. In addition, the fact that the molestation had occurred and had been kept a secret for so long is indicative of serious family issues that also needed attention. Given that the core of Virginia difficulties (abandonment by mother, sexual molestation by uncle) occurred within the familial context, it cannot be denied that she needed the support of her family to work through those issues. Her family also needed support to better understand the implications of the molestation and to work through their own culpability in the maintenance of this secret. Not involving Virginia in more family sessions during this period certainly is a shortcoming of this case.

WHAT I MIGHT HAVE DONE SIMILARLY

Both Lamberti and I approach therapy with families from transitional family therapy and biopsychosocial perspectives. Accordingly, I believe that some similarities exist in the manner in which he and I might have approached therapy with Virginia and her family. For example, I also would have approached Virginia's treatment from a position of strengths rather than deficits. Clearly, Virginia's problems in living began following many stressful personal transitions, especially losses, that occurred within a brief time interval and disequilibrated and overwhelmed her coping abilities. Those tribulations, including the serious life-threatening illness of three close family members, the end of a problematic extramarital relationship, the loss of her fantasy that she would escape her difficulties through this relationship, and the loss of her identity as a high-functioning professional and her ability to work subsequent to a work-related back injury, challenged Virginia's resiliency. Given her history of resiliency in the face of stress, it was appropriate to emphasize her strengths rather than deficits.

Similar to Lamberti, I also would have included extended family members in the therapy to expanded Virginia's support system beyond Eddie, and to hear multiple perspectives of the family's story. As Lamberti discovered during his work with Virginia, her situation was much more complicated than an adjustment disorder secondary to multiple stressors. Each stressor, in its own way, amplified her issues from the past. Thus, her mental health issues became much more devastating and longer lasting. Accordingly, to best understand the severity and persistence of her difficulties it was critical to understand the context of her childhood.

WHAT I MIGHT HAVE DONE DIFFERENTLY

Not having sat in the therapy room with Virginia and her family and knowing this family only through this case report, it is difficult to second-guess Lamberti. Despite this limitation, however, there are some things I might have done differently in working with this family. First, I would have engaged Virginia and her family in additional family therapy. Here, the intent would have been to provide Virginia and her family the opportunity to work through issues of grief and loss. Clearly, everyone in this family had experienced significant losses. It is quite possible that Virginia's continued decompensation in the context of loss may be a reflection of her inability to tolerate loss and perceived abandonment. Perhaps her family would have been a source of support for her as she attempted to learn more effective ways to cope with loss. In addition, other family members may have shared this difficulty and, by improving their ability to cope in the context of losses, likely would have decreased the stress Virginia experienced when faced with loss.

I also would have involved Virginia and Eddie in additional family and couples sessions to deal with the strains in their marital relationship. Clearly, their marital relationship was strained by Virginia's illness. Interestingly, despite their marital difficulties (e.g., Virginia's extramarital relationship), Eddie proved to be a good source of support and comfort for Virginia. However, Virginia's ultimate divorce from Eddie may indicate that she did not feel this support or was unable to accept it.

Additional family/couples sessions also would have provided an opportunity to further assess and address parenting issues with the couple, particularly Virginia. Lamberti notes that Virginia experienced difficulty parenting his daughter. Despite this observation, however, throughout the case report no indications are noted that parenting issues/concerns were directly addressed with the couple. Although improving Virginia's general functioning would likely have improved her functioning as a mother, I believe she needed specific assistance in this area given her history of abuse, emotional volatility (including a diagnosis of bipolar disorder), and chronic health issues. Based on that history, Virginia and her daughter were at least "at risk." Consequently, to minimize that risk, I would have focused Virginia and her family on the future of their family, as represented by her child and the type of childhood (different from Virginia's) they could all work together to create for the child.

Yet still, I would have had more discussions with Virginia about the role of her back injury to better understand how she coped with the pain, how she and her family perceived their support of her, and how illness was managed in the family. Lamberti mentioned the role of Virginia's back injury in her downward mental health spiral but does not tell how he dealt with it in therapy. Since he was working with Virginia from a transitional family therapy approach, which is grounded in the biopsychosocial model, her back pain and its effect on her and her family are viewed as important issues in her treatment. Unfortunately, however, based on the case description, it appears that Virginia's health issues were given short shrift in the context of the sexual abuse. I might have used the metaphor of an "overburdened back" to help Virginia to begin to make connections between her stress, depression, and pain.

OTHER ISSUES AND CONCERNS

A Question for the Therapist

One question raised by this case relates to the management of secrets in family therapy. Reading the case report, I was unclear about how Virginia's sexual abuse secret was managed in therapy. I believe that any time a history of abuse exists, the disclosure of that information needs to be handled with great care by the therapist. How did Virginia "remind" others (family members) of the molestation she had suffered and of which she believed they knew? How would Lamberti have managed therapy if Virginia had not felt safe and able to disclose to her extended family the abuse and its effects on her?

A Matter of Ethics

The lack of cooperation between providers and its impact on the continuity of care afforded Virginia post-Lamberti raises an ethical issue related to this case. Following Lamberti's departure, it appears that each treatment period—particularly periods of intensive day or inpatient treatment—was conducted in a vacuum with relatively poor communication between providers. Specifically, Virginia's care was transferred to a new psychiatric resident who discontinued couples and family/relational therapy in favor of individual and pharmacotherapy and she was shunted between providers and programs. This raises ethical concerns that the change in provider and therapeutic modality was initiated although it was known that Virginia had responded more positively to family therapy than to individual therapy (her discharge summaries support this) and the day treatment program therapist had noted that her attendance was better on the days family therapy was scheduled. It is possible that the new treatment providers were biased against relational therapies and choose not to pursue that approach. Perhaps Virginia's presentation was very complicated and frustrating to her new providers. It is clear that barriers to collaboration existed in the treatment system and prevented the new providers from communicating and working with Lamberti and his team who had experienced some success in treating Virginia.

I can only wonder whether Virginia's care was less than optimal because she could not afford private insurance and was relatively poor. Family therapists who work in large systems have the systemic mind-set and expertise to attempt to create better functioning systems. It is sad that our most damaged and disenfranchised clients often have access to the least functioning systems (in this case, a relatively inexperienced resident in a poorly communicating system) in which to try to heal themselves.

A Comment About Interdisciplinary Recognition

Lamberti identified the critical incident as a significant factor in Virginia's disclosure of the sexual abuse. Although I theoretically can agree that the "It was the dog" discussion did set the stage for Virginia's disclosure, I believe it is important that Virginia's previous therapists and the years she spent in therapy prior to beginning family therapy also be credited with contributing to her disclosure or at least her readiness to disclose. My clinical experiences with sexual abuse victims have taught me that, regardless of the therapeutic modality, such clients will disclose their story in their own time. Oftentimes, it appears that disclosure is directly related to a dialogue in the current therapy or to a family event. Other times, it is less clear. As family therapists, we are less likely to upset our individually oriented colleagues when we acknowledge the role that prior therapy played in major therapeutic movements in therapy of which we are the current therapist of record. Doing so is analogous to giving someone else credit for "loosening" a recalcitrant jar lid when one eventually gets the lid off.

CONCLUDING THOUGHTS

Despite the attributions made and ideas regarding how Virginia's follow-up might have been optimized, Virginia's story is a powerful reminder that "shaking the system" can create positive change. Lamberti's gentle opening of doors too long closed, creation of bridges and communication between people who desperately needed each other, and support of the system's strengths gave Virginia an opportunity she had never had before. Virginia's story also shows how a confluence of many factors can create the opportunity for a critical incident. Virginia did not decompensate and present for therapy because of the occurrence of a single life event; it was the confluence of her childhood traumas, current losses, and lack of emotional support, real or perceived, that set the stage for her back injury to send her into an emotional tail spin. Similarly, it likely was her years of individual therapy, the newfound support of her family, and the opportunity to reexamine her assumptions/verities about her family (particularly her mother) that set the stage for her grandmother's "ridiculous" excuse for the cut-off to allow her to free her secret. The context really does matter.

Index